HAMLET

WILLIAM SHAKESPEARE

TEXT & STUDY NOTES

BRIAN FORRISTAL & KARL WHITE

FORUM PUBLICATIONS

Published by
Forum Publications
23 Washington St., Cork.
Tel: (021) 4270525 · (021) 4270500
Fax: (01) 6335347

Design and layout: Dominic Carroll & Jeremy Bowman

Film stills courtesy of BBC

ISBN: 978-1-906565-08-4

2

WHO WAS WILLIAM SHAKESPEARE?

For all his fame and celebration, we know almost nothing about William Shakespeare. His father, John, was a glover and leather merchant. He married Mary Arden, the daughter of the wealthy Robert Arden of Wilmecote, who owned a sixty-acre farm.

The precise date of Shakespeare's birth is not known, but, traditionally, 23 April – St George's Day – has been accepted as his birthday.

Shakespeare probably began his education at the age of six or seven at the Stratford grammar school. As was the case in all Elizabethan grammar schools, the focus would have been very much on Latin history, poetry and drama.

There are other fragmented and dubious details about Shakespeare's life growing up in Stratford. Many believe that after leaving school he worked as a butcher and in his father's glove business.

When Shakespeare was eighteen he married Anne Hathaway, who was twenty-six and already several months pregnant.

William's first child, Susanna, was baptised in Stratford sometime in May 1583. Baptism records reveal that twins – Hamnet and Judith – were born in February 1592. Hamnet, William's only son, died in 1596, just eleven years old.

No one knows for certain how Shakespeare first started his career in the theatre, but by 1592 he had become an established actor.

By late 1594, Shakespeare was an actor, writer and part-owner of a playing company, known as the Lord Chamberlain's Men. He wrote many great plays, achieving great fame, fortune and the praise of the king and queen. He died on 23 April 1616 at the age of fifty-two.

THE THEATRE IN SHAKESPEARE'S TIME

Going to the theatre in Shakespeare's day was a very different experience from today, with the audience expected to sit in silence and with respect. In Shakespeare's time, a visit to the theatre was more like going to a boxing match! The audience was noisy and expressed its approval or disapproval with no reservations whatsoever. Individual characters were booed or cheered, and bad performances had the audience hissing and shouting their disapproval. The most common way for this to happen was for the crowd to shout 'Mew', which is where we get our expression 'cat call' from.

Eating and drinking during plays was very popular, and sellers of oranges, apples and nuts circulated amongst the audience during performances. You could also buy bottles of beer and tobacco pipes. The throwing of fruit at the stage was another way for the audience to express its disapproval of what they were watching.

The opening of the theatre was signalled by the blowing of a trumpet and the flying of a flag on the roof. A small orchestra would play three flourishes to signal the beginning of the play itself. Then a man dressed in a long black cloak with a false beard and a wreath of leaves would introduce the play and ask for the audience to quieten down.

At the end of each play, the next upcoming drama would be announced, and then prayers would be said for the king or queen, with all the actors kneeling on the stage. After this, there came a comic jig performed by the players that lasted around twenty minutes. This was one of the most popular parts of the theatre experience, with certain actors gaining reputations for being great dancers. It was also a way for both the audience and the actors to unwind and blow off steam, especially if they had been performing a tragedy!

One of the biggest differences between theatre in Shakespeare's time and now is that back then there were no female actors. All the parts were played by men and boys. As can be imagined, this must have created an air of comedy to the plays that doesn't come across when we read them today, especially in big romantic scenes. It must have been very funny when, as happens in quite a few of Shakespeare's plays, the female characters disguise themselves as men. Shakespeare's original audience would have seen a man playing a woman who was supposed to be disguised as a man!

THE GLOBE THEATRE

Most of Shakespeare's most famous plays were performed in the Globe Theatre, built on the south bank of the Thames around 1598. This was made of timber with a thatched roof, in the shape of a polygon. It was roughly 100 feet wide and could hold around 3,500 people.

The stage at the Globe was only a metre or so off the ground, and was surrounded on three sides by the audience. There was a trapdoor in the middle of the stage that led down to the 'underworld' – a space where ghosts and other supernatural characters could make a dramatic appearance during a play. Above the stage was the musicians' gallery, which was also used to represent walls and balconies.

On either side of the gallery were the Lord's Rooms, which were used as viewing points reserved exclusively for noblemen and women. Above all of this was what was called the 'heavens' – an overhanging canopy from which more friendly supernatural characters such as angels and gods could be lowered to the stage.

Compared to the theatrical performances of today, props and special effects in Shakespeare's time were pretty minimal. The audience had to be willing to suspend disbelief and use its imagination to create the play's setting in the mind's eye. If a scene was set, for example, at night, or in a desert or a forest, only the actors' words could convey this.

Although the stage always looked the same, a great deal of importance was placed on elaborate costumes and make-up. Gory special effects were also available. The organs of sheep and pigs were used as human hearts in murder scenes, and sheep's blood was used to suggest human blood on swords, axes and spears.

In 1613 the Globe was completely destroyed by fire when a cannon fired during a performance of *Henry VIII* set fire to the thatched roof!

THE REBUILT GLOBE THEATRE IN LONDON

CAST OF CHARACTERS

THE ROYAL HOUSE OF DENMARK

Hamlet	*Prince of Denmark*
Claudius	*King of Denmark, Hamlet's uncle*
Gertrude	*Queen of Denmark, Hamlet's mother*
Ghost	*of King Hamlet, Hamlet's father*

THE COURT OF DENMARK

Polonius	*Counsellor to the king*
Ophelia	*his daughter*
Laertes	*his son*
Reynaldo	*his servant*
Osric **Lords** **Gentleman** }	*courtiers*
Messengers and Attendants	
Voltemand **Cornelius** }	*ambassadors to Norway*
Marcellus **Barnardo** **Francisco** }	*officers of the watch*
Soldiers and Guards	

FORMER FELLOW STUDENTS OF HAMLET

Horatio	*Hamlet's friend*
Rosencrantz **Guildenstern** }	*Sent for by Claudius to spy on Hamlet*

NORWAY

Fortinbras	*Prince of Norway*
Captain	*in Fortinbras's army*

OTHER CHARACTERS IN THE PLAY

First Player **Other Players** }	*actors visiting Elsinore*
English Ambassadors	
Sailors	
Clown	*gravedigger and sexton*
Second Clown	*his assistant*
Priest	*at Ophelia's funeral*

The action of the play is set in and around the Danish royal palace at Elsinore

ACT 1 SCENE 1

A guard platform at Elsinore Castle

Enter BARNARDO and FRANCISCO, two sentinels

BARNARDO	Who's there?
FRANCISCO	Nay answer me. Stand and unfold yourself.
BARNARDO	Long live the King!
FRANCISCO	Barnardo?
BARNARDO	He.
FRANCISCO	You come most carefully upon your hour.
BARNARDO	'Tis now struck twelve. Get thee to bed Francisco.
FRANCISCO	For this relief much thanks, 'tis bitter cold
	And I am sick at heart.*
BARNARDO	Have you had quiet guard?
FRANCISCO	Not a mouse stirring.
BARNARDO	Well, good night.
	If you do meet Horatio and Marcellus,
	The rivals of my watch, bid them make haste.
FRANCISCO	I think I hear them.

Enter HORATIO and MARCELLUS

	Stand ho! Who is there?
HORATIO	Friends to this ground.
MARCELLUS	And liegemen to the Dane.
FRANCISCO	Give you good night.
MARCELLUS	Oh farewell honest soldier.
	Who hath relieved you?
FRANCISCO	Barnardo hath my place.
	Give you good night.

Exit FRANCISCO

MARCELLUS	Holla, Barnardo!
BARNARDO	Say,
	What, is Horatio there?
HORATIO	A piece of him.
BARNARDO	Welcome, Horatio, welcome, good Marcellus.
HORATIO	What, has this thing appeared again tonight?
BARNARDO	I have seen nothing.
MARCELLUS	Horatio says 'tis but our fantasy,
	And will not let belief take hold of him
	Touching this dreaded sight, twice seen of us.
	Therefore I have entreated him along
	With us to watch the minutes of this night,
	That if again this apparition come
	He may approve our eyes, and speak to it.
HORATIO	Tush, tush, 'twill not appear.
BARNARDO	Sit down a while,
	And let us once again assail your ears,
	That are so fortified against our story,
	What we have two nights seen.
HORATIO	Well, sit we down,
	And let us hear Barnardo speak of this.

---

unfold: identify (by giving the password)

most carefully: punctually

rivals: partners

liegemen: loyal followers; *Dane*: the Danish king

fantasy: imagination

Touching: concerning

approve: believe

assail your ears: tell you forcefully

* 9   *sick at heart*: the first of the play's
       many references to sickness

BARNARDO	Last night of all,	35	*Last night of all*: Only last night
	When yond same star that's westward from the pole		*pole*: pole star (North Star)
	Had made his course t' illume that part of heaven		*t'illume*: to light up
	Where now it burns, Marcellus and myself,		
	The bell then beating one –		

Enter GHOST

MARCELLUS	Peace, break thee off! Look where it comes again,	40	
BARNARDO	In the same figure, like the King that's dead.		
MARCELLUS	Thou art a scholar, speak to it Horatio.*		
BARNARDO	Looks a not like the King? Mark it, Horatio.		
HORATIO	Most like. It harrows me with fear and wonder.		*harrows*: tortures, distresses
BARNARDO	It would be spoke to.		*would be*: wants to be
MARCELLUS	Question it, Horatio.	45	
HORATIO	What art thou that usurp'st this time of night,†		*usurp'st*: wrongfully uses
	Together with that fair and warlike form		
	In which the majesty of buried Denmark		*buried Denmark*: the dead king Hamlet
	Did sometime march? By heaven I charge thee speak.		*sometimes*: once, formally
MARCELLUS	It is offended.		
BARNARDO	See, it stalks away!	50	
HORATIO	Stay! Speak, speak, I charge thee speak!		*charge*: order

Exit GHOST

MARCELLUS	'Tis gone, and will not answer.		
BARNARDO	How now, Horatio? you tremble and look pale.		
	Is not this something more than fantasy?		
	What think you on't?	55	*on't*: of it
HORATIO	Before my God, I might not this believe		*might*: could
	Without the sensible and true avouch		*avouch*: confirmation
	Of mine own eyes.		
MARCELLUS	Is it not like the King?		
HORATIO	As thou art to thyself.		
	Such was the very armour he had on	60	
	When he the ambitious Norway combated;		*Norway*: King of Norway
	So frowned he once when in an angry parle		*parle*: discussion
	He smote the sledded Polacks on the ice.†		*smote*: struck
	'Tis strange.		
MARCELLUS	Thus twice before, and jump at this dead hour,	65	*jump*: exactly
	With martial stalk hath he gone by our watch.		*martial stalk*: military stride
HORATIO	In what particular thought to work I know not,§		
	But in the gross and scope of mine opinion,		*gross and scope*: general view
	This bodes some strange eruption to our state.		
MARCELLUS	Good now, sit down, and tell me, he that knows,	70	*Good now*: Now, my good friends.
	Why this same strict and most observant watch		*watch*: state of alertness
	So nightly toils the subject of the land,		*toils*: puts to toil
	And why such daily cast of brazen cannon,		*brazen*: brass
	And foreign mart for implements of war,		*mart*: trading
	Why such impress of shipwrights, whose sore task	75	*impress*: forced labour
	Does not divide the Sunday from the week,		*divide*: distinguish
	What might be toward, that this sweaty haste		*toward*: in preparation
	Doth make the night joint-labourer with the day:		
	Who is't that can inform me?		

---

* 42   *Thou art a scholar ...*: It was believed that ghosts could not speak until spoken to. It was also thought best that a scholar address a ghost, because such a person could speak Latin, the language required to exorcise a ghost should it prove evil.

† 46   *What art thou ...*: Horatio suggests that the Ghost has no right to be out at this time of night, nor has it a right to assume the form of the great king.

‡ 63   *He smote the sledded Polacks*: A reference to the time the king fought the Poles on icy terrain.

§ 67   *In what ... not*: i.e. I don't know exactly what to think.

HORATIO   That can I –
At least the whisper goes so: our last king,   80   *whisper*: rumour
Whose image even but now appeared to us,
Was as you know by Fortinbras of Norway,
Thereto pricked on by a most emulate pride,   *pricked*: urged, incited; *emulate*: jealous, envious
Dared to the combat; in which our valiant Hamlet –
For so this side of our known world esteemed him –*   85
Did slay this Fortinbras, who, by a sealed compact†   *sealed compact*: treaty
Well ratified by law and heraldy,   *heraldy*: chivalry
Did forfeit (with his life) all those his lands
Which he stood seized of, to the conqueror;   *stood seized of*: controlled
Against the which a moiety competent   90   *moiety competent*: equal amount of land
Was gagèd by our king, which had returned‡   *gagèd*: wagered
To the inheritance of Fortinbras,
Had he been vanquisher; as by the same comart§   *vanquisher*: conqueror
And carriage of the article design,   *article design*: treaty
His fell to Hamlet. Now, sir, young Fortinbras,   95
Of unimprovèd mettle hot and full,   *unimproved mettle*: untested bravery
Hath in the skirts of Norway here and there   *skirts*: outskirts
Sharked up a list of landless resolutes₵   *resolutes*: desperados, bandits
For food and diet to some enterprise
That hath a stomach in't, which is no other,   100
As it doth well appear unto our state,   *doth well appear*: is obvious
But to recover of us, by strong hand
And terms compulsatory, those foresaid lands   *compulsatory*: compulsory
So by his father lost; and this, I take it,
Is the main motive of our preparations,   105
The source of this our watch, and the chief head   *head*: source
Of this post-haste and romage in the land.   *post-haste*: feverish activity
BARNARDO   I think it be no other but e'en so.
Well may it sort that this portentous figure   *portentous*: of ominous significance
Comes armèd through our watch so like the king   110
That was and is the question of these wars.
HORATIO   A mote it is to trouble the mind's eye.   *mote*: irritant
In the most high and palmy state of Rome,
A little ere the mightiest Julius fell,   *Julius*: Julius Caesar
The graves stood tenantless and the sheeted dead   115
Did squeak and gibber in the Roman streets;
As stars with trains of fire, and dews of blood,
Disasters in the sun; and the moist star   *the moist star*: the moon
Upon whose influence Neptune's empire stands
Was sick almost to doomsday with eclipse.   120
And even the like precurse of feared events,
As harbingers preceding still the fates
And prologue to the omen coming on,
Have heaven and earth together demonstrated
Unto our climatures and countrymen.   125

Enter GHOST

But soft, behold! lo where it comes again!   *soft*: stay, peace
I'll cross it though it blast me. Stay, illusion.**   *cross it*: cross its path

It spreads his arms   ....
                                                                        * 85   *this side of our known world*: all Europe
If thou hast any sound or use of voice,   † 86   *a sealed compact*: an agreement to which each
Speak to me.   king gave his seal of approval

                                                 continued

                                                                        ‡ 91   It is interesting how the description here of
                                                                                the single combat between old Hamlet and old
                                                                                Fortinbras corresponds somewhat with the end
                                                                                of the play, where Hamlet and Laertes engage in
                                                                                combat accompanied by wagers.

                                                                        § 93   '*comart*': This is one of a number of words
                                                                                in Shakespeare whose origin and meaning is
                                                                                disputed

                                                                        ₵ 98   *Sharked up*: Fortinbras is seen to gather men in
                                                                                a manner similar to the way a shark indiscrimi-
                                                                                nately gathers fish to eat.

                                                                        ** 127 *cross it*: It was thought that anyone crossing
                                                                                the path of a ghost became subject to its evil
                                                                                influence.

<table>
<tr><td></td><td>If there be any good thing to be done</td><td>130</td></tr>
</table>

	If there be any good thing to be done	130	
	That may to thee do ease, and grace to me,*		
	Speak to me.		
	If thou art privy to thy country's fate,		*privy to*: knowledgeable about
	Which happily foreknowing may avoid,		
	Oh speak.	135	
	Or if thou hast uphoarded in thy life		*uphoarded*: hidden
	Extorted treasure in the womb of earth,		
	For which, they say, you spirits oft walk in death,		
The cock crows			
	Speak of it. Stay and speak! Stop it, Marcellus.		
MARCELLUS	Shall I strike it with my partisan?	140	*partisan*: long-handled spear
HORATIO	Do, if it will not stand.		
BARNARDO	'Tis here!		
HORATIO	'Tis here!		
MARCELLUS	'Tis gone!		
Exit GHOST			
	We do it wrong being so majestical,		
	To offer it the show of violence;		
	For it is as the air invulnerable,	145	
	And our vain blows malicious mockery.		*vain blows*: futile attempts to hit it
BARNARDO	It was about to speak when the cock crew.		
HORATIO	And then it started like a guilty thing†		
	Upon a fearful summons. I have heard		
	The cock, that is the trumpet to the morn,	150	*trumpet*: trumpeter
	Doth with his lofty and shrill-sounding throat		*lofty*: high-sounding
	Awake the god of day, and at his warning,		
	Whether in sea or fire, in earth or air,		
	Th' extravagant and erring spirit hies†		
	To his confine; and of the truth herein	155	
	This present object made probation.		*probation*: proof
MARCELLUS	It faded on the crowing of the cock.		
	Some say that ever 'gainst that season comes		*that season*: Christmas
	Wherein our Saviour's birth is celebrated,		
	This bird of dawning singeth all night long,	160	*bird*: the cock
	And then they say no spirit dare stir abroad,		
	The nights are wholesome, then no planets strike,§		*wholesome*: good for the health
	No fairy takes, nor witch hath power to charm,		
	So hallowed and so gracious is that time.		
HORATIO	So have I heard, and do in part believe it.	165	
	But look, the morn in russet mantle clad		*russet*: reddish-brown
	Walks o'er the dew of yon high eastward hill.		
	Break we our watch up, and by my advice		
	Let us impart what we have seen to-night		
	Unto young Hamlet, for, upon my life,	170	
	This spirit, dumb to us, will speak to him.		
	Do you consent we shall acquaint him with it,		
	As needful in our loves, fitting our duty?₵		
MARCELLUS	Let's do't, I pray, and I this morning know		
	Where we shall find him most conveniently.	175	
Exeunt			

* 131 *to thee do ease and grace to me*: i.e.
       give comfort to you and reflect credit
       on me.
† 148 *And then it started ... summons*: And
       then it fled like an evildoer caught
       redhanded.
‡ 154 *Th'extravagant ... confine*: The
       spirit who strays and wanders out
       of bounds hurries to his place of
       confinement.
§ 162 *no planets strike*: In Shakespeare's
       day planets were believed to be
       capable of striking and blasting men
       and things.
₵ 173 *our loves*: the love each of us feels for
       him.

MARCELLUS, HORATIO & BARNARDO

Guards are keeping watch on the battlements in Elsinore. The ghost of the old king of Denmark has been appearing each night around midnight. One of the guards has brought Horatio to see the Ghost because he is a man of great learning. The Ghost appears, and despite Horatio's efforts to make it speak it remains silent. The guards and Horatio discuss Denmark's recent military build-up. This is occurring because Fortinbras, the young prince of Norway, may be about to attack. Horatio decides to tell Prince Hamlet about the Ghost.

A CLOSER LOOK

LINES 1–39: AN UNEASY WATCH

The play opens at midnight on a battlement of the royal castle of Elsinore, Denmark. It is time for the changing of the watch, and the sentry Barnardo has come to relieve his comrade Francisco. The atmosphere is one of nervousness and fear. Francisco is greatly relieved to see his comrade, and confesses that he is 'sick at heart'. (9) The sentries are nervous because they have seen a ghost the previous two nights while on watch.

Horatio and Marcellus then appear. Horatio does not believe the story about the Ghost: ''tis but our fantasy/ And will not let belief take hold of him'. (23–4) Marcellus has asked Horatio to join them in order that he may see the Ghost for himself. Horatio is sceptical: 'Tush, tush, 'twill not appear'. (30) Barnardo begins to talk about the Ghost.

LINES 40–69: THE GHOST APPEARS

No sooner has Barnardo begun his tale than the apparition appears. (40) It is the ghost of Hamlet, the late king of Denmark, clad in full battle armour. Marcellus urges Horatio to speak to the figure. (42) Horatio is struck by 'fear and wonder', but attempts nonetheless to address the Ghost. (46–9) The Ghost turns and

walks away, in spite of Horatio's further attempts to make it speak. (51)

Horatio's scepticism is destroyed now that he has seen the figure for himself. Marcellus asks him if he believes it to be the ghost of the late king, and Horatio says he does. (59–64) Horatio cannot imagine why it has appeared, but he believes that the spirit heralds dark times for Denmark: 'This bodes some strange eruption to our state'. (69)

LINES 70–125: POLITICAL TROUBLE

Marcellus is troubled by recent developments in the state, and asks Horatio if he knows the reason for the heightened military activity that has recently begun in Denmark. (70–8)

Horatio enlightens Marcellus. The late King Hamlet had defeated King Fortinbras of Norway in single combat. By doing so, he won ownership of some of Norway's territory. The son of the Norwegian king, also named Fortinbras, has gathered together a motley force of men, and is determined to regain the territory lost by his father.

The Danish are gathering their military strength in

case Fortinbras attacks: 'and this, I take it/Is the main motive of our preparations/The source of this our watch, and the chief head/Of this post-haste, and romage in the land'. (104–7) Marcellus remarks that it is fitting that the late king's ghost should be abroad, as he was involved in events that led to the current unrest.

LINES 126–75: THE GHOST REAPPEARS

As Horatio is speaking, the Ghost reappears. (126) Horatio bravely addresses the Ghost again. He urges it to speak, asking it if it has any idea of what the future holds for Denmark: 'If thou art privy to thy country's fate/Which happily foreknowing may avoid/Oh speak.' (133–5) A cock then crows and the Ghost starts to leave. (139)

Dawn begins to break. Horatio says they should tell Prince Hamlet, the late king's son, of what they have seen. Horatio believes that the Ghost will speak to Hamlet: 'for, upon my life,/This spirit, dumb to us, will speak to him'. (170–1) Marcellus agrees to this suggestion, and says that he knows where Hamlet can be found. (174–5)

SOME LINES TO LEARN

But in the gross and scope of mine opinion,
This bodes some strange eruption to our state
Horatio (68–9)

HORATIO

A WISE & LEARNED GENTLEMAN

In the opening scene, Horatio is portrayed as a figure that others turn to and whose learning and opinion is respected. He has been brought to the battlements by Marcellus in order that he may see the Ghost and address it. (26–8) He is an educated university student whose scientific background makes him sceptical about the Ghost. He only believes it when he sees it with his own eyes.

Horatio is a knowledgeable man who can inform Marcellus of the reasons for the military activity in Denmark. (79–107) He also appears to have an extensive knowledge of bad omens, portents and superstitions. He can tell Marcellus of what happened in Rome before the murder of Julius Caesar, and why the Ghost flees when the cock crows. (148–56)

When the Ghost appears, Horatio shows great bravery in attempting to speak with it, though he knows he may be risking his life in doing so: 'I'll cross it though it blast me'. (127)

Trumpet call. Enter CLAUDIUS King of Denmark, GERTRUDE the queen, HAMLET,
POLONIUS, LAERTES, OPHELIA, VOLTEMAND, CORNELIUS, LORDS Attendant

CLAUDIUS   Though yet of Hamlet our dear brother's death
The memory be green, and that it us befitted
To bear our hearts in grief, and our whole kingdom
To be contracted in one brow of woe,
Yet so far hath discretion fought with nature   5
That we with wisest sorrow think on him,
Together with remembrance of ourselves.
Therefore our sometime sister, now our queen,
Th' imperial jointress to this warlike state,
Have we, as 'twere with a defeated joy,   10
With one auspicious and one dropping eye,*
With mirth in funeral and with dirge in marriage,
In equal scale weighing delight and dole,
Taken to wife: nor have we herein barr'd
Your better wisdoms, which have freely gone   15
With this affair along – for all, our thanks.
Now follows, that you know: young Fortinbras,
Holding a weak supposal of our worth,
Or thinking by our late dear brother's death
Our state to be disjoint and out of frame,   20
Colleaguèd with this dream of his advantage,
He hath not failed to pester us with message,
Importing the surrender of those lands
Lost by his father, with all bonds of law,
To our most valiant brother. So much for him.   25
Now for ourself and for this time of meeting
Thus much the business is: we have here writ
To Norway, uncle of young Fortinbras,
Who, impotent and bed-rid, scarcely hears
Of this his nephew's purpose, to suppress   30
His further gait herein; in that the levies,†
The lists and full proportions, are all made‡
Out of his subject: and we here dispatch
You, good Cornelius, and you, Voltemand,
For bearers of this greeting to old Norway;   35
Giving to you no further personal power
To business with the king, more than the scope
Of these dilated articles allow.§
Farewell, and let your haste commend your duty.

---

green: young, fresh

contracted: drawn together

discretion: prudence; *nature*: instinct

sometime: former
jointress: co-owner

dirge: lament, mourning
dole: grief
barr'd: neglected
Your: referring to the Council of State

weak supposal: poor estimate

frame: order
Colleaguèd with: together with

Importing: concerning

impotent: powerless
suppress: curb
gait: proceeding, progress

subject: people

dilated: lengthy and detailed

---

* 11   *one auspicious and one dropping eye*:
a hopeful and a sad eye, representing
conflicting emotions

† 31   *levies*: military troops

‡ 32   *lists and full proportions*: soldiers
enlisted and supplies

§ 36–8   *no further ... allow*: they are only
allowed do what Claudius instructs
in the document

CORNELIUS VOLTEMAND }	In that and all things will we show our duty.	40
CLAUDIUS	We doubt it nothing, heartily farewell.	
	Exeunt VOLTEMAND and CORNELIUS	

And now, Laertes, what's the news with you?
You told us of some suit; what is't, Laertes?
You cannot speak of reason to the Dane,
And loose your voice: what wouldst thou beg Laertes,   45
That shall not be my offer, not thy asking?
The head is not more native to the heart,
The hand more instrumental to the mouth,
Than is the throne of Denmark to thy father.
What wouldst thou have, Laertes?

LAERTES   My dread lord,   50
Your leave and favour to return to France,
From whence though willingly I came to Denmark,
To show my duty in your coronation,
Yet now I must confess, that duty done,
My thoughts and wishes bend again toward France   55
And bow them to your gracious leave and pardon.*

CLAUDIUS   Have you your father's leave? What says Polonius?

POLONIUS   He hath, my lord wrung from me my slow leave
By laboursome petition, and at last
Upon his will I sealed my hard consent,   60
I do beseech you give him leave to go.

CLAUDIUS   Take thy fair hour Laertes, time be thine,
And thy best graces spend it at thy will.
But now, my cousin Hamlet, and my son –

HAMLET   *[Aside]* A little more than kin, and less than kind.†   65

CLAUDIUS   How is it that the clouds still hang on you?

HAMLET   Not so, my lord; I am too much i' the sun.‡

QUEEN   Good Hamlet, cast thy nighted colour off,
And let thine eye look like a friend on Denmark.
Do not for ever with thy vailed lids   70
Seek for thy noble father in the dust:
Thou know'st 'tis common; all that lives must die,§
Passing through nature to eternity.

HAMLET   Ay, madam, it is common.

GERTRUDE   If it be,
Why seems it so particular with thee?   75

---

suit: formal appeal
Dane: King of Denmark
loose your voice: not be heard

more native: closer
instrumental: useful

dread: revered

bow them: entreat themselves

laboursome petition: tiresome, repetitive pleas
sealed: promised

fair hour: opportunity of youth
best graces: gifts of youth

nighted: dark, colour of mourning

vailed lids: downcast eyes, hidden

particular: personal

---

* 55–6   *My thoughts and wishes ... leave and pardon*: My desire is to return to France, for which I beg your permission.

† 65   *A little more than kin, and less than kind*: Hamlet is doubly related to Claudius being both his nephew (a closer relation than cousin) and now also his stepson – however, he feels little kindness towards him. Note the wordplay in kin/kind.

‡ 67   *my lord; I am too much i' the sun*: too much immersed in the sunshine of the marriage celebrations. The word 'sun' also puns on 'son': Hamlet is expressing his distaste for his new role as Claudius' stepson.

§ 72   *common*: this word has two meanings, universal (all must die) and vulgar (it is improper to mourn for too long)

HAMLET	Seems, madam? nay it is; I know not seems.
	'Tis not alone my inky cloak, good mother,
	Nor customary suits of solemn black,
	Nor windy suspiration of forced breath,*
	No, nor the fruitful river in the eye,
	Nor the dejected haviour of the visage,
	Together with all forms, moods, shapes of grief,
	That can denote me truly. These indeed seem,
	For they are actions that a man might play,
	But I have that within which passes show –
	These but the trappings and the suits of woe.
CLAUDIUS	'Tis sweet and commendable in your nature Hamlet,
	To give these mourning duties to your father;
	But, you must know, your father lost a father,
	That father lost, lost his, and the survivor bound
	In filial obligation for some term
	To do obsequious sorrow; but to persevere
	In obstinate condolement is a course
	Of impious stubbornness; 'tis unmanly grief;
	It shows a will most incorrect to heaven,
	A heart unfortified, a mind impatient,
	An understanding simple and unschooled.
	For what we know must be, and is as common
	As any the most vulgar thing to sense,
	Why should we in our peevish opposition
	Take it to heart? Fie, 'tis a fault to heaven,
	A fault against the dead, a fault to nature,
	To reason most absurd, whose common theme
	Is death of fathers, and who still hath cried,
	From the first corse till he that died today,†
	'This must be so.' We pray you throw to earth
	This unprevailing woe, and think of us
	As of a father: for let the world take note,
	You are the most immediate to our throne,
	And with no less nobility of love
	Than that which dearest father bears his son,
	Do I impart toward you. For your intent
	In going back to school in Wittenberg,
	It is most retrograde to our desire,
	And we beseech you bend you to remain
	Here in the cheer and comfort of our eye,
	Our chiefest courtier, cousin, and our son.
GERTRUDE	Let not thy mother lose her prayers, Hamlet:
	I pray thee, stay with us; go not to Wittenberg.
HAMLET	I shall in all my best obey you, madam.
CLAUDIUS	Why, 'tis a loving and a fair reply:
	Be as ourself in Denmark. Madam, come.
	This gentle and unforced accord of Hamlet
	Sits smiling to my heart, in grace whereof,
	No jocund health that Denmark drinks today
	But the great cannon to the clouds shall tell,
	And the king's rouse the heavens all bruit again,
	Respeaking earthly thunder. Come away.

Flourish. Exeunt all but HAMLET

Glossary (right margin)

80

customary: traditional

fruitful river: plentiful tears
haviour: behaviour, expression; *visage:* face

seem: outward show, appearance, falsity

85 *passes show:* exceeds what can be acted
suits of woe: grief's clothing

90

obsequious: compliant, dutiful
obstinate condolement: fixed sorrowing

95 *incorrect to heaven:* against God's command
unfortified: weak
unschool'd: unlearned

100 *peevish:* foolish

105 *corse:* corpse

unprevailing: unpopular

110

retrograde: contrary

courtier: aristocrat

120

accord: agreement
in grace whereof: to celebrate this good
125 *jocund:* cheerful and lighthearted

rouse: toast; *bruit again:* re-announce, echo

---

* 79 *Nor windy suspiration of forced breath:* irrepressible sighs

† 105 *From the first corse:* Adam's son Abel was the first corpse (Genesis 4:8)

15

HAMLET	O! that this too too solid flesh would melt,	
	Thaw and resolve itself into a dew,	130
	Or that the Everlasting had not fixed	
	His canon 'gainst self-slaughter! O God, God,	
	How weary, stale, flat and unprofitable,	
	Seem to me all the uses of this world!	
	Fie on't, ah fie, 'tis an unweeded garden	135
	That grows to seed, things rank and gross in nature	
	Possess it merely. That it should come to this!	
	But two months dead – nay, not so much, not two –	
	So excellent a king, that was to this	
	Hyperion to a satyr; so loving to my mother*	140
	That he might not beteem the winds of heaven	
	Visit her face too roughly – heaven and earth,	
	Must I remember? why, she would hang on him	
	As if increase of appetite had grown	
	By what it fed on, and yet, within a month –	145
	Let me not think on't; frailty, thy name is woman –	
	A little month, or ere those shoes were old	
	With which she follow'd my poor father's body	
	Like Niobe, all tears, why she, even she –	
	O, God, a beast that wants discourse of reason,†	150
	Would have mourn'd longer – married with my uncle,	
	My father's brother, but no more like my father	
	Than I to Hercules – within a month,	
	Ere yet the salt of most unrighteous tears	
	Had left the flushing in her gallèd eyes,	155
	She married. Oh most wicked speed, to post	
	With such dexterity to incestuous sheets.‡	
	It is not, nor it cannot come to good:	
	But break, my heart, for I must hold my tongue.	

Enter HORATIO, MARCELLUS, and BARNARDO

HORATIO	Hail to your lordship.	
HAMLET	I am glad to see you well	160
	Horatio – or I do forget myself.	
HORATIO	The same, my lord, and your poor servant ever.	
HAMLET	Sir, my good friend; I'll change that name with you.	
	And what make you from Wittenberg, Horatio?	
	Marcellus.	165
MARCELLUS	My good lord.	
HAMLET	I am very glad to see you. *[To Barnardo]* Good even sir.	
	But what in faith make you from Wittenberg?	
HORATIO	A truant disposition, good my lord.	
HAMLET	I would not hear your enemy say so,	170
	Nor shall you do mine ear that violence	
	To make it truster of your own report	
	Against yourself. I know you are no truant.	
	But what is your affair in Elsinore?	
	We'll teach you to drink deep ere you depart.	175
HORATIO	My lord, I came to see your father's funeral.	
HAMLET	I pray thee do not mock me fellow-student;	
	I think it was to see my mother's wedding.	

His canon: God's law

Seem to me: his subjective view, uncertain

rank: pungent, stale

beteem: permit

Hercules: son of Zeus, famed for his courage

gallèd: sore from crying

dexterity: skill, apparent ease

truant disposition: skiving nature

truster: believe

* 139–40 *that was ... Hyperion to a satyr*: his father was as an hyperion (sun-god) to a satyr (half-human, half-beast)

† 150 *a beast, that wants discourse of reason*: traditionally, humans are considered superior to beasts because of their ability to reason

‡ 157 *incestuous sheets*: marriage to a brother's widow is considered to be incest

HORATIO	Indeed, my lord, it followed hard upon.
HAMLET	Thrift, thrift, Horatio. The funeral baked meats
	Did coldly furnish forth the marriage tables.*
	Would I had met my dearest foe in heaven
	Or ever I had seen that day, Horatio.
	My father, methinks I see my father –
HORATIO	Where, my lord?
HAMLET	In my mind's eye, Horatio.
HORATIO	I saw him once; he was a goodly king.
HAMLET	He was a man, take him for all in all.
	I shall not look upon his like again.
HORATIO	My lord, I think I saw him yesternight.
HAMLET	Saw? who?
HORATIO	My lord, the king your father.
HAMLET	The king my father!
HORATIO	Season your admiration for a while
	With an attent ear, till I may deliver
	Upon the witness of these gentlemen
	This marvel to you.
HAMLET	For God's love, let me hear.
HORATIO	Two nights together had these gentlemen,
	Marcellus and Barnardo, on their watch,
	In the dead waste and middle of the night,
	Been thus encountered. A figure like your father,
	Armed at point exactly, cap-a-pe,
	Appears before them, and with solemn march
	Goes slow and stately by them. Thrice he walked
	By their oppressed and fear-surprisèd eyes,
	Within his truncheon's length, whilst they, distilled
	Almost to jelly with the act of fear,
	Stand dumb and speak not to him. This to me
	In dreadful secrecy impart they did,
	And I with them the third night kept the watch,
	Where, as they had delivered, both in time,
	Form of the thing, each word made true and good,
	The apparition comes. I knew your father;
	These hands are not more like.†
HAMLET	But where was this?
MARCELLUS	My lord, upon the platform where we watched.
HAMLET	Did you not speak to it?
HORATIO	My lord, I did,
	But answer made it none. Yet once methought
	It lifted up it head and did address
	Itself to motion, like as it would speak;
	But even then the morning cock crew loud,
	And at the sound it shrunk in haste away,
	And vanished from our sight.

180

185

190

195

200

205

210

215

foe: enemy
Or ever: rather than

Season your admiration: calm your excitement
attent: attentive

dead vast: still and empty as death

cap-a-pe: top to toe

oppressed: disheartened
truncheon: baton; *distilled*: reduced

deliver'd: told

---
* 180–1   *the funeral baked meats ... the marriage tables*: food left over from the funeral was served cold at the wedding. Hamlet is exaggerating the speed at which the wedding followed the funeral for ironic effect. Nevertheless, his remark echoes satirically Claudius' earlier comment about 'mirth in funeral' and 'dirge in marriage' (at line 12 of this scene).

† 212   *These hands are not more like*: Horatio is comparing the similarity between his own two hands to the likeness between the Ghost and Hamlet's father.

HAMLET	'Tis very strange.	220
HORATIO	As I do live my honour'd lord 'tis true	
	And we did think it writ down in our duty	
	To let you know of it.	
HAMLET	Indeed, indeed, sirs, but this troubles me.	
	Hold you the watch to-night?	
MARCELLUS BARNARDO }		225
HAMLET	Arm'd, say you?	
MARCELLUS BARNARDO }		
HAMLET	From top to toe?	
MARCELLUS BARNARDO }		
HAMLET	Then saw you not his face?	
HORATIO	Oh yes, my lord, he wore his beaver up.	
HAMLET	What, looked he frowningly?	230
HORATIO	A countenance more in sorrow than in anger.	
HAMLET	Pale, or red?	
HORATIO	Nay very pale.	
HAMLET	And fix'd his eyes upon you?	
HORATIO	Most constantly.	
HAMLET	I would I had been there.	
HORATIO	It would have much amazed you.	235
HAMLET	Very like, very like. Stayed it long?	
HORATIO	While one with moderate haste might tell a hundred.	
MARCELLUS BARNARDO }		
HORATIO	Not when I saw 't.	
HAMLET	His beard was grizzled – no?	
HORATIO	It was, as I have seen it in his life,	240
	A sable silver'd.	
HAMLET	I will watch to-night;	
	Perchance 'twill walk again.	
HORATIO	I warrant it will.	
HAMLET	If it assume my noble father's person,	
	I'll speak to it, though hell itself should gape	
	And bid me hold my peace. I pray you all,	245
	If you have hitherto concealed this sight,	
	Let it be tenable in your silence still,	
	And whatsomever else shall hap to-night,	
	Give it an understanding but no tongue.	
	I will requite your loves. So, fare you well:	250
	Upon the platform, 'twixt eleven and twelve,	
	I'll visit you.	
ALL	Our duty to your honour.	
HAMLET	Your loves, as mine to you. Farewell.	

Exeunt all but HAMLET

                  My father's spirit, in arms! All is not well.
                  I doubt some foul play: would the night were come.   255
                  Till then sit still, my soul. Foul deeds will rise
                  Though all the earth o'erwhelm them to men's eyes.

Exit

Glossary (right margin):

beaver: vizor of helmet

countenance: expression

grizzled: grey

sable silver'd: dark hair lined with grey

gape: open

concealed: kept secret

whatsomever … hap: whatever happens
no tongue: don't speak to it
requite: return your affection

doubt: suspect
rise: come to surface, be revealed
o'erwhelm: bury

* 247   *Let it be tenable in your silence still*:
             keep it as a secret

CLAUDIUS

Claudius, the new king of Denmark, is holding court. He makes a long-winded speech mourning the death of his brother and justifying his marriage to Gertrude. He sends ambassadors to Norway to deal with the threat posed by young Fortinbras, the Norwegian prince. He reluctantly permits Laertes to return to his studies in France.

The king and queen encourage Hamlet to cheer up and put aside his grief for his father. Hamlet makes bitter and sarcastic remarks, revealing his disgust and anger at his mother's hasty remarriage. Hamlet's soliloquy expresses his suicidal thoughts. Life seems disgusting, empty and pointless to the prince.

Horatio arrives and tells him he has seen a ghost resembling his dead father walking on the battlements. They agree to meet that night at twelve, and to encounter the Ghost together.

A CLOSER LOOK

✒ LINES 1–39: CLAUDIUS ADDRESSES HIS SUBJECTS

Claudius begins by justifying his recent marriage to Gertrude, the queen and widow of his brother, the deceased King Hamlet. He states that the memory of the king's death is still raw ('green') and that the country was rightly filled with sorrow at his passing: 'it us befitted/ To bear our hearts in grief, and our whole kingdom/ To be contracted on one brow of woe.' (2–4)

Claudius stresses that he and Gertrude felt mixed emotions when they wed. He says that they felt joy and love for one another, but also sorrow for the deceased king:

With an auspicious and one dropping eye,
With mirth in funeral and with dirge in marriage,
In equal scale weighing delight and dole (11–13)

19

He thanks his subjects for supporting him in his decision to marry Gertrude.

The second part of Claudius' speech concerns the bellicose activities of Fortinbras. Claudius informs the court of Fortinbras' military preparations. Fortinbras wants Denmark to return the lands lost by his father many years ago. (23–5) He thinks that Denmark is in a weakened state because of the king's death. (17–19)

Claudius plans to send messengers to the elderly king of Norway, Fortinbras' uncle, informing him of Fortinbras' aggressive behaviour. (27–31) Claudius hopes that the king will call a halt to the military build-up. (27–33)

✍ LINES 40–63: LAERTES ASKS PERMISSION TO RETURN TO FRANCE

Laertes says that he has done his duty in attending the king's coronation, and asks the king's permission to return to France. Claudius confers with Laertes' father, Polonius, and agrees.

✍ LINES 64–128: THE KING AND QUEEN SPEAK WITH HAMLET

Claudius then turns to his nephew, Prince Hamlet. He addresses him as 'my cousin Hamlet, and my son'. (64) This suggests his complex relationship to the prince, who is his natural nephew, stepson by marriage and heir to the throne.

Hamlet has been behaving in a very mournful manner. Both Claudius and Gertrude urge him to cheer up and put his grief for his father behind

CHARACTER DEVELOPMENT

SOME LINES TO LEARN

How weary, stale, flat and unprofitable,
Seem to me all the uses of this world!
Fie on't, ah fie, 'tis an unweeded garden
That grows to seed, things rank and gross in nature
Possess it merely.

Hamlet (133–7)

CLAUDIUS

A SKILFUL POLITICIAN
Claudius' first speech reveals his skills as a politician. He is careful to acknowledge the greatness of his predecessor. He long-windedly justifies his decision to marry Gertrude, and thanks the court for its support in this matter. The king then discusses the possibility of Fortinbras invading Denmark. By focusing on this external threat, he deflects attention away from his unusual marriage.

Claudius uses the threat posed by Fortinbras to cement his new position as the Danish king. He says that Fortinbras thinks that Denmark is weak and divided. This suggests that the Danish people must rally around their new leader if they are to face down this new threat.

It could be argued that Claudius' shrewdness is evident in sending diplomats to Norway. If possible, he wants to negate the threat of Fortinbras without a fight. Or perhaps he is doing it to buy time in order to continue the arms build-up – described in the first scene – before confronting his enemy.

It could also be argued that Claudius perceives Hamlet as a threat to his fragile new regime. Hamlet, after all, is a member of the royal family with a claim to the throne. He responds to this potential threat by ingratiating himself with the prince, declaring Hamlet as heir, and saying he loves him like his own son. Does he ask Hamlet to remain in Denmark so he can keep this potential threat under close observation?

DECEPTIVE
In this scene, Claudius displays a certain degree of affection and concern for Hamlet, warning him that too much mourning is unhealthy, and urging him not to return to his studies but to remain in Denmark 'in the cheer and comfort of our eye'. (116) However, Claudius might have political reasons for wanting Hamlet to cheer up. The prince's ostentatious grief is an uncomfortable reminder of the old regime.

GERTRUDE

A LOYAL WIFE
Gertrude doesn't say a huge amount in this scene, but what she does say echoes her husband's desire for Hamlet to cheer up and put aside his grief over his father.

MATERNAL FEELING
Gertrude's affection for her son is evident when she asks him not to return to his studies but to remain in Denmark.

LACK OF FEELING
There is a strange lack of feeling in Gertrude's attitude towards Hamlet's grief. She urges Hamlet to snap out of his mourning, telling him death is commonplace. Remember, this is Hamlet's father and her own husband that she is talking about.

him. Gertrude says that death is an everyday occurrence and a natural part of life: 'all that lives must die,/ Passing through nature to eternity.' (72–3) Claudius tells him that the loss of a father is a common experience, and one shouldn't grieve too long. To do so is 'unmanly', and suggests a simple mind and a weak heart. (87–107)

Hamlet's replies suggest the resentment he feels towards his mother and her new husband. When Gertrude asks him why he 'seems' so grief-stricken, Hamlet's reply is aggressive: 'Seems, madam? nay it is; I know not seems'.(76) Hamlet suggests that his feelings of grief are real, while those of Gertrude and Claudius were only a public show of mourning.

Claudius asks Hamlet to consider him his father, and declares him heir to the throne. (106–7) Claudius and Gertrude ask Hamlet to remains at court instead of returning to university. (113–19) Hamlet curtly agrees. (120)

✎ LINES 129–59: HAMLET'S DISGUST AND ANGER

Hamlet is left alone and speaks a soliloquy. He has been experiencing suicidal thoughts. He wishes his flesh would simply melt away or that God had not declared suicide a sin: 'O that this too too solid flesh would melt,/ Thaw and resolve itself into a dew!/ Or that the Everlasting had not fixed/ His canon 'gainst self-slaughter!' (129–32)

To him, life seems pointless, empty and meaningless: 'How weary, stale, flat and unprofitable/ Seem to me all the uses of the world!' (133–4) He regards the world with disgust and contempt, viewing it as an 'unweeded garden' populated by foul beings: 'things rank and gross in nature/ Possess it merely'. (135–7)

Hamlet is distraught at his mother's marriage to Claudius. He feels that his mother married much too soon after his father's death. He can hardly believe that she remarried only a month after mourning behind her husband's coffin. Hamlet considers that this hasty remarriage is an insult to the love that his father bore his mother. He regards Claudius as vastly inferior to his father: 'My father's brother, but no more like my father/ Than I to Hercules'. (152–3) He seems particularly horrified that Gertrude has married his uncle, and regards their union as an 'incestuous' one.

There is a sense in which Hamlet regards his mother as almost animalistic for going through with this hasty marriage. In doing so, she acted like a beast, being guided by passion and instinct rather than by her reason: 'a beast that wants discourse of reason/ Would have mourn'd longer'. (151–2) Her marriage seems to have affected his views of women in general. He sees them as weak and vulnerable in the face of lust and temptation: 'frailty, thy name is woman'. (146)

ANGER & RAGE

Hamlet is filled with rage and bitterness toward his mother because of her remarriage. He feels her remarriage was too hasty, incestuous, and to a far lesser man than his father. This is evident in the bitter, smart remarks Hamlet makes at the beginning of the scene. It is eloquently expressed in his soliloquy, where he describes his anger, shock and disbelief at his mother's decision. It is further expressed when he bitterly remarks to Horatio that the 'funeral baked meats/ Did coldly furnish forth the marriage tables'. (180–1)

NEGATIVE VIEW OF FEMALE SEXUALITY

As we have seen, Gertrude's remarriage has tainted Hamlet's view of female sexuality. His mother, he feels, was guided by animalistic urges rather than by reason. Her behaviour has caused Hamlet to view women in general as 'frail' when it comes to controlling their own lusts.

MENTAL ANGUISH

Hamlet is in a tortured and anguished mental state. He experiences suicidal thoughts, and views life as pointless, and the world as a corrupt and disgusting place. What Hamlet is experiencing here is more than mere bereavement, more than mere anger and disappointment at his mother's behaviour. He has entered an extreme state of mind, one that causes him to view the world through a lens of disgust, contempt and futility.

Horatio's story about the Ghost seems to rouse Hamlet somewhat from his listless depression. He questions Horatio, Marcellus and Barnardo energetically about this apparition, and is eager to encounter the Ghost no matter what dangers this might involve.

DUTIFUL SON

It is obvious that Hamlet had extremely high regard for his father. He tells Horatio, 'I shall not look upon his like again'. (188) In his long soliloquy, he describes him as 'So excellent a king', and praises the intense and tender love he showed his mother. (139–40) It is obvious, then, that this great man's passing would have a negative impact on the prince's emotional state. As he puts it, he continues to see his father in his mind's eye. (185)

LINES 160–257: HAMLET IS TOLD OF THE GHOST

Horatio, Marcellus and Barnardo come to tell Hamlet of their encounter with the Ghost. Horatio tells Hamlet that the Ghost resembles his father. (211–12) He says that he spoke to the Ghost, who looked as if it was going to reply, only to be interrupted by the cock's crowing. (215–18)

Hamlet says that he will watch with them that very night in the hope that the Ghost will speak to him. (224–5) He asks Horatio and the guards to remain silent about what they have seen, and arranges to meet them on the sentry platform before midnight. (246–53) As they leave, Hamlet expresses his forebodings concerning the news: 'My father's spirit in arms! All is not well./ I doubt some foul play'. (254–5)

CHARACTER DEVELOPMENT

HORATIO

HAMLET'S LOYAL FRIEND
Horatio is Hamlet's trusted friend. Their friendship is signalled by the warmth of their greeting. Horatio's loyalty to the prince is demonstrated by the fact that he comes straight-away with news of the Ghost's appearance. He also agrees to remain silent about what he has seen, and to accompany the prince that night when he goes to witness the appar-ition. Throughout the play, Horatio will be the one figure in whom Hamlet has total faith and trust.

HAMLET

Enter LAERTES and his sister, OPHELIA

LAERTES   My necessaries are embarked: farewell.
And, sister, as the winds give benefit
And convoy is assistant, do not sleep,
But let me hear from you.

OPHELIA   Do you doubt that?

LAERTES   For Hamlet and the trifling of his favour,*
Hold it a fashion and a toy in blood,
A violet in the youth of primy nature,
Forward, not permanent, sweet, not lasting,
The perfume and suppliance of a minute,
No more.

OPHELIA   No more but so?

LAERTES   Think it no more.
For nature crescent does not grow alone
In thews and bulk, but, as this temple waxes
The inward service of the mind and soul†
Grows wide withal. Perhaps he loves you now,
And now no soil nor cautel doth besmirch
The virtue of his will: but you must fear,
His greatness weigh'd, his will is not his own,
For he himself is subject to his birth.
He may not, as unvalued persons do,
Carve for himself; for on his choice depends
The safety and health of this whole state,
And therefore must his choice be circumscribed
Unto the voice and yielding of that body
Whereof he is the head. Then if he says he loves you,
It fits your wisdom so far to believe it
As he in his particular sect and place
May give his saying deed, which is no further
Than the main voice of Denmark goes withal.
Then weigh what loss your honour may sustain
If with too credent ear you list his songs,
Or lose your heart, or your chaste treasure open
To his unmaster'd importunity.
Fear it Ophelia, fear it my dear sister,
And keep you in the rear of your affection,‡
Out of the shot and danger of desire.

continued

---

necessaries: personal luggage
winds give benefit: favourable weather
convoy is assistant: means of sending letters

5 *trifling*: insignificant
fashion: changeable; *blood*: humour
violet: flower associated with transience
Forward: blooming early
suppliance: pastime

10

crescent: growing; *alone*: only
thews: muscles; *temple*: body

15 *cautel*: deceit

weigh'd: considered

unvalued persons: people of lower rank
20 *Carve*: choose

circumscribed: limited
body: public body, body politic

25

particular sect and place: his social position

main voice: majority
weigh: consider, judge
30 *credent*: credulous, believing; *list*: listen to
chaste treasure: value of her virginity
unmaster'd: uncontrolled

35 *shot*: from cupid's arrow

....
* 5   *For Hamlet and the trifling of his favour*:
Laertes' comment, which assumes that
Hamlet's interest in Ophelia is minor and
will not last, introduces the love relationship
between Ophelia and Hamlet for the first
time.

† 13–14 *The inward service of the mind and soul/
Grows wide withal*: as the body grows so too
does the inner mind and soul

‡ 34 *keep you in the rear of your affection*: do not let
your emotion and desire rule you

The chariest maid is prodigal enough[*]
If she unmask her beauty to the moon.
Virtue itself scapes not calumnious strokes.
The canker galls the infants of the spring
Too oft before their buttons be disclosed,   40
And in the morn and liquid dew of youth
Contagious blastments are most imminent.
Be wary then; best safety lies in fear:
Youth to itself rebels, though none else near.

OPHELIA   I shall th' effect of this good lesson keep,   45
As watchman to my heart. But good my brother,
Do not, as some ungracious pastors do,
Show me the steep and thorny way to heaven,
Whiles like a puff'd and reckless libertine
Himself the primrose path of dalliance treads,   50
And recks not his own rede.[†]

LAERTES   Oh fear me not.

Enter POLONIUS

I stay too long – but here my father comes.
A double blessing is a double grace;[‡]
Occasion smiles upon a second leave.

POLONIUS   Yet here, Laertes? Aboard, aboard, for shame!   55
The wind sits in the shoulder of your sail,
And you are stayed for. There, my blessing with thee,
And these few precepts in thy memory
Look thou character. Give thy thoughts no tongue,
Nor any unproportioned thought his act.   60
Be thou familiar, but by no means vulgar.
Those friends thou hast, and their adoption tried,
Grapple them to thy soul with hoops of steel,
But do not dull thy palm with entertainment
Of each new-hatched, unfledged courage. Beware   65
Of entrance to a quarrel, but being in,
Bear't that the opposèd may beware of thee.
Give every man thy ear, but few thy voice;
Take each man's censure, but reserve thy judgement.
Costly thy habit as thy purse can buy,   70
But not express'd in fancy; rich, not gaudy.
For the apparel oft proclaims the man,
And they in France of the best rank and station
Are of a most select and generous chief in that.[§]
Neither a borrower nor a lender be,   75
For loan oft loses both itself and friend,
And borrowing dulls the edge of husbandry.
This above all, to thine own self be true,
And it must follow, as the night the day,
Thou canst not then be false to any man.   80
Farewell, my blessing season this in thee.

LAERTES   Most humbly do I take my leave, my lord.
POLONIUS   The time invites you. Go, your servants tend.
LAERTES   Farewell, Ophelia; and remember well
What I have said to you.

---

chariest: most cautious; **prodigal:** reckless

calumnious strokes: slander
canker: caterpillar; **galls:** destroys
buttons: buds

blastments: blights

pastors: shepherd of the flock, priest

puff'd: swollen (with excess)
dalliance: engaging in casual love affairs

sits in the shoulder: is favourable

precepts: guidelines
Look thou: will give to you
unproportioned: unmeasured, inappropriate
vulgar: too familiar, common
adoption tried: friendship tested

dull thy palm: spend money

Bear't: see it through

censure: opinion of others
habit: dress

apparel: clothes

husbandry: careful thrift

---

[*] 36–7   *The chariest maid ... beauty to the moon:* the most virtuous maid is thought to be immoral if she but reveal her beauty to the chaste moon

[†] 51   *recks not his own rede:* doesn't follow his own advice

[‡] 53   *A double blessing is a double grace:* Laertes has already said his farewell to Polonius and received his father's blessing

[§] 74   *Are of a most select and generous chief in that:* French nobles have a most refined style of dress

OPHELIA	'Tis in my memory lock'd,	85
	And you yourself shall keep the key of it.	
LAERTES	Farewell.	

Exit LAERTES

POLONIUS	What is't Ophelia he hath said to you?	
OPHELIA	So please you, something touching the Lord Hamlet.	*touching:* concerning the subject of
POLONIUS	Marry, well bethought:	90 *bethought:* thought of
	'Tis told me, he hath very oft of late	
	Given private time to you, and you yourself	
	Have of your audience been most free and bounteous.*	
	If it be so, as so 'tis put on me,	
	And that in way of caution, I must tell you	95
	You do not understand yourself so clearly	
	As it behooves my daughter and your honour.	
	What is between you? Give me up the truth.	
OPHELIA	He hath my lord of late made many tenders	*tenders:* offers, promises
	Of his affection to me.	100
POLONIUS	Affection! Puh! you speak like a green girl,	*green:* uncultured, inexperienced
	Unsifted in such perilous circumstance.	*Unsifted:* ignorant
	Do you believe his tenders, as you call them?	
OPHELIA	I do not know my lord what I should think.	
POLONIUS	Marry I'll teach you. Think yourself a baby	105
	That you have ta'ne these tenders for true pay,	*ta'en:* taken
	Which are not sterling. Tender yourself more dearly,†	
	Or – not to crack the wind of the poor phrase,	
	Roaming it thus – you'll tender me a fool.	*Roaming it:* playing around with it
OPHELIA	My lord, he hath importuned me with love	110
	In honourable fashion.	
POLONIUS	Ay, fashion you may call it. Go to, go to.	
OPHELIA	And hath given countenance to his speech, my lord,	*countenance:* support
	With almost all the holy vows of heaven.	
POLONIUS	Ay, springes to catch woodcocks. I do know,‡	115
	When the blood burns, how prodigal the soul	
	Lends the tongue vows. These blazes daughter,	
	Giving more light than heat, extinct in both§	
	Even in their promise, as it is a-making,	*a-making:* an art, false
	You must not take for fire. From this time	120
	Be somewhat scanter of your maiden presence.	
	Set your entreatments at a higher rate	*entreatments:* needs
	Than a command to parley. For Lord Hamlet,	*parley:* playful conversation
	Believe so much in him, that he is young	
	And with a larger tedder may he walk	125 *larger tedder:* longer tether/rope
	Than may be given you: in few Ophelia,	
	Do not believe his vows, for they are brokers,	*brokers:* people who buy and sell for gain
	Not of that dye which their investments show,	*dye:* colour, outward appearance
	But mere implorators of unholy suits,	*implorators:* enticers
	Breathing like sanctified and pious bonds,	130
	The better to beguile. This is for all:	
	I would not in plain terms from this time forth,	
	Have you so slander any moment leisure	
	As to give words or talk with the Lord Hamlet.	
	Look to't, I charge you. Come your ways.	135 *Come your ways:* repair your ways
OPHELIA	I shall obey, my lord.	

Exeunt

* 93   *Have of your audience been most free and bounteous:* received him into your company unreservedly

† 107   *Tender yourself more dearly:* put a greater value on yourself

‡ 115   *Ay, springes to catch woodcocks:* the woodcock was famed to be easily snared

§ 117–18 *these blazes … more light than heat, extinct in both:* these passionate vows have no true substance or worth

LAERTES & OPHELIA

Laertes is preparing to leave for France. Both Laertes and Polonius advise Ophelia to be wary of Hamlet's affections. Polonius gives Laertes advice on how he should behave when he is abroad.

A CLOSER LOOK

◆ LINES 5–51: BROTHERLY ADVICE

Laertes is saying farewell to his sister Ophelia before he returns to France. He offers her some brotherly advice. She has told him that Hamlet has made romantic approaches to her. Laertes is deeply suspicious. He says that Ophelia must, for her own protection, not take Hamlet's interest in her seriously.

He warns her that Hamlet's attraction to her is only a passing fancy and will not last: 'Forward, not permanent, sweet not lasting'. (8)

Even if Hamlet's feelings are genuine, he will not be able to marry her. As heir to the throne, he must marry for political gain, not for genuine feeling: 'And therefore must his choice be circumscribed/ Unto the voice and yielding of that body/ Whereof he is the head'. (22–4)

SOME LINES TO LEARN

This above all, to thine own self be true,
And it must follow, as the night the day,
Thou canst not then be false to any man.

Polonius (78–80)

If she yields to Hamlet's approaches, her character and reputation might be damaged: 'Fear it Ophelia, fear it my dear sister'. (33)

Ophelia agrees to follow Laertes' advice, asking only that he too should abide by his own words and not act hypocritically. (45–51)

◆ LINES 58–136: FATHERLY ADVICE

Polonius enters and offers his son some advice before he leaves for France:

- Laertes should be careful in speaking his mind, and never act out of anger. (59–60)
- He should be friendly, but not indiscriminately so, and should make sure to keep his real friends close to him. (62–3)
- He should avoid quarrels, but ensure that his opponents respect him if he does so. (65–7)
- He should listen to all opinions, but be careful about expressing his own. (68–9)
- He should buy good quality clothes, but nothing too flashy. (70–2)
- He should also avoid loaning or borrowing money, the former because of the uncertainty of being repaid and the possibility of losing friends, and the

latter because it damages one's thriftiness. (75–7)

- Finally, he should always act in a way that is genuine and in accord with his feelings: 'to thine own self be true'. (78) In doing so, he will never deceive anyone. (79–80)

Laertes departs, asking his sister once again to remember his advice concerning Hamlet. Ophelia promises to do so. (84–6)

Polonius says that he has heard something of Hamlet's approaches to Ophelia, and demands to know the full story. (90–8) When Ophelia tells him that Hamlet has confessed to having feelings for her, Polonius is scornful, saying she is naive ('green') if she believes the prince's declarations. (101–3) He says that she will disgrace herself and her family if she is not more careful. (105–9)

Ophelia protests that Hamlet's approaches were honourable, saying that Hamlet has sworn his feelings for her are genuine: 'With almost all the holy vows of heaven'. (114) Polonius tells her that Hamlet's vows were only a tactic designed to woo her into bed. He knows from experience how passion makes men declare emotions that they do not have. (115–20) He forbids Ophelia from seeing Hamlet again and she obeys him. (124–36)

POLONIUS & LAERTES

CHARACTER DEVELOPMENT

OPHELIA

INNOCENT & TRUSTING
Ophelia's innocence and trusting nature is evident in the way she listens to the words of her brother and father. She listens without interruption to Laertes' warnings about Hamlet, and promises to take heed of his words: 'I shall th' effect of this good lesson keep'. (45) Similarly, she takes her father's advice and agrees to avoid the prince: 'I shall obey, my lord'. (136)

LAERTES

AN AFFECTIONATE BROTHER
He acts like an affectionate brother. He asks his sister to write to him often when he is away at college in France. He advises her to be wary of Hamlet's affections as they might not be sincere. He also advises her that as prince of Denmark, Hamlet may have to marry a foreign princess for political reasons.

POLONIUS

LONG-WINDED & SELF-IMPORTANT
Polonius is a character who likes the sound of his own voice. This is evident when he gives advice to both Laertes and Ophelia. He puts the advice across in an extremely long-winded and wordy manner. It could be argued that Polonius' self-importance is also evident in this scene. He comes across as someone convinced of his own wisdom, and as someone who always knows best.

However, there can be little doubt that Polonius has genuine affection for his children, and has their interests at heart. Some of the advice he gives is quite sound, even if it is delivered in a long-winded fashion.

27

The gun platform

Enter HAMLET, HORATIO, and MARCELLUS

HAMLET	The air bites shrewdly, it is very cold.
HORATIO	It is a nipping and an eager air.
HAMLET	What hour now?
HORATIO	I think it lacks of twelve.
HAMLET	No, it is struck.
HORATIO	Indeed? I heard it not: then it draws near the season
	Wherein the spirit held his wont to walk.

A flourish of trumpets, and two pieces goes off

What does this mean, my lord?

HAMLET   The king doth wake tonight and takes his rouse,
Keeps wassail, and the swaggering up-spring reels,˙
And, as he drains his draughts of Rhenish down,
The kettle-drum and trumpet thus bray out
The triumph of his pledge.

HORATIO   Is it a custom?

HAMLET   Ay marry is't,
But to my mind, though I am native here
And to the manner born, it is a custom
More honoured in the breach than the observance.†
This heavy-headed revel east and west
Makes us traduced and taxed of other nations:
They clepe us drunkards, and with swinish phrase
Soil our addition; and indeed it takes
From our achievements, though performed at height,
The pith and marrow of our attribute.
So, oft it chances in particular men,
That for some vicious mole of nature in them,
As in their birth – wherein they are not guilty,
Since nature cannot choose his origin –
By the o'ergrowth of some complexion,‡
Oft breaking down the pales and forts of reason,
Or by some habit that too much o'erleavens
The form of plausive manners – that these men,
Carrying I say the stamp of one defect,
Being nature's livery or fortune's star,§
Their virtues else be they as pure as grace,
As infinite as man may undergo,
Shall in the general censure take corruption¢
From that particular fault. The dram of eale˙˙
Doth all the noble substance of a doubt
To his own scandal.

Glosses (right margin):

shrewdly: keenly

eager: sharp

5

takes his rouse: carouses

10   *Rhenish*: wine from the Rhine

pledge: toast

15   *to the manner born*: brought up to it

heavy-headed revel: wits dulled by drink
traduced: exposed to ridicule
clepe: call
20   *Soil our addition*: stain our reputation

vicious mole of nature: natural defect
25   *As*: namely

pales and forts: defences
o'erleavens: corrupts by excess
30   *plausive manners*: approved behaviour

livery: clothes

˙ 9   *Keeps wassail, and the swaggering up-spring reels*: holds a drinking session, and drunkenly dances the upspring (a traditional German dance)

† 16   *More honour'd in the breach than the observance*: it is more honourable to break the tradition that to practise it

‡ 27   *o'ergrowth of some complexion*: excess or imbalance of a particular character trait

§ 32   *Being nature's livery, or fortune's star*: due either to nature's mark or to the influence of ill fortune (associated with destiny, written in the stars)

¢ 35   *general censure*: the evaluation of the man as a whole – may also suggest public opinion

˙˙ 36–8   *eale*: evil; *the dram of eale ... scandal*: the smallest amount of evil brings disgrace to nobility and virtue

Enter GHOST

HORATIO	Look, my lord, it comes!
HAMLET	Angels and ministers of grace defend us!

Be thou a spirit of health or goblin damned,
Bring with thee airs from heaven or blasts from hell,
Be thy intents wicked or charitable,
Thou com'st in such a questionable shape
That I will speak to thee. I'll call thee Hamlet,
King, father, royal Dane. Oh answer me.
Let me not burst in ignorance, but tell
Why thy canonised bones, hearsèd in death,
Have burst their cerements; why the sepulchre,
Wherein we saw thee quietly enurned,
Hath oped his ponderous and marble jaws
To cast thee up again. What may this mean,
That thou, dead corse, again in complete steel
Revisits thus the glimpses of the moon,
Making night hideous, and we fools of nature
So horridly to shake our disposition
With thoughts beyond the reaches of our souls?
Say, why is this? wherefore? What should we do?

GHOST beckons HAMLET

HORATIO	It beckons you to go away with it,
	As if it some impartment did desire
	To you alone.
MARCELLUS	Look, with what courteous action
	It wafts you to a more removèd ground:
	But do not go with it.
HORATIO	No, by no means.
HAMLET	It will not speak; then I will follow it.
HORATIO	Do not, my lord.
HAMLET	Why, what should be the fear?
	I do not set my life in a pin's fee,
	And for my soul, what can it do to that,
	Being a thing immortal as itself?
	It waves me forth again: I'll follow it.
HORATIO	What if it tempt you toward the flood, my lord,
	Or to the dreadful summit of the cliff
	That beetles o'er his base into the sea,
	And there assume some other horrible form
	Which might deprive your sovereignty of reason
	And draw you into madness? Think of it.
	The very place puts toys of desperation,
	Without more motive, into every brain
	That looks so many fathoms to the sea
	And hears it roar beneath.
HAMLET	It wafts me still. Go on; I'll follow thee.
MARCELLUS	You shall not go, my lord.
HAMLET	Hold off your hands.
HORATIO	Be ruled; you shall not go.
HAMLET	My fate cries out,
	And makes each petty arture in this body
	As hardy as the Nemean lion's nerve.
	Still am I called. Unhand me, gentlemen!
	By heaven I'll make a ghost of him that lets me.
	I say, away! – Go on, I'll follow thee.

questionable shape: his form invites question

hearsèd: coffined
cerements: burial clothes
enurned: entombed
his: pronoun refers to the sepulchre

complete steel: full armour

disposition: mind

impartment: communication

removèd ground: separate, quiet place

pin's fee: little worth

beetles: overhangs

sovereignty: rule

toys of desperation: irrational impulses

petty arture: little artery

lets: hinders

* 56   *With thoughts beyond the reaches of our souls*: with such thoughts that evade all reason

† 83   *Nemean lion*: the terrible lion of Nemea – the first labour Hercules had to perform was the killing of this beast

Exit GHOST and HAMLET

HORATIO	He waxes desperate with imagination.
MARCELLUS	Let's follow, 'tis not fit thus to obey him.
HORATIO	Have after. To what issue will this come?
MARCELLUS	Something is rotten in the state of Denmark.
HORATIO	Heaven will direct it.*
MARCELLUS	Nay, let's follow him.

Exeunt

90

waxes desperate: grows mad

Have after: let's pursue

* 91   *Heaven will direct it/ Nay, let's follow him*: let's not leave it to Heaven to do something about it

30

HORATIO, HAMLET & MARCELLUS

Hamlet, Horatio and Marcellus have gone to the palace battlements in the hope of encountering the Ghost. The Ghost appears and beckons Hamlet to go with it so they may talk. Horatio and Marcellus urge Hamlet not to follow the Ghost. Hamlet, however, ignores their warning and heads off after the apparition.

A CLOSER LOOK

It is just gone midnight. Hamlet, Horatio and Marcellus are on the palace battlements waiting to see if the Ghost will appear. Trumpets sound and two cannons go off.

Hamlet is shocked by the Ghost's sudden appearance. The Ghost resembles his father, but in reality it could be a demon from hell come to lure him to his doom. (40–1) Yet he feels he must speak to the Ghost, addressing it as 'Hamlet,/ King, father, royal Dane'. (44–5) He asks it to tell them why it is walking abroad and what it wants. (56–7)

The Ghost beckons Hamlet away. (58–60) Marcellus and Horatio urge Hamlet not to go with it, but the prince is determined, declaring that he does not fear death: 'It will not speak: then I will follow it'. (63)

Horatio and Marcellus attempt to restrain him, but the prince threatens violence if they will not let him go. (84–5) They give up, and Hamlet exits following the Ghost. Horatio and Marcellus follow them, fearing for the prince's safety. (87–91)

CHARACTER DEVELOPMENT

HAMLET

BRAVE & DETERMINED?
In this scene ,Hamlet comes across as brave and determined. He faces the Ghost and addresses it, despite the risks involved. (42–4) He is so determined to follow the Ghost and speak with it, that he threatens his friends with violence if they threaten to restrain him:' Unhand me, gentlemen!/ By heaven I'll make a ghost of him that lets me'. (84–5)

However, it is also possible that Hamlet's feelings of despair and depression lead him to follow the Ghost. Because he places so little value on his own life, he doesn't care if the Ghost leads him to his death: 'I do not set my life in a pin's fee'. (65) As we have seen in Act 1 Scene 2, Hamlet is filled with suicidal thoughts.

HORATIO

LOYAL FRIEND
Horatio once again shows his friendship for Hamlet in this scene. He has Hamlet's best interests at heart when he tries to restrain him and prevent him from following the Ghost.

Enter GHOST and HAMLET

HAMLET	Where wilt thou lead me? Speak; I'll go no further.
GHOST	Mark me.
HAMLET	I will.
GHOST	My hour is almost come
	When I to sulph'rous and tormenting flames
	Must render up myself.
HAMLET	Alas, poor ghost!
GHOST	Pity me not, but lend thy serious hearing
	To what I shall unfold.
HAMLET	Speak, I am bound to hear.
GHOST	So art thou to revenge, when thou shalt hear.
HAMLET	What?
GHOST	I am thy father's spirit,
	Doomed for a certain term to walk the night,
	And for the day confined to fast in fires,
	Till the foul crimes done in my days of nature
	Are burnt and purged away. But that I am forbid
	To tell the secrets of my prison house,
	I could a tale unfold whose lightest word
	Would harrow up thy soul, freeze thy young blood,
	Make thy two eyes, like stars, start from their spheres,
	Thy knotted and combinèd locks to part
	And each particular hair to stand on end
	Like quills upon the fretful porpentine:
	But this eternal blazon must not be
	To ears of flesh and blood. List, list, oh list!
	If thou didst ever thy dear father love –
HAMLET	Oh God!
GHOST	Revenge his foul and most unnatural murder.
HAMLET	Murder?
GHOST	Murder most foul, as in the best it is,
	But this most foul, strange and unnatural.*
HAMLET	Haste me to know't, that I, with wings as swift
	As meditation or the thoughts of love
	May sweep to my revenge.
GHOST	I find thee apt;
	And duller shouldst thou be than the fat weed†
	That roots itself in ease on Lethe wharf,
	Wouldst thou not stir in this. Now Hamlet, hear.‡
	'Tis given out that, sleeping in my orchard,
	A serpent stung me. So the whole ear of Denmark
	Is by a forgèd process of my death
	Rankly abused; but know, thou noble youth,
	The serpent that did sting thy father's life
	Now wears his crown.

Line numbers: 5, 10, 15, 20, 25, 30, 35, 40

sulph'rous and tormenting flames: purgatory

unfold: tell

purged: cleansed

harrow up: rip through
spheres: sockets

porpentine: porcupine
eternal blazon: description of the afterlife
list: listen

Haste me to know't: tell me quickly

Lethe wharf: river of forgetfulness

'Tis given out that: it's said that
whole ear: all
forgèd process: false account of events

* 28   *this most ... unnatural*: repetition of 'unnatural' emphasises the violation of the natural bond between kin

† 32   *duller shouldst thou be than the fat weed*: you would have to be more lethargic than the drug of laziness itself (which grows by the River Lethe in Hades, the underworld)

‡ 34   *Wouldst thou not stir in this*: if this would not move you to action

HAMLET	O my prophetic soul!*	40
	My uncle?	
GHOST	Ay, that incestuous, that adulterate beast,	
	With witchcraft of his wits, with traitorous gifts –	
	O wicked wit and gifts, that have the power	
	So to seduce – won to his shameful lust	45
	The will of my most seeming virtuous queen:	
	O Hamlet, what a falling-off was there,	
	From me whose love was of that dignity	
	That it went hand in hand even with the vow	
	I made to her in marriage, and to decline	50
	Upon a wretch whose natural gifts were poor	
	To those of mine.	
	But virtue as it never will be moved,	
	Though lewdness court it in a shape of heaven,†	
	So lust, though to a radiant angel linked,	55
	Will sate itself in a celestial bed,	
	And prey on garbage.	
	But, soft, methinks I scent the morning air;	
	Brief let me be. Sleeping within my orchard,	
	My custom always of the afternoon,	60
	Upon my secure hour thy uncle stole,	
	With juice of cursèd hebenon in a vial,	
	And in the porches of my ears did pour	
	The leprous distilment, whose effect	
	Holds such an enmity with blood of man	65
	That swift as quicksilver it courses through	
	The natural gates and alleys of the body,‡	
	And with a sudden vigour doth posset	
	And curd, like eager droppings into milk,	
	The thin and wholesome blood: so did it mine,	70
	And a most instant tetter barked about,§	
	Most lazar-like, with vile and loathsome crust,	
	All my smooth body.	
	Thus was I, sleeping, by a brother's hand	
	Of life, of crown, of queen, at once dispatched:	75
	Cut off even in the blossoms of my sin,	
	Unhouseled, disappointed, unaneled,⸰	
	No reckoning made, but sent to my account	
	With all my imperfections on my head –	
	Oh horrible, oh horrible, most horrible!	80
	If thou hast nature in thee, bear it not;	
	Let not the royal bed of Denmark be	
	A couch for luxury and damnèd incest.	
	But, howsomever thou pursues this act,	
	Taint not thy mind, nor let thy soul contrive	85
	Against thy mother aught. Leave her to heaven	
	And to those thorns that in her bosom lodge	
	To prick and sting her. Fare thee well at once!	
	The glow-worm shows the matin to be near,	
	And gins to pale his uneffectual fire:**	90
	Adieu, adieu, adieu. Remember me.	

Exit

Glossary

sate: satisfy to the point of excess

secure: free from concern
hebenon: poison, possibly henbane (disputed)

distilment: concentrated liquid
enmity: hate
quicksilver: mercury

vigour: strength; posset: thicken
eager: acid, causing curdling
thin and wholesome: healthy
tetter: skin eruptions
lazar-like: like leprosy

dispatched: deprived of life
blossoms: fullness

reckoning: sorting of debts (sins)

nature: human feeling

contrive: scheme
to heaven: to God's judgement
those thorns: guilty conscience

gins: begins

*   40   *O my prophetic soul*: suggests Hamlet's foreknowledge of his uncle's base nature

†   54   *Though lewdness court it in a shape of heaven*: the devil has power to disguise himself by changing his outward form

‡   67   *The natural gates and alleys of the body*: the interior passages of the human body are metaphorically described as 'alleys' of a city

§   71   *And a most instant … crust*: immediately the skin erupted with disgusting scabs

⸰   77   *Unhouseled … unaneled*: without receiving the eucharist or being anointed with holy oil

**   89–90   *The glow-worm … fire*: the glow-worm only gives off light (pale form of fire) in the dark – because its light is fading, morning must be near

HAMLET	O all you host of heaven! O earth! what else?
	And shall I couple hell? Oh fie! Hold, hold, my heart;
	And you, my sinews, grow not instant old
	But bear me stiffly up. Remember thee? 95
	Ay thou poor ghost, while memory holds a seat
	In this distracted globe. Remember thee?
	Yea, from the table of my memory
	I'll wipe away all trivial fond records,
	All saws of books, all forms, all pressures past, 100
	That youth and observation copied there;*
	And thy commandment all alone shall live
	Within the book and volume of my brain,†
	Unmixed with baser matter: yes, by heaven!
	O most pernicious woman! 105
	O villain, villain, smiling, damnèd villain!
	My tables – meet it is I set it down,
	That one may smile, and smile, and be a villain;
	At least I'm sure it may be so in Denmark.
Writing	
	So, uncle, there you are. Now to my word: 110
	It is 'Adieu, adieu, remember me.'
	I have sworn 't.
HORATIO	*[Within]* My lord, my lord!
MARCELLUS	*[Within]* Lord Hamlet!
Enter HORATIO and MARCELLUS	
HORATIO	Heavens secure him!
HAMLET	So be it.
MARCELLUS	*[Within]* Illo, ho, ho, my lord! 115
HAMLET	Hillo, ho, ho, boy! Come bird, come.
MARCELLUS	How is't, my noble lord?
HORATIO	What news, my lord?
HAMLET	Oh, wonderful!
HORATIO	Good my lord, tell it.
HAMLET	No, you will reveal it.
HORATIO	Not I my lord, by heaven.
MARCELLUS	Nor I my lord. 120
HAMLET	How say you then, would heart of man once think it –
	But you'll be secret?
HORATIO }	
MARCELLUS }	
HAMLET	There's ne'er a villain dwelling in all Denmark
	But he's an arrant knave.
HORATIO	There needs no ghost, my lord, come from the grave, 125
	To tell us this.
HAMLET	Why, right; you are i' th' right;
	And so, without more circumstance at all
	I hold it fit that we shake hands and part –
	You, as your business and desire shall point you;
	For every man has business and desire, 130
	Such as it is, and for mine own poor part,
	Look you, I'll go pray.
HORATIO	These are but wild and whirling words, my lord.
HAMLET	I'm sorry they offend you, heartily;
	Yes faith, heartily.

couple hell: embrace evil
instant old: immediately frail

globe: his head (microcosm of the world)
table: tablet, writing material
trivial fond records: unimportant memories
saws: sayings, quotations

baser: less important
pernicious: deadly

tables: writing material

Illo, ho, ho: falconer's cry to recall hawk
come, bird: mock of his friend's call

wonderful: full of wonder, strange

would heart of man once think it: unthinkable

circumstance: ado, detail

whirling: passionate, nonsensical

* 100–1 *All saws of books … copied there*: all previous impressions, whether made by books or youthful experience, that have been printed on the memory

† 103 *Within the book and volume of my brain*: the memory, which like writing material can be written on, is situated in the brain, imaged as a book

HORATIO	There's no offence, my lord.	135
HAMLET	Yes by Saint Patrick but there is, Horatio,	

Saint Patrick: associated with Purgatory

HAMLET   And much offence too. Touching this vision here,
It is an honest ghost, that let me tell you.
For your desire to know what is between us,
O'ermaster't as you may. And now good friends,   140
As you are friends, scholars, and soldiers,
Give me one poor request.

O'ermaster't: control it

HORATIO   What is't, my lord? we will.
HAMLET   Never make known what you have seen to-night.
HORATIO ⎫
MARCELLUS ⎭
HAMLET   Nay but swear't.
HORATIO   In faith   145
My lord not I.
MARCELLUS   Nor I, my lord, in faith.
HAMLET   Upon my sword.
MARCELLUS   We have sworn, my lord, already.
HAMLET   Indeed, upon my sword, indeed.

GHOST cries under the stage

GHOST   Swear.
HAMLET   Ha, ha, boy, say'st thou so? art thou there, truepenny?   150
Come on, you hear this fellow in the cellarage,
Consent to swear.

cellarage: down below

HORATIO   Propose the oath, my lord.
HAMLET   Never to speak of this that you have seen,
Swear by my sword.
GHOST   Swear.   155
HAMLET   *Hic et ubique?* then we'll shift our ground.
Come hither, gentlemen,
And lay your hands again upon my sword.
Never to speak of this that you have heard,
Swear by my sword.   160

Hic et ubique: 'here and everywhere' (Latin)

GHOST   Swear.
HAMLET   Well said old mole, canst work i' th' earth so fast?
A worthy pioneer. Once more remove, good friends.

pioneer: miner

HORATIO   O day and night, but this is wondrous strange.
HAMLET   And therefore as a stranger give it welcome.   165
There are more things in heaven and earth, Horatio,
Than are dreamt of in your philosophy.
But come –

your philosophy: your rational thought

Here as before, never so help you mercy,
How strange or odd some'er I bear myself,   170
As I perchance hereafter shall think meet
To put an antic disposition on –*

odd: strangeness reflected in his syntax
meet: appropriate

That you at such times seeing me never shall,
With arms encumbered thus, or this head-shake,
Or by pronouncing of some doubtful phrase,   175
As 'Well, well, we know,' or 'We could, and if we would,'
Or 'If we list to speak,' or 'There be and if they might,'
Or such ambiguous giving out, to note

encumber'd: folded

ambiguous: unclear

That you know aught of me: this not to do,
So grace and mercy at your most need help you,   180
Swear.
GHOST   Swear.

* 172   *To put an antic disposition on*: To
avoid detection of his true intentions, Hamlet tells his trusted
friends that he will feign madness

HAMLET   Rest, rest, perturbèd spirit. So, gentlemen,
                         With all my love I do commend me to you,
                         And what so poor a man as Hamlet is   185
                         May do, t'express his love and friending to you,
                         God willing shall not lack. Let us go in together,
                         And still your fingers on your lips, I pray. –
                         The time is out of joint: O cursèd spite,   *out of joint*: out of order
                         That ever I was born to set it right. –   190
                         Nay come, let's go together.

Exeunt

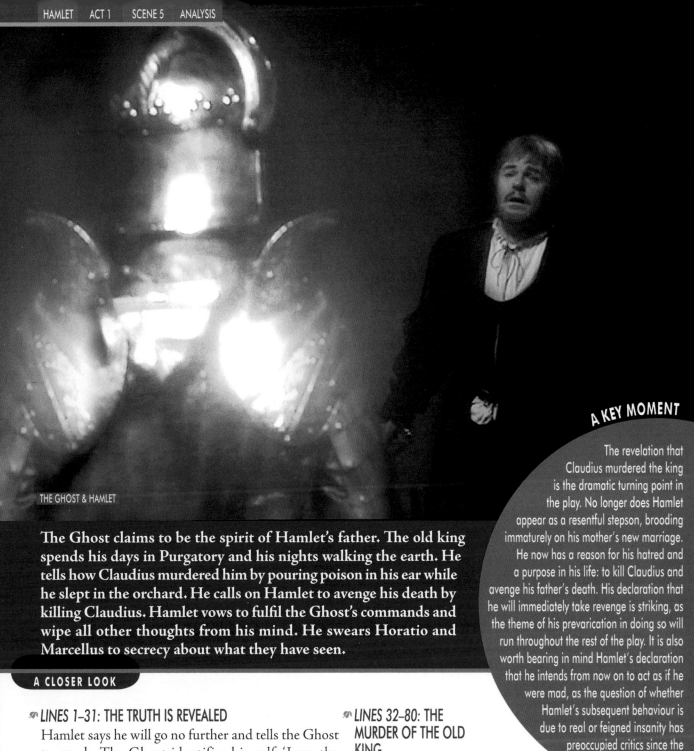

THE GHOST & HAMLET

A KEY MOMENT

The revelation that Claudius murdered the king is the dramatic turning point in the play. No longer does Hamlet appear as a resentful stepson, brooding immaturely on his mother's new marriage. He now has a reason for his hatred and a purpose in his life: to kill Claudius and avenge his father's death. His declaration that he will immediately take revenge is striking, as the theme of his prevarication in doing so will run throughout the rest of the play. It is also worth bearing in mind Hamlet's declaration that he intends from now on to act as if he were mad, as the question of whether Hamlet's subsequent behaviour is due to real or feigned insanity has preoccupied critics since the play first appeared.

The Ghost claims to be the spirit of Hamlet's father. The old king spends his days in Purgatory and his nights walking the earth. He tells how Claudius murdered him by pouring poison in his ear while he slept in the orchard. He calls on Hamlet to avenge his death by killing Claudius. Hamlet vows to fulfil the Ghost's commands and wipe all other thoughts from his mind. He swears Horatio and Marcellus to secrecy about what they have seen.

A CLOSER LOOK

⌖ LINES 1–31: THE TRUTH IS REVEALED

Hamlet says he will go no further and tells the Ghost to speak. The Ghost identifies himself: 'I am thy father's spirit'. (9) He says he is condemned to burn in the flames of Purgatory by day and walk the earth by night until the sins of his life are purged. (9–13) He is forbidden to describe his tortures, but if he could the description would horrify his son. (13–22)

The Ghost emphasises the unnatural nature of his death: 'Murder most foul, as in the best it is;/ But this most foul, strange and unnatural'. (27–8) He states that if Hamlet ever loved him, he must 'Revenge his foul and most unnatural murder'. (25) Hamlet demands to know the truth at once so he can immediately avenge his murder. (29–31) The Ghost is pleased with Hamlet's reaction: 'I find thee apt'. (31)

⌖ LINES 32–80: THE MURDER OF THE OLD KING

The Ghost says that all of Denmark believes his death was due to being stung by a serpent while sleeping in his orchard. (35–7) The truth, however, is that he was murdered by Claudius: 'The serpent that did sting thy father's life/ Now wears his crown'. (39–40)

The Ghost condemns Claudius, calling him an 'incestuous', 'adulterate beast' who used his 'wicked wit and gifts' to seduce Gertrude. (44–5) But the Ghost saves his most damning words for Gertrude. He tells Hamlet that Gertrude is not a good and virtuous person, but only seems so: 'seeming virtuous'. (46) He calls her a slave to her sexual desire. (55–7)

The Ghost then recounts the full story of his death. He was taking his customary afternoon sleep in his orchard when Claudius poured poison in his ear: 'And in the porches of my ears did pour/ That leprous distilment'. He died instantly. (63–73)

With one stroke, Claudius stole his wife, his kingdom and his life: 'by a brother's hand/ Of life, of crown, of queen, at once dispatched'. (74–5) Crucially, the king died with his sins un-confessed and un-atoned for: 'No reckoning made, but sent to my account/ With all my imperfections on my head'. (78–9) This is why he burns in Purgatory and walks the earth by night.

♥ LINES 81–91: HAMLET IS URGED TO VENGEANCE

The Ghost begs Hamlet to avenge his death, as the royal throne of Denmark must not be tainted. (82–3) He also asks Hamlet not to harm Gertrude, claiming that she will be punished in the afterlife and that her own conscience will torment her while she lives: 'leave her to heaven/ And to those thorns that in her bosom lodge/ To prick and sting her'. (86–8) The Ghost then says it must depart, as dawn approaches. He begs Hamlet to not forget him: 'Remember me'. (91)

♥ LINES 92–112: HAMLET SWEARS REVENGE

Hamlet vows that he will make avenging his father's death his only purpose: 'And thy commandment all alone shall live/ Within the book and volume of my brain'. (102–3) He will wipe all other thoughts from his mind. The prince then condemns Claudius and Gertrude, describing his mother 'pernicious', or sinful, and Claudius as a 'smiling damnèd villain'. (105–8)

♥ LINES 113–192: HAMLET'S STRANGE BEHAVIOUR

Horatio and Marcellus catch up with Hamlet and are eager to know about his encounter with the Ghost. Hamlet is in a strange mood and he speaks to his friends in a way that is giddy, excited and confused, causing Horatio to remark on his 'wild and whirling words'. (133) Hamlet refuses to tell them what the Ghost said. He also insists that they swear on his sword not to reveal what they have seen this night. The Ghost joins in with him, shouting 'Swear' from beneath the ground. (155) Hamlet seems amused at the Ghost's behaviour, referring to it as an 'old mole'. (162)

Hamlet tells his friends that he may behave in a strange or mad fashion in the coming days and weeks: 'I perchance hereafter shall think meet/ To put an antic disposition on'. (171–2) His friends must not let on that this 'antic disposition' is only an act.

38

CHARACTER DEVELOPMENT

HAMLET

A LOYAL SON

Hamlet once again reveals the intense love and loyalty he feels for his father. He seems horrified by the sufferings his father's spirit must undergo. He immediately vows to avenge his father's death, and says that he will wipe all other thoughts from his mind. However, as we shall see, there are a number of factors that prevent Hamlet from simply and quickly avenging his father's murder.

ANGER & RAGE

Hamlet vocalises once again the anger he feels towards his mother, calling her a 'most pernicious woman'. (105) He also expresses deep anger towards Claudius, referring to him as a 'smiling damned villain'. (106) The resentment he feels towards his uncle has found a concrete focus. He has been given a real reason to hate Claudius.

EXULTANT

It is not surprising, then, that when Hamlet meets Horatio and Marcellus he is in a strange and agitated state of mind. He speaks in a giddy and confused fashion, with what Horatio describes as 'wild and whirling words'. (133) Hamlet is no doubt shaken and disturbed by the supernatural encounter he has just experienced. But he also seems exhilarated and excited by the meeting with the Ghost, and the task it has given him.

Hamlet is in a state of mind where life seems futile and pointless. In Act 1 Scene 2 he described how he saw life as futile and pointless. It could be argued that the Ghost's visit has given him a mission and a sense of purpose. However, he also seems to feel daunted by the task that now faces him and uncertain about how he will accomplish it: 'O cursèd spite/ That ever I was born to set it right'. (189–90)

HORATIO

HAMLET'S LOYAL FRIEND

Horatio once again shows his loyalty to Hamlet in this scene. He follows Hamlet to make sure that he is all right, and swears not to reveal what he has seen this night.

Enter POLONIUS and REYNALDO

POLONIUS	Give him this money, and these notes, Reynaldo.
REYNALDO	I will my lord.
POLONIUS	You shall do marvellous wisely, good Reynaldo,
	Before you visit him, to make inquire
	Of his behavior.
REYNALDO	My lord, I did intend it.

5

POLONIUS	Marry well said, very well said. Look you sir,
	Inquire me first what Danskers are in Paris;
	And how, and who, what means, and where they keep,
	What company, at what expense; and finding
	By this encompassment and drift of question
	That they do know my son, come you more nearer*
	Than your particular demands will touch it.
	Take you as 'twere some distant knowledge of him;
	As thus, 'I know his father and his friends,
	And in part him' – do you mark this, Reynaldo?
REYNALDO	Ay, very well, my lord.
POLONIUS	'And in part him, but' – you may say – 'not well,
	But, if 't be he I mean, he's very wild,
	Addicted so and so' – and there put on him
	What forgeries you please; marry, none so rank
	As may dishonour him, take heed of that;
	But sir, such wanton, wild, and usual slips
	As are companions noted and most known
	To youth and liberty.
REYNALDO	As gaming, my lord?
POLONIUS	Ay, or drinking, fencing, swearing,
	Quarrelling, drabbing: you may go so far.
REYNALDO	My lord, that would dishonour him.
POLONIUS	Faith no, as you may season it in the charge.
	You must not put another scandal on him,
	That he is open to incontinency,
	That's not my meaning: but breathe his faults so quaintly†
	That they may seem the taints of liberty,
	The flash and outbreak of a fiery mind,
	A savageness in unreclaimèd blood,
	Of general assault.
REYNALDO	But, my good lord –
POLONIUS	Wherefore should you do this?
REYNALDO	Ay, my lord,
	I would know that.

10

15

20

25

30

35

Danskers: Danes
keep: lodge

encompassment: skirting round

distant: vague

forgeries: fictions; *rank*: vile

drabbing: whoring

season it: tone it down

incontinency: promiscuity
quaintly: skillfully

unreclaimed: unreformed
general assault: attacks all indiscriminately

* 11   *come you ... will touch it*: come closer to the specific concerns of your inquiry

† 30–1   *That he is open to incontinency ... not my meaning*: Polonius distinguishes between promiscuity and 'drabbing', suggesting perhaps a difference between a wanton, habitual promiscuity and the natural lust of youth

POLONIUS	Marry sir, here's my drift;
	And I believe it is a fetch of warrant:
	You laying these slight sullies on my son,
	As 'twere a thing a little soiled i' the working,
	Mark you,
	Your party in converse, him you would sound,
	Having ever seen in the prenominate crimes
	The youth you breathe of guilty, be assured
	He closes with you in this consequence;
	'Good sir', or so, or 'friend', or 'gentleman',
	According to the phrase or the addition
	Of man and country.
REYNALDO	Very good, my lord.
POLONIUS	And then, sir, does a this – a does – what was I about to say?
	By the mass I was about to say something: where did I leave?
REYNALDO	At 'closes in the consequence', at 'friend, or so', and 'gentleman'.
POLONIUS	At 'closes in the consequence' – ay, marry,
	He closes with you thus: 'I know the gentleman,
	I saw him yesterday, or th' other day,
	Or then, or then, with such, or such, and as you say,
	There was a gaming; there o'ertook in's rouse;
	There falling out at tennis', or perchance,
	'I saw him enter such a house of sale',
	Videlicet, a brothel – or so forth. See you now,
	Your bait of falsehood takes this carp of truth,
	And thus do we of wisdom and of reach,
	With windlasses and with assays of bias,
	By indirections find directions out.
	So, by my former lecture and advice,
	Shall you my son. You have me, have you not?
REYNALDO	My lord, I have.
POLONIUS	God buy ye, fare ye well.
REYNALDO	Good my lord!
POLONIUS	Observe his inclination in yourself.†
REYNALDO	I shall, my lord.
POLONIUS	And let him ply his music.‡
REYNALDO	Well, my lord.
POLONIUS	Farewell.

Exit REYNALDO
Enter OPHELIA

	How now, Ophelia! what's the matter?
OPHELIA	O my lord, my lord, I have been so affrighted!
POLONIUS	With what, i' th' name of God?
OPHELIA	My lord, as I was sewing in my closet,
	Lord Hamlet with his doublet all unbraced;
	No hat upon his head, his stockings fouled,
	Ungartered, and down-gyvèd to his ankle;
	Pale as his shirt, his knees knocking each other;
	And with a look so piteous in purport
	As if he had been loosèd out of hell
	To speak of horrors – he comes before me.

drift: meaning
fetch of warrant: justified

40 soil'd i' the working: soiled by worldly contact

prenominate: before-named

45 closes with you: confides

addition: attributes

50 By the mass: an oath

55

o'ertook in's rouse: too drunk

Videlicet: that is to say (abbreviated 'viz.')

60

indirections: indirect means

65 You have me: You understand me

70

75 closet: room
doublet all unbraced: jacket unfastened

down-gyvèd: fallen down

80 in purport: in expression

* 62 *With windlasses and with assays of bias*: with roundabout ways and devious tests

† 68 *Observe his inclination in yourself*: act according to his liking

‡ 70 *And let him ply his music*: and let him apply himself to his music. Music was one of the accomplishments of a gentleman. This phrase may also be understood metaphorically: let him 'call his own tune' – that is, carry on in his particular style of living.

POLONIUS   Mad for thy love?

OPHELIA   My lord I do not know;
But truly I do fear it.

POLONIUS   What said he?

OPHELIA   He took me by the wrist, and held me hard;   85
Then goes he to the length of all his arm,*
And with his other hand thus o'er his brow
He falls to such *perusal* of my face
As he would draw it. Long stayed he so;
At last, a little shaking of mine arm   90
And thrice his head thus waving up and down,
He raised a sigh so piteous and profound
As it did seem to shatter all his *bulk*,
And end his being. That done, he lets me go,
And, with his head over his shoulder turned,   95
He seemed to find his way *without his eyes*;
For out-a-doors he went without their helps,
And to the last bended *their light* on me.

POLONIUS   Come, go with me, I will go seek the king.
This is the very *ecstasy* of love,   100
Whose violent property fordoes itself†
And leads the will to desperate undertakings
As oft as any *passion* under heaven
That does afflict our natures. I am sorry.
What, have you given him any hard words of late?   105

OPHELIA   No my good lord; but as you did command,
I did repel his letters, and denied
His access to me.

POLONIUS   That hath made him mad.‡
I am sorry that with better heed and judgement
I had not *quoted* him: I feared he did but trifle,   110
And meant to *wrack* thee; but beshrew my jealousy.§
By heaven, it is as proper to our age⁋
To cast beyond ourselves in our opinions
As it is common for the younger sort
To lack discretion. Come, go we to the king.   115
This must be known, which being kept close, might move
More grief to hide than hate to utter love.**
Come.

Exeunt

perusal: scrutiny

bulk: chest

without his eyes: kept his eyes on her as he left

their light: light thought to emanate from eyes

ecstasy: reason in suspense, altered state

passion: violent emotion

quoted: observed
wrack: dishonour, seduce

* 86   *Then goes he to the length of all his arm*: he holds her at arm's length

† 101   *Whose violent property fordoes itself*: the forceful nature of love in its extreme or obsessive state destroys itself

‡ 108   *That ... mad*: Ophelia's refusal to see Hamlet is what has 'driven him over the edge'

§ 111   *beshrew my jealousy*: curse my suspicion

⁋ 112   *it is as proper ... opinions*: it is a trait of old age to suspect more than we know

** 116–17 *being kept close ... hate to utter love*: the king may be offended to hear of Hamlet's love for Ophelia – however, concealing it might cause more grief, because of what Hamlet in his madness might do

POLONIUS & REYNALDO

Polonius sends Reynaldo to spy on Laertes while he is away studying. Ophelia tells Polonius that Hamlet has been behaving in a very strange fashion towards her. Polonius is convinced that Hamlet's love for Ophelia has driven him mad. He rushes to tell the king this news.

A CLOSER LOOK

LINES 1–73: POLONIUS SPIES ON HIS SON

Polonius is sending his servant Reynaldo to visit Laertes and deliver some money. He wishes to know whether Laertes is behaving himself in Paris. He asks Reynaldo to make the acquaintance of some of Laertes' friends. He should tell these friends that Laertes is fond of drinking, fencing and going to brothels: 'such wanton, wild, and usual slips/ As are companions noted and most known/ To youth and liberty'. (21–3) The friends' responses will reveal how Laertes is really spending his time.

LINES 73–100: OPHELIA IS DISTRESSED

Ophelia enters in a frightened and confused state. She tells how she was visited by a deranged Hamlet. The prince's jacket was undone, he wore no cap and his stockings were down to his ankles; he appeared pale and his body was shaking. (77–81) He had 'a look so piteous in purport/ As if he had been loosèd out of hell'. (82–3)

Ophelia reports that Hamlet held her by the wrist and studied her face intently. 'Long stayed he so'. (91) He then sighed deeply: 'As it did seem to shatter all his bulk/ And end his being'. (95–6) He nodded his head and left the chamber, all the time looking at her over his shoulder: 'He seemed to find his way without his eyes'. (98) He did all this without ever saying a word.

LINES 101–20: POLONIUS THINKS HE KNOWS WHY HAMLET IS 'INSANE'

Polonius immediately decides that Hamlet's strange behaviour is due to his love for Ophelia: 'This is the very ecstasy of love'. (102) He asks Ophelia if she has said anything harsh to the prince lately. She says that she has been refusing to see him, as her father instructed. Polonius thinks that by forbidding Ophelia from seeing Hamlet he has pushed the prince over the edge: 'That hath made him mad'. (110)

Polonius no longer thinks the prince has only lustful designs on his daughter, but really loves her: 'I feared he did but trifle/ And meant to wrack thee'. (112–13) He decides that Claudius must be informed immediately, as to keep Hamlet's behaviour secret would only lead to more trouble: 'This must be known, which, being kept close, might move/ More grief to hide than hate to utter love'. (118–19)

POLONIUS

LONG-WINDED & SELF-IMPORTANT
Polonius' love of his own voice is again evident in the long-winded instructions he gives to Reynaldo. As in Act 1 Scene 3, he comes across as being convinced of his own wisdom, telling Reynaldo how best to spy on Laertes and assuming to know immediately the cause of Hamlet's madness. His self-importance makes him long to be at the centre of the court's affairs, and sends him rushing to the king and queen with news of Hamlet's strange behaviour.

A MEDDLING SCHEMER
Polonius has an inbuilt tendency toward plotting and scheming. We see this when he sends Reynaldo to spy on his son. Polonius is also something of a meddler who can't resist involving himself in other people's business. We see this when he rushes to tell Claudius about Hamlet's strange behaviour. Instead of focusing on the concerns of his own daughter, he seems more eager to involve himself in royal affairs.

OPHELIA

INNOCENT & TRUSTING
Ophelia comes across as an innocent and obedient daughter, doing exactly as her father would have wished her to do, coming straight to him with news of Hamlet's strange behaviour. She seems to have followed her father's instructions to distance herself from Hamlet.

HAMLET

ACTING INSANE?
Ophelia's report suggests that Hamlet is behaving in an extremely strange fashion. He seems to be acting on the warning he gave in Act 1 Scene 5 when he said that he would put an 'antic disposition' on and begin to act in an insane manner. (1.5.172)

OPHELIA & POLONIUS

SOME LINES TO LEARN

And thus do we of wisdom and of reach,
With windlasses and with assays of bias,
By indirections find directions out.
Polonius (64–6)

CONSIDER THIS

In this scene we learn that Hamlet has begun to act like a madman. From this point forward, he will often act like a madman when in public. But we might ask ourselves the following questions:

- What exactly does he hope to achieve by pretending to be mad?
- Why should he choose to torment the innocent Ophelia?
- Was his strange behaviour toward Ophelia completely an act? Or is it also possible that he was genuinely disturbed and distraught when he approached her in this dishevelled and bizarre manner?

43

Trumpet call

Enter KING *and* QUEEN, ROSENCRANTZ *and* GUILDENSTER, with others

CLAUDIUS   Welcome, dear Rosencrantz and Guildenstern!
Moreover that we much did long to see you,   *Moreover that*: especially as
The need we have to use you did provoke
Our hasty sending. Something have you heard
Of Hamlet's transformation – so call it,   5
Sith nor th' exterior nor the inward man   *Sith nor*: since neither
Resembles that it was. What it should be,   *What it should be*: what its cause is
More than his father's death, that thus hath put him
So much from the understanding of himself,
I cannot dream of. I entreat you both,   10
That, being of so young days brought up with him,
And sith so neighboured to his youth and haviour,   *neighboured*: close; *haviour*: behaviour
That you vouchsafe your rest here in our court   *vouchsafe*: agree to
Some little time: so by your companies   *Some little time*: for a little while
To draw him on to pleasures, and to gather   15
So much as from occasion you may glean,   *occasion*: opportunity; *glean*: discover
Whether aught to us unknown afflicts him thus,
That, opened lies within our remedy.   *open'd*: revealed
GERTRUDE   Good gentlemen, he hath much talked of you;
And sure I am, two men there is not living   20
To whom he more adheres. If it will please you   *more adheres*: feels closer
To show us so much gentry and good will   *gentry*: courtesy
As to expend your time with us a while,   *expend*: spend
For the supply and profit of our hope,*
Your visitation shall receive such thanks   25
As fits a king's remembrance.
ROSENCRANTZ   Both your majesties
Might, by the sovereign power you have of us
Put your dread pleasures more into command   *dread*: deeply revered
Than to entreaty.
GUILDENSTERN   But we both obey,
And here give up ourselves, in the full bent†   30   *give up ourselves*: give up our time and labour
To lay our service freely at your feet
To be commanded.
CLAUDIUS   Thanks Rosencrantz and gentle Guildenstern.
GERTRUDE   Thanks Guildenstern and gentle Rosencrantz.
And I beseech you instantly to visit   35
My too much changed son. Go some of you
And bring these gentlemen where Hamlet is.
GUILDENSTERN Heavens make our presence and our practises
Pleasant and helpful to him.
GERTRUDE   Ay, amen.

---

* 24   *For the supply and profit of our hope*:
       for the purpose of securing our goal

† 30   *in the full bent*: completely commit-
       ted, like a drawn bow

Exeunt ROSENCRANTZ and GUILDENSTERN and some Attendants
Enter POLONIUS

POLONIUS	Th' ambassadors from Norway, my good lord,
	Are joyfully returned.
CLAUDIUS	Thou still hast been the father of good news.
POLONIUS	Have I, my lord? Assure you, my good liege,
	I hold my duty, as I hold my soul,
	Both to my God and to my gracious king;
	And I do think, or else this brain of mine
	Hunts not the trail of policy so sure˚
	As it hath used to do, that I have found
	The very cause of Hamlet's lunacy.
CLAUDIUS	Oh speak of that, that do I long to hear.
POLONIUS	Give first admittance to th' ambassadors;
	My news shall be the fruit to that great feast.
CLAUDIUS	Thyself do grace to them, and bring them in.

Exit POLONIUS

	He tells me, my dear Gertrude, he hath found
	The head and source of all your son's distemper.
GERTRUDE	I doubt it is no other but the main:
	His father's death, and our o'erhasty marriage.
CLAUDIUS	Well, we shall sift him.

Re-enter POLONIUS, VOLTEMAND and CORNELIUS

	Welcome, my good friends.
	Say Voltemand, what from our brother Norway?
VOLTEMAND	Most fair return of greetings and desires.
	Upon our first, he sent out to suppress
	His nephew's levies, which to him appeared
	To be a preparation 'gainst the Polack;
	But better looked into, he truly found
	It was against your highness; whereat grieved,
	That so his sickness, age and impotence
	Was falsely borne in hand, sends out arrests
	On Fortinbras, which he in brief obeys;
	Receives rebuke from Norway, and in fine
	Makes vow before his uncle never more
	To give th' assay of arms against your majesty.
	Whereon old Norway, overcome with joy,
	Gives him three thousand crowns in annual fee,
	And his commission to employ those soldiers,
	So levied as before, against the Polack;
	With an entreaty, herein further shown,
	That it might please you to give quiet pass
	Through your dominions for this enterprise,
	On such regards of safety and allowance
	As therein are set down.

Gives a document

CLAUDIUS	It likes us well,
	And at our more considered time we'll read,†
	Answer, and think upon this business.
	Meantime, we thank you for your well-took labour.
	Go to your rest; at night we'll feast together:
	Most welcome home.

Exeunt Ambassadors

40
45
50
55
60
65
70
75
80
85

fruit: best of
do grace to them: greet them with honour

distemper: malady

sift: listen carefully

our brother: fellow king

nephew's levies: troop described earlier

falsely borne in hand: taken advantage of

assay: challenge

quiet pass: peaceful passage
dominions: lands
regards: conditions

˚ 47   *Hunts not the trail of policy*: does not pursue the craft of politics
† 82   *at our more considered time*: when we've more time to consider

POLONIUS   This business is well ended.
My liege, and madam, to expostulate
What majesty should be, what duty is,
Why day is day, night night, and time is time,   90
Were nothing but to waste night, day and time.
Therefore, since brevity is the soul of wit
And tediousness the limbs and outward flourishes,
I will be brief. Your noble son is mad.
Mad call I it; for, to define true madness,   95
What is't but to be nothing else but mad?
But let that go.
GERTRUDE   More matter, with less art.*
POLONIUS   Madam, I swear I use no art at all.
That he is mad, 'tis true; 'tis true 'tis pity;,
And pity 'tis 'tis true – a foolish figure,   100
But farewell it, for I will use no art.
Mad let us grant him then, and now remains
That we find out the cause of this effect,
Or rather say, the cause of this defect,†
For this effect defective comes by cause.   105
Thus it remains, and the remainder thus.†
Perpend.
I have a daughter – have while she is mine –
Who in her duty and obedience, mark,
Hath given me this. Now gather and surmise.   110

Reads the letter

'To the celestial, and my soul's idol, the most beautified
Ophelia,' –
That's an ill phrase, a vile phrase, 'beautified' is a vile
phrase – but you shall hear. Thus:
'In her excellent white bosom, these, et cetera.'   115
GERTRUDE   Came this from Hamlet to her?
POLONIUS   Good madam, stay awhile, I will be faithful.
    'Doubt thou the stars are fire,
    Doubt that the sun doth move,
    Doubt truth to be a liar,   120
    But never doubt I love.
'O dear Ophelia, I am ill at these numbers, I have not art
to reckon my groans: but that I love thee best,
    O most best, believe it. Adieu.
    'Thine evermore, most dear lady, whilst this machine
                        is to him, HAMLET.'   125
This in obedience hath my daughter shown me,
And more above, hath his solicitings,
As they fell out, by time, by means, and place,
All given to mine ear.
CLAUDIUS   But how hath she
Received his love?
POLONIUS   What do you think of me?   130
CLAUDIUS   As of a man faithful and honourable.

---

expostulate: illustrate, debate

comes by cause: there is a reason for it

Perpend: consider what I have to say
while she is mine: until she marries
mark: note
gather and surmise: listen and conclude

machine: body
is to him: remains living, owned by his soul

fell out: occurred
given to mine ear: told to me

---

*   97   *More matter, with less art*: stick to the
             point, and cut the frilly language

†   103–4 *this effect … defect*: Polonius is play-
             ing on word similarity, making his
             language tangled and less plain

†   106   *Thus it remains, and the remainder
             thus*: it remains that he is mad, and
             what is left to be done is as follows

POLONIUS	I would fain prove so. But what might you think,	
	When I had seen this hot love on the wing –	*on the wing*: in flight
	As I perceived it, I must tell you that,	
	Before my daughter told me – what might you,	135
	Or my dear majesty your queen here, think,	
	If I had played the desk or table-book,*	
	Or given my heart a winking, mute and dumb,	*a winking*: deliberate closing of the eyes
	Or looked upon this love with idle sight –	*idle sight*: seeing, but doing nothing
	What might you think? No, I went round to work,	140
	And my young mistress thus I did bespeak:	
	'Lord Hamlet is a prince out of thy star.	*out of thy star*: out of your reach
	This must not be.' And then I precepts gave her,	*precepts*: orders
	That she should lock herself from his resort,	*resort*: visits
	Admit no messengers, receive no tokens.	145
	Which done, she took the fruits of my advice,	*fruits*: wisdom
	And he, repulsed – a short tale to make –	
	Fell into a sadness, then into a fast,	
	Thence to a watch, thence into a weakness,	*to a watch*: to wakefulness, unable to sleep
	Thence to a lightness, and by this declension,	150 *declension*: decline
	Into the madness wherein now he raves,	
	And all we mourn for.	
CLAUDIUS	Do you think 'tis this?	
GERTRUDE	It may be, very like.	
POLONIUS	Hath there been such a time, I'ld fain know that,	*I'd fain*: I'd like
	That I have positively said, 'tis so,	155
	When it proved otherwise?	
CLAUDIUS	Not that I know.	
POLONIUS	Take this from this, if this be otherwise.	*this from this*: my head from my body
	If circumstances lead me, I will find	*lead*: allow
	Where truth is hid, though it were hid indeed	
	Within the centre.†	
CLAUDIUS	How may we try it further?	160
POLONIUS	You know, sometimes he walks four hours together	
	Here in the lobby.	
GERTRUDE	So he does indeed.	
POLONIUS	At such a time I'll loose my daughter to him.	*loose*: release
	Be you and I behind an arras then.	*arras*: tapestry hanging
	Mark the encounter: if he love her not,	165
	And be not from his reason fallen thereon,	*thereon*: on account of his love
	Let me be no assistant for a state,	
	But keep a farm and carters.	
CLAUDIUS	We will try it.	

Enter HAMLET reading on a book

GERTRUDE	But look where sadly the poor wretch comes reading.	*reading*: signals his detachment
POLONIUS	Away, I do beseech you both, away.	170
	I'll board him presently.	*board him presently*: approach him now

Exeunt CLAUDIUS and GERTRUDE, and Attendants

	Oh give me leave.	
	How does my good Lord Hamlet?	
HAMLET	Well, God-a-mercy.	*God-a-mercy*: traditional polite response
POLONIUS	Do you know me, my lord?	175

---

*   137   *If I had played the desk or table-book*: if I had served as a means of communication between the lovers, thus assisting their affair by taking notes and storing information secretly

†   160   *the centre*: centre of the earth, remotest place

HAMLET	Excellent well, y'are a fishmonger.*
POLONIUS	Not I my lord.
HAMLET	Then I would you were so honest a man.
POLONIUS	Honest, my lord?
HAMLET	Ay, sir. To be honest, as this world goes, is to be one man 180 picked out of ten thousand.
POLONIUS	That's very true my lord.
HAMLET	For if the sun breed maggots in a dead dog, being a good kissing carrion – Have you a daughter?†
POLONIUS	I have, my lord. 185
HAMLET	Let her not walk i' th' sun. Conception is a blessing, but as your daughter may conceive – Friend, look to 't.‡
POLONIUS	*Aside* How say you by that? Still harping on my daughter. Yet he knew me not at first, a said I was a fishmonger – a is far gone, far gone. And 190 truly, in my youth I suffered much extremity for love, very near this. I'll speak to him again. – What do you read my lord?
HAMLET	Words, words, words.
POLONIUS	What is the matter, my lord? 195
HAMLET	Between who?
POLONIUS	I mean, the matter that you read, my lord.
HAMLET	Slanders, sir: for the satirical rogue says here that old men have grey beards, that their faces are wrinkled, their eyes purging thick amber and plumtree gum, and that 200 they have a plentiful lack of wit, together with most weak hams. All which sir, though I most powerfully and potently believe, yet I hold it not honesty to have it thus set down, for yourself, sir, should be old as I am, if like a crab you could go backward. 205
POLONIUS	*Aside* Though this be madness, yet there is method in 't. – Will you walk out of the air, my lord?
HAMLET	Into my grave?
POLONIUS	Indeed, that is out o' the air. *Aside* How pregnant sometimes his replies are! a happiness that often madness 210 hits on, which reason and sanity could not so prosperously be delivered of. I will leave him, and suddenly contrive the means of meeting between him and my daughter. – My honourable lord, I will most humbly take my leave of you. 215
HAMLET	You cannot sir, take from me any thing that I will more willingly part withal; except my life, except my life, except my life.
POLONIUS	Fare you well my lord.
HAMLET	These tedious old fools! 220

purging: discharging

hams: thighs

set down: in print

method: logic, reason

pregnant: full of meaning and wit

suddenly: immediately

withal: with

* 176   *you are a fishmonger*: Hamlet's 'antic disposition' (Act 1, Scene 5, line 172) is in play. By calling Polonius a fishmonger, Hamlet may be suggesting that he smells of corruption – or perhaps implying that Polonius is trading his daughter ('fishmonger' was an Elizabethan slang word for pimp)

† 183–4   *if the sun breed maggots ... good kissing carrion*: It was an ancient belief that the sun gave life to the maggots that appeared suddenly on dead matter. Hamlet is suggesting that the sun is like a god that by kissing flesh (carrion) breeds maggots.

‡ 186–7   *Let her not walk ... may conceive*: the sense of these lines derives from the earlier image of the sun as impregnator. There is a pun on conception, meaning both the forming of ideas and impregnation. The second sense of impregnation comes to the fore at the mention of how his daughter may conceive. These lines are deliberately riddling.

Enter ROSENCRANTZ and GUILDENSTERN

POLONIUS	You go to seek the Lord Hamlet, there he is.
ROSENCRANTZ	God save you, sir!

Exit POLONIUS

GUILDENSTERN	My honoured lord!
ROSENCRANTZ	My most dear lord!
HAMLET	My excellent good friends! How dost thou Guildenstern? Ah, Rosencrantz! Good lads, how do you both?
ROSENCRANTZ	As the indifferent children of the earth.
GUILDENSTERN	Happy, in that we are not over-happy; On Fortune's cap we are not the very button.
HAMLET	Nor the soles of her shoe?
ROSENCRANTZ	Neither, my lord.
HAMLET	Then you live about her waist, or in the middle of her favours?
GUILDENSTERN	Faith, her privates we.
HAMLET	In the secret parts of Fortune? Oh most true; she is a strumpet. What news?
ROSENCRANTZ	None, my lord, but that the world's grown honest.
HAMLET	Then is doomsday near – but your news is not true. Let me question more in particular. What have you, my good, friends deserved at the hands of Fortune, that she sends you to prison hither?
GUILDENSTERN	Prison, my lord?
HAMLET	Denmark's a prison.
ROSENCRANTZ	Then is the world one.
HAMLET	A goodly one; in which there are many confines, wards, and dungeons; Denmark being one o' the' worst.
ROSENCRANTZ	We think not so my lord.
HAMLET	Why then 'tis none to you, for there is nothing either good or bad, but thinking makes it so. To me it is a prison.
ROSENCRANTZ	Why then your ambition makes it one; 'tis too narrow* for your mind.
HAMLET	O God, I could be bounded in a nutshell and count myself a king of infinite space, were it not that I have bad dreams.
GUILDENSTERN	Which dreams indeed are ambition, for the very substance of the ambitious is merely the shadow of a dream.†
HAMLET	A dream itself is but a shadow.
ROSENCRANTZ	Truly, and I hold ambition of so airy and light a quality that it is but a shadow's shadow.
HAMLET	Then are our beggars bodies, and our monarchs and out-stretched heroes the beggars' shadows. Shall we to† the court? for by my fay I cannot reason.
ROSENCRANTZ GUILDENSTERN}	
HAMLET	No such matter: I will not sort you with the rest of my servants; for to speak to you like an honest man, I am most dreadfully attended. But in the beaten way of friendship, what make you at Elsinore?

Margin line numbers and glosses:

225

indifferent: ordinary

very button: at the very peak

230 *Nor the soles*: Nor at the very bottom

her favours: sexual connotation
privates: private parts of the body

235

is a strumpet: is fickle with her favours

240

to prison hither: here to prison

245 *confines*: places of confinement

250

255

but a shadow's shadow: insubstantial
260 *our beggars*: those without ambition

fay: faith
wait upon: accompany (Hamlet misinterprets)

265

beaten: well-tested

* 250 *your ambition makes it one*: an attempt to find out the reason for Hamlet's melancholy

† 254–6 *the very substance … dream*: what the ambitious man actually achieves is only a shadow of his desire for success

‡ 261 *out-stretched heroes*: men whose ambition stretches them – also elongated, like shadows cast from the beggars

ROSENCRANTZ	To visit you, my lord, no other occasion.
HAMLET	Beggar that I am, I am even poor in thanks, but I thank you – and sure, dear friends, my thanks are too dear a halfpenny. Were you not sent for? Is it your own inclining? Is it a free visitation? Come, deal justly with me: come, come. Nay, speak.
GUILDENSTERN	What should we say, my lord?
HAMLET	Why, anything but to the purpose. You were sent for – and there is a kind of confession in your looks which your modesties have not craft enough to colour. I know the good kind and queen have sent for you.
ROSENCRANTZ	To what end, my lord?
HAMLET	That you must teach me. But let me conjure you, by the rights of our fellowship, by the consonancy of our youth, by the obligation of our ever-preserved love, and by what more dear a better proposer could charge you withal, be even and direct with me, whether you were sent for or no.
ROSENCRANTZ	*Aside to GUILDENSTERN* What say you?
HAMLET	*Aside* Nay then I have an eye of you. – If you love me, hold not off.
GUILDENSTERN	My lord, we were sent for.
HAMLET	I will tell you why; so shall my anticipation prevent your discovery, and your secrecy to the king and queen moult no feather. I have of late – but wherefore I know not – lost all my mirth, forgone all custom of exercises; and indeed it goes so heavily with my disposition that this goodly frame, the earth, seems to me a sterile promontory; this most excellent canopy, the air, look you, this brave o'erhanging firmament, this majestical roof fretted with golden fire – why, it appeareth no other thing to me than a foul and pestilent congregation of vapours. What a piece† of work is a man! how noble in reason, how infinite in faculties, in form and moving how express and admirable, in action how like an angel, in apprehension how like a god! The beauty of the world, the paragon of animals – and yet to me, what is this quintessence of dust? Man delights not me – no, nor woman neither, though by your smiling you seem to say so.
ROSENCRANTZ	My lord, there was no such stuff in my thoughts.
HAMLET	Why did ye laugh then, when I said man delights not me?
ROSENCRANTZ	To think, my lord, if you delight not in man, what lenten entertainment the players shall receive from you: we coted them on the way; and hither are they coming to offer you service.
HAMLET	He that plays the king shall be welcome; his majesty shall have tribute of me; the adventurous knight shall use his foil and target, the lover shall not sigh gratis, the humorous man shall end his part in peace; the clown shall make those laugh whose lungs are tickle o'th'sere; and the lady shall say her mind freely – or the blank verse shall halt for't. What players are they?
ROSENCRANTZ	Even those you were wont to take such delight in, the tragedians of the city.

270

275

280

285

290

295

300

305

310

315

320

Beggar: unambitious

to the purpose: to the point, honestly

craft … colour: deceit enough to hide

conjure you: put before you, suggest
consonancy: harmony

a better proposer: one more adept

I have an eye of you: I see you
hold not off: don't hide the truth

moult no feather: unbroken, intact

goodly frame: earth as ordered structure
sterile promontory: barren peninsula, prison

fretted: adorned
golden fire: stars, heavenly bodies
piece of work: God's artistic masterpiece

apprehension: powers of comprehension
paragon: model of excellence

smiling: could be interpreted as smirking

lenten entertainment: little delight
coted: passed them

tribute: honour

not sigh gratis: not miss payment

tickle o'th'sere: easily amused; *freely*: loosely

halt: limp; *for't*: forth

tragedians: actors of tragedy

* 289–90 *anticipation … discovery*: my fore-knowledge of the truth will save you from accusations of having disclosed the information to me

† 298 *foul … vapours*: mass of diseases carried by the air and spread by the wind

HAMLET	How chances it they travel? their residence, both in reputation and profit, was better both ways.	*their residence*: their staying put in the city
ROSENCRANTZ	I think their inhibition comes by the means of the late innovation.	*inhibition*: reserve against staying in the city *late innovation*: recent censorship
HAMLET	Do they hold the same estimation they did when I was in the city? Are they so followed?	325 *estimation*: regard
ROSENCRANTZ	No, indeed are they not.	
HAMLET	How comes it? Do they grow rusty?	
ROSENCRANTZ	Nay, their endeavour keeps in the wonted pace, but there is sir an eyrie of children, little eyases, that cry out on the top of question and are most tyrannically clapped for't. These are now the fashion, and so be-rattle the common stages – so they call them – that many wearing rapiers are afraid of goose-quills and dare scarce come thither.	*wonted pace*: as good as ever 330 *eyases*: hawks *tyrannically*: vehemently *be-rattle*: assail *rapiers*: swords *goose-quills*: pens for writing
HAMLET	What, are they children? who maintains 'em? How are they escoted? Will they pursue the quality no longer than they can sing? Will they not say afterwards, if they should grow themselves to common players – as it is most like, if their means are no better, their writers do them wrong to make them exclaim against their own succession?*	335 *escoted*: paid for 340
ROSENCRANTZ	Faith, there has been much to do on both sides, and the nation holds it no sin to tar them to controversy. There was for a while no money bid for argument unless the poet and the player went to cuffs in the question.	*tar*: incite *bid*: offered
HAMLET	Is't possible?	345
GUILDENSTERN	Oh there has been much throwing about of brains.	*throwing about of brains*: battle of wits
HAMLET	Do the boys carry it away?	*carry it away*: win the argument
ROSENCRANTZ	Ay that they do, my lord, Hercules and his load too.†	
HAMLET	It is not very strange, for mine uncle is king of Denmark, and those that would make mouths at him while my father lived give twenty, forty, fifty, a hundred ducats‡ apiece for his picture in little. 'Sblood, there is something in this more than natural, if philosophy could find it out.	350 *make mouths*: mocking expression *ducats*: gold coins
A flourish		
GUILDENSTERN	There are the players.	
HAMLET	Gentlemen, you are welcome to Elsinore. Your hands, come then. Th'appurtenance of welcome is fashion and ceremony. Let me comply with you in this garb, lest my§ extent to the players, which I tell you must show fairly outward, should more appear like entertainment than yours. You are welcome – but my uncle-father and aunt-mother are deceived.	355 *appurtenance*: proper way to behave *ceremony*: offers a show of formality *my extent*: the welcome I extend 360 *are deceived*: in thinking him mad
GUILDENSTERN	In what, my dear lord?	
HAMLET	I am but mad north-north-west. When the wind is southerly, I know a hawk from a handsaw.‖	*north-north-west*: a little off compass *handsaw*: heron (also 'hernshaw')
Enter POLONIUS		
POLONIUS	Well be with you, gentlemen.	365
HAMLET	Hark you Guildenstern, and you too – at each ear a hearer. That great baby you see there is not yet out of his swaddling-clouts.	

* 336–40 *Will they pursue … succession?*: Will they continue acting only until their voice breaks? Will they not then say that the writers did them wrong, by making them, as child actors, deny themselves a future in the profession?

† 348 *Hercules and his load too*: This was the symbol for the Globe Theatre, where Shakespeare's plays were performed – Hercules bearing up the globe.

‡ 351 *picture in little*: miniature portrait

§ 357 *comply with you in this garb*: shake hands as ceremony and fashion demand

‖ 364 *I know a hawk from a handsaw*: In cryptic language, Hamlet is saying he still has judgement – by distinguishing between similar things (hawk and heron), he has his wits about him.

ROSENCRANTZ	Happily he's the second time come to them; for they say an old man is twice a child.
HAMLET	I will prophesy: he comes to tell me of the players, mark it. –You say right sir, a Monday morning, 'twas then indeed.
POLONIUS	My lord, I have news to tell you.
HAMLET	My lord, I have news to tell you. When Roscius was an actor in Rome –
POLONIUS	The actors are come hither, my lord.
HAMLET	Buzz, buzz!
POLONIUS	Upon my honour.
HAMLET	Then came each actor on his ass –
POLONIUS	The best actors in the world, either for tragedy, comedy, history, pastoral, pastoral-comical, historical-pastoral, tragical-historical, tragical-comical-historical-pastoral, scene individable or poem unlimited: Seneca cannot be too heavy, nor Plautus too light. For the law of writ and the liberty, these are the only men.
HAMLET	O Jephtha judge of Israel, what a treasure hadst thou!*
POLONIUS	What a treasure had he, my lord?
HAMLET	Why – 'One fair daughter and no more, The which he lovèd passing well.'†
POLONIUS	*Aside* Still on my daughter.
HAMLET	Am I not i'th'right, old Jephtha?
POLONIUS	If you call me Jephtha my lord, I have a daughter that I love passing well.
HAMLET	Nay, that follows not.
POLONIUS	What follows, then, my lord?
HAMLET	Why – 'As by lot God wot,' and then you know – 'It came to pass, as most like it was,' – the first row of the pious chanson will show you more, for look where my abridgement comes.

Enter the Players

You are welcome masters, welcome, all. I am glad to see thee well. Welcome, good friends. O, my old friend! why, thy face is valenced since I saw thee last; com'st thou to beard me in Denmark? What, my young lady and mistress – byrlady, your ladyship is nearer to heaven than when I saw you last by the altitude of a chopine. Pray God, your voice, like a piece of uncurrent gold be not cracked within the ring. Masters, you are all welcome.‡ We'll e'en to't like French falconers, fly at any thing§ we see: we'll have a speech straight. Come give us a taste of your quality: come, a passionate speech.

When … actor: pre-empts Polonius

Buz, buz!: contemptuous exclamation

Seneca: classical writer of tragedy
Plautus: classical comic playwright

passing: more that

wot: know

row: stanza; *chanson*: song
abridgement: cutting short

valenced: covered with a beard
lady: boy-actor who takes female roles
nearer to heaven: grown taller
a chopine: the high sole of a woman's shoe

---

* 387 *O Jephtha, judge of Israel, what a treasure hadst thou*: biblical reference (Judges 2:9–40). Jephtha promised Jehovah that he would sacrifice the first living thing that came to meet him if he conquered the Ammonites. This turned out to be his daughter.

† 390–1 *'One fair daughter … loved passing well'*: Hamlet quotes from a popular ballad about Jephthah's daughter at her death

‡ 410–11 *your voice … the ring*: Hamlet is mocking the boy actor, saying that he hopes his voice hasn't cracked like the gold coins that are no longer of value because they have been clipped ('cracked') around their circular edges.

§ 412 *French falconers*: supposed in Elizabethan England to be careless about their prey

| FIRST PLAYER | What speech, my lord? | 415 |
| HAMLET | I heard thee speak me a speech once, but it was never | |

FIRST PLAYER   What speech, my lord?   415

HAMLET   I heard thee speak me a speech once, but it was never
acted, or if it was, not above once; for the play I remember,
pleased not the million; 'twas caviary to the general. But it
was, as I received it, and others whose judgements in such
matters cried in the top of mine, an excellent play, well   420
digested in the scenes, set down with as much modesty as
cunning. I remember one said there were no sallets in the
lines to make the matter savoury, nor no matter in the
phrase that might indict the author of affectation, but
called it an honest method, as wholesome as sweet, and   425
by very much more handsome than fine. One speech in't
I chiefly loved: 'twas Aeneas' tale to Dido, and thereabout
of it especially where he speaks of Priam's slaughter:
if it live in your memory, begin at this line, let me see,
let me see –   430
   'The rugged Pyrrhus, like th'Hyrcanian beast' –
'Tis not so, it begins with Pyrrhus –
   'The rugged Pyrrhus, he whose sable arms,
   Black as his purpose, did the night resemble
   When he lay couchèd in the ominous horse,   435
   Hath now this dread and black complexion smeared
   With heraldry more dismal. Head to foot
   Now is he total gules; horridly tricked
   With blood of fathers, mothers, daughters, sons,
   Baked and impasted with the parching streets,*   440
   That lend a tyrannous and damnèd light
   To their lord's murder. Roasted in wrath and fire,
   And thus o'er-sizèd with coagulate gore,
   With eyes like carbuncles, the hellish Pyrrhus
   Old grandsire Priam seeks –'   445
So, proceed you.

POLONIUS   'Fore God, my lord, well spoken, with good accent
and good discretion.

FIRST PLAYER   'Anon he finds him,
   Striking too short at Greeks; his antique sword,   450
   Rebellious to his arm, lies where it falls,
   Repugnant to command. Unequal matched,
   Pyrrhus at Priam drives, in rage strikes wide,
   But with the whiff and wind of his fell sword
   The unnervèd father falls. Then senseless Ilium,   455
   Seeming to feel this blow, with flaming top
   Stoops to his base, and with a hideous crash
   Takes prisoner Pyrrhus' ear; for lo, his sword,
   Which was declining on the milky head
   Of reverend Priam, seemed i'th'air to stick.   460
   So, as a painted tyrant, Pyrrhus stood,
   And like a neutral to his will and matter,†
   Did nothing.
   But, as we often see against some storm,
   A silence in the heavens, the rack stand still,   465
   The bold winds speechless, and the orb below
   As hush as death, anon the dreadful thunder
   Doth rend the region; so after Pyrrhus' pause,

continued

---

digested: arranged, shaped; *modesty*: propriety
sallets: ribaldries

Aeneas' tale: Virgil's Aeneid
Priam's slaughter: Murder of King Priam

rugged: hairy

sable: black

ominous horse: fateful horse of Troy

heraldry more dismal: dreadful armorial marks
gules: red

damnèd light: like the flames of hell
their lord's: King Priam's

carbuncles: fiery red stones

Anon: soon
too short: missing their mark
Rebellious to his arm: defying his intent
Repugnant to: resisting

fell: cruel
unnervèd: enfeebled; *Ilium*: Troy

hideous: frightening

milky: white

against: just before
rack: clouds
orb below: earth
anon: soon after

---

*   440   *Baked and impasted with the parching streets*: the blood on his face congealed by the heat of the city

†   462   *like a neutral to his will and matter*: inactive, reduced to passivity, despite his intent and duty to act – in this stance he becomes like a 'painted tyrant' caught in a pose

	A rousèd vengeance sets him new a-work,		470	*A rousèd*: newly awakened
	And never did the Cyclops' hammers fall			
	On Mars's armour, forged for proof eterne,*			
	With less remorse than Pyrrhus' bleeding sword			
	Now falls on Priam.			
	Out, out, thou strumpet, Fortune! All you gods,			
	In general synod take away her power;		475	*synod*: assembly
	Break all the spokes and fellies from her wheel,			*fellies*: rims; *wheel*: fortune's wheel
	And bowl the round nave down the hill of heaven,			*nave*: centre of wheel, naval
	As low as to the fiends.'			

POLONIUS This is too long.

HAMLET It shall to th' barber's, with your beard. Prithee say on. [480]
He's for a jig or a tale of bawdry, or he sleeps. Say on:† come to Hecuba.

Hecuba: King Priam's wife

FIRST PLAYER 'But who – ah woe! – had seen the mobled queen – '

mobled: veiled

HAMLET The mobled queen?

POLONIUS That's good, 'mobled queen' is good. [485]

FIRST PLAYER 'Run barefoot up and down, threat'ning the flames

the flames: the burning city of Troy

With bisson rheum, a clout upon that head

bisson rheum: blinding tears

Where late the diadem stood, and, for a robe,

diadem: jewelled hair piece, crown

About her lank and all o'er-teemèd loins,

o'er-teemèd: worn-out with childbirth

A blanket, in the alarm of fear caught up – [490]
Who this had seen, with tongue in venom steeped,

tongue in venom steeped: satirical words

'Gainst Fortune's state would treason have pronounced.
But if the gods themselves did see her then,
When she saw Pyrrhus make malicious sport
In mincing with his sword her husband's limbs, [495]
The instant burst of clamour that she made,

burst of clamour: loud outburst

Unless things mortal move them not at all,

them: the gods

Would have made milch the burning eyes of heaven,‡
And passion in the gods.

POLONIUS Look, whether he has not turned his colour and has [500]
tears in's eyes. Pray you, no more.

he: referring to Hamlet

HAMLET 'Tis well: I'll have thee speak out the rest soon. – Good
my lord, will you see the players well bestowed? Do you

bestowed: accommodated

hear, let them be well used; for they are the abstract and
brief chronicles of the time. After your death you were [505]

abstract and brief chronicles: summary

better have a bad epitaph than their ill report while you
live.

POLONIUS My lord, I will use them according to their desert.

HAMLET God's bodkin man, much better. Use every man after his

God's bodkin: expletive, curse

desert, and who should scape whipping? Use them after [510]
your own honour and dignity; the less they deserve, the
more merit is in your bounty. Take them in.

bounty: goodness, generosity

POLONIUS Come sirs.

Exit POLONIUS

HAMLET Follow him, friends: we'll hear a play to-morrow. – Dost
thou hear me, old friend; can you play The Murder of [515]
Gonzago?

FIRST PLAYER Ay, my lord.

---

* 470–1 **Cyclops' hammers ... proof eterne**: the Cyclops were giants hired by Vulcan to make armour for the god of war, Mars

† 480–1 *tale of bawdry ... sleeps*: he wouldn't complain of its length if he was listening to a bawdy tale

‡ 498 *Would have made milch the burning eyes of heaven*: would have turned the celestial bodies' eyes to milky tears

HAMLET	We'll ha't to-morrow night. You could for a need study a speech of some dozen or sixteen lines, which I would set in down and sert in't, could you not?
FIRST PLAYER	Ay my lord.
HAMLET	Very well. Follow that lord, and look you mock him not.

Exeunt PLAYERS

	My good friends, I'll leave you till night. You are welcome to Elsinore.
ROSENCRANTZ	Good my lord.

Exeunt ROSENCRANTZ and GUILDENSTERN

HAMLET	Ay so, God bye to you. Now I am alone.

O what a rogue and peasant slave am I!*
Is it not monstrous that this player here,
But in a fiction, in a dream of passion,
Could force his soul so to his own conceit†
That from her working all his visage wanned,‡
Tears in his eyes, distraction in's aspect,
A broken voice, and his whole function suiting
With forms to his conceit? And all for nothing?
For Hecuba!
What's Hecuba to him, or he to Hecuba,
That he should weep for her? What would he do,
Had he the motive and the cue for passion
That I have? He would drown the stage with tears,
And cleave the general ear with horrid speech,
Make mad the guilty and appal the free,
Confound the ignorant, and amaze indeed
The very faculties of eyes and ears. Yet I,
A dull and muddy-mettled rascal, peak
Like John-a-dreams, unpregnant of my cause,§
And can say nothing – no, not for a king,
Upon whose property and most dear life
A damn'd defeat was made. Am I a coward?
Who calls me villain, breaks my pate across,
Plucks off my beard, and blows it in my face,
Tweaks me by th'nose, gives me the lie i'th'throat,
As deep as to the lungs? Who does me this?
Ha, 'swounds, I should take it, for it cannot be
But I am pigeon-livered and lack gall
To make oppression bitter, or ere this◖
I should ha' fatted all the region kites
With this slave's offal. Bloody, bawdy villain!
Remorseless, treacherous, lecherous, kindless villain!
Oh, vengeance!
Why, what an ass am I! This is most brave,
That I, the son of the dear murderèd,

continued

Glossary / notes:

520

ha't: have it; *for a need*: if necessary
study: learn

mock: mimic

525

530

her working: his soul's passion;
aspect: countenance
function suiting: faculties conforming
Forms: expression

535

cue for passion: prompt to revenge

540   *cleave*: smite
the free: those free from guilt, innocent
Confound: mystify
faculties: senses
muddy-mettled: lethargic, sluggish
545   *John-a-dreams*: a dreamer

damn'd defeat: unholy conquest

550

gives me the lie i'th'throat: calls me liar
who does me this?: who so insults me?
'swounds: by God's wounds

555   *or ere this*: or before now
region kites: birds of prey
this slave's offal: his own remains

560

* 527   *O, what a rogue and peasant slave am I*: How cunning and artful I am on the one hand, yet lowly and submissive, lacking the courage to take action against the king, on the other.

† 530   *force ... conceit*: align his self's core to a fiction

‡ 531   *wann'd*: grew wan or pale

§ 545   *unpregnant of my cause*: without the potential to bring to fruition the desire for revenge, which has just grounds for action

◖ 545–5   *But I am pigeon-liver'd and lack gall ... bitter*: the pigeon is associated with meekness. Gall, the source of bitter anger, was believed to reside in the liver. Thus, Hamlet describes himself as lacking the necessary courage to make his uncle regret his tyrannous act.

Prompted to my revenge by heaven and hell,
Must, like a whore unpack my heart with words,
And fall a-cursing, like a very drab,
A scullion!   565
Fie upon't! foh! About, my brains. Hum, I have heard
That guilty creatures sitting at a play
Have by the very cunning of the scene
Been struck so to the soul, that presently
They have proclaimed their malefactions;   570
For murder, though it have no tongue, will speak
With most miraculous organ. I'll have these players
Play something like the murder of my father
Before mine uncle. I'll observe his looks,
I'll tent him to the quick. If a do blench,   575
I know my course. The spirit that I have seen
May be a devil – and the devil hath power
T'assume a pleasing shape. Yea, and perhaps,
Out of my weakness and my melancholy,
As he is very potent with such spirits,   580
Abuses me to damn me. I'll have grounds
More relative than this. The play's the thing
Wherein I'll catch the conscience of the king.

Exit

by heaven and hell: by justice and fury

drab: prostitute
scullion: kitchen-maid
About: get going

proclaim'd: admitted; *malefactions*: misdeeds

miraculous: because it has no tongue

tent: a medical probe; *blench*: flinch
spirit: ghost

he: the devil

More relative: more material

GERTRUDE, CLAUDIUS, GUILDENSTERN & ROSENCRANTZ

Claudius has summoned Rosencrantz and Guildenstern, two old school friends of Hamlet's. He wants them to talk to the prince and discover the reasons for his apparent insanity. Polonius reveals his theory that Hamlet's 'lunacy' is caused by love for Ophelia. Polonius has a conversation with Hamlet during which the prince speaks in an irrational manner. Hamlet greets Rosencrantz and Guildenstern warmly. He tells them about the mental anguish that has gripped him. He guesses Claudius has summoned them to Elsinore. Initially, his two friends deny this. Eventually, however, Hamlet persuades them to admit the truth.

A troop of players, or actors, arrives at the castle. Hamlet greets them extremely warmly and asks them to perform a speech straight away. He also asks them to perform a play called *The Murder of Gonzago* the following evening. Hamlet gives a moving soliloquy in which he condemns himself for failing to take action against Claudius. He plans to use the players to prove Claudius' guilt to himself. *The Murder of Gonzago* has a plot very similar to the murder of Hamlet's father. Hamlet will observe Claudius during the play. If Claudius reacts guiltily, Hamlet will know he did indeed commit the old king's murder.

A CLOSER LOOK

LINES 1–39: ROSENCRANTZ AND GUILDENSTERN

Rosencrantz and Guildenstern are fellow students and friends of Hamlet. The king and queen have summoned them to Elsinore in the hope that they might be able to cheer Hamlet up and discover the cause of his recent strange behaviour. The king tells Rosencrantz and Guildenstern that Hamlet is greatly changed: 'Sith nor th' exterior nor the inward man/ Resembles that it was'. (6–7) Claudius says that Hamlet has lost his reason, has been removed from the 'understanding of himself'. (9)

Claudius can think of no other reason but the recent death of Hamlet's father for the prince's strange behaviour. (7–10) It is the king's hope that if anything else is causing Hamlet's madness then his friends will discover it: 'you may gleam,/ Whether aught to us unknown afflicts him thus'. (16–17) Rosencrantz and Guildenstern agree to do their best. (29–32)

LINES 40–86: THE AMBASSADORS RETURN FROM NORWAY

Polonius announces the return of the ambassadors to Norway. He also informs the king that he believes he knows the reason for Hamlet's strange behaviour. However, he wishes to wait until after the ambassadors have delivered their report to reveal it: 'My news shall be the fruit to that great feast'. (52)

PRETENDING TO BE MAD

In the previous scene Ophelia described how Hamlet behaved in an extremely bizarre fashion toward her. Now Claudius tells us the prince has undergone a 'transformation'. Hamlet, he says, is behaving as though he has lost his reason, as though he has been removed 'from the understanding of himself'. (9) Polonius refers to the 'lunacy' that has begun to characterise the prince's behaviour. (49)

Hamlet also behaves in a deranged fashion during his encounter with Polonius. He seems to think that Polonius is a 'fishmonger'. (176) He asks Polonius if he has a daughter even though he knows Ophelia well. (184) He says some strange things about maggots, dogs and women getting pregnant if they walk in the sun. He seems to suggest that he is older than Polonius when in fact he is much younger: 'for yourself, sir, shall grow old as I am, if, like a crab you could go backward'. (204–5)

There can be little doubt that Hamlet's mad behaviour is largely an act. He admits to Rosencrantz and Guildenstern that he is 'but mad north-north-west', suggesting that at most he is only the tiniest bit mad. (363) Hamlet comes across as rational and perceptive in his conversation with his two old friends, quickly guessing that they have been summoned to spy on him by Claudius.

The prince also comes across as very sane in his dealings with the players, giving them a warm welcome to Elsinore and enthusiastically requesting a favourite speech. (413–14) Furthermore, his soliloquy at the end of the scene also reveals the workings of a rational, logical mind. There can be no doubt, therefore, that Hamlet is sane, and that the peculiar behaviour he exhibits is an act.

MENTAL ANGUISH

In Act 1 Hamlet expressed what can only be described as suicidal thoughts, wishing that his body would simply dissolve and melt away. Similar sentiments are expressed here. When Polonius leaves him, he says that there is nothing he would part with more readily than his life: 'You cannot sir, take from me anything that I will not more willingly part withal; except my life'. (216–18) Such suicidal thoughts are perhaps also evident when he says that he might walk into his grave. (208)

As in Act 1, Hamlet expresses his disgust at the world in which he is forced to live. He describes the world as a prison and Denmark as the worst of its 'many confines, wards and dungeons'. (245–6) The earth, he says, is nothing but a 'sterile promontory' and the air no more than 'a foul and pestilent congregation of vapours'. (298) Even other human beings have ceased to bring him pleasure: 'Man delights not me – no, nor woman neither'. (303–4)

Hamlet movingly expresses how futile and pointless life seems to him. Humankind is often considered the 'paragon of animals', an almost God-like creature. Yet to him it is no more than a 'quintessence of dust'. (303) This sense of futility is perhaps also evident when he tells Polonius that the book he is reading contains only 'Words, words, words'. (194)

PROCRASTINATION & SELF-ACCUSATION

In the scene's final soliloquy, Hamlet gives full vent to the feelings of self-disgust caused by his lack of action against Claudius. Hamlet lists the very good reasons he has for taking Claudius' life. And yet the prince has done nothing. As we noted above, he is disgusted by his own inaction, and calls himself all sorts of names. He is particularly repelled by his tendency to analyse and intellectualise, to be a man of words rather than a man of action, wondering why he must 'like a whore unpack my heart with words'. (563)

We get a sense in this powerful soliloquy that Hamlet wishes he could be driven by raw emotion rather than having to think about and analyse every situation. He seems to feel that he lacks the 'gall', the bitter, raw emotional drive to avenge his father's death. (554)

However, it is possible that Hamlet is being a little too hard on himself here. As he himself notes, he has no proof of Claudius' guilt. It is possible that the Ghost is in reality a devil, trying to ensnare his soul by getting him to murder an innocent man. (576–81).

LOVE OF THEATRE

In this scene Hamlet displays his deep and passionate love of theatre. Rosencrantz first signals this when he remarks that the players' arrival will bring him joy, and remarks how much Hamlet has enjoyed the 'tragedians of the city'. (319–20)

Hamlet immediately remarks how the players

Elsinore. (324–31) He stresses this to Polonius, insisting that the players must be 'well bestowed' during their stay. (503–4) When the players arrive, he welcomes them warmly, calling them 'masters' and 'good friends'. (404–5)

The prince displays an excellent knowledge of the theatrical world:

- He is curious about the new fashion for child performers that threaten to drive the established theatre companies out of business. (335–44)
- It is obvious that he is familiar with this particular troupe and has seen them perform before. (405–9)
- He immediately asks to hear a speech and asks them to perform *The Murder of Gonzago* later at court. (414, 515–6)
- He asks about an obscure play, one that was almost never performed because it was considered too deep and complex to gain popularity with the general public. (417–20)
- He seems to know entire speeches off by heart, and is clearly a good speaker of theatrical verse, earning Polonius' praise for his recital. (447–8)
- He is also capable of writing for the theatre, asking the First Player if he can insert 'some dozen or sixteen lines' into the performance of *The Murder of Gonzago*. (519)

Importantly, as we noted above, he feels that the arrival of the players will allow him to prove that Claudius is guilty of his father's murder. He has asked them to perform *The Murder of Gonzago*, a play whose plot closely resembles the murder of his father. By observing Claudius' reaction, Hamlet will be able to tell if the king is guilty of the murder or not: 'The play's the thing/ Wherein I'll catch the conscience of the king'. (582–3)

Voltemand and Cornelius are ambassadors. We may remember that in Act 1 Scene 2 they were sent to meet with the king of Norway. They were to tell the Norwegian king that young Prince Fortinbras, his nephew, is planning to attack Denmark without his permission. They have just returned from their mission and are ready to report to the king.

They tell Claudius that the king of Norway was surprised and angry to learn of his nephew's plan. He ordered Fortinbras not to attack Denmark, but instead to lead a force against Poland. The Norwegian king now requests Claudius to let Fortinbras' army pass through Denmark on its way to attack the Poles. Claudius is pleased with the ambassadors' news, and declares that he will give the matter some thought. (81–2)

LINES 86–160: POLONIUS REVEALS HIS THEORY OF HAMLET'S 'MADNESS'

Polonius tells in a frustratingly long-winded manner how he believes Hamlet's love for Ophelia brought about his apparent insanity. He produces a letter from Hamlet to Ophelia in which the prince declares his love for her: 'Doubt thou the stars are fire;/ Doubt that the sun doth move;/ Doubt truth to be a liar;/ But never doubt I love'. (118–21)

Claudius asks how Ophelia responded to the prince's declarations. Polonius says that he himself took the initiative and acted like any responsible father by ordering her to cease all communication with Hamlet. (132–45) He told his daughter that Hamlet is above her social station and therefore out of the question as a marriage partner. (140–2) Polonius believes that as a result of Ophelia's refusal to see him, Hamlet descended into his present state of insanity: 'Into the madness wherein now he raves,/ And all we mourn for'. (151–2)

LINES 160–70: POLONIUS SUGGESTS A PLAN

Polonius proposes a plan to prove his theory. He tells the king and queen how Hamlet regularly walks in the lobby for

CLAUDIUS, GERTRUDE & POLONIUS

hours on end. (161–2) Polonius suggests that Ophelia should meet him while he walks there. Both he and the king will conceal themselves behind a tapestry and observe the encounter: 'At such a time I'll loose my daughter to him./ Be you and I behind an arras then./ Mark the encounter'. (163–5)

Polonius believes that Hamlet's reaction to Ophelia will prove his love for her has driven him mad. (165–8) Claudius agrees to the plan. At this moment, Hamlet enters, reading a book. Polonius urges the royal couple to leave so that he may engage Hamlet in conversation. (170–1)

LINES 171–220: POLONIUS SPEAKS WITH HAMLET

Polonius asks the prince if he recognises him, and Hamlet says Polonius is a fish-monger. (175–6) Hamlet remark about how the sun breeds maggots in dead dogs. He then asks Polonius 'Have you a daughter?' (184) When Polonius says he has, Hamlet advises him not to let her walk 'i' th' Sun', lest she conceive. (186–7) Clearly, the prince is again playing on the double meaning of 'sun'.

Polonius asks Hamlet what he is reading. Hamlet replies that he has been reading a description of how old men age, and bizarrely describes himself as an old man, though he is just a young student: 'for yourself, sir, should be as old as I am, if like a crab you could go backward'. (204–5)

Polonius is now utterly convinced of Hamlet's madness, believing that he is 'far gone, far gone'. (90) And yet he acknowledges that Hamlet's replies are often strangely meaningful. Sometimes, he says, mad people can speak with more clarity and meaning than sane people: 'which reason and sanity could not so prosperously be delivered of'. (211–12)

Polonius is sure that Hamlet's insanity is due to his frustrated love for Ophelia. Polonius asks his leave of Hamlet, to which the prince replies that he would part with nothing so gladly, 'except my life, except my life, except my life'. (217–18)

LONG-WINDED

Polonius once again comes across as someone who loves the sound of his own voice. He tells the royal couple that Ophelia is the cause of Hamlet's apparent madness in what can only be described as an irritatingly long-winded manner. In the early part of this scene, he speaks in a particularly elaborate and over-the-top fashion. An irritated Gertrude tells him get to the point: 'More matter, with less art'. (97)

SELF-IMPORTANT

Polonius' sense of self-importance is once again evident in this scene. He is convinced of his own wisdom, telling the king that he has never been proved wrong in anything before. (157–9) He is certain that his theory about the prince's madness is correct, saying that if he's wrong he's only fit to work as a farmer. (168)

His conversations with the prince further convince him that he's right in thinking Hamlet's been driven mad by love for Ophelia. He interprets several of Hamlet's remarks as references to her. 'How say you by that? Still harping on my daughter'. (188–9) These conversations convince him that Hamlet is 'far gone, far gone' with love for his daughter, and even remind him of a similar love affair he himself had when he was a younger man. (190–2)

As we noted in the previous scene, Polonius' self-importance makes him long to be at the centre of royal affairs. He seems delighted to have information relevant to the royal family. He prolongs this moment of importance, telling them he has found the 'cause of Hamlet's lunacy', but then not sharing his theory till after the ambassadors have departed: 'My news shall be the fruit to that great feast'. (52) A similar tendency is arguably evident when he excitedly brings Hamlet news of the players' arrival.

A MEDDLING SCHEMER

Polonius' scheming tendencies are once again evident in this scene. He comes up with a plan to observe Hamlet while he encounters Ophelia, thereby proving his theory of Hamlet's 'madness'. (163–5) He ushers Claudius and Gertrude away so he can speak to Hamlet alone and presumably learn more about the prince's state of mind: 'both, away./ I'll board him presently'. (170–1)

Essentially Polonius is meddling in the affairs of the royal family, matters that have absolutely nothing to do with him. To make matters worse, he intends to uses his own daughter as bait in his scheming, declaring that he will 'loose' her to Hamlet as if she was some kind of animal. (163) His meddling and scheming will have grave consequences for him and his family.

LINES 220–89: HAMLET MEETS ROSENCRANTZ AND GUILDENSTERN

Rosencrantz and Guildenstern arrive at Elsinore. Hamlet seems delighted to see them, and greets them warmly. (222–5) They engage in some witty banter, but the prince is immediately suspicious about their reason for coming to Denmark, a place he describes as 'a prison'. (242)

Rosencrantz and Guildenstern insist that they have come to visit the prince of their own accord. Hamlet, however, is convinced that they have been sent for by the king and queen: 'Were you not sent for? Is it your own inclining? Is it a free visitation?' (271–2) Eventually, he pressures them into admitting that this is the case. (288)

LINES 289–307: HAMLET DESCRIBES HIS NEGATIVE STATE OF MIND

Hamlet tells his friends that he will explain why they were sent for, therefore preventing them having to conduct their mission in secrecy. He explains that for some unknown reason he has lost his usual good humour and abandoned all of his customary habits and activities: 'I have of late – but wherefore I know not – lost all my mirth, forgone all custom of exercises'. (291–2)

The world fills him with disgust and despair. The earth seems like a barren piece of land, and the sky a disgusting and polluted mixture of gases, 'a foul and pestilent congregation of vapours'. (298) He can also take no pleasure in his fellow human beings: 'Man delights not me – no, nor woman neither'. (303–4)

Mankind can appear almost godlike, and is capable of extraordinary understanding and accomplishments. Yet to Hamlet, humanity's grace and achievements mean nothing because we are doomed to die and turn eventually to dust: 'and yet to me, what is this quintessence of dust?' (303)

LINES 308–403: PLAYERS ARE COMING TO ELSINORE

Rosencrantz says that if Hamlet feels this way about life, he will give a poor reception to the theatrical company that is on it way to Elsinore: 'if you delight not in man, what lenten entertainment the players shall receive from you'. (308–9) Hearing that a group of players is coming appears to rejuvenate Hamlet. He declares that they will be greeted warmly and speaks enthusiastically and knowingly about the latest trends in theatre. (312–44)

CHARACTER DEVELOPMENT

ROSENCRANTZ & GUILDENSTERN

Rosencrantz and Guildenstern are Hamlet's old school friends. As Claudius puts it, they have known him since they were children: 'being of so young days brought up with him'. (11) Their familiar relationship is evident when they meet the prince. He greets them as his 'most excellent good friends', asking them 'Good lads, how do you both?' (226) Their closeness is also evident when the three engage in 'laddish' banter of a sexual nature. (They refer to fortune or luck as a woman, and make reference to her 'middle' or 'private' parts.)

Rosencrantz and Guildenstern have been placed in a difficult position. The king has summoned them and asked them to speak with Hamlet so as to determine the cause of his apparent madness, and to report back to him. To put it bluntly, they have been asked to spy on their old friend.

Hamlet guesses straight away what they are up to: 'I know the good king and queen have sent for you'. (277–8) He knows them so well that he can tell by their demeanor they have been sent to discover the reasons for his recent peculiar behaviour: 'there is a kind of confession in your looks'. (276) Initially, Rosencrantz and Guildenstern insist they have come to Elsinore of their own accord. By referring to their friendship, however, Hamlet more or less shames them into admitting the truth. (288)

Rosencrantz and Guildenstern, therefore, find themselves torn between the king who has summoned them and the friend with whom they share an 'ever-preserved love'. (282) As they themselves put it, how can they disobey the 'sovereign power' and 'dread pleasure' of Claudius, the most powerful man in the realm? (27–9) Yet, can they betray Hamlet's friendship by continuing to spy and inform on him?

CONSIDER THIS

At the beginning of the scene Claudius says that Hamlet's mad behaviour must have been caused by his father's death. He says he 'cannot dream of' any other reason for Hamlet's apparent lunacy. (10) What are we to make of this?

It is possible that Claudius is telling the truth, that he simply cannot imagine any other reason for the prince's bizarre actions. He might also suspect that Hamlet's madness is partially cause by his marriage to Gertrude, but is unwilling to admit this in public in order to avoid drawing attention to his somewhat 'irregular' marital arrangements. Gertrude herself suspects that her marriage might be partially responsible for Hamlet's 'madness'. (56–7)

It is extremely unlikely that at that this stage Claudius suspects Hamlet of knowing anything about the old king's murder. After all, Claudius carried out the 'perfect crime', leaving behind no evidence and no witnesses.

Hearing the players arriving at court, Hamlet bids farewell to Rosencrantz and Guildenstern. He tells them that Claudius and Gertrude are being fooled, and that he is only mad some of the time: 'I am but mad north-north-west. When the wind is southerly, I know a hawk from a handsaw'. (363–4) North-north-west is the smallest compass point away from true north. Hamlet is suggesting, therefore, that he is at most only the tiniest bit insane.

Polonius arrives and reads out a leaflet advertising the players. Hamlet once again torments him with mockery and wordplay. He refers to Jephthah, an Old Testament figure who was forced to kill his own daughter. This seems a mocking reference to Polonius' own daughter, Ophelia.

LINES 404–513: THE PLAYERS ARRIVE

Hamlet seems delighted at the players' arrival. He greets them warmly and asks to hear a speech immediately: 'We'll have a speech straight'. (413) He requests a speech about the murder of Priam, king of Troy, by the Greek hero, Pyrhus. (426–46)

Hamlet begins the speech himself. The speech describes Pyrrhus as a warrior coated in the blood of those he has slaughtered: 'horridly tricked/With blood of fathers, mothers, daughters, sons'. (438-9) It goes on to tell how he hunts down the old King Priam in order to kill him. (455–60) Polonius is impressed and compliments Hamlet on his delivery. (441–2)

The First Player takes over the speech. He vividly describes Priam's pathetic attempts to stave off Pyrhus. He then describes the hysterical grief of Prima's wife Hecuba as she witnesses her husband's bloody death at Pyrhus' hands. The Player becomes so caught up in his own delivery that he moves himself to tears.

Hamlet instructs Polonius to escort the players to their quarters and treat them well. (501–4) In response to Polonius' lukewarm answer, Hamlet grows angry, declaring that there is great honour in treating someone well. (509–12) Polonius and all but one of the players exit.

LINES 514–25: HAMLET'S REQUEST TO THE PLAYERS

Hamlet asks the First Player if the company can perform a play called *The Murder of Gonzago* the following night. (514–6) Furthermore, he asks the Player to learn a speech that he himself has written and wishes to put in the play. (518–20) The First Player agrees to do this, and Hamlet bids him leave.

LINES 526–583: HAMLET'S SELF-ACCUSATION

The prince is amazed that the player could move himself to tears while speaking about Hecuba, a fictional character: 'What's Hecuba to him, or he to Hecuba,/ That he should weep for her?' (536–7) Hamlet has a much greater 'motive and cue for passion' than the player, yet so far he has done nor said nothing against the murderer of his father. (538–65)

He mentions all the reasons he has for taking action:

- He has been asked to avenge his 'dear father' on whose 'property and most dear life/A damn'd defeat was made'. (547–8)
- He has been commanded to act by a presence from beyond the grave: 'Prompted to my revenge by heaven and hell'. (562)
- The man he's been asked to kill is nothing but a 'Remorseless, treacherous, lecherous, kindless villain!' (558)

Despite all this, however, he has done nothing. He bitterly accuses himself of being a procrastinator, someone who thinks too much and over-analyses situations rather than taking direct action. He is disgusted by what he sees as this negative aspect of his personality, wondering why he must 'like a whore unpack my heart with words'(563).

This disgust at his own procrastination is evident in the stream of insults the prince throws at himself. He bitterly describes himself as a 'rogue' and a 'peasant slave', an 'ass', a 'drab' and a 'scullion'. He condemns himself as weak-willed and unreliable, a 'dull and muddy-mettled rascal'. (544) He declares that he must be a coward for not having already killed the king:

> But I am pigeon-livered and lack gall
> To make oppression bitter, or ere this
> I should ha' fatted all the region kites
> With this slave's offal. (554–7)

Hamlet's delay is at least partially due to the fact that he has no concrete evidence against Claudius. He is concerned that Claudius might in fact be innocent. He worries that the ghost may be the devil in disguise trying to trick him into murdering an innocent man. (576–81)

Now, however, he believes he has a way of determining whether his uncle is guilty or not. He has heard that criminals sometimes react guiltily to a theatrical performance resembling their own crime:

> *guilty creatures sitting at a play*
> *Have by the very cunning of the scene*
> *Been struck so to the soul, that presently*
> *They have proclaimed their malefactions* (567–70)

Hamlet has asked the company to perform a play with a storyline that closely resembles his father's murder. It will include a short speech specially written by him. During the performance, Hamlet will carefully observe Claudius to see if his reaction betrays his guilt. (592–4) If Claudius reacts guiltily to the play Hamlet will have proof that he killed the old king: 'The play's the thing/ Wherein I'll catch the conscience of the king'. (582–3) Confident of Claudius' guilt, he will be able to take his revenge.

Enter KING, QUEEN, POLONIUS, OPHELIA, ROSENCRANTZ, GUILDENSTERN, LORDS

CLAUDIUS	And can you, by no drift of circumstance,	
	Get from him why he puts on this confusion,	
	Grating so harshly all his days of quiet	
	With turbulent and dangerous lunacy?	
ROSENCRANTZ	He does confess he feels himself distracted,	5
	But from what cause a will by no means speak.	
GUILDENSTERN	Nor do we find him forward to be sounded,	
	But with a crafty madness keeps aloof	
	When we would bring him on to some confession	
	Of his true state.	
GERTRUDE	Did he receive you well?	10
ROSENCRANTZ	Most like a gentleman.	
GUILDENSTERN	But with much forcing of his disposition.	
ROSENCRANTZ	Niggard of question; but, of our demands,	
	Most free in his reply.	
GERTRUDE	Did you assay him	
	To any pastime?	15
ROSENCRANTZ	Madam, it so fell out, that certain players	
	We o'er-raught on the way; of these we told him,	
	And there did seem in him a kind of joy	
	To hear of it. They are about the court,	
	And, as I think, they have already order	20
	This night to play before him.	
POLONIUS	'Tis most true,	
	And he beseech'd me to entreat your majesties	
	To hear and see the matter.	
CLAUDIUS	With all my heart, and it doth much content me	
	To hear him so inclined.	25
	Good gentlemen, give him a further edge,	
	And drive his purpose on to these delights.	
ROSENCRANTZ	We shall, my lord.	

Exeunt ROSENCRANTZ and GUILDENSTERN

CLAUDIUS	Sweet Gertrude, leave us too,	
	For we have closely sent for Hamlet hither,	
	That he, as 'twere by accident, may here	30
	Affront Ophelia. Her father and myself,	
	Lawful espials,	
	Will so bestow ourselves, that seeing unseen,	
	We may of their encounter frankly judge,	
	And gather by him, as he is behaved,	35
	If't be th'affliction of his love or no	
	That thus he suffers for.	
GERTRUDE	I shall obey you.	
	And for your part Ophelia, I do wish	
	That your good beauties be the happy cause	
	Of Hamlet's wildness. So shall I hope your virtues	40
	Will bring him to his wonted way again,	
	To both your honours.	

Glossary (right margin):

drift of circumstance: direction of conversation
confusion: disorder of his wit and senses
Grating: jarring
turbulent: violent turmoil

forward to be sounded: willing to be questioned

assay: persuade

fell out: happened
o'er-raught: overtook

the matter: the play

edge: push

closely: recently

Affront: come face to face with
lawful espials: rightful spies
bestow: position

wonted way: usual spirits, now wanting

OPHELIA   Madam, I wish it may.

Exit GERTRUDE with LORDS

POLONIUS   Ophelia, walk you here. – Gracious, so please you,
We will bestow ourselves. – Read on this book,
That show of such an exercise may colour   45   *colour*: provide an excuse for
Your loneliness. – We are oft to blame in this:
'Tis too much proved, that with devotion's visage,   *devotion's visage*: appearance of devotion
And pious action, we do sugar o'er   *sugar o'er*: hide with sweetness
The devil himself.

CLAUDIUS   *Aside*   O, 'tis too true.
How smart a lash that speech doth give my conscience!   50   *smart a lash*: stinging blow
The harlot's cheek, beautied with plastering art,   *plastering art*: cosmetics
Is not more ugly to the thing that helps it
Than is my deed to my most painted word: *painted word*: artful deceit
O heavy burden!

POLONIUS   I hear him coming: let's withdraw, my lord.   55

Exeunt CLAUDIUS and POLONIUS

Enter HAMLET

HAMLET   To be, or not to be, that is the question –   *To be*: to have being, to live
Whether 'tis nobler in the mind to suffer †
The slings and arrows of outrageous fortune,   *outrageous*: capricious, unbearably fickle
Or to take arms against a sea of troubles,   *sea of troubles*: an unconquerable force
And by opposing end them. To die, to sleep –   60   *end them*: by ending his life
No more; and by a sleep to say we end
The heart-ache and the thousand natural shocks
That flesh is heir to – 'tis a consummation   *consummation*: consumed by death
Devoutly to be wished. To die, to sleep –   *Devoutly to be wished*: deeply desired
To sleep: perchance to dream. Ay, there's the rub;   65   *dream*: vision; *rub*: obstacle
For in that sleep of death what dreams may come
When we have shuffled off this mortal coil,   *shuffled*: cast; *mortal coil*: bodily concern (i.e. death)
Must give us pause. There's the respect   *respect*: fear
That makes calamity of so long life, ‡   *calamity*: disaster
For who would bear the whips and scorns of time,   70
The oppressor's wrong, the proud man's contumely,   *contumely*: arrogant rudeness
The pangs of disprized love, the law's delay,   *disprized*: not regarded as valuable or 'prized'
The insolence of office, and the spurns   *office*: those who hold official positions
That patient merit of th'unworthy takes,   *patient merit*: the deserving who endure
When he himself might his quietus make   75   *quietus*: discharge, pun on 'quiet'
With a bare bodkin? Who would fardels bear, §   *bare bodkin*: mere dagger
To grunt and sweat under a weary life,
But that the dread of something after death,
The undiscover'd country from whose bourn   *bourn*: boundary
No traveller returns, puzzles the will   80   *puzzles*: bewilders
And makes us rather bear those ills we have
Than fly to others that we know not of?
Thus conscience does make cowards of us all,   *conscience*: inner moral reflection
And thus the native hue of resolution   *native hue of*: natural instinct to act
Is sicklied o'er with the pale cast of thought,   85   *sicklied ...*: thought makes resolution weak
And enterprises of great pitch and moment   *pitch / moment*: aspiration / importance
With this regard their currents turn awry ₵   *regard*: melancholy thought, meditation
And lose the name of action. Soft you now!   *Soft you now*: be quiet now
The fair Ophelia. – Nymph, in thy orisons   *thy orisons*: thy prayers
Be all my sins remembered.

OPHELIA   Good my lord,   90
How does your honour for this many a day?

HAMLET   I humbly thank you, well, well, well.

---

*   50   *smart a lash ... heavy burden*: this is the first indication the king gives of his guilty conscience

†   57–8   *whether 'tis nobler ... fortune*: whether it's more virtuous (noble) to suffer silently in a stoic fashion the
misfortunes that fate – depicted here as a warrior
with weapons – flings at us

‡   69   *That makes calamity of so long life*: makes one willing
to endure calamity for so long. There is also a sense
that a 'long life' is a calamity, if it results from refusing to act or take risks

§   76   *who would fardels bear*: who would bear heavy
burdens

₵   87   *their currents turn awry*: the natural course of action
is diverted

| 65

| OPHELIA | My lord, I have remembrances of yours | | *remembrances*: gifts as symbols of affection |

OPHELIA My lord, I have remembrances of yours
That I have longèd long to re-deliver.
I pray you, now receive them.

HAMLET   No, not I,   95
I never gave you aught.

OPHELIA My honoured lord, you know right well you did,
And with them words of so sweet breath composed
As made the things more rich. Their perfume lost,   100
Take these again, for to the noble mind
Rich gifts wax poor when givers prove unkind.
There my lord.

HAMLET Ha, ha, are you honest?

OPHELIA My lord?

HAMLET Are you fair?   105

OPHELIA What means your lordship?

HAMLET That if you be honest and fair, your honesty should admit
no discourse to your beauty.*

OPHELIA Could beauty, my lord, have better commerce than with
honesty?   110

HAMLET Ay truly, for the power of beauty will sooner transform
honesty from what it is to a bawd, than the force of
honesty can translate beauty into his likeness. This was
sometime a paradox, but now the time gives it proof. I did
love you once.   115

OPHELIA Indeed my lord you made me believe so.

HAMLET You should not have believed me, for virtue cannot so†
inoculate our old stock but we shall relish of it. I loved
you not.

OPHELIA I was the more deceived.   120

HAMLET Get thee to a nunnery – why wouldst thou be a breeder
of sinners? I am myself indifferent honest, but yet I could
accuse me of such things, that it were better my mother
had not borne me. I am very proud, revengeful, ambitious,
with more offences at my beck than I have thoughts to   125
put them in, imagination to give them shape, or time to
act them in. What should such fellows as I do crawling
between earth and heaven? We are arrant knaves all,‡
believe none of us. Go thy ways to a nunnery. Where's
your father?   130

OPHELIA At home, my lord.

HAMLET Let the doors be shut upon him, that he may play the fool
nowhere but in's own house. Farewell.

OPHELIA Oh help him you sweet heavens!

HAMLET If thou dost marry, I'll give thee this plague for thy dowry: 135
be thou as chaste as ice, as pure as snow, thou shalt not
escape calumny. Get thee to a nunnery, go. Farewell. Or, if
thou wilt needs marry, marry a fool, for wise men know
well enough what monsters you make of them. To a
nunnery, go, and quickly too. Farewell.   140

perfume: his 'sweet breath'

wax: grow

honest: truthful, chaste

fair: beautiful, virtuous

commerce: relations

a bawd: woman in charge of a brothel
his: honesty's
paradox: seeming contradiction

nunnery: house of nuns
indifferent honest: reasonably good-living

my beck: at my call, waiting to be committed

plague: disease, curse

calumny: slander, lies

monsters: cuckolds

....
* 107–8 *If you be honest … no discourse to
your beauty*: if you stay chaste and
beautiful, your chastity should
permit no one to commune with, or
have access to, your beauty

† 117–18 *for virtue cannot … but we shall
relish*: virtue can't make us so
immune to our natural (original)
instinct to sin that we lose all of our
taste for it

‡ 128 *between earth and heaven*: dual con-
flicted nature

OPHELIA	O heavenly powers, restore him!	
HAMLET	I have heard of your paintings too, well enough; God hath	*your paintings*: women's cosmetics
	given you one face, and you make yourselves another. You	
	jig, you amble, and you lisp, you nickname God's creatures,	*jig*: dance; *amble*: swagger
	and make your wantonness your ignorance. Go to, I'll no 145	*wantonness*: arts of seduction
	more on't, it hath made me mad. I say, we will have no	*ignorance*: pretence to knowing no better
	more marriages. Those that are married already, all but	
	one shall live; the rest shall keep as they are. To a nunnery,	
	go.	

Exit

OPHELIA	Oh what a noble mind is here o'erthrown! 150	
	The courtier's, soldier's, scholar's, eye, tongue, sword,	
	Th'expectancy and rose of the fair state,	*expectancy ... state*: Hamlet as future king
	The glass of fashion and the mould of form,	*glass ...*: virtuous model for all to copy
	Th'observed of all observers, quite, quite down,	*observed*: most honoured, significant
	And I of ladies most deject and wretched, 155	
	That sucked the honey of his music vows,	
	Now see that noble and most sovereign reason,	*sovereign reason*: reason's rightful rule
	Like sweet bells jangled, out of time and harsh;	*out of time*: out of order
	That unmatched form and feature of blown youth	
	Blasted with ecstasy. Oh woe is me * 160	
	T'have seen what I have seen, see what I see.	

Enter KING and POLONIUS

CLAUDIUS	Love? His affections do not that way tend;	*affections*: emotions
	Nor what he spake, though it lacked form a little,	
	Was not like madness. There's something in his soul,	
	O'er which his melancholy sits on brood, 165	
	And I do doubt the hatch and the disclose	*doubt*: fear; *hatch*: result of brooding
	Will be some danger; which for to prevent,	
	I have in quick determination	*quick determination*: speedily decided
	Thus set it down: he shall with speed to England	*with speed*: go quickly
	For the demand of our neglected tribute 170	*neglected tribute*: unpaid dues
	Haply the seas, and countries different,	*Haply*: it may happen that
	With variable objects, shall expel	*variable objects*: new variety of sights
	This something-settled matter in his heart,	
	Whereon his brains still beating puts him thus	
	From fashion of himself. What think you on't? 175	*fashion of himself*: his usual way of being
POLONIUS	It shall do well. But yet do I believe	
	The origin and commencement of his grief	
	Sprung from neglected love. How now, Ophelia?	
	You need not tell us what Lord Hamlet said;	
	We heard it all. My lord, do as you please; 180	
	But, if you hold it fit, after the play,	
	Let his queen mother all alone entreat him	
	To show his grief. Let her be round with him,	*grief*: grievance; *round*: plain-spoken
	And I'll be placed, so please you, in the ear	*in the ear*: within earshot
	Of all their conference. If she find him not, 185	*find him not*: fails to find his true self
	To England send him; or confine him where	
	Your wisdom best shall think.	
CLAUDIUS	It shall be so:	
	Madness in great ones must not unwatched go.	

Exeunt

* 159–60 *unmatched form ... with ecstasy*: Hamlet, in the prime of his man-hood (considered to be the most ideal state) is withered with mad passion

OPHELIA, POLONIUS & CLAUDIUS

Rosencrantz and Guildenstern report to Claudius on their meeting with Hamlet. Claudius and Polonius arrange for Hamlet to meet Ophelia, and prepare to spy on their conversation. Hamlet gives a moving soliloquy in which he ponders the trials of life and the attractions of suicide. He pretends to be mad during his meeting with Ophelia. He verbally abuses her and reveals an extremely negative attitude toward women. Ophelia is distraught at the prince's behaviour.

A CLOSER LOOK

LINES 1–28: ROSENCRANTZ AND GUILDENSTERN REPORT TO CLAUDIUS

Claudius asks Rosencrantz and Guildenstern if they have been able to learn the cause of Hamlet's apparently mad behaviour. (1–4) They report that although Hamlet confessed to being out of sorts, he would not tell them why. (5–6) Every time they broached the subject with him, the prince would dodge the issue with a 'crafty madness'. (8) Claudius tells them to continue their efforts to learn what lies behind the prince's 'madness'. (26–7)

Gertrude asks if they persuaded Hamlet to distract himself with some pastime or other. Rosencrantz tells her of the arrival of the players, and how Hamlet reacted with a 'kind of joy'. (18) Polonius confirms this. He adds that the prince wishes the royal couple to attend the players' performance that night.

Claudius is glad to hear this news, probably believing it a sign that his stepson is returning to normality. He promises that he and Gertrude will attend: 'With all my heart, and it doth much content me/ To hear him so inclined'. (24–5)

CHARACTER DEVELOPMENT

HAMLET

PRETENDING TO BE MAD

When Hamlet encounters Ophelia in this scene, he seems to deliberately alter his behaviour. Having only moments before spoken in a clear and rational way about suicide and the trials of life, his speech suddenly takes on a disconnected and disjointed quality, making what he says to Ophelia sound like the products of an irrational mind. He denies he ever gave her gifts, though he obviously did, and repeatedly switches from saying he never loved her to telling her that he once did. (95–151)

It is important to realise that Hamlet does not act like someone who has gone completely and utterly insane. As Claudius puts it after observing the prince's encounter with Ophelia, 'what he spake, though it lacked form a little,/ Was not like madness'. (163–4) Though what he says is disjointed and peculiar, it makes a strange kind of sense. His crazy remarks are often sharp and punning observations of the world around him.

A NEGATIVE STATE OF MIND

In this scene, Hamlet continues to think about suicide. He wonders whether it is better to be dead than alive: 'To be, or not to be, that is the question'. (56) He regards death as a restful sleep that soothes us after the toil and hardship of living. (60–5) He himself longs for the soothing sleep of death: ''tis a consummation/ Devoutly to be wished'. (63–4) He wonders why we endure the trials of living, why we 'bear the whips and scorns of time' (70), when we could end it all with a dagger: 'When he himself might his quietus make/ With a bare bodkin'. (75–6)

According to Hamlet, all that stops us from committing suicide is fear of what awaits us in the next life. We do not know what awaits us in the 'undiscover'd country' of death. (79) There is always a possibility that the eternity of death will be filled with terrible dreams. Therefore, we prefer to stick with the devil we know, enduring the ills of this world rather than risking what awaits us in the next.

In the 'To be, or not to be' soliloquy, Hamlet also expounds upon the sense of futility he expressed in Acts 1 and 2. He depicts life as being full of trials and difficulties, wondering why any of us continue to bear the 'whips and scorns of time'. (70) A similar attitude seems evident when he tells Ophelia to become a nun and not bother having any children: 'Get thee to a nunnery – why wouldst thou be a breeder of sinners?' (121–2) It's as though Hamlet thinks there is no point bringing children into the world. He considers the world to be full of 'arrant knaves', none of whom are to be trusted. (128–9)

NEGATIVE FEELINGS TOWARDS WOMEN

Though Hamlet pretends to be mad during his meeting with Ophelia, his speech reveals a genuine anger and bitterness towards women and marriage, and a disgust of female sexuality:

+ He considers women to be deliberately deceptive and manipulative: 'God hath given you one face, and you make yourselves another'. (142–3)
+ He says that women are a corrupting force and make 'monsters' out of men. (139)
+ He repeatedly tells Ophelia to take herself off to a nunnery and damns her if she decides to marry.(137–9)
+ He calls for no more marriages to take place, and hints at his wish to destroy his mother's marriage to Claudius: 'I say, we will have no more marriages. Those that are married already, all but one shall live'. (148–50)
+ It is hard to know if Hamlet has always held these opinions of women and marriage, or if they stem from his recent anger and bitterness towards his mother's remarriage.

A SENSE OF SUPERIORITY

In his rant at Ophelia, we get a sense of the prince's feelings of superiority. He berates Ophelia and damns her as a woman whilst suggesting that he, though flawed, is a virtuous and noble man. (124-7) He dismisses Ophelia when he has had enough of ranting, as though she were his social inferior, which she is, and not the woman that he once loved: 'Go to, I'll no more on't, it hath made me mad'. (145–6) He also expresses his opinions as though he were establishing laws: 'I say, we will have no more marriages'. (146–7)

HAMLET & OPHELIA

69

⌖LINES 28–49: CLAUDIUS AND POLONIUS PREPARE TO SPY ON HAMLET

Claudius and Polonius prepare to spy on a meeting between Hamlet and Ophelia. The prince's reaction to Ophelia will tell them if frustrated love for her is the cause of his strange behaviour. (35–7) Gertrude departs, telling Ophelia she hopes it is indeed Hamlet's love for her that has made him mad. She hopes a successful romance between them might bring Hamlet back to his usual self: 'so shall I hope your virtues/ Will bring him to his wonted way again,/ To both your honours'. (40–2)

⌖LINES 49–54: CLAUDIUS DESCRIBES HIS GUILT

Polonius instructs his daughter to walk up and down the hall, with the appearance of intently reading a book. This will make her seem pious and holy. (44–9) Polonius remarks how a devoted and religious appearance often disguises a sinister intent: 'with devotion's visage,/ And pious action, we do sugar o'er/ The devil himself'. (47–9)

This remark strikes a chord with Claudius, who draws aside to express his guilty conscience: 'How smart a lash that speech doth give my conscience'. (50) He conceals his guilt with elegant words and phrases just as a prostitute might conceal her ugliness with make-up: 'The harlot's cheek, beautied with plastering art,/ Is not more ugly to the thing that helps it/ Than is my deed to my most painted word'. (51–3)

⌖LINES 56–88: TO BE OR NOT TO BE

Hamlet wonders if it's better to be dead than alive: 'To be, or not to be, that is the question'. (56) He says that death is like sleep, an easeful rest after life's sufferings and difficulties: 'To die, to sleep –/ No more; and by a sleep to say we end/ The heart-ache and the thousand natural shocks/ That flesh is heir to'. (60–3) He finds the thought of death's eternal sleep an attractive one: ''tis a consummation/ Devoutly to be wished'. (63–4)

Hamlet says we are put off dying by the fear of the unknown. We are uncertain what the sleep of death might bring, fearing it might be filled with terrible dreams:

> Ay, there's the rub;
> For in that sleep of death what dreams may come
> When we have shuffled off this mortal coil,
> Must give us pause. There's the respect
> That makes calamity of so long life (65–9)

Hamlet then lists some of the ills we must endure on our journey through life: the evildoing of oppressors, the scorn and abuse of the proud, the pain of unrequited love, the arrogance of bureaucracy, and the insults that worthy people have to endure from the unworthy.

He wonders why we endure the pain of living when it is so easy for us to kill ourselves: 'When he himself might his quietus make/ With a bare bodkin?' (75–6) He suggests that we go on living only because we are afraid of what might await us after death. We would rather

CHARACTER DEVELOPMENT

A SHREWD POLITICIAN

We saw in the previous scene that Claudius regards Hamlet's seemingly deranged behaviour as a potential threat to Claudius' rule. In this scene, he becomes even more convinced that Hamlet's 'madness' could have dire consequences for his new regime: 'There's something in his soul/ O'er which his melancholy sits on brood'. (164–5)

Claudius is pleased, therefore, to hear of Hamlet's enthusiasm for the players, and agrees immediately to attend their performance. He seems to hope that Hamlet's interest in the players is a sign he's returning to normal. He asks Rosencrantz and Guildenstern to continue their efforts to improve Hamlet's mood.

Claudius continues his efforts to discover the cause of the prince's apparent madness. He listens to Rosencrantz and Guildenstern's report and orders them to continue their efforts. He spies on Hamlet's meeting with Ophelia. He also permits Polonius to spy on a meeting between Hamlet and his mother. The king displays his decisiveness and ruthlessness when he declares that if he cannot get to the bottom of the prince's strange behaviour, he will remove this potential threat by sending Hamlet to England.

CLAUDIUS' GUILT

In this scene, Claudius gives the first indication of the intense guilt he feels for the terrible deed he has committed. Claudius, then, is not a one-dimensional villain but a killer with a conscience, someone who is tormented with guilt for the murder of his brother.

suffer the pains of this world than face something worse in the afterlife. (81–2)

Hamlet says that thinking too much about the consequences of our actions prevents us from taking any action at all. Once we have an urge to do something, we should act straightaway. If we stop and think, our resolve will falter and we will fail to act: 'And thus the native hue of resolution/ Is sicklied o'er with the pale cast of thought,/ And enterprises of great pitch and moment/ With this regard their currents turn awry/ And lose the name of action'. (84–8)

LINES 90–149: HAMLET TORMENTS OPHELIA

Ophelia enters, interrupting Hamlet's reflections. Ophelia tells Hamlet that she has gifts and tokens ('remembrances') from him that she wishes to return. (93–5) She remarks on the eloquence of his love letters: 'words of so sweet breath composed'. (95) She states that his gifts have now lost their charm because Hamlet has apparently changed his mind about her: 'For to the noble mind/ Rich gifts wax poor when givers prove unkind'. (100–1)

Hamlet denies that he ever gave her anything and then becomes quite aggressive:

- He tells her that he loves her and then quickly changes his mind. Ophelia says that she was taken in by his declarations of love.
- He tells her repeatedly that she should enter a 'nunnery', or convent. He tells her not to have any children, saying that by doing so she will only be bringing more sinners into the world: 'Why wouldst thou be a breeder/ of sinners?' (120–1)
- He asks Ophelia if she is honest and beautiful, a question that confuses her. (107–8) He suggests that it is impossible for beautiful people to be honest.
- He describes himself as an evil person, saying he has more evil intentions than he can possibly carry out: 'more offences at my beck than I have thoughts to put them in, imagination to give them shape, or time to act them in'. (125–7)
- He says that if she ever marries, she should marry a fool, because intelligent men know the degrading effects women have upon their characters; 'marry a fool; for wise men know well enough what monsters you make of them'. (138–9)
- He says that women are false and deceitful, making special mention of the way they use make-up to disguise their true appearance: 'God hath given you one face, and you make yourselves another'. (142–3)
- He attacks the way women dance, walk and speak; the way they use fashionable names instead of natural ones; and how they claim ignorance when they deny their efforts at seduction. (143–5)

POLONIUS

SELF IMPORTANT
As we have already observed, Polonius relishes being at the centre of court affairs. In this scene, he is constantly at the king's side, listening to Rosencrantz and Guildenstern's report and observing Hamlet's meeting with Ophelia. He backs up what Rosencrantz and Guildenstern have to say about Hamlet's enthusiasm for the players, and adds that the prince wishes for the royal couple to attend the performance. (22–3)

A MEDDLING SCHEMER
Polonius must be happy that the king has agreed to his plan to spy on Hamlet and Ophelia. He takes charge of the operation, telling Ophelia where to walk and how she should behave. After observing the prince's encounter with Ophelia, Polonius is still absolutely convinced of his opinion that Hamlet's madness stems from 'neglected love'. (178) He immediately calls for further surveillance, suggesting that he observe a meeting between Hamlet and Gertrude after the play.

AN UNCARING FATHER
Polonius is well capable of telling his children how they ought to behave. In Act 1 Scene 3 he gave long-winded advice to Laertes as he was departing to France, and insisted that Ophelia cease all contact with Hamlet upon hearing of the prince's strange behaviour. However, we must question whether Polonius actually cares deeply about his son and daughter.

In this scene he certainly displays a distinct lack of care for Ophelia. Polonius selfishly uses his daughter's troubles with Hamlet to demonstrate his theory regarding the prince's madness. He uses Ophelia like a prop in his plan, telling her where to walk and what to do: 'Ophelia, walk you here … Read on this book'. (43–4) And despite the fact that he hears all the terrible things that Hamlet says to Ophelia, and that his daughter is visibly distraught after her encounter with the prince, Polonius offers her no emotional support. He is already thinking of further schemes, and barely turns aside from his discussions with the king to acknowledge his heart-broken daughter: 'How now, Ophelia?/ You need not tell us what Lord Hamlet said;/ We heard it all'. (178–81) She has served her purpose in his plan and it seems of no consequence to him that it has caused her so much grief.

He condemns the institute of marriage: 'I say, we will have no more marriages'. (146–7)

At several points throughout this rant, Hamlet says farewell to Ophelia as if he is about to stop, only to continue berating her and women in general. Finally, Hamlet says that he will cease ranting, as he has driven himself mad with anger: 'it hath made me mad'. (146)

LINES 150–61: OPHELIA'S LAMENT

Ophelia is left distraught by the prince's performance. She believes he has gone mad: 'Oh, what a noble mind is here o'erthrown!' (150) Hamlet, she says, was once the pride of Denmark, but now he has disintegrated: 'The courtier's, soldier's, scholar's eye, tongue, sword,/Th'expectancy and rose of the fair state,/The glass of fashion and the mould of form,/Th'observed of all observers, quite, quite down!' (150–4) She describes herself as the most unfortunate of women: 'of ladies most dejected and wretched'. (155)

LINES 162–88: CLAUDIUS AND POLONIUS CONTINUE TO SCHEME

The king and Polonius emerge from the place where they have been secretly observing Hamlet. Claudius is now convinced that Hamlet's troubles are not caused by his love for Ophelia: 'Love? His affections do not that way tend'. (162) He also suspects that Hamlet is not really mad: 'Nor what he spake, though it lacked form a little,/Was not like madness'. (163–4)

Claudius is starting to worry about what is going on in Hamlet's mind. (164–9) He fears that the troubled prince may prove a danger to himself and to others. He thinks a change of scene might soothe Hamlet's troubled mind, and decides to send him to England. (168–9) Does Claudius suspect that Hamlet knows something about his father's murder?

Claudius asks Polonius his opinion of the plan. Polonius thinks it a good one, but persists stubbornly in believing that frustrated love for Ophelia is the cause of Hamlet's derangement: 'But yet do I believe/ The origin and commencement of this grief/ Sprung from neglected love'. (176–8)

Polonius then has another idea. Before Hamlet is sent abroad, Claudius must arrange for Hamlet to have an audience alone with Gertrude. Polonius will spy on the meeting in the hope that Hamlet will tell his mother what has been troubling him. (183–5) The king agrees. He says that Hamlet must be constantly observed: 'It shall be so:/ Madness in great ones must not unwatched go'. (187–8)

CHARACTER DEVELOPMENT

OPHELIA

INNOCENT & TRUSTING

Ophelia once again appears as an innocent and trusting daughter, willingly going along with her father's plans to spy on Hamlet. Whilst for Polonius the planned encounter with Hamlet provides the perfect means for him to appear important in the eyes of the king, for Ophelia the meeting is deeply personal and emotional. She is devastated by the prince's strange and callous behaviour. Clearly devastated after the encounter, Ophelia is offered no emotional support by her father. Whilst all eyes are on the prince, there seems to be nobody watching out for this unfortunate, innocent girl.

LOVE FOR HAMLET

Ophelia's response to Hamlet's wild and angry behaviour shows how deeply she feels for the prince. She is devastated to see how Hamlet has changed so dramatically from a noble, much-admired and talented youth to a ranting, bitter madman: 'Oh woe is me/ T'have seen what I have seen'. (160–1) She is the only character to express such heartfelt concern for this obviously troubled man.

ROSENCRANTZ & GUILDENSTERN

As we observed in Act 2 Scene 2 Hamlet's old school friends have been put in a difficult position, being asked by the king to spy on their friend. It seems, however, that duty to the king is outweighing loyalty to a friend, and in this scene we find them dutifully reporting on their meeting with Hamlet to Claudius. They tell the king in a succinct and honest manner that Hamlet is acting mad, but will give no hint why he is doing so. They also tell Claudius that Hamlet's mood greatly improved upon hearing that the players were on their way to Elsinore. The king is pleased with their report, and asks that they continue to encourage Hamlet's good spirits.

Enter HAMLET and two or three of the PLAYERS

HAMLET Speak the speech I pray you as I pronounced it to you, trippingly on the tongue; but if you mouth it as many of our players do, I had as lief the town-crier spoke my lines. Nor do not saw the air too much with your hand thus, but use all gently; for in the very torrent, tempest, and, as I may say, whirlwind of your passion, you must acquire and beget a temperance that may give it smoothness. Oh, it offends me to the soul to hear a robustious periwig-pated fellow tear a passion to tatters, to very rags, to split the ears of the groundlings, who for the most part are capable of nothing but inexplicable dumbshows and noise. I would have such a fellow whipped for o'erdoing Termagant – it out-herods Herod. Pray you avoid it.

FIRST PLAYER I warrant your honour.

HAMLET Be not too tame neither, but let your own discretion be your tutor. Suit the action to the word, the word to the action, with this special observance, that you o'erstep not the modesty of nature. For anything so o'erdone is from the purpose of playing, whose end both at the first and now, was and is, to hold, as 'twere, the mirror up to nature; to show virtue her own feature, scorn her own image, and the very age and body of the time his form and pressure. Now this overdone, or come tardy off, though it make the unskilful laugh, cannot but make the judicious grieve, the censure of the which one must in your allowance o'erweigh a whole theatre of others. Oh, there be players that I have seen play, and heard others praise and that highly, not to speak it profanely, that neither having the accent of Christians nor the gait of Christian, pagan, nor man, have so strutted and bellowed that I have thought some of nature's journeymen had made men, and not made them well, they imitated humanity so abominably.

FIRST PLAYER I hope we have reformed that indifferently with us, sir.

HAMLET Oh reform it altogether. And let those that play your clowns speak no more than is set down for them, for there be of them that will themselves laugh, to set on some quantity of barren spectators to laugh too, though in the meantime some necessary question of the play be then to be considered. That's villanous, and shows a most pitiful ambition in the fool that uses it. Go make you ready.

Exeunt PLAYERS

Enter POLONIUS, ROSENCRANTZ, and GUILDENSTERN

How now, my lord, will the king hear this piece of work?

Line numbers: 5, 10, 15, 20, 25, 30, 35, 40

mouth: speak without feeling
I had as lief: I'd be as happy
saw the air: be overly dramatic in gesture

temperance: restraint the top
robustious: boisterous, over
periwig-pated: wig-wearing

Termagant: figure of violence in medieval plays
Herod: biblical tyrant
warrant: will do as you ask
discretion: prudence

mirror: represent by imitation

body of: society of
his form and pressure: his likeness
the judicious: the serious critic

praise and that highly: highly praise

indifferently: to some degree

be then: needs next

*   10 *groundlings*: poor audience standing on the ground
†   23 *come tardy off*: played inadequately through mis-timing of lines
‡   25 *censure of the which one*: the critic's judgement
§   31 *nature's journeymen*: not nature but her workmen
¶   36–7 *set on some quantity of barren spectators to laugh*: improvise and add to their set speeches to make those without wit and judgement laugh at their antics

POLONIUS	And the queen too, and that presently.
HAMLET	Bid the players make haste.

Exit POLONIUS

Will you two help to hasten them?

ROSENCRANTZ }
GUILDENSTERN

Exeunt ROSENCRANTZ and GUILDENSTERN

HAMLET	What ho, Horatio!	45

Enter HORATIO

HORATIO	Here sweet lord, at your service.	
HAMLET	Horatio, thou art e'en as just a man	
	As e'er my conversation coped withal.	
HORATIO	Oh my dear lord.	
HAMLET	Nay, do not think I flatter,	
	For what advancement may I hope from thee,	50
	That no revenue hast but thy good spirits	
	To feed and clothe thee? Why should the poor be flattered?*	
	No, let the candied tongue lick absurd pomp	
	And crook the pregnant hinges of the knee	
	Where thrift may follow fawning. Dost thou hear?†	55
	Since my dear soul was mistress of her choice,	
	And could of men distinguish her election,	
	Hath sealed thee for herself, for thou hast been	
	As one in suffering all that suffers nothing,	
	A man that Fortune's buffets and rewards	60
	Hast tane with equal thanks. And blest are those	
	Whose blood and judgement are so well commeddled‡	
	That they are not a pipe for Fortune's finger	
	To sound what stop she please. Give me that man	
	That is not passion's slave, and I will wear him	65
	In my heart's core, ay in my heart of heart,	
	As I do thee. Something too much of this.	
	There is a play to-night before the king:	
	One scene of it comes near the circumstance	
	Which I have told thee of my father's death:	70
	I prithee, when thou seest that act afoot,	
	Even with the very comment of thy soul	
	Observe my uncle. If his occulted guilt	
	Do not itself unkennel in one speech,	
	It is a damnèd ghost that we have seen,	75
	And my imaginations are as foul	
	As Vulcan's stithy. Give him heedful note;§	
	For I mine eyes will rivet to his face,	
	And after we will both our judgements join	
	In censure of his seeming.¶	
HORATIO	Well my lord:	80
	If he steal aught the whilst this play is playing,	
	And scape detecting, I will pay the theft.	
HAMLET	They are coming to the play; I must be idle.	
	Get you a place.	

Glossary (right margin):

just: well-balanced, fair
e'er: ever; *coped withal*: encountered

advancement: gain

mistress of her choice: his soul's in charge
election: choice
sealed thee: chosen you as her soulmate
As one: unchanging

Hast tane: Has taken
blood and judgement: passion and reason
a pipe: hollow, without true substance
what stop: what tune
passion's slave: slave to whatever passion moves him

comes near: closely enacts

afoot: being acted out
comment of thy soul: closest judgement
occulted: dark and hidden
unkennel: reveal
damnèd ghost: evil spirit
imaginations: suspicions

steal aught: hide emotion
scape detecting: escape detection
idle: unoccupied, as opposed to conspiring

Footnotes (right margin):

* 52   *Why ... flatter'd?*: Who'd flatter the poor?

† 53–5   *No, let the candied tongue... follow fawning*: let the flatterer with his sugar-coated tongue lick and fawn with bended knee the ridiculously pompous and wealthy, where economic profit is the desired result

‡ 64   *commeddled*: mixed together

§ 77   *Vulcan's stithy*: blacksmith god's anvil, symbol of the smith's profession

¶ 80   *In censure of his seeming*: in judgement of how he acts

Danish march (trumpets and kettle-drums). Enter KING, QUEEN, POLONIUS, OPHELIA,
ROSENCRANTZ, GUILDENSTERN, and other LORDS attendant, with his GUARD
carrying torches.

CLAUDIUS	How fares our cousin Hamlet?	85
HAMLET	Excellent, i'faith, of the chameleon's dish: I eat the air, promise-crammed. You cannot feed capons so.*	
CLAUDIUS	I have nothing with this answer, Hamlet, these words are not mine.	
HAMLET	No, nor mine now. – My lord, you played once i' the,† university you say?	90
POLONIUS	That did I my lord, and was accounted a good actor.	
HAMLET	What did you enact?	
POLONIUS	I did enact Julius Caesar: I was killed i'th' Capitol. Brutus killed me.	95
HAMLET	It was a brute part of him to kill so capital a calf there. – Be the players ready?	
ROSENCRANTZ	Ay, my lord; they stay upon your patience.	
GERTRUDE	Come hither my dear Hamlet, sit by me.	
HAMLET	No good mother, here's metal more attractive.	100
POLONIUS	Oh ho! do you mark that?	
HAMLET	Lady, shall I lie in your lap?	
OPHELIA	No my lord.	
HAMLET	I mean, my head upon your lap?	
OPHELIA	Ay my lord.	105
HAMLET	Do you think I meant country matters?	
OPHELIA	I think nothing, my lord.	
HAMLET	That's a fair thought to lie between maids' legs.	
OPHELIA	What is, my lord?	
HAMLET	Nothing.	110
OPHELIA	You are merry, my lord.	
HAMLET	Who, I?	
OPHELIA	Ay, my lord.	
HAMLET	O God, your only jig-maker. What should a man do but be merry? for look you how cheerfully my mother looks, and my father died within's two hours.	115
OPHELIA	Nay, 'tis twice two months my lord.	
HAMLET	So long? Nay then let the devil wear black, for I'll have a suit of sables. O heavens! die two months ago, and not forgotten yet? Then there's hope a great man's memory may outlive his life half a year: but, byrlady a must build‡ churches then, or else shall a suffer not thinking on, with the hobby-horse, whose epitaph is, 'For O, for O, the hobby-horse is forgot.'§	120

Hoboys play. The dumb-show enters.⹁

Enter a KING and a QUEEN, very lovingly, the Queen embracing him. She kneels and makes
show of protestation unto him. He takes her up, and declines his head upon her neck. He lies him
down upon a bank of flowers. She, seeing him asleep, leaves him. Anon comes in another man,
takes off his crown, kisses it, pours poison in the sleeper's ears, and leaves him. The Queen returns,
finds the King dead, and makes passionate action. The Poisoner, with some two or three Mutes,
comes in again, seeming to condole with her. The dead body is carried away. The Poisoner woos the
Queen with gifts. She seems harsh awhile, but in the end accepts his love.
Exeunt

---

nothing with: no understanding of

brute … capital: Hamlet plays with words

metal … attractive: more magnetic, desirable

lie in your lap: sexual innuendo

my head upon your lap: traditional custom

country matters: physical lovemaking

sables: luxurious furs

not thinking on: oblivion

---

* 86–7 *the chameleon's dish … feed capons so*: Hamlet's response to the king's question deliberately misinterprets 'how fares' to mean 'how eats' instead of 'how does'. The chameleon was believed to feed on air – Hamlet states that the air he feeds on is crammed full of promises, perhaps alluding to the king's earlier promise that he is heir to the throne.

† 90 *nor mine now*: once spoken, they're no longer his

‡ 121 *build churches*: so prayers may be said for him

§ 124 *hobby-horse*: figure of a horse, easily forgotten

⹁ 124–5 *hoboys*: oboes (musical instruments)

OPHELIA	What means this my lord?	125
HAMLET	Marry this is miching mallecho; it means mischief.	
OPHELIA	Belike this show imports the argument of the play?	

Enter PROLOGUE

HAMLET	We shall know by this fellow; the players cannot keep, counsel they'll tell all.	
OPHELIA	Will a tell us what this show meant?	130
HAMLET	Ay, or any show that you'll show him. Be not you ashamed to show, he'll not shame to tell you what it means.	
OPHELIA	You are naught, you are naught: I'll mark the play.	
PROLOGUE	For us, and for our tragedy,	
	Here stooping to your clemency,	135
	We beg your hearing patiently.	
HAMLET	Is this a prologue, or the posy of a ring?	
OPHELIA	'Tis brief, my lord.	
HAMLET	As woman's love.	

Enter the PLAYER KING and QUEEN

PLAYER KING	Full thirty times hath Phoebus' cart gone round	140
	Neptune's salt wash and Tellus' orbèd ground,	
	And thirty dozen moons with borrowed sheen*	
	About the world have times twelve thirties been,	
	Since love our hearts and Hymen did our hands	
	Unite commutual in most sacred bands.	145
PLAYER QUEEN	So many journeys may the sun and moon	
	Make us again count o'er ere love be done!	
	But woe is me, you are so sick of late,	
	So far from cheer and from your former state,	
	That I distrust you. Yet, though I distrust,	150
	Discomfort you my lord it nothing must.	
	For women's fear and love holds quantity,	
	In neither aught, or in extremity.†	
	Now, what my love is, proof hath made you know;	
	And as my love is sized, my fear is so.	155
	Where love is great, the littlest doubts are fear;	
	Where little fears grow great, great love grows there.	
PLAYER KING	Faith, I must leave thee love, and shortly too:	
	My operant powers their functions leave to do;	
	And thou shalt live in this fair world behind,	160
	Honoured, beloved; and haply one as kind	
	For husband shalt thou –	
PLAYER QUEEN	O, confound the rest!	
	Such love must needs be treason in my breast.	
	In second husband let me be accurst:	
	None wed the second but who killed the first.	165
HAMLET	That's wormwood, wormwood.	
PLAYER QUEEN	The instances that second marriage move‡	
	Are base respects of thrift, but none of love.	
	A second time I kill my husband dead	
	When second husband kisses me in bed.	170

miching mallecho: underhand villainy
imports the argument: suggests the plot

counsel: secret

naught: naughty, improper; *mark*: watch

clemency: kindness

posy of a ring: verse imprinted inside a ring

Phoebus' cart: sun's chariot
Neptune ... ground: sea and earth, entire globe

Hymen: pagan god of marriage
commutual: mutually committed

distrust: am anxious about you
Discomfort: put you out, upset

sized: measured

operant powers: vital faculties
behind: without me
haply: hopefully

Such love: love for another husband

wormwood: plant associated with bitterness

* 142 *moons with borrowed sheen*: it was known that the moon reflected the sun's brightness rather than generating its own light

† 152–3 *women's fear and love ... aught, or in extremity*: women experience fear and love in equal measure – neither emotion is present, or both are present to an extreme

‡ 167 *The instances that second marriage move*: the motives that move one to marry a second time

PLAYER KING	I do believe you think what now you speak,	
	But what we do determine oft we break.	
	Purpose is but the slave to memory,	
	Of violent birth, but poor validity,*	
	Which now like fruit unripe sticks on the tree;	175
	But fall unshaken when they mellow be.	
	Most necessary 'tis that we forget	
	To pay ourselves what to ourselves is debt.	
	What to ourselves in passion we propose,	
	The passion ending, doth the purpose lose.	180
	The violence of either grief or joy	
	Their own enactures with themselves destroy†	
	Where joy most revels, grief doth most lament;	
	Grief joys, joy grieves, on slender accident.	
	This world is not for aye, nor 'tis not strange	185
	That even our loves should with our fortunes change,	
	For 'tis a question left us yet to prove,	
	Whether love lead fortune, or else fortune love.	
	The great man down, you mark his favourite flies;‡	
	The poor advanced makes friends of enemies,	190
	And hitherto doth love on fortune tend;	
	For who not needs shall never lack a friend,	
	And who in want a hollow friend doth try	
	Directly seasons him his enemy.	
	But, orderly to end where I begun,	195
	Our wills and fates do so contrary run	
	That our devices still are overthrown;	
	Our thoughts are ours, their ends none of our own.§	
	So think thou wilt no second husband wed,	
	But die thy thoughts when thy first lord is dead.	200
PLAYER QUEEN	Nor earth to me give food, nor heaven light,	
	Sport and repose lock from me day and night,	
	To desperation turn my trust and hope,	
	An anchor's cheer in prison be my scope,	
	Each opposite that blanks the face of joy	205
	Meet what I would have well, and it destroy;	
	Both here and hence pursue me lasting strife,	
	If, once a widow, ever I be wife.	
HAMLET	If she should break it now!	
PLAYER KING	'Tis deeply sworn. Sweet, leave me here awhile;	210
	My spirits grow dull, and fain I would beguile	
	The tedious day with sleep.	

Sleeps

PLAYER QUEEN	Sleep rock thy brain,	
	And never come mischance between us twain.	

Exit

HAMLET	Madam, how like you this play?	
GERTRUDE	The lady doth protest too much methinks.	215
HAMLET	Oh but she'll keep her word.	
CLAUDIUS	Have you heard the argument? Is there no offence in't?	

Most necessary 'tis: it's inevitable

pay ... debt: fulfil our promises to ourselves

Grief ... grieves: grief turns to joy, joy to grief
for aye: for ever

lead: is followed by

advanced: promoted
hitherto: to this extent
not needs: is well provided for

Directly seasons: favours him towards

so contrary run: run in opposite directions
devices: designs, plans
thoughts: opinions

anchor's cheer: the female hermit's meagre joy

offence: cause for objection

....

*   173–4 *Purpose is ... poor validity*: our
            intended actions depend on our
            remembering of them. When we first
            form our intentions they are full of
            force – however, they rarely last.

†   182   *Their own enactures ... destroy*: the
            process of translating a passion into
            action destroys it

‡   189   *his favourite flies*: his closest follower
            leaves him

§   198   *their ends*: death or purposes

HAMLET	No, no, they do but jest, poison in jest, no offence i' the world.
CLAUDIUS	What do you call the play?
HAMLET	*The Mousetrap.* Marry how? Tropically. This play is the image of a murder done in Vienna. Gonzago is the duke's name, his wife, Baptista: you shall see anon. 'Tis a knavish piece of work, but what o' that? Your majesty, and we that have free souls, it touches us not. Let the galled jade winch,†

Enter LUCIANUS

	our withers are unwrung. This is one Lucianus, nephew to‡ the king.
OPHELIA	You are as good as a chorus, my lord.
HAMLET	I could interpret between you and your love, if I could see the puppets dallying.
OPHELIA	You are keen my lord, you are keen.
HAMLET	It would cost you a groaning to take off mine edge.§
OPHELIA	Still better and worse.
HAMLET	So you mistake your husbands. Begin, murderer. Pox,€ leave thy damnable faces and begin. Come, the croaking raven doth bellow for revenge.
LUCIANUS	Thoughts black, hands apt, drugs fit, and time agreeing, Confederate season, else no creature seeing. Thou mixture rank, of midnight weeds collected, With Hecat's ban thrice blasted, thrice infected, Thy natural magic and dire property On wholesome life usurp immediately.

Pours the poison in his ears

HAMLET	A poisons him i'th'garden for's estate. His name's Gonzago. The story is extant, and written in very choice Italian. You shall see anon how the murderer gets the love of Gonzago's wife.
OPHELIA	The king rises.
HAMLET	What, frighted with false fire?
GERTRUDE	How fares my lord?
POLONIUS	Give o'er the play.
CLAUDIUS	Give me some light. Away!
ALL	Lights, lights, lights!

Exeunt all but HAMLET and HORATIO

HAMLET	Why, let the stricken deer go weep, The hart ungallèd play; For some must watch, while some must sleep, So runs the world away. Would not this, sir, and a forest of feathers, if the rest of my fortunes turn Turk with me, with two provincial roses on my razed shoes, get me a fellowship in a cry of players, sir?

offence: wrongdoing

knavish: workmanlike

free souls: innocent, no guilt

chorus: interpreter of action in classical play
interpret: be the voice
puppets: Ophelia and her love
keen: sharp
my edge: my desire
better and worse: more keen, and offensive

Confederate season: season acts as accomplice
mixture rank: poison
Hecat: queen of witches
natural magic: inherent dark powers
usurp: takes possession of, invade

for's estate: for his kingship and lands

false fire: fiction, passions acted in a play

stricken: wounded
hart ungallèd: unhurt deer, pun on hart/heart
watch: stay awake, on guard

feathers: worn on actors' hats
turn Turk: turn renegade, false
roses: rosettes, part of actor's costume;
fellowship: partnership

* 221   *The Mouse-trap*: the title reflects Hamlet's intent to 'catch the conscience of the king' (Act 3, Scene 1, line 583).

† 225   *galled jade*: horse sore from rub of saddle, guilty

‡ 226   *withers ... unwrung*: horse's shoulders not tensed, by analogy not affected by gut-wrenching emotion

§ 232   *groaning*: pangs of childbirth

€ 234   *So ... husbands*: marriage vows, for better and worse

HORATIO	Half a share.
HAMLET	A whole one I.
	For thou dost know, O Damon dear,
	This realm dismantled was
	Of Jove himself, and now reigns here
	A very, very – pajock.*
HORATIO	You might have rhymed.
HAMLET	O good Horatio, I'll take the ghost's word for a thousand pound. Didst perceive?
HORATIO	Very well, my lord.
HAMLET	Upon the talk of the poisoning?
HORATIO	I did very well note him.

Enter ROSENCRANTZ and GUILDENSTERN

HAMLET	Ah, ha! – Come, some music! Come, the recorders!
	For if the king like not the comedy,†
	Why then – belike, he likes it not, perdy.
	Come, some music!
GUILDENSTERN	Good my lord, vouchsafe me a word with you.
HAMLET	Sir, a whole history.
GUILDENSTERN	The king, sir, –
HAMLET	Ay sir, what of him?
GUILDENSTERN	Is in his retirement marvellous distempered.
HAMLET	With drink, sir?
GUILDENSTERN	No, my lord, rather with choler.
HAMLET	Your wisdom should show itself more richer to signify this to his doctor, for, for me to put him to his purgation would perhaps plunge him into far more choler.‡
GUILDENSTERN	Good my lord, put your discourse into some frame, and start not so wildly from my affair.
HAMLET	I am tame sir, pronounce.
GUILDENSTERN	The queen your mother, in most great affliction of spirit, hath sent me to you.
HAMLET	You are welcome.
GUILDENSTERN	Nay good my lord, this courtesy is not of the right breed. If it shall please you to make me a wholesome answer, I will do your mother's commandment: if not, your pardon and my return shall be the end of my§ business.
HAMLET	Sir, I cannot.
GUILDENSTERN	What, my lord?
HAMLET	Make you a wholesome answer; my wit's diseased. But, sir, such answer as I can make, you shall command, or rather, as you say, my mother. Therefore no more, but to the matter. My mother, you say.

265

270

275   *perdy*: by God

   vouchsafe: grant

280

   distempered: out of temper, imbalanced, ill

   wisdom ... richer: you would be wiser to
285   *purgation*: cleansing

   some frame: some order
   affair: concern
   tame: calm; *pronounce*: speak

290

   courtesy: manner of speaking
   breed: kind, sort; *wholesome*: reasonable
295

   pardon: permission to leave

300

---

*   263–6   *O Damon ... pajock*: in pastoral poetry Damon is a shepherd who has all the virtues associated with the golden age, before the world's corruption. The image of Jove's realm being usurped by a peacock is an analogy for his father's kingdom being usurped by Claudius.

†   274   *comedy*: Hamlet is being ironic in describing the play as a comedy

‡   285–6   *doctor ... more choler*: whereas a doctor would attempt to cure the king's anger by physically eliminating the excess of bile from his body (perhaps by blood-letting, a common curative in this period), for Hamlet, to cleanse (purge) the king would necessitate extracting a confession from him, thereby purifying his soul from guilt. However, Hamlet's cure would have the effect of making the king even more upset and angry. Hamlet's words make sense once 'purgation' is understood as a form of both physical and spiritual cleansing.

§   296   *return*: to the queen

ROSENCRANTZ	Then thus she says. Your behaviour hath struck her into amazement and admiration.	
HAMLET	O wonderful son, that can so astonish a mother! But is there no sequel at the heels of this mother's admiration? Impart.	
ROSENCRANTZ	She desires to speak with you in her closet, ere you go to bed.	310
HAMLET	We shall obey, were she ten times our mother. Have you any further trade with us?	
ROSENCRANTZ	My lord, you once did love me.	
HAMLET	So I do still, by these pickers and stealers.	
ROSENCRANTZ	Good my lord, what is your cause of distemper? You do surely bar the door upon your own liberty if you deny your griefs to your friend.	315
HAMLET	Sir, I lack advancement.	
ROSENCRANTZ	How can that be, when you have the voice of the king himself for your succession in Denmark?	320
HAMLET	Ay, but sir, while the grass grows – the proverb is something musty.	

Enter the PLAYERS with recorders

	Oh, the recorders. Let me see one. To withdraw with you – Why do you go about to recover the wind of me, as if you would drive me into a toil?	325
GUILDENSTERN	O my lord, if my duty be too bold, my love is too unmannerly.†	
HAMLET	I do not well understand that. Will you play upon this pipe?	
GUILDENSTERN	My lord, I cannot.	
HAMLET	I pray you.	330
GUILDENSTERN	Believe me, I cannot.	
HAMLET	I do beseech you.	
GUILDENSTERN	I know no touch of it my lord.	
HAMLET	'Tis as easy as lying: govern these ventages with your fingers and thumb, give it breath with your mouth, and it will discourse most eloquent music. Look you, these are the stops.	335
GUILDENSTERN	But these cannot I command to any utterance of harmony; I have not the skill.	
HAMLET	Why look you now how unworthy a thing you make of me. You would play upon me, you would seem to know my stops, you would pluck out the heart of my mystery, you would sound me from my lowest note to the top of my compass – and there is much music, excellent voice, in this little organ, yet cannot you make it speak. 'Sblood, do you think I am easier to be played on than a pipe? Call me what instrument you will, though you can fret me, you cannot play upon me.	340 345

Enter POLONIUS

	God bless you, sir.	
POLONIUS	My lord, the queen would speak with you, and presently.	350
HAMLET	Do you see yonder cloud that's almost in shape of a camel?	
POLONIUS	By the mass, and 'tis like a camel indeed.	
HAMLET	Methinks it is like a weasel.	
POLONIUS	It is backed like a weasel.	
HAMLET	Or like a whale?	355

admiration: wonder, incredulity

sequel at the heels: further development

closet: room

trade: business, use; *us*: royal pronoun

these pickers and stealers: these hands

deny: refuse to unburden

voice of the king: the king's word
succession: ascension to the throne
'*While the grass grows, the horse starves*'
musty: old, stale

withdraw: to speak privately
recover the wind: hunting metaphor
toil: net

govern … ventages: control these holes

play upon: manipulate
my stops: my notes
mystery: life, secret; *compass*: range
little organ: recorder

fret: irritate

* 316   *bar … liberty*: refuse to be free
† 326-7   *duty … unmannerly*: If I'm too forward or insolent in my communications with you, it is only because of the strength of my love for you

POLONIUS	Very like a whale.*
HAMLET	Then I will come to my mother by and by. – They fool me
	to the top of my bent. – I will come by and by.
POLONIUS	I will say so.
HAMLET	By and by is easily said. – Leave me, friends.

to ... bent: to the utmost of what I can bear

360

Exeunt all but HAMLET

'Tis now the very witching time of night,
When churchyards yawn, and hell itself breathes out
Contagion to this world. Now could I drink hot blood,
And do such bitter business as the day
Would quake to look on. Soft, now to my mother.
O heart, lose not thy nature; let not ever
The soul of Nero enter this firm bosom.
Let me be cruel, not unnatural:
I will speak daggers to her but use none;
My tongue and soul in this be hypocrites;†
How in my words somever she be shent,
To give them seals never my soul consent!‡

365

370

Contagion: disease, infectious evil

quake: shake
thy nature: human feeling
Nero: Roman emperor who killed his mother

shent: shamed
seals: as a seal on a letter, which ratifies it

Exit

<hr>

* 351–6 *camel ... weasel ... whale*: Hamlet is
testing how far Polonius is willing to
humour him in his madness

† 370 *be hypocrites*: say one thing and do
another

‡ 371–2 *How in my words ... consent*: no
matter how my words, which are as
spoken daggers, shame her, and thus
confirm her guilt, I will never allow
myself to take revenge by using a real
dagger to kill her

HAMLET & THE PLAYERS

Hamlet speaks with the players who are soon to perform at court. He has given them some lines to insert into their performance, and he tells them how they ought to be delivered. The court gathers for the performance of the play, and Hamlet resumes his act of madness, joking in a crude manner with Ophelia. The play that the players perform has the effect that Hamlet desired. Claudius is disturbed by having to watch a performance that closely resembles the way he murdered Hamlet's father, and walks out of the room. The play is called to a halt, and Hamlet is left utterly convinced of the king's guilt. He is in a violent mood, and now seems ready to avenge his father's murder. First, however, he must visit the queen in her bedroom.

A CLOSER LOOK

LINES 1–44: HAMLET SPEAKS WITH THE PLAYERS

Hamlet speaks with some of the players who are set to perform shortly at court. He has given them a speech that he wishes to have inserted into their performance. He is hoping that the these lines will enhance the similarity between the plot of the play and the Ghost's account of the murder. If what the Ghost said is true, then Claudius ought to show signs of guilt at seeing a performance resembling his murderous deed.

The prince has a great love and knowledge of theatre, and he tells the players exactly how they ought to perform their lines. He asks them to speak the lines clearly and with feeling. (1–2) He insists that they don't use unnecessary or overly dramatic hand gestures as they speak. (2–7) Hamlet despises over-the-top performances: 'Oh, it offends me to the soul to hear a robustious periwig-pated fellow tear a passion to

tatters'. (8–9) Such overacting, he says, might raise a few laughs from the mob but they will be scorned by the more discerning elements of the audience. (23–6)

The purpose of theatre, Hamlet states, is to reflect life. Drama should mirror the times in which we live, and critically comment on our customs and values. 'Playing' should:

> hold, as 'twere, the mirror up to nature; to show virtue her own feature, scorn her own image, and the very age and body of the time his form and pressure. (20–2)

LINES 45–67: HAMLET PAYS TRIBUTE TO HORATIO

Horatio arrives and is greeted warmly and enthusiastically by Hamlet. The prince seems to be in good form, and he lavishes praise on his loyal and trusted friend:

- He says that Horatio is the most honest and well-balanced man he has ever dealt with. (47–8)
- Horatio is the man that he prizes above all others. (55)
- Hamlet praises Horatio's ability to remain calm and level-headed regardless of whether things are going well or badly for him. (57–61)

CHARACTER DEVELOPMENT

Hamlet considers it a blessing for a person to have a good mix of passion and reason: 'blest are those/ Whose blood and judgement are so well commeddled [commingled]'. (61–2) It is not good if somebody is a 'slave' to their passions. The prince values those who can temper their passion with reason, of whom Horatio is one:

> *Give me that man*
> *That is not passion's slave, and I will*
> *wear him*
> *In my heart's core, ay in my heart of*
> *heart,*
> *As I do thee.* (64–7)

Horatio is embarrassed by Hamlet's lavish praise. Hamlet insists, however, that his words stem from his deep love and trust of Horatio, and that he is not flattering him with some other motive in mind. After all, he reminds his friend, why would a prince flatter someone of significantly lower status. (56–9)

LINES 67–83: HAMLET'S PLAN TO TEST THE TRUTH OF THE GHOST'S STORY

It seems that Hamlet has already confided the Ghost's story to Horatio. (70) He now tells his friend that a play will be performed tonight in which one scene will closely resemble the death of his father, as recounted by the Ghost: 'One scene of it comes near the circumstance/ Which I have told thee of my father's death'. (68–9) He asks Horatio to watch Claudius' face closely at this point of the play in order to observe his reaction. If Claudius shows no undue reaction, then the Ghost is evil and Hamlet's suspicions will prove to

A LOVE OF THEATRE

In Act 2 Scene 2 we witnessed Hamlet's great excitement upon hearing of the players coming to court. In this scene he reveals just how knowledgeable he is about theatrical performance, describing in great detail how he wishes the players to perform their lines. He is confident of his views and opinions, and tells them exactly what he likes and dislikes in a performance. The prince is deeply passionate about theatre, and loathes to see bad acting.

PRETENDING TO BE MAD

Hamlet again continues to act mad before the king and queen and members of the court. As the royal couple arrive to watch the show, Hamlet tells Horatio that it is time for him to 'be idle' once more, meaning that he must once again pretend to be insane.

- He responds to Claudius' greeting with what seems like gibberish. (86–7)
- He makes a similar response when Polonius tells him that he once played the part of Julius Caesar in a play: 'It was a brute part of him to kill so capital a calf there'. (96–)
- He makes several comments about Ophelia's genitalia that are both highly socially inappropriate and weird and disjointed.
- He pretends to not know how long it has been since his father's death. (116)

Hamlet gives a similar performance when he meets Rosencrantz and Guildenstern after the players have performed. He speaks to them in a manner that is somehow wild and disconnected, telling them that his 'wit's diseased'. (300) Rosencrantz is baffled and frustrated by Hamlet's strange talk and asks him to speak normally: 'put your discourse into some frame, and start not so wildly from my affair'. (287–8)

NEGATIVE ATTITUDE TOWARDS WOMEN

Though more playful than when he met her in the previous scene, Hamlet continues to speak to Ophelia in a very unpleasant manner. His joking is bawdy and offensive, and again reveals the prince's negative attitude towards women. He treats Ophelia as though she were a common prostitute, though she has done nothing to earn such contempt. We can only imagine how hurtful his words must be to Ophelia, the woman that he once swore to love.

A RUTHLESS STREAK

Hamlet is now certain that the Ghost spoke the truth and that Claudius is guilty of murder. At the end of the scene, he speaks in a dark and violent manner, suggesting that he could 'drink hot blood'. (363) This is the first time in the play when Hamlet seems to be in the right frame of mind to avenge his father's death. The prince is highly conscious of this, but he must first visit his mother before he can act. He cannot afford to lose the violent anger that will enable him to go through with the killing, and yet he cannot allow his rage to be directed against his mother. Hamlet speaks to himself at the end of the scene in an effort to restrain himself from causing his mother harm: 'Let me be cruel, not unnatural:/ I will speak daggers to her but use none'. (368–9)

have been unfounded. (71–7) Hamlet will also be observing Claudius, and the two will meet afterwards to swap notes. (79–80)

LINES 84–124: THE COURT GATHERS FOR THE PERFORMANCE OF THE PLAY

The royal court arrive for the performance of the play. Once again, Hamlet begins to act in an eccentric and peculiar manner. He responds playfully and cryptically when speaking to both Claudius and Polonius. When Gertrude asks her son to sit with her, Hamlet declines, saying that he prefers to sit with Ophelia: 'No good mother, here's metal more attractive'. (100)

Hamlet speaks to Ophelia in a crude and offensive manner. He asks her if he should lie with his head on her lap, and makes a series of puns based on slang relating to genitalia. (106–8) Ophelia suffers this patiently, remarking only that Hamlet seems merry. (111) Hamlet speaks bitterly about his mother, saying how she is merry though she has only recently been widowed: 'for look you how cheerfully my mother looks, and my father died within's two hours'. (115–16) Ophelia corrects him, saying that it has been four months. (117) Hamlet feigns shock, and bitterly suggests that all a great man can hope for is that his memory 'may outlive his life half/ a year'. (120–1)

LINES 125–247: THE PLAYERS PERFORM THE PLAY

The players enter and perform a brief mime. The mime represents the plot of the play to come. They act out the poisoning of a king by a man who then goes on to woo the initially reluctant queen.

The play then begins with two players, dressed as a king and queen, appearing on stage. The Player King tells us that they have been married for thirty years. (140–3) The Player Queen speaks of

CHARACTER DEVELOPMENT

CLAUDIUS

CLAUDIUS' GUILT

The fact that the king walked out of the performance convinces Hamlet of his guilt. The play had exactly the effect that the prince intended. Seeing an enactment of the very crime he committed deeply disturbs Claudius. We must bear in mind, however, that although we have heard Claudius' confession in the previous scene, no one else but Hamlet and Horatio knows of his crime. Although the prince is convinced that the walkout is a confession of guilt, we may easily imagine that a member of the court might think Claudius took offence at the slanderous nature of the performance and left in protest at the insult.

A SHREWD POLITICIAN

It could be argued that the king's decision to walk out of the performance reveals political shrewdness. A less composed person might have responded in a more emotional manner and even confronted Hamlet publicly. Claudius silently leaves the room to consider how best to act. Though he is obviously shaken by what he sees, he does not give anyone but Hamlet any reason to be suspicious.

HAMLET & THE PLAYERS

her love for the king, and of how she is very anxious over the state of his health. (146-9) The Player King declares that he will soon be dead, but that his queen will find another husband. (158-61) The Player Queen protests sharply, denying she will ever remarry. (162-70) Only those who kill their husbands marry a second time. (165) The Player Queen says that second marriages are often made for reasons of security and not for love. (167-8)

The Player King says that although his queen undoubtedly believes what she says, promises often change with circumstances. This can sometimes be a necessary and good thing as promises are often made in moments of high emotion which are short-lived. Circumstances change and our feelings with them. (171-200) The Player King then asks that he be left to sleep as he is growing tired. (210-12) The Player Queen departs, hoping that misfortune should never come between them.

Hamlet asks Gertrude what she thinks of the play at this point. (214) The queen replies that the Player Queen seems to be over-doing it with her vows of loyalty: 'The lady doth protest too much methinks'. (215) Claudius asks Hamlet if the play contains any offensive material, to which Hamlet replies: 'No, no, they do but jest'. (218) He tells the king that the play is called *The Mousetrap*, though the play is actually called *The Murder of Gonzago*. (221)

✒ LINES 248-72: THE KING IS STARTLED BY WHAT HE SEES ON STAGE

Another Player, Lucianus, makes a speech describing his murderous intent. (237-42) He then pours poison into the sleeping Player King's ear. At this point, Claudius abruptly rises from his seat, calls for light and leaves the room. (251) Polonius orders the play to be brought to a halt, and everyone exits except Hamlet and Horatio.

Hamlet is convinced that the king's abrupt exit is proof of his guilt. He now has full faith in what the Ghost told him: 'I'll take the ghost's word for a thousand pound'. (268-9) Hamlet asks Horatio if he saw the king's reaction, and Horatio says that he 'did very well note him'. (272) Hamlet is delighted with the outcome of his plan, and asks for some music to be played. (276)

✒ LINES 273-360: HAMLET SPEAKS ANGRILY WITH ROSENCRANTZ AND GUILDENSTERN

Rosencrantz and Guildenstern come to tell the prince that the king is in a bad temper. (281) They also report that the queen is bewildered by the prince's behaviour, and that she wishes to speak with him in her chamber. (291)

Hamlet responds in a mad and confusing manner. Guildenstern is confused by the prince's replies, and asks him to speak in a more coherent fashion: 'put your discourse into some frame, and start not so wildly from my affair'. (287-8) Hamlet says that it is impossible for him to speak in a sensible or rational manner

CHARACTER DEVELOPMENT

ROSENCRANTZ & GUILDENSTERN

Rosencrantz and Guildenstern are behaving more and more like the king's servants and less and less like Hamlet's long-time friends. In this scene they are sent to tell the prince that the king and queen are angered and upset by his behaviour and that the queen wishes to speak with him in her room. Hamlet accuses them of speaking falsely and playing games, dismissing their suggestions that they are acting out of regard for him. He berates them for presuming to think that they could get him to reveal his inner thoughts: 'You would play upon me, you would seem to know my stops, you would pluck out the heart of my mystery'. (341-2) In the prince's eyes they are no longer his friends. From now on, he will treat their actions and motives with suspicion.

HORATIO

HAMLET'S LOYAL FRIEND
Horatio seems to be the one person that Hamlet completely trusts. We discover in this scene that he has told Horatio what the Ghost said upon the battlements. He has also confided in Horatio his plan to discover whether Claudius is really guilty of murder, and asks him to observe the king's face throughout the performance of the play. (73-80)

Hamlet lavishes his trusted friend with praise. The prince considers Horatio to possess the ideal temperament. He is a man who can 'suffer the slings and arrows of outrageous fortune' while still maintaining his level-headedness and good character. Unlike Hamlet himself, Horatio is not at the mercy of his changing emotions, 'not a pipe for fortune's finger', and Hamlet idealises him for that fact: 'I will wear him/ In my heart's core, ay, in my heart of heart,/ As I do thee'. (63-7)

A KEY MOMENT

Hamlet is now convinced he has objective proof of Claudius' guilt, and his fears about the Ghost being the devil in disguise have been dispelled. From now on, the issue of whether Hamlet shows unjustifiable hesitancy and delay in killing Claudius will become more acute. Should Hamlet kill Claudius immediately or does he have good grounds for waiting?

85

GUILDENSTERN, ROSENCRANTZ & HAMLET

SOME LINES TO LEARN

the purpose of playing, whose end both at the first and now, was and is, to hold, as 'twere the mirror up to nature

Hamlet (19–20)

Give me that man
That is not passion's slave, and I will wear him
In my heart's core

Hamlet (64–6)

Where love is great, the littlest doubts are fear;
Where little fears grow great, great love grows there

Player Queen (156–7)

Our wills and fates do so contrary run
That our devices still are overthrown;
Our thoughts are ours, their ends none of our own

Player King (196–8)

there is much music, excellent voice, in this little organ, yet cannot you make it speak

Hamlet (344–5)

because his mind is 'diseased'. (300)

Rosencrantz and Guildenstern attempt to understand the prince and get to the bottom of his strange behaviour. They tell him that it might help if he opened up to his friends. (316–28) However, the prince no longer views them as his friends. He believes that they are acting purely out of duty to the king, and that their claims to be his loving friends are false.

Hamlet tells them that he will not fall for their tricks and lies. He is not someone that can be so easily toyed with and made to say what they wish to hear. Rosencrantz and Guildenstern, he says, seem to think he is like a musical instrument that can be played upon: 'You would play upon me; you would seem to know my stops; you would pluck out the heart of my mystery'. (341–2) He taunts them for their inability to get him to

expose his inner thoughts: 'there is much music, excellent voice, in this little organ; yet cannot you make it speak'. (344–5) They will never be able to understand him: 'Call me what/ instrument you will, though you can fret me, yet you/ cannot play upon me'. (346–8)

Polonius comes to remind Hamlet that his mother is waiting for him in her room. Hamlet teases him, asking him if he can see 'yonder cloud that's almost in the shape of a camel?' (351) Polonius agrees that the cloud is indeed like a camel, only for Hamlet to say that it is more like a weasel and a whale. Hamlet agrees to go to his mother and asks to be left alone.

LINES 361–72: HAMLET IS READY TO KILL CLAUDIUS

Hamlet is clearly worked up after the excitement of the play and the king's display of guilt. He is ready now to avenge his father's death, and his speech reveals his violent mood: 'now could I drink hot blood,/ And do such bitter business as the day/ Would quake to look on'. (363–5)

However, Hamlet must first visit his mother. He knows that in his highly emotional and violent state he could easily do her harm. He speaks to himself and urges self-control. He vows to 'speak daggers' to Gertrude but use none. (384)

ACT 3 SCENE 3

The king's private chapel

Enter CLAUDIUS, ROSENCRANTZ and GUILDENSTERN

CLAUDIUS   I like him not, nor stands it safe with us
                To let his madness range. Therefore prepare you:
                I your commission will forthwith dispatch,
                And he to England shall along with you:
                The terms of our estate may not endure   5
                Hazard so dangerous as doth hourly grow
                Out of his brows.

GUILDENSTERN   We will ourselves provide.
                Most holy and religious fear it is
                To keep those many many bodies safe
                That live and feed upon your majesty.   10

ROSENCRANTZ   The single and peculiar life is bound,
                With all the strength and armour of the mind
                To keep itself from noyance; but much more
                That spirit upon whose weal depends and rests
                The lives of many. The cess of majesty   15
                Dies not alone, but like a gulf, doth draw
                What's near it with it. It is a massy wheel,
                Fixed on the summit of the highest mount,
                To whose huge spokes ten thousand lesser things
                Are mortised and adjoined, which when it falls, * 20
                Each small annexment, petty consequence,
                Attends the boisterous ruin. Never alone†
                Did the king sigh, but with a general groan.

CLAUDIUS   Arm you I pray you, to this speedy voyage;
                For we will fetters put upon this fear   25
                Which now goes too free-footed.

ROSENCRANTZ }
GUILDENSTERN }

Exeunt ROSENCRANTZ and GUILDENSTERN

Enter POLONIUS

POLONIUS   My lord, he's going to his mother's closet.
                Behind the arras I'll convey myself
                To hear the process. I'll warrant she'll tax him home,‡
                And, as you said, and wisely was it said,   30
                'Tis meet that some more audience than a mother,
                Since nature makes them partial, should o'erhear
                The speech of vantage. Fare you well, my liege,
                I'll call upon you ere you go to bed,
                And tell you what I know.

---

like him not: not comfortable with him

range: have free reign

forthwith dispatch: quickly send out

terms of our estate: my position as king

provide: put ourselves forward for your use

holy and religious fear: sacred duty

live and feed: depend (the image is of parasites)

single ... life: that of the private individual

noyance: harm

weal: welfare

cease: end, death

gulf: whirlpool

massy: massive

mount: mountain

mortised ... adjoin'd: fitted, as joints of wood

annexment: addition

Arm you: prepare

fetters: restraints, imprison

arras: hanging tapestry

of vantage: from a vantage (concealed) point

....

* 17–20 *a massy wheel ...mortised and adjoined*: the image is that of the king as a massive wheel of fortune, and of all other lesser individuals within society (such as Rosencrantz and Guildenstern) forming the spokes of the wheel, who are about to suffer the same fate as the wheel itself when it falls

† 22 *Attends ... ruin*: is part of the ruin of the whole

‡ 29 *warrant she'll tax him home*: I guarantee she'll bring him to his senses

CLAUDIUS   Thanks, dear my lord.   35

Exit POLONIUS

Oh my offence is rank, it smells to heaven;
It hath the primal eldest curse upon't, *
A brother's murder. Pray can I not, †
Though inclination be as sharp as will.
My stronger guilt defeats my strong intent,   40
And, like a man to double business bound,
I stand in pause where I shall first begin,
And both neglect. What if this cursèd hand
Were thicker than itself with brother's blood, ‡
Is there not rain enough in the sweet heavens   45
To wash it white as snow? Whereto serves mercy §
But to confront the visage of offence?
And what's in prayer but this two-fold force,
To be forestalled ere we come to fall, ⊄
Or pardoned being down? Then I'll look up,   50
My fault is past. But oh, what form of prayer **
Can serve my turn? 'Forgive me my foul murder'?
That cannot be; since I am still possess'd
Of those effects for which I did the murder,
My crown, mine own ambition, and my queen.   55
May one be pardoned and retain the offence? ††
In the corrupted currents of this world
Offence's gilded hand may shove by justice,
And oft 'tis seen the wicked prize itself
Buys out the law. But 'tis not so above;   60
There is no shuffling, there the action lies
In his true nature, and we ourselves compell'd,
Even to the teeth and forehead of our faults, ‡‡
To give in evidence. What then? What rests? §§
Try what repentance can. What can it not?   65
Yet what can it when one cannot repent?
Oh wretched state! Oh bosom black as death!
Oh limèd soul that struggling to be free ⊄⊄
Art more engaged! Help, angels! – Make assay!
Bow stubborn knees, and heart with strings of steel   70
Be soft as sinews of the new-born babe.
All may be well.

He kneels

A brother's murder: Cain's killing of Abel

pause … begin: paralysing indecision
both: his guilt and his desire to pray

pardon'd being down: forgive our fall/sin

those effects: the resulting benefits

gilded: gold-covered; *shove by*: push aside

above: in Heaven
shuffling: trickery, cheating
In his true nature: exposed, naked to the eye

more engaged: more entangled in sin
heart … steel: heart of iron
Be soft: reference to 'heart strings'

---

* 37   *primal … curse*: the oldest curse on humankind

† 38–9   *Pray …will*: though I both desire to pray and will myself to do it, I cannot

‡ 44   *thicker … blood*: covered with his brother's blood

§ 46–7   *Whereto serves mercy …of offence?*: What is mercy's role but to meet with (confront, as in a battle) the face of sin

⊄ 49   *forestalled … fall*: save us from temptation to sin

** 50–1   *Then I'll look up/ My fault is past*: Then I'll look to God and pray for forgiveness, my sin is done

†† 56   *retain the offence*: keep the benefits of their crime

‡‡ 63   *teeth … forehead*: to confront our faults, face to face

§§ 64   *To give in evidence*: act as witness (to our own sins)

⊄⊄ 68   *limèd*: trapped, as a bird trapped with lime (sticky substance traditionally used to catch birds)

Enter HAMLET

HAMLET   Now might I do it pat, now a is a-praying;
              And now I'll do't – and so he goes to heaven,
              And so am I revenged. That would be scanned: 75
              A villain kills my father, and for that,
              I his sole son, do this same villain send
              To heaven.
              Why, this is hire and salary, not revenge.
              He took my father grossly, full of bread,*   80
              With all his crimes broad blown, as flush as May,†
              And how his audit stands who knows save heaven?
              But in our circumstance and course of thought†
              'Tis heavy with him. And am I then revenged
              To take him in the purging of his soul,§   85
              When he is fit and seasoned for his passage?
              No.
              Up sword, and know thou a more horrid hent:ᶜ
              When he is drunk asleep, or in his rage,
              Or in th'incestuous pleasure of his bed;   90
              At gaming, swearing, or about some act
              That has no relish of salvation in't –
              Then trip him that his heels may kick at heaven**
              And that his soul may be as damned and black
              As hell whereto it goes. My mother stays.   95
              This physic but prolongs thy sickly days.

Exit

CLAUDIUS   My words fly up, my thoughts remain below.
              Words without thoughts never to heaven go.

Exit

to heaven: because of his prayers
scann'd: thought through, looked at

broad blown: in full bloom
audit: account of himself

him: Claudius
seasoned: prepared

relish: taste, flavour

This physic: Claudius' healing prayers

---

* 80   *full ... bread*: physical appetite
       indulged, unprepared
† 81   *flush*: red, colour of sin
‡ 83   *circumstance ... thought*: limited
       earthly opinion
§ 85   *purging*: cleansing by prayer
ᶜ 88   *more horrid hent*: more terrible
       design/use
** 93 *heels...heaven*: the image is of
       Claudius plunging head first from
       Heaven into hell

HAMLET & CLAUDIUS

Claudius has gone to his private chamber after witnessing Hamlet's play. Convinced that Hamlet is a threat to his regime, he decides to act on his idea of sending the prince away to England. Polonius goes to Gertrude's chamber to spy on Hamlet while he talks to his mother. Left alone, Claudius describes the intense guilt he feels for murdering his brother. He attempts to pray for forgiveness. Hamlet sneaks into the chamber prepared to kill the king. However, he decides to postpone this bloody deed. Because Claudius is praying, killing him now would send his soul directly to Heaven, when Hamlet wants to send him to hell.

A CLOSER LOOK

⟋ LINES 1–7: CLAUDIUS DECIDES HAMLET MUST BE SENT AWAY

Claudius has returned to his quarters, having left the performance of *The Murder of Gonzago*. Throughout Acts 2 and 3, Claudius has considered Hamlet's apparent madness a threat to his new regime. He is now even more convinced that this is case: 'I like him not, nor stands it safe with us/ To let his madness range'. (1–2) Having seen *The Murder of Gonzago*, he must also suspect that Hamlet knows something about the murder of the old king.

In Act 3 Scene 1 he considered sending the prince to England in order to neutralise the threat posed by his erratic behaviour. He now decides to put this plan into action, and orders Rosencrantz and Guildenstern to escort him there: 'Therefore prepare you;/ I your commission will forthwith dispatch,/ And he to England shall along with you'. (2–4)

⟋ LINES 8–27: CLAUDIUS IS FAWNED UPON

Rosencrantz and Guildenstern behave like fawning lackeys. Guildenstern declares that it is a sacred duty to protect the king, whose safety is vital to all. (8–10) Rosencrantz launches into a long speech about how the king's life is intertwined with those of his subjects. (14–15) When the king suffers or dies, so do his subjects: 'Never alone/ Did the king sigh, but with a general groan'. (22–3) The king answers by reiterating that Hamlet must be dealt with: 'For we will fetters put upon this fear,/ Which now goes too free-footed'. (25–6) Rosencrantz and Guildenstern exit to do Claudius' bidding.

⟋ LINES 27–35: POLONIUS PREPARES TO SPY ON HAMLET

In Act 1 Scene 3 Polonius suggested he would spy on a meeting between Hamlet and Gertrude, in the hope that the prince would reveal to his mother the cause of his apparent lunacy.

He now enters Claudius' chamber and says he is about to put this plan into action. Hamlet, he says, is on his way to his mother's chamber for a private audience.

SOME LINES TO LEARN

In the corrupted currents of this world
Offence's gilded hand may shove by justice,
And oft 'tis seen the wicked prize itself
Buys out the law.

Claudius (57–60)

My words fly up, my thoughts remain below:
Words without thoughts never to heaven go

Claudius (97–8)

Polonius will conceal himself there and listen to what takes place: 'Behind the arras I'll convey myself/ To hear the process'. (28–9) He leaves, promising to return to Claudius to tell him what transpires. (34–5)

LINES 36–72: CLAUDIUS' SPIRITUAL TORMENT

Claudius is left alone, and we witness his spiritual agony as he contemplates his murder of the old king. He is fully aware of the horror of his crime: 'Oh my offence is rank, it smells to heaven'. He compares his crime to the first ever murder, that of Abel by his brother Cain: 'It hath the primal eldest curse upon't,/ A brother's murder'. (37–8) The king reveals the crushing guilt from which he suffers:

· He wants to pray for forgiveness but his intense guilt stops him from doing so: 'Pray can I not … My stronger guilt defeats my strong intent'. (38–40) He feels there's no point in praying because his sin is so great: 'Whereto serves mercy/ But to confront the visage of offence'. (46–7)
· He feels he cannot be forgiven as he is still benefiting from the rewards of his crime: 'Forgive my foul murder?/ That cannot be; since I am still possess'd/ Of those effects for which I did the murder,/ My crown, mine own ambition, and my queen'. (52–5)
· He realises that while he may get away with his crimes in this life, he will eventually be punished in the next. (57–60) In the next life, we must admit our sins and suffer the consequences. (61–4)
· He is in state of despair, desperate for forgiveness but unable to repent.

He tries to convince himself that prayer can indeed save him. Prayer, he reminds himself, not only protects people from temptation but also redeems them after they have actually sinned. (47–50) Eventually, he forces himself to kneel and pray, hoping that in spite of everything he might be forgiven: 'Bow stubborn knees, and heart with strings of steel/ Be soft as sinews of the new-born babe./ All may be well'. (70–1)

LINES 73–96: HAMLET DECIDES TO DELAY KILLING CLAUDIUS

Hamlet enters unnoticed. He sees Claudius praying and defenceless. This is the perfect opportunity to kill Claudius and avenge his father's death: 'Now might I do it pat, now he is a-praying:/ And now I'll do't … And so am I revenged'. (73–5) Yet he stops to think. Claudius is praying, therefore he is in a state of grace. If he is killed at this moment, he will go to Heaven: 'A villain kills my father; and for that,/ I his sole son, do this same villain send/ To heaven'. (76–8) It would be wrong, he feels, to send Claudius directly to Heaven while his father suffers

CLAUDIUS

A SHREWD POLITICIAN

In this scene Claudius once again demonstrates his political acumen. Throughout Acts 2 and 3, Claudius has regarded Hamlet's apparent madness and erratic behaviour as a threat to his new regime. Having seen *The Murder of Gonzago*, he must now also suspect that the prince somehow knows the truth about old Hamlet's death. He is determined to 'fetter', or control, the threat Hamlet presents to them. (25)

Claudius behaves in a decisive manner, acting immediately on his plan to send Hamlet to England. (He first considered this idea in Act 3 Scene 1.) A shrewd political operator, Claudius knows that Hamlet is too poplar with the people to have him executed. The next best thing is to remove him from the scene by sending him abroad. He cleverly justifies his decision by stating that his position as king, and therefore the safety of the realm as a whole, is threatened by Hamlet's madness 'The terms of our estate may not endure/ Hazard so dangerous as doth hourly grow/ out of his brows'. (5–7)

It is possible, however, that Claudius makes a slip-up when he allows Polonius to go and spy on Hamlet's meeting with Gertrude. The king must suspect that Hamlet somehow knows about his crime. What if Polonius overhears Hamlet sharing this knowledge with Gertrude?

CLAUDIUS' GUILT

In this scene we see another side of Claudius as he reveals his intense guilt for killing old Hamlet. He is not a two-dimensional villain, unconcerned by the moral consequences of what he's done. Instead, he is tortured by guilt and seems disgusted by the terrible act he has committed: 'Oh my offence is rank, it smells to heaven'.

He knows he has committed murder, the worst of crimes, and that he faces eternal damnation. He expresses a deep desire to receive God's forgiveness for his crime. Yet he cannot bring himself to truly pray: 'Pray can I not,/ Though inclination be as sharp as will'. (38–9) He fears that there is no mercy strong enough to absolve him: 'Is there not rain enough in the sweet heavens/ To wash it white as snow? (45–6)

The reason he cannot pray or be forgiven is that he still holds the rewards of the crime: the throne and Gertrude. Although Claudius is tormented by guilt, it is important to note that he never considers renouncing these ill-gotten gains and seeking true heavenly forgiveness.

in the fires of Purgatory: 'Am I then revenged/ To take him in the purging of his soul,/ When he is fit and seasoned for his passage? No.' (84–7)

Hamlet decides he will kill Claudius when the king is committing a sinful act, such as drinking, swearing or making love to Gertrude:

> Up sword; and know thou a more horrid hent:
> When he is drunk asleep, or in his rage,
> Or in th'incestuous pleasure of his bed;
> At gaming, swearing, or about some act
> That has no relish of salvation in't.
> (88–92)

That way, Claudius will die damned and burn in hell forever: 'Then trip him that his heels may kick at heaven/ And that his soul may be as damned and black/ As hell whereto it goes'. (93–5) Hamlet remembers that his mother is waiting for him, and he leaves. (95–6)

The king rises, unaware how close he was to death. Hamlet believed Claudius was praying and therefore in a state of sinless grace. Ironically, however, the king reveals that he was unable to pray with conviction: 'My words fly up, my thoughts remain below./ Words without thoughts never to heaven go'. (97–8)

CONSIDER THIS

This is the first time the audience can be absolutely certain that Claudius actually killed old Hamlet. We may have been convinced by the Ghost's revelations and even more convinced by the king's reaction to the play. He also expressed feelings of guilt in Act 3 Scene 1, without specifying exactly what he felt guilty about. Yet it is only now that the culprit and only living witness to old Hamlet's murder finally and unambiguously reveals his guilt to the audience.

CHARACTER DEVELOPMENT

HAMLET

HAMLET'S RUTHLESS STREAK?

Hamlet's decision not to murder Claudius reveals the ruthless side of his personality. His father was murdered in cold blood, without the opportunity to confess his sins, and suffers torment in Purgatory as a result. If Hamlet murders Claudius while he's praying, the king's soul will be in a state of grace and will go straight to Heaven. Hamlet feels it's wrong that Claudius should go straight to paradise while his own father languishes in Purgatory. He wants Claudius not only to die but also to suffer in the next life.

Some readers feel that Hamlet displays not ruthlessness but softness in this scene, squandering a gilt-edged opportunity to dispatch his foe. They suggest that when the crucial moment comes, Hamlet lacks the necessary ruthlessness to kill his uncle in cold blood. On this reading, Hamlet uses the fact that Claudius is praying to justify his hesitation to himself.

There may also be a practical reason for Hamlet's hesitation. How would it look if he murdered the king in cold blood claiming that his father's ghost had told him to do so? Given his behaviour in court, it would be regarded as an act of total insanity. For murdering the king, he would most likely be locked up or put to death. In order to avoid this, Hamlet would have to stage a coup and seize the throne himself – something he is at this point in no position to achieve.

POLONIUS

SELF-IMPORTANT

In deciding to spy on Hamlet, Polonius once again displays complete confidence in his own abilities (although to date his spying and scheming has proved far from effective). His overconfidence will prove fatal.

MEDDLING SCHEMER

In this scene Polonius yet again indulges his tendencies toward meddling and scheming. We get the impression that he is absolutely in his element when rushing around the palace in order to plot and spy, and involving himself as per usual in the internal affairs of the royal family.

FAWNING

Polonius also displays his tendency to fawn on those in power. He gives Claudius the credit for coming up with the idea of spying on Hamlet when he goes to meet his mother: 'And, as you said, and wisely was it said'. (30–3) It was in fact Polonius himself who suggested doing this back in Act 3 Scene 1.

ROSENCRANTZ & GUILDENSTERN

In this scene Rosencrantz and Guildenstern show themselves to be willing servants of the king. Their fawning and flattering behaviour toward Claudius leaves a strongly negative impression. What both the prince and the audience suspected in the previous scene has been proved true: they have taken Claudius' side and betrayed their old school friend. It is important to remember, however, that they have been placed in a difficult situation. Disobeying Claudius, the most powerful man in the realm, is simply not an option.

Enter GERTRUDE and POLONIUS

POLONIUS	A will come straight. Look you lay home to him.
	Tell him his pranks have been too broad to bear with,
	And that your grace hath screened and stood between
	Much heat and him. I'll silence me e'en here.
	Pray you be round with him.
HAMLET	*Within* Mother, mother, mother!
GERTRUDE	I'll warrant you, fear me not. Withdraw, I hear him coming.

POLONIUS hides himself behind the arras

Enter HAMLET

HAMLET	Now, mother, what's the matter?
GERTRUDE	Hamlet, thou hast thy father much offended.
HAMLET	Mother, you have my father much offended.
GERTRUDE	Come, come, you answer with an idle tongue.
HAMLET	Go, go, you question with a wicked tongue.
GERTRUDE	Why, how now, Hamlet!
HAMLET	What's the matter now?
GERTRUDE	Have you forgot me?
HAMLET	No, by the rood, not so.
	You are the queen, your husband's brother's wife;
	And, would it were not so, you are my mother.
GERTRUDE	Nay, then, I'll set those to you that can speak.
HAMLET	Come, come, and sit you down; you shall not budge;
	You go not till I set you up a glass
	Where you may see the inmost part of you.
GERTRUDE	What wilt thou do? thou wilt not murder me?
	Help, help, ho!
POLONIUS	*Behind* What, ho! Help, help, help!
HAMLET	*Drawing* How now, a rat? Dead, for a ducat, dead.

Kills Polonius

POLONIUS	*Behind* O, I am slain!

Falls and dies

GERTRUDE	Oh me, what hast thou done?
HAMLET	Nay I know not, is it the king?
GERTRUDE	Oh what a rash and bloody deed is this!
HAMLET	A bloody deed! Almost as bad, good mother,
	As kill a king and marry with his brother.
GERTRUDE	As kill a king?

lay home: tax him severely, as a parent
broad: unrestrained

heat: trouble, anger at his behaviour
round: plain-speaking, direct

thy father: Claudius, Hamlet's stepfather
my father: the dead King Hamlet
idle: irresponsible, loose

the rood: Christ's wooden cross

can speak: can make you listen

Dead … ducat: I bet a coin that I'll kill it

HAMLET	Ay lady, 'twas my word.	30

Lifts up the array and reveals the body of POLONIUS

Thou wretched, rash, intruding fool, farewell.
I took thee for thy better. Take thy fortune.
Thou find'st to be too busy is some danger. –
Leave wringing of your hands. Peace! Sit you down,*
And let me wring your heart, for so I shall   35
If it be made of penetrable stuff,†
If damnèd custom have not brazed it so,
That it be proof and bulwark against sense.‡

GERTRUDE   What have I done, that thou dar'st wag thy tongue
In noise so rude against me?

HAMLET   Such an act   40
That blurs the grace and blush of modesty,
Calls virtue hypocrite, takes off the rose
From the fair forehead of an innocent love
And sets a blister there, makes marriage vows§
As false as dicers' oaths. Oh such a deed¶   45
As from the body of contraction plucks**
The very soul, and sweet religion makes
A rhapsody of words. Heaven's face doth glow:††
Yea, this solidity and compound mass,‡‡
With tristful visage, as against the doom,   50
Is thought-sick at the act.§§

GERTRUDE   Ay me, what act,
That roars so loud, and thunders in the index?¶¶

busy: interfering

bulwark: barricade

blurs: smears

glow: blush

tristful visage: sad, forlorn face
thought-sick: ill at the thought, horrified

* 34   *Leave …*: Hamlet has turned his
       attention to the queen
† 36   *If it be made of penetrable stuff*: if your
       heart is open and receptive
‡ 37–8 *If damned custom … sense*: if habitual
       vice has not converted your heart
       to brass, making it impenetrable to
       natural feeling
§ 44   *blister*: whores, branded, had a blis-
       tered forehead
¶ 40–5 *Such an act … dicers' oaths*: an act
       that makes a mockery of all things
       good and turns them to evil – an
       act that turns modesty's blush to
       a smear; *that makes a hypocrite of
       virtue*: that turns romantic love into
       a form of prostitution – that makes
       marriage vows as empty as gamblers'
       promises
** 46 *contraction*: marriage contract as
       symbol of union
†† 46–8 *body of … rhapsody of words*:
       removes the soul from its union
       with the body, breaking the contract
       between the two – without the soul,
       the practice of religion and prayer
       becomes empty, as words without
       meaning
‡‡ 49 *solidity … mass*: earth, compounded
       of four elements
§§ 48–51 *Heaven's face …at the act*: the queen's
       act takes on cosmological propor-
       tions, embodying all the sins of the
       earth. It makes Heaven blush, and
       causes the earth to become sick at
       heart as if the day of judgement were
       at hand.
¶¶ 52 *index*: beginning (as table of contents
       in a book)

HAMLET	Look here upon this picture, and on this,	*and on this*: a second picture
	The counterfeit presentment of two brothers.*	
	See what a grace was seated on this brow; 55	*brow*: forehead
	Hyperion's curls, the front of Jove himself,	*Hyperion*: sun god; *front of Jove*: Jove's forehead
	An eye like Mars, to threaten and command;	*Mars*: god of war
	A station like the herald Mercury,†	
	New-lighted on a heaven-kissing hill;	*heaven-kissing hill*: Mount Atlas
	A combination and a form indeed, 60	
	Where every god did seem to set his seal,	*his seal*: his mark
	To give the world assurance of a man.‡	
	This was your husband. Look you now, what follows.	
	Here is your husband, like a mildewed ear,	*mildewed ear*: diseased ear (of corn)
	Blasting his wholesome brother. Have you eyes? 65	*Blasting*: Blighting
	Could you on this fair mountain leave to feed	
	And batten on this moor? Ha! have you eyes?	*batten*: fatten; *moor*: uncultivated heath
	You cannot call it love, for at your age	
	The heyday in the blood is tame, it's humble,	*blood*: associated with passion, animal spirits
	And waits upon the judgement; and what judgement 70	*judgement*: seated in the rational brain
	Would step from this to this? Sense sure, you have,	
	Else could you not have motion, but sure that sense	
	Is apoplexed, for madness would not err,	*apoplexed*: paralysed
	Nor sense to ecstasy was ne'er so thralled,	*ecstasy*: passion; *ne'er*: never; *thralled*: enslaved
	But it reserved some quantity of choice 75	*choice*: judgement
	To serve in such a difference. What devil was't	
	That thus hath cozened you at hoodman-blind?§	
	Eyes without feeling, feeling without sight,	
	Ears without hands or eyes, smelling sans all,	
	Or but a sickly part of one true sense 80	
	Could not so mope.	*so mope*: behave with so little awareness or aim
	O shame, where is thy blush? Rebellious hell,€	
	If thou canst mutine in a matron's bones,**	*mutine*: revolt
	To flaming youth let virtue be as wax	*flaming*: fiery, hot-blooded
	And melt in her own fire. Proclaim no shame†† 85	
	When the compulsive ardour gives the charge,‡‡	
	Since frost itself as actively doth burn,	*frost*: old age; *doth burn*: with the fires of lust
	And reason panders will.	*panders will*: gives in to desire
GERTRUDE	O Hamlet, speak no more:	
	Thou turn'st mine eyes into my very soul,	
	And there I see such black and grainèd spots 90	*grainèd*: ingrained
	As will not leave their tinct.	*As ... tinct*: as cannot be cleansed of stain
HAMLET	Nay, but to live	
	In the rank sweat of an enseamèd bed,	*enseamèd*: greasy with animal fat
	Stewed in corruption, honeying and making love	*Stewed*: cooked, also slang for brothel
	Over the nasty sty.	*sty*: pigsty
GERTRUDE	Oh speak to me no more;	
	These words like daggers enter in mine ears. 95	
	No more sweet Hamlet.	

---

* 54   *counterfeit presentment*: pictorial representation

† 58   *station ...*: stance like the messenger of the gods

‡ 62   *give ... man*: making real the ideal of manhood

§ 77   *cozened ... blind*: tricked you at blind man's buff

€ 82   *Rebellious hell*: lower senses rebel against higher

** 83   *matron's bones*: mature female body

†† 85   *melt ... fire*: virtue melts as wax in the fire of youth

‡‡ 86   *compulsive ardour ...*: lust reverses proper order

HAMLET   A murderer and a villain,
A slave that is not twentieth part the tithe
Of your precedent lord, a vice of kings,
A cutpurse of the empire and the rule,
That from a shelf the precious diadem stole   100
And put it in his pocket.

GERTRUDE   No more!

Enter GHOST

HAMLET   A king of shreds and patches –
Save me, and hover o'er me with your wings,
You heavenly guards! – What would your gracious figure?

GERTRUDE   Alas, he's mad!   105

HAMLET   Do you not come your tardy son to chide,
That lapsed in time and passion lets go by
Th' important acting of your dread command? Oh say!

GHOST   Do not forget. This visitation
Is but to whet thy almost blunted purpose.   110
But look, amazement on thy mother sits:
Oh step between her and her fighting soul:
Conceit in weakest bodies strongest works.
Speak to her, Hamlet.

HAMLET   How is it with you, lady?

GERTRUDE   Alas, how is't with you,   115
That you do bend your eye on vacancy
And with th'incorporal air do hold discourse?
Forth at your eyes your spirits wildly peep,*
And, as the sleeping soldiers in th'alarm,
Your bedded hair, like life in excrements,   120
Starts up, and stands on end. O gentle son,†
Upon the heat and flame of thy distemper
Sprinkle cool patience. Whereon do you look?

HAMLET   On him, on him! Look you how pale he glares!
His form and cause conjoined, preaching to stones,   125
Would make them capable. – Do not look upon me;‡
Lest with this piteous action you convert
My stern effects. Then what I have to do
Will want true colour: tears perchance for blood.

GERTRUDE   To whom do you speak this?   130

HAMLET   Do you see nothing there?

GERTRUDE   Nothing at all, yet all that is I see.

HAMLET   Nor did you nothing hear?

GERTRUDE   No, nothing but ourselves.

HAMLET   Why, look you there – look, how it steals away –   135
My father in his habit as he lived –
Look, where he goes, even now, out at the portal.

Exit Ghost

---

murderer and a villain: speaking of Claudius
tithe: tenth part

cutpurse: thief

diadem: crown

shreds and patches: rags

tardy: late (in taking his revenge)
lapsed: failed
important: urgent

whet: sharpen
amazement: bewildered distraction
fighting soul: inner struggle
Conceit: images, imagination

vacancy: emptiness
incorporal: bodiless

alarm: call to arms

heat … distemper: passionate outburst

convert: transform (through pity)
My stern effects: my hardened resolve
want: lack

habit: clothing
portal: doorway

---

* 118   *eyes … peep:* your madness shines
        through your eyes

† 119–21 *bedded hair … on end:* your hair,
        which normally lies flat, is standing
        on end. This phenomenon was
        generally ascribed to the visitation of
        a spirit. Hair is described as 'like life
        in excrements' because though it has
        no sense (life) yet it grows out of the
        body, it is paradoxically both dead
        and alive

‡ 125–6 *His form and cause… capable:* his
        ghostly appearance, together with
        his reason for seeking revenge, would
        be enough to make even stones
        capable of obeying his command

GERTRUDE	This the very coinage of your brain.[*]
	This bodiless creation ecstasy
	Is very cunning in.
HAMLET	Ecstasy?
	My pulse as yours doth temperately keep time,[†]
	And makes as healthful music. It is not madness
	That I have uttered. Bring me to the test,
	And I the matter will reword, which madness
	Would gambol from. Mother, for love of grace,
	Lay not that flattering unction to your soul,[‡]
	That not your trespass, but my madness speaks;[§]
	It will but skin and film the ulcerous place,
	Whilst rank corruption, mining all within,
	Infects unseen. Confess yourself to heaven,
	Repent what's past; avoid what is to come,
	And do not spread the compost on the weeds
	To make them ranker. Forgive me this my virtue,[ℂ]
	For in the fatness of these pursy times
	Virtue itself of vice must pardon beg,
	Yea, curb and woo for leave to do him good.
GERTRUDE	Oh Hamlet, thou hast cleft my heart in twain.
HAMLET	Oh throw away the worser part of it,
	And live the purer with the other half.
	Good night – but go not to mine uncle's bed;
	Assume a virtue, if you have it not.[**]
	That monster custom, who all sense doth eat,
	Of habits devil, is angel yet in this,
	That to the use of actions fair and good
	He likewise gives a frock or livery
	That aptly is put on. Refrain tonight,[††]
	And that shall lend a kind of easiness
	To the next abstinence, the next more easy;
	For use almost can change the stamp of nature,
	And either [curb] the devil, or throw him out,[‡‡]
	With wondrous potency. Once more, good night:
	And when you are desirous to be blessed,
	I'll blessing beg of you. For this same lord,
	I do repent: but heaven hath pleased it so,
	To punish me with this, and this with me,
	That I must be their scourge and minister.
	I will bestow him, and will answer well
	The death I gave him. So, again, good night.
	I must be cruel, only to be kind;
	Thus bad begins, and worse remains behind.
	One word more, good lady.

140
145
150
155
160
165
170
175
180

bodiless …: imagination, linked with madness

skin and film: finely cover
mining: undermining
Infects unseen: spreads the disease, unnoticed

pursy: greedy

curb … woo: bend and beg; *him:* vice
cleft … twain: broken my heart in two

use: practice
frock or livery: covering (as in clothing)

stamp of nature: animal instinct

this same lord: Polonius

with this: with the visitation of the Ghost
scourge and minister: agents of Heaven's will
bestow: dispose of

* 138 *coinage of your brain:* creation (mere figment) of your imagination

† 141 *temperately …:* heart pulses in steady, measured beats rather than madly

‡ 146 *lay that flattering unction:* put an oily veneer on to give yourself a merely superficial sense of well-being

§ 147 *Lay not that … speaks:* do not convince yourself, as a soothing balm to your own troubled soul, that my madness is at fault rather than your own transgressions

ℂ 153 *make them ranker:* make the weeds more deadly

** 161 *Assume:* pretend to be virtuous, even if you aren't in fact

†† 162–6 *That monster … put on:* routine is a devilish monster that eats away our awareness of the evil nature of our habits. However, it can also be as an angel in that it can create a habitual mode of doing good

‡‡ 170 The word 'curb' here is uncertain, and Shakespeare scholars dispute the correct interpretation

GERTRUDE	What shall I do?
HAMLET	Not this by no means that I bid you do:
	Let the bloat king tempt you again to bed;
	Pinch wanton on your cheek, call you his mouse,*
	And let him for a pair of reechy kisses,
	Or paddling in your neck with his damned fingers,
	Make you to ravel all this matter out,†
	That I essentially am not in madness,
	But mad in craft. 'Twere good you let him know,‡
	For who that's but a queen, fair, sober, wise,
	Would from a paddock, from a bat, a gib,
	Such dear concernings hide? Who would do so?
	No, in despite of sense and secrecy,
	Unpeg the basket on the house's top.
	Let the birds fly, and, like the famous ape,
	To try conclusions, in the basket creep,
	And break your own neck down.§
GERTRUDE	Be thou assured, if words be made of breath,
	And breath of life, I have no life to breathe
	What thou hast said to me.
HAMLET	I must to England; you know that?
GERTRUDE	Alack,
	I had forgot. 'Tis so concluded on.
HAMLET	There's letters sealed, and my two schoolfellows,
	Whom I will trust as I will adders fanged,
	They bear the mandate. They must sweep my way
	And marshal me to knavery. Let it work,
	For 'tis the sport to have the engineer
	Hoist with his own petar, an't shall go hard
	But I will delve one yard below their mines,
	And blow them at the moon. Oh 'tis most sweet
	When in one line two crafts directly meet.
	This man shall set me packing.
	I'll lug the guts into the neighbour room.
	Mother, good night. Indeed this counsellor
	Is now most still, most secret, and most grave,
	Who was in life a foolish prating knave.
	Come sir, to draw toward an end with you.
	Good night mother.

Exit HAMLET tugging in POLONIUS; GERTRUDE remains

---

bloat: bloated, diseased
mouse: playful term
185 *reechy*: reeky, smoky, dirty

in craft: in design, cunning
190 *queen ... wise*: her wisdom is to keep his secret
paddock (toad) ... bat ... gib: witches' familiars

195

no life to breathe: I'll keep your secret
200

205 *mandate*: command; *sweep*: prepare
marshal ... knavery: guide me into some trap
engineer: designer, maker of engines of war
Hoist: hoisted, blown up; *petar*: bomb
delve ... mines: build a counter-mine below theirs
210
crafts: cunning plots
packing: packing to leave / plotting
lug the guts: referring to Polonius' body
this counsellor: Polonius
215

....

* 186 *Pinch wanton on your cheek*: his caresses leave a mark on your cheek, branding you as licentious

† 187 *Make ... out*: to clear up the subject of my madness

‡ 189 *'Twere good*: sarcasm

§ 193–7 *No, in despite ... break your own neck down*: nobody would go against sense and secrecy to, first, let the birds fly out of the basket on the roof top, and next attempt the same, as the ape was famed to do – for it would result in their own death. In other words, Hamlet is warning his mother not to disclose his secret.

HAMLET & GERTRUDE

Hamlet is on the way to his mother's chamber. Polonius conceals himself to observe their meeting. Hamlet kills him, thinking it is Claudius hidden behind the screen. Hamlet tells his mother how angry he is at her for marrying Claudius. He says she has committed a terrible and sinful act. He cannot understand how she could marry Claudius, who he rages at and describes as a parasite, a murderer and a thief.

The Ghost reappears to remind Hamlet of the task it gave him. Gertrude cannot see the Ghost and assumes Hamlet has finally gone completely mad. Hamlet assures her he has only been pretending to be mad all the time, but asks her not to share this information with Claudius. He also pleads with her not to sleep with Claudius anymore. He leaves, taking the body of Polonius with him.

A CLOSER LOOK

LINES 1–6: POLONIUS BRIEFS GERTRUDE

The queen is in her chamber. Polonius tells her that Hamlet is on his way. He advises her to tell the prince that his mad behaviour has been over-the-top: 'Tell him his pranks have been too broad to bear with'. (2) She should say that so far Claudius has been protected from facing the consequences of his bizarre actions: 'that your grace hath screened and stood between/ Much heat and him'. (3–4) Polonius urges the queen to be blunt with her son, and conceals himself upon hearing Hamlet approach.

LINES 7–22: HAMLET REVEALS HIS ANGER TOWARD HIS MOTHER

Hamlet enters in aggressive mood. The queen tells him she has summoned him because he has greatly offended the king, referring to Claudius as Hamlet's father. (9) The prince answers that she herself has offended his real father. (10) The queen accuses Hamlet of having a loose, or 'idle', tongue, while he says she has

a wicked one. (11–12) Gertrude asks if he has forgotten that she is his mother. (14) The prince answers sarcastically, referring to what he regards as her incestuous second marriage: 'You are the queen, your husband's brother's wife'. (15)

Gertrude, taken aback by Hamlet's angry words, makes to leave. Hamlet responds angrily, telling her she isn't going anywhere until he has made her look within herself and confront her guilt:

> *Come, come, and sit you down; you shall not budge;*
> *You go not till I set you up a glass*
> *Where you may see the inmost part of you.* (18–20)

Gertrude is terrified by the intensity of Hamlet's rage. Fearing for her life, she calls for help: 'What wilt thou do? Thou wilt not murder me?/ Help, help, ho!' (21–2)

HAMLET

ANGER AND BITTERNESS

From the very beginning of the play, Hamlet has been filled with rage caused by his mother's remarriage. Let's remind ourselves that the remarriage upset Hamlet for three different reasons: he felt that it came much too soon after his father's death, that Claudius isn't half the man his father was, and that the union is incestuous.

In this scene Hamlet expresses this anger towards his mother in no uncertain terms, essentially raging at her for its entire first half. In Act 3 Scene 2 he vowed to verbally torment his mother for what he perceives as her great sin. Now he does so, attempting to 'wring her heart' with his harsh words. (35) His aim is to 'set up a glass' or mirror in which Gertrude 'may see the inmost part' of herself. (19-20) He refuses to let her leave until his rage is vented: 'you shall not budge'. (18)

His volcanic anger is evident when he describes his mother as having a 'wicked tongue', and especially when he cruelly wishes she was not his mother at all. (10, 14) He violently rants at Gertrude, saying how her actions have stolen the very soul from the institution of marriage, have branded 'innocent love' like a prostitute, and have made even Heaven blush. (40-51)

He seems filled with incomprehension at his mother's actions, simply failing to understand how she could marry Claudius having previously been with a great man like his father. Repeatedly he asks her 'Have you eyes?' (65-7) Either her reason was paralysed when she made this choice or she must have been possessed by a devil. (71-5)

Hamlet also vents his anger at Claudius in this scene, referring to him as 'a murderer and a villain,/ A slave'. (96-7) He describes the king in no uncertain terms as a thief or 'cutpurse' who stole the 'empire and the rule' from its rightful owner. (99)

NEGATIVE ATTITUDE TOWARD WOMEN

In this scene Hamlet once again displays a negative attitude toward women. In particular he displays a disgust or discomfort with female sexuality:

- He declares that it's impossible for an older woman like Gertrude to love for another man: 'You cannot call it love … at your age'. (68)
- He says that women of Gertrude's age feel little passion or sexual desire: 'The heyday in the blood is tame, it's humble'. (69)

- He describes her marriage bed as a sewer of lust and corruption: 'but to live/ In the rank sweat of an enseamèd bed,/ Stewed in corruption, honeying and making love/ Over the nasty sty'. (91-4)
- He presents her sexual relations with Claudius as being sinful and corrupt, describing how the king caresses her with his 'damned fingers'. (186)

It is notable that while Hamlet regards his mother's sexual behaviour as disgusting, sinful and corrupt, he cannot avoid dwelling on it and describing it in some detail. He is simultaneously repelled and fascinated by his mother's sexuality.

Hamlet's unease with female sexuality was also evident in Act 1 Scene 3, where he continually urged Ophelia to avoid sexuality by going to a 'nunnery'. We also saw it in the vulgar sexual comments he made to her in Act 3 Scene 2.

A SENSE OF SUPERIORITY

Throughout this scene Hamlet displays what many feel is an unpleasant sense of superiority. He credits himself as being more or less the only person in Elsinore to have any virtue: 'Forgive me this my virtue/ For in the fatness of these pursy times/ Virtue itself of vice must pardon beg'. (153-5) We may remember that he made a similar remark to Ophelia in Act 3 Scene 1.

The prince behaves in an extremely preachy and self-righteous manner. This is evident when he tells Gertrude he will force her to look into her very soul. We also see it when he urges her to 'Confess yourself to heaven/ Repent what's past; avoid what is to come'. (150-1) A similar preachiness is evident when he advises his mother that she can overcome her sinful lust by getting into the habit of not sleeping with Claudius: 'Refrain tonight,/ And that shall lend a kind of easiness/ To the next abstinence, the next more easy'. (166-8)

He rages against his mother, pointing out what he perceives as her faults. However, he offers her no chance to explain or justify herself. Instead, he is a self-appointed judge and jury. Hamlet seems convinced that he and only he knows what is right and proper.

RUTHLESS STREAK

We saw the prince's ruthless streak in the previous scene, when he delayed killing Claudius because the king was praying. Killing him would therefore send him directly to Heaven when Hamlet wants to send him to hell. The death of Polonius provides further evidence of this ruthlessness.

Hamlet assumes that Claudius is spying on him from behind the screen. (32) Yet he doesn't bother to lift the screen before driving his sword into it. If there's even a chance the hidden observer is Claudius, then that person is going to die. At this stage, the prince definitely means business.

Hamlet claims to regret killing Polonius: 'I do repent'. (174) His regret, however, seems a little insincere, especially given the way he taunts the corpse. He refers to Polonius as a 'fool' and a as a 'foolish prating knave'. (31, 216) He spends only a moment contemplating Polonius' demise before turning his attention back to his mother. We get the impression that Hamlet's only regret is that it wasn't the king he killed.

This steely side to his character is also evident when he says he plans to deal clinically with Rosencrantz and Guildenstern. He claims that their betrayal of him will 'marshal' or lead him to 'knavery' of his own. He seems to admit he will take a kind of pleasure in the prospect of dealing them back in kind: 'For 'tis the sport to have the engineer/ Hoist with his own petar'. (207-8) He ominously says that it will 'go hard' with his two old school friends. (208)

LOYALTY TO HIS FATHER
This scene stresses once again just how much Hamlet reveres and misses his father. His depiction of the dead king is unreserved in its admiration and respect: 'A combination and a form indeed,/ Where every god did seem to set his seal,/ To give the world assurance of a man'. (60-2) His love for his father is evident when he is almost moved to tears by the Ghost's terrible state. (124-5)

PRETENDING TO BE MAD
Throughout Acts 2 and 3 Hamlet has pretended to be mad. Now he admits to his mother that his madness is an act. We might ask ourselves why Hamlet chooses this moment to come clean to Gertrude. He urges his mother not to share this information with the king, who has been desperate to discover the reasons behind the prince's apparent lunacy. Once again, we might ask ourselves why Hamlet is so keen for Claudius not to know what lies behind his 'madness'.

LINES 21-38: HAMLET KILLS POLONIUS
Polonius, hidden behind a screen, has been listening all the while. Now he too calls for help. (23) Hamlet draws his sword and, apparently believing it is Claudius behind the screen, eagerly runs his weapon through the cover. (24) Polonius falls down dead, pulling the screen over his body.

The queen is shocked: 'what hast thou done … Oh what a rash and bloody deed is this!' (25, 27) Hamlet, however, seems only eager to know if it is Claudius he has murdered. (26)

When he lifts the screen, he seems disappointed to see the body of Polonius rather than the king. Though Polonius is dead, Hamlet cannot resist taunting him: 'Thou wretched, rash, intruding fool, farewell./ I took thee for thy better'. (31-2)

LINES 40-101: HAMLET CRITICISES HIS MOTHER FOR MARRYING CLAUDIUS
Hamlet seems unaffected by the 'bloody deed' he's just committed. He's more interested in confronting his mother: 'let me wring your heart'. (35) He tells her to sit down and listen to what he has to say. (34-5) Hamlet goes on in a poetic and long-winded fashion about the terrible sin Gertrude has committed. (40-51) Gertrude is confused, however, because Hamlet has yet to specify exactly what she has done wrong; 'Ay me, what act,/ That roars so loud, and thunders in the index?' (51-2)

Hamlet produces miniature portraits of his father and of Claudius. (53) The dead king was handsome and dignified, an example of perfect manliness: 'See what a grace was seated on this brow … To give the world assurance of a man'. (55, 62) Claudius is greatly inferior, a kind of parasite that fed on old Hamlet's greatness: 'like a mildew'd ear,/ Blasting his wholesome brother. (64-5) Hamlet simply cannot under-

GERTRUDE

MATERNAL FEELING

In this scene it is clear that Gertrude loves her son. During the ghost's visit she fears for his sanity, desperately urging him to calm himself: 'O gentle son,/ Upon the heat and flame of thy distemper/ Sprinkle cool patience'. (121–3) She promises not to betray Hamlet by telling the king he's only feigning madness:

Be thou assured, if words be made of
*   breath,*
And breath of life, I have no life to
*   breathe*
What thou hast said to me. (198–200)

Gertrude, then, finds herself torn between loyalty to her husband and loyalty to her son. Claudius has been desperately attempting to discover the reasons behind the prince's apparent madness, and would dearly love to know that the prince is only faking insanity. Yet Gertrude has promised Hamlet not to reveal this information.

DID GERTRUDE SUSPECT THAT CLAUDIUS KILLED HER PREVIOUS HUSBAND?

Hamlet refers to Claudius as a murderer and accuses him of stealing the kingdom. (96) Notably, Gertrude never asks him to elaborate on these accusations. She doesn't express astonishment or horror at the charges Hamlet has leveled. She doesn't even defend her husband against them.

This lack of response is possibly because Gertrude is in a very stressful situation. Her son is raging at her in her own bedroom and has just murdered her counsellor. It is possible that Gertrude says nothing to avoid aggravating the prince further. It's also possible that she's in such a state of shock she doesn't properly take in her son's accusations. Yet is it also possible that on some level Gertrude suspects Claudius might have been involved in her previous husband's death?

GUILT FOR MARRYING CLAUDIUS

Hamlet accuses Gertrude of having committed a terrible sin when she married Claudius. Initially, however, he doesn't actually specify what her sin is, merely that she's done something so terrible it makes even the heavens blush. (48) Gertrude claims to have no idea what the prince is talking about: 'What have I done, that thou dar'st wag thy tongue/ In noise so rude against me?' (39–40) She says she has know idea 'what act' she might have committed to upset the prince so much. (51)

Yet Gertrude clearly feels guilty about her remarriage. Three times in quick succession she pleads with her son to 'speak no more', declaring that his criticisms of her remarriage cut her 'like daggers'. (88, 94, 101) She reveals the deep guilt this decision has caused her, saying her very soul is marked by 'black and grainèd spots' that cannot be washed away. (90) In Act 2 Scene 2 she referred to her marriage to Claudius as being 'overhasty'. It is also possible that deep down she shares Hamlet's view of the union as being incestuous and inappropriate.

Does her guilt make her listen silently when Hamlet tells her to avoid Claudius' bed? Does she contemplate taking Hamlet's advice and refraining from sex with her husband? It is also possible, however, that she remains silent in order to avoid aggravating the prince. Hamlet, after all, has violently raged at her, has murdered Polonius before her very eyes, and has been talking to himself with a crazed expression on his face.

SOME LINES TO LEARN

Eyes without feeling, feeling without sight,
Ears without hands or eyes, smelling sans all
Hamlet (78–9)

For use almost can change the stamp of nature,
And either curb the devil, or throw him out
With wondrous potency
Hamlet (169–71)

I must be cruel, only to be kind:
Thus bad begins, and worse remains behind
Hamlet (179–80)

For 'tis the sport to have the engineer
Hoist with his own petar, an't shall go hard
But I will delve one yard below their mines,
And blow them at the moon.
Hamlet (207–10)

POLONIUS

SELF-IMPORTANT

Polonius' self-importance is once again evident in this scene. At the beginning of the scene he appears confident in his plan to spy on Hamlet. As usual, he seems convinced that he knows best, telling Gertrude what she should say to the prince when he arrives.

A MEDDLING SCHEMER

Polonius' scheming tendencies are evident in this scene as he puts into action his plan to observe the prince talking with his mother. He once again meddles in affairs that have nothing to do with him. He involves himself as per usual in the business of the royal family, this time with fatal results. It is difficult not to agree with Hamlet that he is a 'wretched, rash, intruding fool'. (31)

stand how his mother could have chosen Claudius as a husband, when she had previously been with a great man like the old king. (66–7) He repeatedly asks her if she has eyes, feeling she must have been blind to make such a choice.

Gertrude's choice of second husband should have been governed by judgement, by her faculty of reason. (70) Yet what kind of logic makes a woman chose a parasite like Claudius when she had previously been with a noble king like old Hamlet? (70–1) Not even madness or physical passion could impair someone's judgement in such a way. (73–6) Hamlet feels his mother's faculty of reason must have been completely 'apoplexed', or paralysed, when she made this choice: 'but sure that sense/ Is apoplexed'. (72–3) She must have been under the influence of some devil or evil spirit: 'What devil was't/ That thus hath cozened you'. (76–7)

Gertrude is cut by her son's words and repeatedly asks him to stop berating: 'Oh speak to me no more;/ These words like daggers enter in mine ears; No more sweet Hamlet!' (94–6)

His words, she says, have forced her to confront the guilt that stains her soul: 'Thou turn'st mine eyes into my very soul;/ And there I see such black and grainèd spots/ As will not leave their tinct'. (89–91)

Hamlet, however, continues to rant. He turns his wrath to Claudius, describing him as a 'murderer and a villain' who became king through crime and theft: 'a vice of kings,/ A cutpurse of the empire and rule,/ That from a shelf the precious diadem stole/ And put it in his pocket!' (98–101) His tirade is brought to an abrupt end, however, as he suddenly sees the Ghost of his father in the room.

LINES 102–38: THE GHOST REAPPEARS
Hamlet is shocked by the Ghost's sudden appearance, and calls on angels to protect him. (103–4) He asks the Ghost what it wants, fearing it has come to criticise him for his delay in killing Claudius: 'Do you not come your tardy son to chide'. (105–7) The Ghost has indeed come to remind Hamlet of his mission: 'Do not forget. This visitation/ Is but to whet thy almost blunted purpose'. (109–10)

Gertrude cannot see the Ghost, and thinks Hamlet's gone completely insane because he seems to be talking to himself: 'Alas, he's mad!' (105) The Ghost instructs Hamlet to comfort her. (111–12) Gertrude is horrified

to see her son staring at nothing and talking to the empty air: 'you do bend your eye on vacancy/ And with th'incorporal air do hold discourse?' (116–117) She says Hamlet's hair is standing on end and that he has a crazed look in her eye. (120–4)

Hamlet points at the Ghost, expressing how its worn appearance fills him with compassion and pity. (124–6) He worries that these emotions will make him soft, weakening his resolve to kill Claudius. (126–8) He describes his father's spirit walking out the door of the chamber: 'Look, where he goes, even now, out at the portal.' (137)

Gertrude is still baffled and confused. She can see no ghost of her dead husband and has no idea who Hamlet's talking to: 'To whom do you speak this?' (130) She thinks Hamlet is speaking only to a figment of his own crazed imagination: 'This the very coinage of your brain'. (138) Hamlet, however, denies that he is insane: 'It is not madness/ That I have uttered'. (142–3)

LINES 139–201: HAMLET URGES HIS MOTHER TO REPENT
With the departure of the Ghost, Hamlet turns his attention back to his mother, urging her to repent of her sins. He urges her not to soothe her conscience by dismissing his criticisms as the words of a madman. (145–7) Doing so will only allow her sin to fester and become worse: 'rank corruption, mining all within/ Infects unseen': (149–51)

HAMLET & GERTRUDE

- She must confess the great sin she has committed by being with Claudius: 'Confess yourself to heaven; repent what's past'. (150–1))
- She must be guided by the purer side of her nature: 'Oh throw away the worser part of,/ And live the purer with the other half'. (158–59)
- She must not sleep with Claudius tonight or in the future: 'avoid what is to come'. (151) She must not encourage the 'weeds' of sin that have infected her soul: 'And do not spread the compost on the weeds/ To make them ranker'. (152–3)

Hamlet's tone in these lines is extremely ironic and sarcastic. Superficially, it might seem that he's actually telling Gertrude to sleep with Claudius and reveal his secrets. A close reading of line 182, however, reveals that he is telling her not to do these things.

Before departing, Hamlet urges Gertrude not to let Claudius kiss and fondle as per usual, not to 'Let the bloat king tempt you again to bed/ Pinch wanton on your cheek; call you his mouse'. (183–4) He also asks her not to tell Claudius what has been said between them, and specifically the fact that he is only pretending to be mad, is only 'mad in craft'. (188–89) Doing so will lead her into danger. (197) Gertrude promises she will remain silent. (198–20)

CONSIDER THIS

DOES GERTRUDE THINK HAMLET IS INSANE?
In this scene Hamlet admits to his mother that he's only 'mad in craft', that his lunatic behaviour has all been an act. Gertrude appears to believe him and promises not to share this information with Claudius. Yet does she really think her son is sane? After all, throughout this scene Hamlet has behaved in a fairly crazed fashion:

- He's just killed Polonius in cold blood.
- He's violently raged at her and called her a terrible sinner.
- He's accused her husband of murdering his father.
- He claims to be speaking to the ghost of his father when all she can see is empty air.
- He has, she says, a deranged look in his eye.

It is possible that Gertrude genuinely believes Hamlet when he says he's sane. However, it's also possible she thinks he really has lost his reason. She may pretend to believe his admission of sanity in order to avoid aggravating him further. After all, the prince is in such a state of rage and high emotion that she fears for her safety. (21–3)

WHAT DID GERTRUDE KNOW ABOUT THE OLD KING'S MURDER?
Hamlet accuses Gertrude of being involved in the old king's murder: 'A bloody deed! Almost as bad, good mother,/ As kill a king and marry with his brother'. (28–9) There is a sense here that Hamlet is attempting to judge by Gertrude's reaction if she was involved in or knew about his father's murder. Her reply ('As kill a king?') seems to reveal astonishment, as if she genuinely doesn't know what Hamlet is talking about. Do we find her response to this accusation satisfactory? Most readers are convinced that Gertrude had nothing to do with her husband's murder. This view is perhaps supported by the fact that the Ghost urges Hamlet to comfort her.

WHY CAN'T GERTRUDE SEE THE GHOST?
In its previous appearances, the ghost was visible to everyone who came across it. In this scene, however, only Hamlet can see it. To Gertrude, it remains invisible. Why is this? It is possible that the ghost is not really present, that Hamlet, overcome by stress and rage, hallucinates its arrival in his mother's chamber. It is also possible that the Ghost is really present but remains invisible to Gertrude for some reason. Why might this be? Some critics suggest it's because she offended her former husband's spirit by marrying the brother who murdered him.

- Even if she does not feel inwardly repentant, she must do the right thing and avoid her husband's bed: 'Assume a virtue, if you have it not'. (161)
- Over time, it will become easier and easier for her to refrain from sleeping with her husband: 'Refrain tonight,/ And that shall lend a kind of easiness/ To the next abstinence: the next more easy'. (166–8)

Hamlet stresses that the force of habit is a powerful thing: 'That monster custom, who all sense doth eat'. (162) We can develop bad habits, becoming addicted to sinful practices. Yet we can also develop good habits, which make it easier and easier to commit 'actions fair and good' and 'curb the devil, or throw him out'. (164, 170)

LINES 202–18: HAMLET VOWS TO THWART CLAUDIUS' PLANS
Hamlet asks Gertrude if she knows he is being sent to England. (201) He has either learned about or guessed Claudius' plan to have him removed. He bitterly declares that Claudius' scheme will backfire: 'Let it work;/ For 'tis the sport to have the engineer/ Hoist with his own petar'. (206–8)

He also knows that Rosencrantz and Guildenstern are acting as puppets of the king. (206) He warns that their betrayal will lead him to commit dirty tricks of his own: 'they must sweep my way,/ And marshal me to knavery'. (204–6)

Hamlet then declares that he must dispose of Polonius' body: 'I'll lug the guts into the neighbouring room'. (213) He cannot resist having another dig at the dead counsellor, saying he is 'now most still, most secret, and most grave,/ Who was in life a foolish prating knave'. (215–16) He bids Gertrude goodnight, dragging the corpse away with him.

Enter CLAUDIUS, with ROSENCRANTZ and GUILDENSTERN

CLAUDIUS   There's matter in these sighs, these profound heaves.
You must translate, 'tis fit we understand them.
Where is your son?

GERTRUDE   Bestow this place on us a little while.

Exeunt ROSENCRANTZ and GUILDENSTERN

Ah, mine own lord, what have I seen tonight!

CLAUDIUS   What, Gertrude? How does Hamlet?

GERTRUDE   Mad as the sea and wind, when both contend
Which is the mightier. In his lawless fit,
Behind the arras hearing something stir,
Whips out his rapier, cries, 'A rat, a rat!'
And in this brainish apprehension kills
The unseen good old man.

CLAUDIUS   Oh heavy deed!
It had been so with us had we been there.
His liberty is full of threats to all,
To you yourself, to us, to everyone.
Alas, how shall this bloody deed be answered?
It will be laid to us, whose providence*
Should have kept short, restrained and out of haunt,†
This mad young man. But so much was our love,
We would not understand what was most fit,
But, like the owner of a foul disease,
To keep it from divulging, let it feed
Even on the pith of life. Where is he gone?

GERTRUDE   To draw apart the body he hath killed:
O'er whom his very madness, like some ore
Among a mineral of metals base,
Shows itself pure; a weeps for what is done.

CLAUDIUS   Oh Gertrude, come away!
The sun no sooner shall the mountains touch
But we will ship him hence, and this vile deed
We must with all our majesty and skill
Both countenance and excuse. Ho, Guildenstern!

Enter ROSENCRANTZ and GUILDENSTERN

Friends both, go join you with some further aid.
Hamlet in madness hath Polonius slain,
And from his mother's closet hath he dragged him:
Go seek him out, speak fair, and bring the body
Into the chapel. I pray you haste in this.

Exeunt ROSENCRANTZ and GUILDENSTERN

Come Gertrude, we'll call up our wisest friends;
And let them know both what we mean to do,
And what's untimely done. So haply, slander
Whose whisper o'er the world's diameter,
As level as the cannon to his blank,‡
Transports his poisoned shot, may miss our name
And hit the woundless air. Oh, come away,§
My soul is full of discord and dismay.

Exeunt

---

matter: meaning
translate: explain

brainish apprehension: headstrong delusion

us … we: Claudius is using the royal plural

answered: explained
laid to us: blamed on me
short: under control

understand: give credence to; *fit*: important

divulging: being known publicly
pith: marrow

ore: precious metal
mineral: mine

sun … touch: at dawn (it's still nighttime)
vile deed: the killing of Polonius

countenance: support

haply: it may happen that

. . . .
* 17   *providence*: foresight/influence
† 18   *out … haunt*: away from society
‡ 42   *to his blank*: to his mark, aim
§ 40–4 *slander …hit the woundless air*: we may direct
        slanderous whispers, which carry their
        poisonous arrows as far as the wide world
        (and as straight as the cannon to its aim), so
        that they miss blaming us and instead target
        the invincible air

CLAUDIUS & GERTRUDE

Claudius finds Gertrude upset after her meeting with Hamlet. She tells him how Hamlet killed Polonius and that the prince is insane. The king fears for his own safety and decides that Hamlet should be sent away to England this very night. He will summon his best advisors to ensure that this messy situation is dealt with in the best possible manner.

A CLOSER LOOK

Claudius finds Gertrude alone and very upset. He realises that something significant has happened to cause the queen such grief: 'There's matter in these sighs, these profound heaves'. (1) He quickly asks about Hamlet.

Gertrude tells Claudius that Hamlet is insane: 'Mad as the sea and wind'. (7) She describes how he killed Polonius in a fit of madness and that he has now gone to dispose of the body. (24) Gertrude then lies and says that Hamlet 'weeps for what is done' and that his feelings of remorse reveal his essential worth and integrity. (25–7)

Claudius' realises that he could just as easily have been the victim: 'It had been so with us had we been there'. (13) He is fearful now of what Hamlet is capable of doing. He declares that if Hamlet is allowed to roam free he will be a threat to everyone: 'His liberty is full of threats to us all'. (14)

However, the king also knows that this murder will have to be accounted for, and realises that he will be blamed for allowing an obviously disturbed prince such freedom: 'It will be laid to us'. (17) The king claims that it was because of his great love for Hamlet that he did not act to restrain him sooner: 'so much was our love'. (19) Claudius swiftly decides what needs to be done:

- He declares that Hamlet will be sent to England that very night. (30–1)
- He will use all of his political skill to explain away the murder: 'We must, with all our majesty and skill,/ Both countenance and excuse'. (31–2)
- He will summon his counsellors and explain to them what has happened and what he intends to do. (38–40) It is his hope that this incident will not damage his reputation.
- He instructs Rosencrantz and Guildenstern to find his stepson and take Polonius' corpse to the chapel. (33–7)

The incident has, however, shaken and troubled the king. He declares that his soul is 'full of discord and dismay'. (45)

CLAUDIUS

The performance of the play revealed to Claudius that the prince knows he murdered old Hamlet. He has now just heard how Hamlet killed Polonius. Had the king been in the bedroom instead of his counsellor, he would now likely be dead. Hamlet, therefore, poses a serious threat to Claudius. He could ruin the king by exposing his terrible secret. He also now seems capable of taking bloody revenge for the death of his father.

In spite of the pressure he must be feeling, Claudius retains his composure and acts in a decisive manner. He has already stated that Hamlet will be sent to England. (3.1.170) He now needs to make this happen as quickly as possible. However, the king must make it seem that his decision to send the prince away is warranted and reasonable, not only to Gertrude but to the general public. He therefore declares that Hamlet now poses a threat to everyone: 'His liberty is full of threats to us all;/ To you yourself, to us, to everyone'. (14–15)

The king also anticipates how he might be partially blamed for Polonius' death. He will be asked why the prince was permitted to freely roam the palace when he knew that Hamlet was of unsound mind. Claudius will explain this by saying that he loved his stepson too much to confine him: 'But so much was our love,/ We would not understand what was most fit'. (19–20)

Claudius is, however, ultimately dealing with a very messy and tricky situation. It is easy to see how rumours and stories will start spreading through Denmark as people discuss these strange events. It is vital that the king control the message and protect his reputation. He therefore decides to summon the royal couple's wisest friends for an emergency conference on how to 'spin' or explain to the world at large the recent dramatic events at Elsinore. (38–40)

GERTRUDE

In the previous scene Hamlet told Gertrude that he is not really insane, only 'mad in craft'. He asked his mother not to reveal this fact to Claudius.

In this scene Gertrude tells the king that Hamlet is utterly insane: 'Mad as the sea and wind, when both contend/ Which is the mightier'. (7–8) She also says that it was because of his madness that he killed Polonius and that he now weeps for what he has done. (27)

It is hard to know whether Gertrude tells Claudius that Hamlet is insane because she wants to stay loyal to her promise to her son or because she really believes that the prince has lost the plot. Her claim that Hamlet weeps for what he has done is plainly false and perhaps this is said for the benefit of her son, in the hope that the king will be more lenient.

Of the prince's claim that Claudius is a murderer, she says nothing. Of course, we might also ask ourselves if this is because she does not believe, or refuses to entertain the possibility, that the accusation could be true.

Because of all these uncertainties, it is hard to gauge how strong Gertrude's maternal feelings actually are for her son.

Enter HAMLET

HAMLET　Safely stowed.

ROSENCRANTZ　} *Within*　Hamlet! Lord Hamlet!
GUILDENSTERN

HAMLET　But soft, what noise? Who calls on Hamlet? Oh here they
come.

Enter ROSENCRANTZ and GUILDENSTERN

ROSENCRANTZ　What have you done, my lord with the dead body?　　5

HAMLET　Compounded it with dust whereto 'tis kin.

Compounded: mixed; kin: of the same kind

ROSENCRANTZ　Tell us where 'tis, that we may take it thence and bear
it to the chapel.

HAMLET　Do not believe it.

ROSENCRANTZ　Believe what?　　10

HAMLET　That I can keep your counsel and not mine own. Besides,
to be demanded of a sponge, what replication should be
made by the son of a king?

ROSENCRANTZ　Take you me for a sponge my lord?

HAMLET　Ay sir, that soaks up the king's countenance, his rewards,　　15
his authorities. But such officers do the king best service
in the end: he keeps them like an ape in the corner of his
jaw, first mouthed to be last swallowed. When he needs
what you have gleaned, it is but squeezing you, and,*
sponge, you shall be dry again.　　20

countenance: favour

like: the king is being compared to an ape
ape: reputed to store apples in his mouth

gleaned: learned

ROSENCRANTZ　I understand you not my lord.

HAMLET　I am glad of it, a knavish speech sleeps in a foolish ear.†

knavish: sarcastic

ROSENCRANTZ　My lord, you must tell us where the body is, and go
with us to the king.

HAMLET　The body is with the king, but the king is not with the body.‡　　25
The king is a thing –

king: the king is the body politic

GUILDENSTERN　A thing my lord?

HAMLET　Of nothing. Bring me to him. Hide fox, and all after!

Exeunt

---

* 18–19　*needs … squeezing you:* Hamlet is
warning them that they're playing a
dangerous game, that the king will
use them, and perhaps destroy them,
for his gain

† 22　*sleeps:* isn't heard/understood; *foolish
ear:* implies that Rosencrantz is a
fool

‡ 25　*the king is not with the body:* in speaking of the king, Hamlet is thinking of
his dead father who is now 'a thing …
of nothing'

HAMLET

Rosencrantz and Guildenstern find Hamlet but are unable to get him to disclose the location of Polonius' body. The prince continues to speak to his one-time friends in a mad fashion and warns them that the king is only using them for his own advantage. Hamlet then asks to be brought before Claudius before running away and calling on the two courtiers to chase him.

A CLOSER LOOK

Hamlet has just hidden the body of Polonius. He hears Rosencrantz and Guildenstern approaching, calling his name. (1–3) They have been sent by the king to find out where the body is so that it can be taken to the chapel.

Hamlet's responses to their enquiries are strange and elusive. When asked what he has done with Polonius' body, he says that he has 'Compounded it with dust whereto 'tis kin'. (6) When Rosencrantz presses for information regarding the location of the body, Hamlet says that 'The body is with the king, but the king is not with the body'. (25)

Hamlet believes that Rosencrantz and Guildenstern are simply the king's agents and no longer his friends to be trusted. He is angered by the fact that he, the 'son of a King', should be subjected to such questioning. (13–15) He compares Rosencrantz and Guildenstern to sponges, saying that they soak up the king's orders and rewards. (15–16) He warns them that the king will dispose of them when he has 'gleaned' what he needs to know. (18–20)

Hamlet eventually asks to be lead to Claudius only to then run away from Rosencrantz and Guildenstern, crying 'Hide fox, and all after'. (28)

CHARACTER DEVELOPMENT

HAMLET

PRETENDING TO BE MAD
Hamlet again acts in a mad and peculiar manner. He has just killed a man and is attempting to hide the body. However, he seems to be in a highly excited and somewhat playful state, not too dissimilar to how he was after he spoke to the Ghost on the ramparts (Act 1 Scene 5). He speaks in a strange and sometimes cryptic manner to Rosencrantz and Guildenstern, and runs away from them at the end of the scene as though they are playing some schoolyard game: 'Hide fox, and all after'. (28)

However, though his former schoolmates are bamboozled by what he says, the prince's words are at times sharp and pertinent. He tells Rosencrantz and Guildenstern that they are little more than the king's 'sponges'. Claudius will flatter and reward them while they are useful to him, but he will also quickly discard them when he has gotten what he needs.

A FEELING OF SUPERIORITY
We are reminded of Hamlet's status as prince and heir to the throne when he grows angry with Rosencrantz's interrogation. He asks why he, 'the son of a king', should answer their questions. (12–13) It is noticeable how Rosencrantz and Guildenstern quickly begin to address Hamlet as 'my lord', which they had not always done previously. It is clear that any friendship that might have existed between these fellow-students has now completely vanished. Hamlet demands the respect that he has a right to expect from those of a lower status.

Enter CLAUDIUS and two or three ATTENDANTS

CLAUDIUS I have sent to seek him, and to find the body.
How dangerous is it that this man goes loose,
Yet must not we put the strong law on him;
He's loved of the distracted multitude,
Who like not in their judgement, but their eyes;*   5
And where tis so, th' offender's scourge is weighed,
But never the offence. To bear all smooth and even,†
This sudden sending him away must seem
Deliberate pause. Diseases desperate grown
By desperate appliance are relieved,   10
Or not at all.

Enter ROSENCRANTZ

          How now, what hath befallen?
ROSENCRANTZ Where the dead body is bestowed, my lord,
We cannot get from him.
CLAUDIUS   But where is he?
ROSENCRANTZ Without, my lord, guarded, to know your pleasure.‡
CLAUDIUS Bring him before us.
ROSENCRANTZ   Ho! bring in my lord.   15

Enter HAMLET and GUILDENSTERN

CLAUDIUS Now, Hamlet, where's Polonius?
HAMLET At supper.
CLAUDIUS At supper? Where?
HAMLET Not where he eats, but where a is eaten. A certain convocation
of politic worms are e'en at him. Your worm is your only   20
emperor for diet: we fat all creatures else to fat us, and we fat§
ourselves for maggots. Your fat king and your lean beggar‖
is but variable service, two dishes, but to one table; that's the end.**
CLAUDIUS Alas, alas.
HAMLET A man may fish with the worm that hath eat of a king,   25
and eat of the fish that hath fed of that worm.

---

distracted multitude: irrational mob

scourge: punishment

Deliberate pause: of unhurried consideration
appliance: remedy, treatment

bestowed: hidden

convocation of politic: parliament of shrewd
fat: fatten;
maggots: we'll in turn be eaten by worms

---

* 5   *their eyes*: Hamlet is popular because he is good-looking

† 7   *bear ... even*: to be seen to conduct this affair with fair judgement and thus rule without causing any offence or opposition

‡ 14   *Without, my lord; guarded, to know your pleasure*: outside under guard, waiting on your command

§ 21   *creatures ... us*: other creatures to feed ourselves

‖ 22   *variable service*: different courses of food served in a formal way

** 23 *worm is your only emperor for diet*: the emperor is food for worms, thus the worm is emperor-like, at the top of the food chain. The word 'diet' also alludes to the Diet (legislative assembly) at the German city of Worms, presided over by the emperor, Charles V, in 1521.

CLAUDIUS	What dost you mean by this?	
HAMLET	Nothing but to show you how a king may go a progress through the guts of a beggar.	*progress*: state journey
CLAUDIUS	Where is Polonius?	30
HAMLET	In heaven, send hither to see. If your messenger find him not there, seek him i'th'other place yourself. But if indeed you find him not within this month, you shall nose him as you go up the stairs into the lobby.	*nose him*: smell him
CLAUDIUS	Go seek him there.	35
HAMLET	A will stay till you come.	

Exeunt Attendants

CLAUDIUS	Hamlet, this deed, for thine especial safety,	
	Which we do tender, as we dearly grieve	*tender*: care for; *as*: even as
	For that which thou hast done, must send thee hence	
	With fiery quickness. Therefore prepare thyself.	40 *fiery quickness*: energetic speed
	The bark is ready, and the wind at help,	*bark*: ship; *at help*: favourable
	Th'associates tend, and everything is bent	*bent*: in place, like a drawn bow
	For England.	
HAMLET	For England!	
CLAUDIUS	Ay Hamlet.	
HAMLET	Good.	
CLAUDIUS	So is it if thou knew'st our purposes.	
HAMLET	I see a cherub that sees them. But, come; for England!	45 *cherub*: spirit of Heaven, with special vision
	Farewell dear mother.	
CLAUDIUS	Thy loving father, Hamlet.	
HAMLET	My mother. Father and mother is man and wife; man and wife is one flesh, and so, my mother. Come, for England.	

Exit

CLAUDIUS	Follow him at foot, tempt him with speed aboard.	50 *at foot*: closely
	Delay it not, I'll have him hence to-night.	
	Away, for everything is sealed and done*	
	That else leans on th'affair. Pray you, make haste.	*leans … affair*: depends on this business

Exeunt ROSENCRANTZ and GUILDENSTERN

	And England, if my love thou hold'st at aught,	
	As my great power thereof may give thee sense,	55
	Since yet thy cicatrice looks raw and red	*cicatrice*: scar
	After the Danish sword, and thy free awe	
	Pays homage to us – thou mayst not coldly set	*homage*: respect; *coldly set*: undervalue
	Our sovereign process; which imports at full,	
	By letters congruing to that effect,	60 *congruing*: agreeing
	The present death of Hamlet. Do it, England;	
	For like the hectic in my blood he rages,	*hectic*: fever
	And thou must cure me. Till I know 'tis done,	
	Howe'er my haps, my joys were ne'er begun.	*haps*: luck

Exit

* 52   *sealed … done*: refers to letters ordering Hamlet's death

HAMLET & CLAUDIUS

Claudius discusses the difficulties he faces in punishing Hamlet, a popular figure with the Danish people. Hamlet is brought before the king and finally reveals the location of Polonius' body, but only after first delivering a strange speech about death and decay. The prince seems unconcerned upon hearing that he is to be sent immediately to England, and hints that he knows it is Claudius' intention to have him killed there. Left alone at the end of the scene, Claudius reveals his anxiety. He desperately hopes that England will carry out his command to execute the prince.

A CLOSER LOOK

LINES 1–11: CLAUDIUS CAREFULLY CONSIDERS HOW TO DEAL WITH HAMLET

Claudius speaks to his counsellors about the difficulty he faces in dealing with Hamlet. He would like to punish Hamlet severely for killing Polonius but knows that the general public would disapprove of any harsh action. The king is well aware of how much the public loves Hamlet, and he cannot afford to lose their support.

The king, however, has a low opinion of the general public. He considers them confused and irrational: 'the distracted multitude'. (4) Claudius says that they judge by appearance and are incapable of rational judgement. He knows that if he is seen to act severely with Hamlet, the public will be outraged at his pun-

ishment and give little heed to the fact that the prince has murdered another man: 'th' offender's scourge is weighed/ But never the offence'. (6–7) His decision to exile Hamlet to England must, therefore, appear like a carefully considered and just act: 'To bear all smooth and even,/ This sudden sending him away must seem/ Deliberate pause' (7–9)

LINES 12–36: CLAUDIUS INTERROGATES HAMLET

Rosencrantz tells the king that Hamlet refuses to reveal the location of Polonius' body. Claudius decides to do the interrogating himself, and orders that the prince be brought before him. (15) Hamlet is brought in under guard, and frustrates and taunts the king with his strange answers.

CHARACTER DEVELOPMENT

CLAUDIUS

A SHREWD POLITICIAN

Claudius knows that the situation he is dealing with is a sensitive one and calls for careful management. He is aware that Hamlet is extremely popular with the Danish people, and that his punishment could easily cause a public outcry and be damaging to the king: 'Yet must not we put the strong law on him:/ He's loved of the distracted multitude'. (3–4) Hamlet's exile must look like a carefully weighed political decision that serves the good of the state: 'This sudden sending him away must seem/ Deliberate pause'. (8–9)

FALSE

When speaking with Hamlet, Claudius continues to act like a loving and considerate stepfather. He tells the prince that he is being sent to England 'for thine especial safety'. (37)

It must be Claudius' hope that he will appear before his people as an innocent and dutiful king who is being tormented by his mad and dangerous stepson.

ANXIOUS AND FEARFUL

Though he appears composed when he is dealing with Hamlet and speaking publicly before the court, Claudius reveals his anxiety when he is alone at the end of the scene. He desperately hopes that England will carry out his command to execute the prince. Hamlet has deeply unsettled the king: 'For like the hectic in my blood he rages'. (62) Until he knows that Hamlet is dead, he will not be able to relax: 'Till I know 'tis done,/ Howe'er my haps, my joys were ne'er begun'. (63–4)

RUTHLESS

Claudius has little compunction about dispatching the son of the woman he loves to his death. He appears willing to threaten England to ensure that his instructions are obeyed. (61–3) The king's aim now is to hold on to power at all costs.

HAMLET

PRETENDING TO BE MAD

In this scene Hamlet continues to act in a mad fashion. His responses to Claudius' questions are strange. When asked where Polonius is, the prince replies 'At supper'. He then speaks about worms and maggots, and describes how 'a king may go a progress through the guts of a beggar'.

However, as we have said before, though the prince may be acting somewhat madly, what he says is not mindless gibberish. His responses to the king are certainly bizarre, but they contain sharp and logical observations about death. Also, by speaking in this rather peculiar manner, Hamlet can say things that he might not be permitted to say if he was speaking normally and clearly. His speech about worms essentially makes the point that kings are no better than beggars once they die. Publicly likening a king to a beggar ought to deeply offend a monarch, who believes that he is essentially divine.

CONFIDENT AND BOLD

Although Hamlet is now at the mercy of the king, he does not appear greatly distressed. He greets Claudius' news that he is to be sent to England with a nonchalant 'Good', though he seems quite aware that his stepfather is plotting his death.

Hamlet seems energised since discovering that the Ghost's story is true. He no longer has any doubts regarding Claudius' guilt, and he seems quite willing and capable of taking revenge. His confident behaviour before the king in this scene seems designed to unsettled Claudius. Hamlet knows that he will not be harmed openly before the court, and that he can say more or less what he wants.

However, the prince lost the advantage he gained after the play's performance when he killed Polonius. The king now has a sound reason to have Hamlet removed from Denmark. We must wonder what Hamlet is thinking now regarding the possibilities of avenging his father's death.

A NEGATIVE STATE OF MIND

Though delivered in a somewhat playful manner and obviously designed to trouble the king, Hamlet's speech about worms and maggots eating the bodies of kings and beggars once again reveals his preoccupation with death and decay. What he says seems well considered, and suggests that the prince is spending an unhealthy amount of time contemplating the fate of our bodies once we die.

SOME LINES TO LEARN

We fat all creatures else to fat us,
and we fat ourselves for maggots
Hamlet (21–2)

A man may fish with the worm
that hath eat of a king, and eat of
the fish that hath fed of that worm
Hamlet (25–6)

When asked where Polonius is, Hamlet replies 'At supper'. (17) When Claudius asks Hamlet to explain his answer, the prince speaks in a dark-humoured and cynical way about death and the futility of life: Polonius is now 'At supper', he says, in the sense that he is being eaten by worms. Hamlet suggests that it is ironic how we fatten animals in order to make ourselves fat. The way he sees it, we are in turn only fattening ourselves for the worms that will consume our bodies when we are dead and buried in the ground.

Death, Hamlet states, is a great leveller. It does not matter if a man was a king or a beggar in life, as both ultimately become food for worms in death: 'Your fat king and your lean beggar is but variable service, two dishes, but to one table'. (22–3) The fact that we are eaten by worms when we die can lead to rather bizarre and grotesque scenarios. Hamlet imagines how a 'man may fish with the worm that hath eat of a king,/ and eat of the fish that hath feed of that worm'. (25–6)

Claudius again asks where Polonius is, only to be told that he is 'In heaven'. Hamlet instructs the king to send a messenger there to confirm this. If the messenger cannot find Polonius there, then Claudius ought to seek him in hell himself: 'seek him i'th'other place yourself'. (31–2) Hamlet finally reveals to the king that Polonius' body is in the lobby up the stairs. Rosencrantz is sent to recover it. (37)

LINES 37–49: THE KING TELLS HAMLET HE IS TO BE SENT TO ENGLAND

Claudius tells Hamlet that he is being sent away to England. The king says that he is doing this for his stepson's protection: 'for thine especial safety/ Which we do tender'. (37–8) He instructs Hamlet to prepare himself. (40)

Hamlet was already aware that he would be sent to England, and he expresses no surprise or outrage at his punishment. (43) His rather cheery response to the news leads Claudius to hint at his darker plans for the prince: 'So is it if thou knew'st our purposes'. (44) Hamlet, however, intimates that he knows Claudius' real intentions: 'I see a cherub that sees them'. (45) As he departs, he frustrates Claudius by referring to him as his mother: 'Farewell dear mother'. (46) The king orders Rosencrantz and Guildenstern to follow him and make sure they leave for England that night. (50–3)

LINES 50–64: CLAUDIUS REVEALS HIS TRUE INTENTIONS

Left alone, Claudius discloses his real plan for Hamlet. He has given a letter to Rosencrantz and Guildenstern addressed to the king of England in which there are instructions for Hamlet to be murdered. England has been recently defeated by Denmark in battle, and Claudius is confident his 'request' will be obeyed. The king is desperate for Hamlet to be eliminated, as the prince poses an intolerable threat: 'Do it, England;/ For like the hectic in my blood he rages,/ And thou must cure me'. (61–3) He cannot rest easy until he knows his troublesome stepson is out of the way: 'Till I know 'tis done,/ Howe'er my haps, my joys were ne'er begun'. (63–4)

Enter FORTINBRAS, a Captain, and Soldiers, marching

FORTINBRAS	Go captain, from me greet the Danish king.
	Tell him that, by his licence, Fortinbras
	Craves the conveyance of a promised march
	Over his kingdom. You know the rendezvous.
	If that his majesty would aught with us,
	We shall express our duty in his eye;
	And let him know so.
CAPTAIN	I will do't, my lord.
FORTINBRAS	Go softly on.

Exit FORTINBRAS, with the army

Enter HAMLET, ROSENCRANTZ, etc.

HAMLET	Good sir, whose powers are these?
CAPTAIN	They are of Norway, sir.
HAMLET	How purposed sir I pray you?
CAPTAIN	Against some part of Poland.
HAMLET	Who commands them sir?
CAPTAIN	The nephew to old Norway, Fortinbras.
HAMLET	Goes it against the main of Poland sir,
	Or for some frontier?
CAPTAIN	Truly to speak, and with no addition,
	We go to gain a little patch of ground
	That hath in it no profit but the name.
	To pay five ducats, five, I would not farm it,
	Nor will it yield to Norway or the Pole
	A ranker rate, should it be sold in fee.
HAMLET	Why then the Polack never will defend it.
CAPTAIN	Yes, it is already garrisoned.
HAMLET	Two thousand souls and twenty thousand ducats
	Will not debate the question of this straw.
	This is th'imposthume of much wealth and peace,
	That inward breaks, and shows no cause without
	Why the man dies. I humbly thank you sir.
CAPTAIN	God buy you, sir.

Exit

ROSENCRANTZ	Will't please you go, my lord?

licence: permission

conveyance: safe passage, escort

aught: meet
in his eye: in his presence

softly: slowly, safely

powers: army, troops

How purposed: what's their purpose

addition: exaggeration

no profit: no worth

ranker rate: higher interest; *fee:* freehold

garrisoned: readied for defence

imposthume: inner corruption, like an abscess
shows ... without: does not show externally

God buy you: God be with you

* 25–6 *Two thousand ... this straw:* the high cost of fighting, in both lives and money, will not be enough to settle this trivial dispute

5

10

15

20

25

30

HAMLET   I'll be with you straight; go a little before.

Exeunt all but HAMLET

How all occasions do inform against me,*   *occasions*: events;

And spur my dull revenge! What is a man   *dull*: tediously slow, blunt

If his chief good and market of his time

Be but to sleep and feed? A beast, no more.   35   *beast … more*: no more than a beast

Sure, he that made us with such large discourse,   *discourse*: faculties, such as speech and reason

Looking before and after, gave us not†

That capability and god-like reason

To fust in us unused. Now whether it be   *fust*: to go mouldy, smell stale

Bestial oblivion, or some craven scruple‡   40

Of thinking too precisely on th'event –   *event*: action and consequence

A thought which quartered hath but one part wisdom   *quarter'd*: dissected, examined

And ever three parts coward – I do not know

Why yet I live to say this thing's to do,§

Sith I have cause, and will, and strength, and means   45   *Sith*: since

To do't. Examples gross as earth exhort me: *exhort*: urge

Witness this army of such mass and charge,   *mass and charge*: size and expense

Led by a delicate and tender prince,

Whose spirit with divine ambition puffed   *puff'd*: swollen

Makes mouths at the invisible event,   50   *Makes mouths*: shows contempt, scorns

Exposing what is mortal and unsure

To all that fortune, death and danger dare,

Even for an egg-shell. Rightly to be great𝄐**   *egg-shell*: something very delicate

Is not to stir without great argument,

But greatly to find quarrel in a straw††   55

When honour's at the stake. How stand I then,   *honour's at the stake*: honour is at risk

That have a father killed, a mother stained,

Excitements of my reason and my blood,   *Excitements*: incitements

And let all sleep, while to my shame I see

The imminent death of twenty thousand men,   60

That for a fantasy and trick of fame   *fantasy … fame*: illusion of honour

Go to their graves like beds, fight for a plot

Whereon the numbers cannot try the cause,

Which is not tomb enough and continent

To hide the slain? Oh from this time forth,††   65

My thoughts be bloody or be nothing worth.

Exit

---

*   32   *inform … me*: accuse, show me up

†   37   *Looking … after*: understanding cause and effect

‡   40   *Bestial oblivion, or some craven scruple*: animal-like unawareness, or cowardly pang of consciousness

§   44   *Why yet I live to say 'This thing's to do'*: why I am still just talking about revenge, rather than performing it, still saying: 'This must be done'

𝄐   53   *Makes mouths at the invisible event … egg-shell*: scorns at the unforeseen outcome of war, by placing life at risk for such a trivial matter

**   53   *Rightly to be great*: true greatness

††   55   *greatly … straw*: discover even a trivial reason to act

‡‡   62–5   *fight for a plot … hide the slain*: the land they fight over is not large enough to hold the army, nor big enough to provide a plot of burial ground for all that will be killed on it

FORTINBRAS

As he is being led to the ship that will take him to England, Hamlet sees the army of Fortinbras, the prince of Norway, on its way to fight Poland. Hearing how Fortinbras is willing to fight the Poles over an insignificant piece of land causes Hamlet to criticise himself for his inability to act and take vengeance against Claudius. He vows to act with more violence and determination from now on.

A CLOSER LOOK

✏ LINES 1–8: FORTINBRAS ENTERS DENMARK

Fortinbras, the prince of Norway, is leading his army to fight Poland. He needs to pass through Denmark in order to reach his destination. He must seek the permission of the Danish king before he can do this. He sends one of his captains to Elsinore to ask permission on his behalf.

✏ LINES 9–31: HAMLET SPEAKS TO A NORWEGIAN ARMY CAPTAIN

Hamlet is being taken by Rosencrantz and Guildenstern to the ship that will take him to England. As they make their way across a plain in Denmark, they encounter the Norwegian captain. Hamlet asks the captain whose army it is, and is also curious to know the purpose of its presence in Denmark. (9, 11)

The captain tells Hamlet they are Norwegian forces, under the command of the young Fortinbras. They are on their way to Poland to fight for a small piece of land on the Polish border. According to the captain, this is a worthless piece of land.

Hamlet is amazed to hear that the Polish have already amassed an army to defend this insignificant piece of land. He finds it hard to believe that so much blood will be shed over such a trifle. He considers such a battle to be the result of rich and restless rulers having too much time on their hands and too little to do. (27–9)

✏ LINES 32–66: HAMLET BERATES HIMSELF

Hearing how the young Norwegian prince is marching

into battle over something small and insignificant has a profound impression upon Hamlet. He thinks about how great men ought to behave, and berates himself for his own inability to act.

Hamlet considers man to be no more than an animal if all he does is eat and sleep. (33–5) We have been blessed with great mental faculties in order to do great thing. (36–9) He views Fortinbras' action against the Poles with some admiration. His Norwegian counterpart is 'a delicate and tender prince' who is unafraid to march into battle and risk his life over something insignificant: 'Exposing what is mortal and unsure/ To all that fortune, death and danger dare,/ Even for an eggshell'. (51–3) The prince believes that the appearance of Fortinbras serves as yet another reminder of his own lack of action. (32–3)

SOME LINES TO LEARN

What is a man,
If his chief good and market of his time
Be but to sleep and feed? A beast, no more
Hamlet (33–5)

Rightly to be great
Is not to stir without great argument,
But greatly to find quarrel in a straw
When honour's at the stake
Hamlet (53–6)

Oh from this time forth,
My thoughts be bloody or be nothing worth!
Hamlet (65–6)

Hamlet thinks that the truly great man will not take up arms without an important motive, but will do so if his honour is being challenged: 'Rightly to be great/ Is not to stir without great argument,/ But greatly to find quarrel in a straw/ When honour's at the stake'. (53–6) Hamlet wonders why, having great motives, he is still incapable of taking real action to avenge his father's murder. He speculates that he is either slow-witted, too analytical or too cowardly. (39–44) His procrastination is especially puzzling as he believes he has 'cause, and will, and strength, and means/ To do't'. (45–6) He swears that from now on he will act ruthlessly and directly. The time for hesitation is over: 'Oh from this time forth,/ My thoughts be bloody or be nothing worth.' (65–6)

CHARACTER DEVELOPMENT

HAMLET

SELF-CRITICAL
After the performance of the play which exposed the king's guilt, Hamlet seemed energised and puposeful (Act 3 Scene 2). He was full of anger and violence, and seemed ready to act and kill Claudius. However, believing the king to be at prayer and not wanting his soul to go to Heaven when he died, he let the moment pass (Act 3 Scene 3). He then killed Polonius in his mother's room, thus handing the advantage back to Claudius.

Hamlet now seems to have once again lost the rage and violence that he felt after the play, and which enabled him to act in a bloody manner. His speech upon seeing Fortinbras leading an army to Poland is reminiscent of his soliloquy in Act 2 Scene 2 after witnessing the player's emotional performance of lines from a play about Hecuba. Again, Hamlet berates himself for his lack of action. He is appalled that he – having greater personal motivation than Fortinbras seems to have for attacking Poland – cannot kill Claudius. He vows once again to act in a determined and bloody manner: 'Oh from this time forth,/ My thoughts be bloody or be nothing worth.' (65–6)

FORTINBRAS

THE AMBITIOUS PRINCE
Although we have heard Fortinbras talked of before, this is the first occasion when we meet him in the play. In spite of the fact that he does not say a great deal, his words convey determination and single-mindedness. With his willingness to march against Poland over an insignificant piece of land, Fortinbras' ability to act decisively, even if the consequences are great and bloody, can be effectively contrasted with Hamlet's prevarication and self-reflection. The prince recognises how he differs from Fortinbras, and he seeks to use the Norwegian prince's example as a motivation to act more decisively and violently in the future.

Enter HORATIO, GERTRUDE, and a GENTLEMAN

GERTRUDE	I will not speak with her.
GENTLEMAN	She is importunate, indeed distract:
	Her mood will needs be pitied.
GERTRUDE	What would she have?
GENTLEMAN	She speaks much of her father, says she hears
	There's tricks i'th'world, and hems, and beats her heart,
	Spurns enviously at straws, speaks things in doubt*
	That carry but half sense. Her speech is nothing,
	Yet the unshapèd use of it doth move
	The hearers to collection. They yawn at it,†
	And botch the words up fit to their own thoughts,
	Which, as her winks and nods and gestures yield them,
	Indeed would make one think there might be thought,
	Though nothing sure, yet much unhappily.
HORATIO	'Twere good she were spoken with, for she may strew
	Dangerous conjectures in ill-breeding minds.
GERTRUDE	Let her come in.

Exit GENTLEMAN

	Aside To my sick soul, as sin's true nature is,
	Each toy seems prologue to some great amiss:
	So full of artless jealousy is guilt,
	It spills itself in fearing to be spilt.

Enter OPHELIA distracted

OPHELIA	Where is the beauteous majesty of Denmark?
GERTRUDE	How now, Ophelia!
OPHELIA	*She sings*
	How should I your true love know
	From another one?
	By his cockle hat and staff
	And his sandal shoon.
GERTRUDE	Alas sweet lady, what imports this song?
OPHELIA	Say you? Nay, pray you mark.
	Song
	He is dead and gone, lady,
	He is dead and gone;
	At his head a grass-green turf,
	At his heels a stone.
	Oho!
GERTRUDE	Nay, but, Ophelia –
OPHELIA	Pray you mark.
	Song
	White his shroud as the mountain snow –

Enter KING CLAUDIUS

GERTRUDE	Alas, look here my lord.
OPHELIA	Larded with sweet flowers
	Which bewept to the grave did not go
	With true-love showers.
CLAUDIUS	How do you, pretty lady?

Glossary (right margin):

importunate: persistent, unrelenting
mood: state of mind

5 *hems*: makes 'hmm' noise
in doubt: without clear sense
is nothing: has no meaning
unshapèd: uncontrolled
collection: assemble, put together (meaning)
10 *botch*: patch together badly
Which: her words; *yield*: express

15 *conjectures*: speculations

toy: trivial matter
artless jealousy: inherent distrust
20 *spills*: betrays, destroys

25 *cockle … staff*: as worn by a pilgrim
shoon: shoes
what imports: what is the relevance of
pray you mark: pay attention

30

35

Larded: strewn

40 *showers*: tears

* 6 *Spurns enviously at straws*: spitefully kicks out at trifles
† 9 *they yawn at it*: they have to guess what it means

OPHELIA Well, good dild you! They say the owl was a baker's daughter.
Lord, we know what we are, but know not what we may
be. God be at your table.

CLAUDIUS Conceit upon her father.   45

OPHELIA Pray you, let's have no words of this; but when they ask
you what it means, say you this:

Song

Tomorrow is Saint Valentine's day,
　　All in the morning betime,
And I a maid at your window,   50
　　To be your Valentine.
Then up he rose, and donned his clothes,
　　And dupped the chamber door;
Let in the maid that out a maid
　　Never departed more.   55

CLAUDIUS Pretty Ophelia!

OPHELIA Indeed la! Without an oath, I'll make an end on't:
By Gis and by Saint Charity,
　　Alack and fie for shame,
Young men will do't if they come to't;   60
　　By cock, they are to blame.
Quoth she, 'Before you tumbled me,
　　You promised me to wed.'
He answers –
So would I ha' done, by yonder sun,   65
　　And thou hadst not come to my bed.

CLAUDIUS How long hath she been thus?

OPHELIA I hope all will be well. We must be patient: but I cannot
choose but weep, to think they should lay him i'th'cold
ground. My brother shall know of it, and so I thank you   70
for your good counsel. Come, my coach! Good night,
ladies; good night, sweet ladies, good night, good night.

Exit

CLAUDIUS Follow her close; give her good watch, I pray you.

Exit HORATIO

Oh this is the poison of deep grief; it springs
All from her father's death, and now behold –   75
Oh Gertrude, Gertrude,
When sorrows come, they come not single spies
But in battalions. First, her father slain;
Next, your son gone, and he most violent author
Of his own just remove; the people muddied,   80
Thick and unwholesome in their thoughts and whispers,
For good Polonius' death; –and we have done but greenly
In hugger-mugger to inter him: poor Ophelia
Divided from herself and her fair judgement,
Without the which we are pictures, or mere beasts;   85
Last, and as much containing as all these,
Her brother is in secret come from France,
Feeds on his wonder, keeps himself in clouds,
And wants not buzzers to infect his ear
With pestilent speeches of his father's death,   90
Wherein necessity, of matter beggared,
Will nothing stick our person to arraign†

continued

Glossary (right column)

good dild: God yield, reward

Conceit: fanciful thought

Valentine: patron saint of lovers
betime: early

dupped: opened
maid: young girl, virgin
more: again

end on't: finish it
Gis: Jesus

tumbled: bed

ha': have
And thou: if you

battalions: troops
author: creator
muddied: confused

greenly: foolishly
hugger-mugger: hurried secrecy

Last: final cause of Ophelia's grief

wonder: amazement
wants: lacks; *buzzers*: rumour-mongers

matter beggared: without substance

* 85 *Without the which we are pictures, or
mere beasts*: without judgement we
are but images of ourselves, or mere
beasts (as bodies without souls)

† 92 *Will … arraign*: will stop at nothing
to accuse us

	In ear and ear. O my dear Gertrude, this,	*ear and ear*: to one listener after another
	Like to a murdering piece, in many places	*murdering piece*: weapon
	Gives me superfluous death.	95

A noise within

| GERTRUDE | Alack, what noise is this? |
| CLAUDIUS | Attend! Where are my Swissers? Let them guard the door. | *Swissers*: Swiss soldiers, employed in court |

Enter a MESSENGER

	What is the matter?	
GENTLEMAN	Save yourself, my lord:	
	The ocean, overpeering of his list,	*overpeering ... list*: overflowing his banks
	Eats not the flats with more impituous haste	100 *Eats*: consumes; *impituous*: violent
	Than young Laertes in a riotous head	*head*: onset
	O'erbears your officers. The rabble call him lord,	*rabble*: masses, mob
	And, as the world were now but to begin,	
	Antiquity forgot, custom not known,	
	The ratifiers and props of every word,*	105
	They cry 'Choose we! Laertes shall be king.'	*They*: the rabble
	Caps, hands, and tongues, applaud it to the clouds,	
	'Laertes shall be king, Laertes king!'	
GERTRUDE	How cheerfully on the false trail they cry!	*False ... cry*: like hounds following a scent
	O, this is counter, you false Danish dogs!	110 *counter*: a backward trail, hunting a false scent

Noise within

| CLAUDIUS | The doors are broke. |

Enter LAERTES with others

LAERTES	Where is this king? – Sirs, stand you all without.
ALL	No, let's come in.
LAERTES	I pray you, give me leave.
ALL	We will, we will.	115
LAERTES	I thank you: keep the door.

Exeunt followers

	O thou vile king,	
	Give me my father!	
GERTRUDE	Calmly, good Laertes.	
LAERTES	That drop of blood that's calm proclaims me bastard,	
	Cries cuckold to my father, brands the harlot	
	Even here, between the chaste unsmirched brow	120 *Even here*: in this of all places
	Of my true mother.†	
CLAUDIUS	What is the cause, Laertes,	
	That thy rebellion looks so giant-like? –	
	Let him go, Gertrude, do not fear our person:	
	There's such divinity doth hedge a king,	*hedge*: protect
	That treason can but peep to what it would,‡	125
	Acts little of his will. – Tell me, Laertes,	
	Why thou art thus incensed. – Let him go, Gertrude. –	*incensed*: angry
	Speak man.	
LAERTES	Where is my father?	
CLAUDIUS	Dead.	
GERTRUDE	But not by him.	
CLAUDIUS	Let him demand his fill.	

---

* 105   *ratifiers ... word*: the 'ratifiers' and 'props' are
        'antiquity' and 'custom' – which give authority
        and stability to civilisation

† 118–21 *That drop of blood ... mother*: to be calm in
        these circumstances would prove that I'm not
        my father's son. Such calmness would argue
        that my virtuous mother was actually an
        unfaithful whore, and that Polonius wasn't my
        true father

‡ 125   *peep ... would*: glance at what it would like to
        do

LAERTES	How came he dead? I'll not be juggled with.	130 *juggled with:* deceived
	To hel allegiance, vows to the blackest devil!	
	Conscience and grace to the profoundest pit!	
	I dare damnation. To this point I stand,	*I stand:* I am committed
	That both the worlds I give to negligence,	
	Let come what comes, only I'll be revenged	135
	Most thoroughly for my father.	
CLAUDIUS	Who shall stay you?	*stay:* stop
LAERTES	My will, not all the world.	*will:* decision
	And for my means, I'll husband them so well,	*means:* resources; *husband:* control
	They shall go far with little.	
CLAUDIUS	Good Laertes,	
	If you desire to know the certainty	140
	Of your dear father, is't writ in your revenge	*is't writ:* is it determined
	That, soopstake, you will draw both friend and foe,	*soopstake:* take all in one swoop
	Winner and loser?	
LAERTES	None but his enemies.	
CLAUDIUS	Will you know them then?	
LAERTES	To his good friends thus wide I'll ope my arms,	145 *ope:* open
	And like the kind life-rendering pelican,	
	Repast them with my blood.	*repast:* feed
CLAUDIUS	Why, now you speak	
	Like a good child and a true gentleman.	
	That I am guiltless of your father's death,	
	And am most sensible in grief for it,	150 *most sensible:* most feelingly
	It shall as level to your judgement pierce	*level:* plain, direct
	As day does to your eye.	*Day ... eye:* as daylight enters your eye

A noise within: 'Let her come in'

LAERTES	How now, what noise is that?

Enter OPHELIA

	O heat dry up my brains, tears seven times salt	
	Burn out the sense and virtue of mine eye!	155
	By heaven, thy madness shall be paid by weight,	*paid by weight:* paid for in full measure
	Till our scale turn the beam. O rose of May,	
	Dear maid, kind sister, sweet Ophelia!	
	O heavens, is't possible, a young maid's wits	
	Should be as mortal as an old man's life?	160 *as mortal:* as prone to decay and death
	Nature is fine in love, and where 'tis fine,	
	It sends some precious instance of itself	
	After the thing it loves.	
OPHELIA	*Song*
	They bore him barefaced on the bier	
	Hey non nonny, nonny, hey nonny,	165
	And in his grave rained many a tear –	
	Fare you well, my dove.	

*   134   *both ...:* I care nothing for this world or the next

†   131-6   the contrast here between Laertes and Hamlet in similar circumstances is striking

‡   146   *pelican:* the pelican is a symbol of self-sacrifice: it was believed that the pelican fed her young with the blood from her own breast

§   155   *O heat ... mine eye:* heat is associated with anger. Laertes, on seeing Ophelia's deranged state, asks for anger to dry up his brain, for the brain, associated with the element of water, interprets the senses, which he can no longer tolerate. He asks for his salted (thus scalding) tears to burn out the image of his sister, and to replace his sight (the virtue of his eye) with blinding anger

¶   157   *Till our scale turn the beam:* till our revenge overbalances the harm

**   162-3   *Nature ... loves:* these lines suggest that as human nature, when in love, sends a part of itself after the object of its love, so Ophelia's love is demonstrated by her losing of her mind after the death of her father.

LAERTES	Hadst thou thy wits, and didst persuade revenge,
	It could not move thus.*
OPHELIA	*Song*
	You must sing a-down a-down, and you call him a-down-a. 170
	O, how the wheel becomes it. It is the false steward that
	stole his master's daughter.
LAERTES	This nothing's more than matter.
OPHELIA	There's rosemary, that's for remembrance – pray you, love,
	remember – and there is pansies, that's for thoughts. 175
LAERTES	A document in madness, thoughts and remembrance fitted.
OPHELIA	There's fennel for you, and columbines. There's rue for you,†
	and here's some for me; we may call it herb of grace a
	Sundays. Oh you must wear your rue with a difference.
	There's a daisy. I would give you some violets, but they 180
	withered all when my father died: they say he made a
	good end.
Sings	
	For bonny sweet Robin is all my joy.
LAERTES	Thought and affliction, passion, hell itself,‡
	She turns to favour and to prettiness.
OPHELIA	*Song*
	And will a not come again? 185
	And will a not come again?
	No, no, he is dead,
	Go to thy death-bed:
	He never will come again.
	His beard was as white as snow, 190
	All flaxen was his poll,
	He is gone, he is gone,
	And we cast away moan,
	God-a-mercy on his soul.
	And of all Christian souls, I pray God. God buy you. 195
Exit	
LAERTES	Do you see this, O God?
CLAUDIUS	Laertes, I must commune with your grief,
	Or you deny me right. Go but apart,
	Make choice of whom your wisest friends you will,
	And they shall hear and judge 'twixt you and me. 200
	If by direct or by collateral hand§
	They find us touched, we will our kingdom give,
	Our crown, our life, and all that we can ours,
	To you in satisfaction. But if not,
	Be you content to lend your patience to us,‖ 205
	And we shall jointly labour with your soul
	To give it due content.
LAERTES	Let this be so;
	His means of death, his obscure funeral –
	No trophy, sword, nor hatchment o'er his bones,**
	No noble rite, nor formal ostentation, 210
	Cry to be heard, as 'twere from heaven to earth,
	That I must call't in question.
CLAUDIUS	So you shall.
	And where the offence is, let the great axe fall.
	I pray you go with me.
Exeunt	

matter: without meaning

A document: an instruction

rue: symbol of repentance
violets: symbol of faithfulness

Thought: associated with melancholy

commune with: participate in

whom: whichever among

touched: stained, with guilt

in satisfaction: as recompense

means of death: manner in which he died

ostentation: ceremony

call't in question: demand an explanation

* 169   *could … thus*: could not move me as much as this
† 177   *fennel … columbines*: representing marital infidelity
‡ 183   *hell*: torment
§ 201   *collateral*: (indirect agent) another person's hand
‖ 205   *content …*: wait a while before acting, give us time
** 209   *trophy, sword, nor hatchment*: memorial emblems

| 123

CLAUDIUS, GERTRUDE & LAERTES

Ophelia appears before the queen in a mad and troubled state. She sings fragments of songs about heartbreak and death. The king speaks of the troubles that have befallen the court in recent times, and suggests that the pressure is becoming too much. Laertes storms the castle seeking revenge for his father's death. The king manages to calm him down and says that he will explain the circumstances surrounding Polonius' murder. When Ophelia re-enters the room, Laertes is devastated to see his sister's condition.

A CLOSER LOOK

☙ LINES 1–20: THE QUEEN HEARS OF OPHELIA'S DETERIORATION

A courtier is trying to convince the queen to speak with Ophelia. It seems that Ophelia's mental health has deteriorated and she is acting very strangely. The courtier describes Ophelia's condition to the queen:

- Ophelia 'speaks much of her father' and says that she is hearing talk of deceptions and plots: 'says she hears/ There's tricks i'th' world'. (4–5)
- She makes inarticulate noises and strikes her chest. (5)
- She reacts with suspicion to incidental things ('Spurns enviously at straws') and says things that have no meaning ('speaks things in doubt'). (6)
- Those who hear her speak attempt to make sense of her words, and confuse themselves trying to do so. (8–10)

Horatio suggests to the queen that it is best she see

Ophelia, lest rumours damaging to the royal couple start to circulate in the minds of the people: "Twere good she were spoken with; for she may strew/ Dangerous conjectures in ill-breeding minds'. (14–15)

Just as Ophelia enters, the queen speaks in an 'aside' that seems to reveal she is suffering from a guilty conscience since her encounter with Hamlet. She seems concerned that her paranoia might somehow reveal her sense of guilt to others: 'So full of artless jealousy is guilt,/ It spills itself in fearing to be spilt'. (19–20) However, she does not suggest why she is feeling guilty.

☙ LINES 21–73: OPHELIA'S MADNESS

Ophelia is brought into the room. She seems mentally and emotionally troubled and communicates through fragments of song and enigmatic lines. What she sings and says seems to relate to the recent loss of her father and the demise of her relationship with Hamlet:

- She sings a song that tells the story of a man who seduced a virgin on Valentine's day. (48–55) The song may be making reference to the possibility that she feels betrayed by Hamlet after his declarations of love for her came to nothing.
- She sings another song that describes how young men seduce girls by falsely promising to marry them, but renege after sexual intercourse. (60–6) Again, she may be making an oblique reference to Hamlet.
- She speaks of her grief at Polonius' death: 'I cannot choose but weep, to think they should lay him i'th'cold ground'. (68–70) She warns that Laertes will hear of it ('My brother shall know of it'). (70)
- Her madness is reflected in her farewell: 'Good night, ladies; good night, sweet ladies;/ good night, good night'. (71–2)

Claudius orders her to be followed. (73–4) He is certain that her madness is a result of her deep grief over her father's death. (75–6)

⮥ LINES 74–95: CLAUDIUS IS BEGINNING TO FEEL THE PRESSURE

Left alone with the queen, Claudius expresses sympathy for Ophelia, naming the troubles that have befallen her in recent times: her father's death and the fact that Hamlet was sent away. He laments the fact that troubles always come in groups, never alone. (77–8)

However, Claudius quickly drifts from consideration of Ophelia's griefs to his own. He says that the people of Denmark are growing suspicious over the circumstances of Polonius' death. (80–2) He regrets the fact that Polonius was buried hastily and in secret: 'we have done but greenly/ In hugger-mugger to inter him'. (81–2) The king also mentions how Ophelia's brother has secretly returned from France and is angry at the circumstances of his father's death. Laertes is apparently surrounded by rumour-mongers hostile to Claudius who are feeding him inflammatory stories about recent events: 'And wants not buzzers to infect his ear/ With pestilent speeches of his father's death'. (89–90)

Things are not going too well for the king, and he is starting to feel the pressure. He feels that he is being attacked from many different directions and being killed many times over: 'O my dear Gertrude, this,/ Like to a murdering piece, in many places/ Gives me superfluous death'. (93–5)

⮥ LINES 96–152: LAERTES STORMS THE CASTLE

Just as the king completes his lament, a commotion erupts. Claudius, fearing the worst, calls for his bodyguard. (97) A courtier informs him that Laertes has overcome the king's officers and is leading a popular rebellion: 'The rabble call him lord … They cry "Choose we! Laertes shall be king". (102–6) The queen is disgusted to hear that the Danish people have given their allegiance to Laertes. She considers them to be misguided and confused, like

OPHELIA

AN INNOCENT VICTIM

In this scene we see how recent events have taken their toll on Ophelia. Her father has been killed and his body buried in haste and secrecy. The man she loved was responsible for his death and has now been sent away to England.

It appears that Ophelia has been left alone to suffer these terrible misfortunes. The queen hardly wants to see her at the start of the scene, and the one person who seems to genuinely care for her, Laertes, has been away at university in France.

Whereas Hamlet made a conscious decision to act mad because of his father's murder, Ophelia seems to have actually gone insane since her own father was killed. She sings fragments of songs and hands out flowers to Laertes and the king and queen. When Laertes eventually arrives at Elsinore, he is horrified to see how changed his sister is.

OPHELIA

125

a hunting dog following the wrong scent: 'O, this is counter, you false Danish dogs!' (110)

The doors of the chamber are broken in and an armed Laertes enters with a group of his followers. (111) He asks his men to leave him alone with the royal couple and guard the door outside. (114) He then addresses Claudius angrily, demanding his father's body: 'O thou vile king,/ Give me my father!' (115–16)

The queen asks Laertes to act calmly and attempts to physically restrain him. (117) She says that Claudius was not responsible for Polonius' death. (128) Laertes says that if he were now to be calm, he would not be his father's true son: 'That drop of blood that's calm proclaims me bastard,/ Cries cuckold to my father'. (118–19)

Claudius tells the queen to let go of Laertes. He says that he has no fear of being killed because of his divine status as king. The king's divinity, Claudius states, acts almost like a shield, preventing any would-be assassin from acting: 'There's such divinity doth hedge a king'. (124) He asks Laertes why he is so 'incensed'. (127)

Laertes demands to know the circumstances of Polonius' death. He is desperate for revenge, and says that nothing will prevent him achieving it: 'Let come what comes; only I'll be revenged/ Most thoroughly for my father'. (135–6)

Claudius remains perfectly calm. He asks Laertes if his desire for revenge is so great that he wishes to indiscriminately kill both friends and enemies in his quest. (141–3) Laertes answers that he only desires vengeance on his enemies. The king

praises this sentiment, saying that he is 'guiltless' of Polonius' murder and much agrieved that the man was killed. He promises that these facts will become very clear to Laertes. (147–52)

LINES 153–214: LAERTES SEES OPHELIA

At this moment, Ophelia enters the room with flowers in her hand. Laertes is shocked by the sight of his sister: 'O heat dry up my brains, tears seven times salt/ Burn out the sense and virtue of mine eye!' (154–5) He expresses incredulity that his sister could be transformed so rapidly, and swears vengeance for her madness. (156–63)

Ophelia breaks into song and distributes different flowers to those present in the room. As she hands out the flowers, she mentions what each symbolises: 'There's rosemary: that's for remembrance –pray you, love, remember – and there is pansies, that's for thoughts'. (174–5)

Claudius tells Laertes that he feels his pain at seeing his sister in such a terrible condition. He asks him to gather together some of his wisest and trusted friends so that they may hear the circumstances of Polonius' death and decide whether Claudius is to be held responsible. (197–200) If they find the king guilty, he will forfeit everything to Laertes, including his life. (201–4) If they find him innocent, Laertes will join with Claudius in seeking vengeance: 'Be you content to lend your patience to us,/ And we shall jointly labour with your soul/ To give it due content'. (205–7)

Laertes agrees to the king's proposition. He says that both his father's death and the fact that he was not given an appropriate burial must be accounted for.

LAERTES

VENGEFUL
Laertes reappears in a very dramatic fashion. Enraged at hearing of his father's death and inexplicably quick and undignified burial, he secretly returns from his studies in France to Denmark. Rumours are rife in Denmark that the king had something to do with Polonius' death, and so Laertes quickly gathers together an army of men willing to revolt against Claudius. It seems that it is Laertes' intention to kill the king and seize the throne. In this scene, he manges to storm the castle and gain entry to the king and queen. Only Claudius' composure and carefully measured words prevent the king's death.

Laertes' remarkable action and his adamant desire for revenge stand in sharp contrast with Hamlet's procrastination and lack of action after hearing of his own father's murder. With no greater evidence that Claudius was responsible for his father's death, Laertes has taken it upon himself to storm the castle and kill the king. The rage and desire for bloody vengeance that he feels seems unnatural to Hamlet. The prince has to make an effort to feel such intense anger and even then it seems a short-lived emotion.

A LOVING BROTHER
Not only is Laertes obviously devastated by his father's death, he is brutally exposed without any forewarning to the sight of his sister's insanity. What he says seems to reveal how genuinely and deeply he cared for her: 'O heat, dry up my brain, tears seven times salt/ Burn out the sense and virtue of mine eye!' (154–5)

CHARACTER DEVELOPMENT

CHARACTER DEVELOPMENT

CLAUDIUS

ANXIOUS AND FEARFUL

Although Hamlet has been sent away to England where he is to be executed, Claudius' anxieties and fears for his kingship have not abated. Polonius' death and his hasty and secret burial have resulted in rumours counter to the king spreading throughout Denmark. There is also talk of Laertes having returned from France and of a planned revolt. Despite his consumate political skill, Claudius seems to be unable to control the mood and thoughts of his people. The pressure of recent events is almost too much for him. Left alone with his wife, he allows himself to lament his misfortunes: 'O my dear Gertrude, this,/ Like to a murdering piece, in many places/ Gives me superfluous death'. (93–5)

CALM AND COMPOSED

However, just as things seem to be getting too much for the king, he is given an opportunity to face down his greatest immediate threat. When Laertes storms into the palace accompanied by armed men and threatening violence, the king is the model of self-assured calm and right-eousness. He displays no fear in the face of possible death, and is certain of the sanctity of his position: 'Let him go, Gertrude, do not fear our person:/ There's such divinity doth hedge a king'. (123–4)

A SHREWD POLITICIAN

By letting Laertes give expression to his anger and determination for vengeance, Claudius diffuses a potentially fatal situation. He asks Laertes a series of short questions that makes the latter realise he has no proof of the king's guilt. Through his calm and soothing performance, he placates Laertes and becomes almost patronising in his manner toward the bereaved son: 'Why, now you speak/ Like a good child and a true gentleman./ That I am guilt-less of your father's death'. (146–8) It is an extraordinarily confident and impressive performance from a man under so much pressure.

MANIPULATIVE

Claudius is finally rescued from any possible danger by the reappearance of Ophelia. Laertes is so distraught by the sight of his sister that the king is able to suggest a means by which his innocence can be proven. He proposes that Laertes' wisest friends should question him in order to discover if he is indeed responsible for Polonius' death. He appears to be thoroughly genuine in his suggestion, offering to renounce the kingdom, the throne and his own life if found guilty. (199–204)

GERTRUDE

UNSYMPATHETIC?

Gertrude's behaviour continues to be ambiguous. At the beginning of the scene she seems to heartlessly refuse to see Ophelia. Her refusal may be due to the fact that she is still in a state of confusion and uncertainty after her confrontation with Hamlet, and cannot face what she knows will be a difficult meeting. The descrip-tion of Ophelia's madness must also strike her as bearing an uncanny resemblance to Hamlet's ranting: 'She speaks much of her father, says she hears/ There's tricks i'th'world'. (4–5) Only when Horatio tells her it is in her best political interest to grant an audience to Ophelia does she agree to speak with her.

A GUILTY CONSCIENCE?

That the queen may be starting to feel culpability about her marriage to Claudius is suggested by her short reflection on guilty souls: 'So full of artless jealousy is guilt,/ It spills itself in fearing to be spilt'. (19–20) She may be worried that she will say something to Ophelia in front of her courtiers that will reveal her fears and suspicions.

A LOYAL QUEEN

Whatever doubts or guilty feelings she may have been experiencing regarding her marriage to Claudius seem quickly forgotten, however, upon learning of the popular Danish insurrection in support of Laertes. She immediately expresses her contempt for the people and her loyalty to the king: 'How cheer-fully on the false trail they cry!/ O, this is counter, you false Danish dogs!' (109–10)

In addition, when Laertes threatens the king, she restrains him in a bid to protect her husband. When Claudius tells Laertes that Polonius is dead, she immediately adds: 'But not by him'. (128) It seems that Hamlet's accusations have not been strong enough to overcome her instinctive loyalty to the king.

SOME LINES TO LEARN

So full of artless jealousy is guilt,
It spills itself in fearing to be spilt
Gertrude (19–20)

When sorrows come, they come not single spies
But in battalions
Claudius (77–8)

There's such divinity doth hedge a king
That treason can peep to what it would,
Acts little of his will
Claudius (124–6)

Enter HORATIO with an ATTENDANT

HORATIO   What are they that would speak with me?

ATTENDANT   Sailors, sir: they say they have letters for you.

HORATIO   Let them come in.

Exit Attendant

I do not know from what part of the world
I should be greeted, if not from Lord Hamlet.   5

Enter Sailors

FIRST SAILOR   God bless you, sir.

HORATIO   Let him bless thee too.

FIRST SAILOR   A shall sir, and please him. There's a letter for you sir, it
came from th'ambassador that was bound for England, if
your name be Horatio, as I am let to know it is.   10

HORATIO   *Reads the letter*   'Horatio, when thou shalt have overlooked
this, give these fellows some means to the king; they have
letters for him. Ere we were two days old at sea, a pirate
of very warlike appointment gave us chase. Finding
ourselves too slow of sail, we put on a compelled valour,   15
and in the grapple I boarded them. On the instant they
got clear of our ship, so I alone became their prisoner.
They have dealt with me like thieves of mercy, but they
knew what they did: I am to do a good turn for them. Let
the king have the letters I have sent, and repair thou to   20
me with as much speed as thou wouldest fly death. I have
words to speak in thine ear will make thee dumb, yet are
they much too light for the bore of the matter. These
good fellows will bring theewhere I am. Rosencrantz and
Guildenstern hold their course for England. Of them I   25
have much to tell thee. Farewell.

    He that thou knowest thine,
       HAMLET.'
Come, I will give you way for these your letters;
And do't the speedier, that you may direct me   30
To him from whom you brought them.

Exeunt

overlooked: read
means: access

appointment: purpose
compelled valour: forced courage

thieves of mercy: they treated me well

repair: return
in thine ear: in private

*22   much too light for the bore of the
matter*: Hamlet's words are unable to
match the enormity of what he has
to relate

HORATIO

A KEY MOMENT

The unexpected intervention by the pirates has upset Claudius' carefully laid plans. Thanks to his being taken hostage, Hamlet has now returned to Denmark. Given his apparently new streak of courage and impulsiveness, we wait to see if he will take swift action against his father's murderer.

A group of sailors delivers a letter to Horatio from Hamlet. In the letter the prince tells how his ship was attacked by pirates en route to England. Hamlet boarded the pirates' ship and seems to have somehow negotiated his return to Denmark. He has also written to the king to inform him of his return.

A CLOSER LOOK

LINES 1–31: HAMLET HAS MANAGED TO RETURN TO DENMARK

A group of sailors arrive at the castle bearing a letter for Horatio. The letter is from Hamlet. It tells of dramatic events that occured as Hamlet was sailing to England.

The ship carrying Hamlet to England was at sea for two days when it was pursued by a pirate vessel. Unable to escape, the Danish ship was forced to give combat. During the fight, Hamlet single-handedly boarded the pirates' ship, but became a prisoner once the ships disengaged. (15–18) He was treated well, however, and has presumably struck a deal for his release. It seems that the prince is back ashore in Denmark. The sailors are also carrying letters for Claudius, and Hamlet tells Horatio that once he has read his news he should give the sailors access to the king. (12–13)

Hamlet instructs Horatio to come to him, telling him to go with the sailors when they are returning. (20) He says that he has momentous news that he cannot write in the letter ('I have words to speak in thine ear will make thee dumb' (21–2)). He also tells Horatio that Rosencrantz and Guildenstern are still on course for England, and that he has news of them. (24–5) Horatio tells the sailors that he will bring them to Claudius and that he will accompany them on their return journey to Hamlet. (29–31)

CHARACTER DEVELOPMENT

HAMLET

RUTHLESS

In Act 4 Scene 4 Hamlet vowed that he would look to act in a more ruthless and decisive manner. In this scene we hear how the ship he was aboard en route to England was attacked by pirates. Hamlet's letter to Horatio tells how he single-handedly fought his way onto the pirates' ship. He then somehow managed to arrange to be brought back to Denmark.

Enter CLAUDIUS and LAERTES

CLAUDIUS	Now must your conscience my acquittance seal,
	And you must put me in your heart for friend,
	Sith you have heard, and with a knowing ear,
	That he which hath your noble father slain
	Pursued my life.[*]
LAERTES	It well appears: but tell me
	Why you proceeded not against these feats,
	So crimeful and so capital in nature,
	As by your safety, wisdom, all things else.
	You mainly were stirred up.
CLAUDIUS	Oh for two special reasons,
	Which may to you, perhaps, seem much unsinewed,
	But yet to me they are strong. The queen his mother
	Lives almost by his looks, and for myself,
	My virtue or my plague, be it either which,
	She's so conjunctive to my life and soul,
	That, as the star moves not but in his sphere,
	I could not but by her. The other motive,
	Why to a public count I might not go,
	Is the great love the general gender bear him,
	Who, dipping all his faults in their affection,
	Work like the spring that turneth wood to stone,
	Convert his gyves to graces, so that my arrows,
	Too slightly timbered for so loud a wind,
	Would have reverted to my bow again,
	And not where I had aimed them.
LAERTES	And so have I a noble father lost,
	A sister driven into desperate terms,
	Whose worth, if praises may go back again,
	Stood challenger on mount of all the age
	For her perfections. But my revenge will come.[†]
CLAUDIUS	Break not your sleeps for that. You must not think
	That we are made of stuff so flat and dull
	That we can let our beard be shook with danger[‡]
	And think it pastime. You shortly shall hear more.[§]
	I loved your father, and we love ourself,
	And that I hope will teach you to imagine –

my acquittance seal: confirm my innocence
you … friend: you must trust I'm your friend
knowing: knowledgeable

5   *It well appears*: so it seems
feats: wicked deeds
crimeful: criminal; *capital*: punishable by death

mainly: mightily

10   *unsinewed*: weak, without force

by his looks: for him

conjunctive: closely connected
15   *sphere*: the fixed orbit of each planet

count: reckoning, trial
general gender: ordinary kind

20

gyves to graces: fetters to honours
slightly timbered: light; *loud*: the mob's clamour
reverted: returned (to harm me)

25

terms: circumstances
back again: to what she used to be

30   *Break … sleeps*: do not worry about that
flat and dull: insipid

35

[*]   1–5   This scene returns to the conversation between Laertes and the king, which was broken off at the end of Act 4 Scene 5; in the interval, the king, it seems, has given Laertes an account of Hamlet's misdeeds

[†]   28–9   *Stood challenger … perfections*: her worth was plain for all to see, and her perfections had no equal in all time

[‡]   32   *let our beard be shook with danger*: let danger come so close

[§]   33   *You shortly shall hear more*: presumably, Claudius is thinking of the expected news from England that Hamlet is killed

Enter a MESSENGER with letters

How now? what news?

MESSENGER   Letters, my lord, from Hamlet.
This to your majesty, this to the queen.

CLAUDIUS   From Hamlet? Who brought them?

MESSENGER   Sailors my lord they say, I saw them not;
They were given me by Claudio – he received them   40
Of him that brought them.

CLAUDIUS   Laertes, you shall hear them. –
Leave us.

Exit MESSENGER

Reads 'High and mighty, You shall know I am set naked on
your kingdom. Tomorrow shall I beg leave to see your
kingly eyes, when I shall, first asking your pardon   45
thereunto, recount th'occasion of my sudden and more
strange return.
          HAMLET.'
What should this mean? Are all the rest come back?
Or is it some abuse, and no such thing?   50

LAERTES   Know you the hand?

CLAUDIUS   'Tis Hamlet's character. Naked?
And in a postscript here he says alone.
Can you devise me?

LAERTES   I'm lost in it my lord. But let him come –
It warms the very sickness in my heart   55
That I shall live and tell him to his teeth,
'Thus didest thou!'

CLAUDIUS   If it be so, Laertes –
As how should it be so? – how otherwise? –*
Will you be ruled by me?

LAERTES   Ay, my lord;
So you will not o'errule me to a peace.†   60

CLAUDIUS   To thine own peace. If he be now returned,‡
As checking at his voyage, and that he means
No more to undertake it, I will work him
To an exploit, now ripe in my device,
Under the which he shall not choose but fall,   65
And for his death no wind of blame shall breathe,
But even his mother shall uncharge the practice
And call it accident.

LAERTES   My lord, I will be ruled;
The rather if you could devise it so
That I might be the organ.

CLAUDIUS   It falls right.   70
You have been talked of since your travel much,
And that in Hamlet's hearing, for a quality
Wherein they say you shine. Your sum of parts
Did not together pluck such envy from him
As did that one, and that in my regard   75
Of the unworthiest siege.

naked: stripped of his belongings

abuse: deception

character: handwriting
postscript: appendix
devise: give me help

checking at: stopping short

ripe in my device: fully thought out in my plan

uncharge: find no blame, exonerate

the organ: the agent

sum of parts: all your talents

siege: rank

*   58   *As how should it be so? how otherwise?:* These questions indicate Claudius' bewilderment between thinking Hamlet cannot have returned and that he has

†   60   *So you will not o'errule me to a peace:* provided that you will not counteract my desire for revenge by ruling me to a peaceful reconciliation

‡   61   *thine … peace:* peace of mind, achieved by reprisal

LAERTES		What part is that my lord?
CLAUDIUS	A very riband in the cap of youth,	

CLAUDIUS A very riband in the cap of youth,
Yet needful too, for youth no less becomes
The light and careless livery that it wears
Than settled age his sables and his weeds
Importing health and graveness. Two months since
Here was a gentleman of Normandy.
I've seen myself, and served against, the French,
And they can well on horseback, but this gallant
Had witchcraft in't; he grew unto his seat;
And to such wondrous doing brought his horse,
As he had been incorpsed and demi-natured
With the brave beast. So far he topp'd my thought,*
That I, in forgery of shapes and tricks†
Come short of what he did.

LAERTES   A Norman was't?

CLAUDIUS A Norman.

LAERTES Upon my life, Lamond.

CLAUDIUS   The very same.

LAERTES I know him well, he is the brooch indeed
And gem of all the nation.

CLAUDIUS He made confession of you,
And gave you such a masterly report
For art and exercise in your defence,
And for your rapier most especial,
That he cried out, 'twould be a sight indeed
If one could match you. Th'escrimers of their nation‡
He swore had had neither motion, guard, nor eye,
If you opposed them. Sir, this report of his
Did Hamlet so envenom with his envy
That he could nothing do but wish and beg
Your sudden coming o'er to play with you.
Now out of this, –

LAERTES   What out of this, my lord?

CLAUDIUS Laertes, was your father dear to you?
Or are you like the painting of a sorrow,
A face without a heart?

LAERTES   Why ask you this?

CLAUDIUS Not that I think you did not love your father,
But that I know love is begun by time,
And that I see, in passages of proof,
Time qualifies the spark and fire of it.
There lives within the very flame of love
A kind of wick or snuff that will abate it,
And nothing is at a like goodness still,§
For goodness, growing to a pleurisy,
Dies in his own too much. That we would do
We should do when we would, for this 'would' changes,
And hath abatements and delays as many

80
85
90
95
100
105
110
115
120

continued

very riband: mere ribbon

livery: garments
sables and his weeds: sober clothes, fur-lined
Importing health: signifying prosperity

can well: have great skill
witchcraft in't: more than natural skill

topp'd ... thought: surpassed my estimate

Come short: didn't measure up

brooch: honour

confession: tell

defence: fencing and sword play
rapier: slender, long-bladed sword

escrimers: fencers
motion, guard, nor eye: fencing moves

envenom: make poisonous

play: fight with swords

painting: image, without substance

begun ... time: created by a progress of events
passages of proof: incidents that prove
qualifies: makes less absolute, moderates

snuff: charred part of the wick; *abate*: end

pleurisy: disease linked to excess
too much: excess
when we would: when we have the will to
abatements: diminutions of will and energy

* 88   *As he had been incorpsed ... brave beast*: as if he had grown to share one body with the beast, and so become half-man and half-beast, like a centaur

† 89   *forgery ... tricks*: fabrication of postures and feats

‡ 100   *If one could match you*: if an equal opponent could be found

§ 116   *nothing is at a like goodness still*: nothing remains at the same level of goodness, unchanged

As there are tongues, are hands, are accidents;*
And then this 'should' is like a spendthrift sigh,†
That hurts by easing. But, to the quick o' th'ulcer –‡
Hamlet comes back; what would you undertake
To show yourself in deed your father's son   125   *deed*: action
More than in words?

LAERTES   To cut his throat i'th'church.§

CLAUDIUS   No place indeed should murder sanctuarize;   *sanctuarize*: give sanctuary to
Revenge should have no bounds. But good Laertes,   *bounds*: limits
Will you do this, keep close within your chamber;
Hamlet, returned, shall know you are come home;   130
We'll put on those shall praise your excellence,   *put on*: arrange
And set a double varnish on the fame
The Frenchman gave you; bring you in fine together,   *in fine*: finally
And wager on your heads. He being remiss,   *remiss*: careless
Most generous, and free from all contriving,   135   *generous*: magnanimous, large-minded
Will not peruse the foils, so that with ease,   *peruse … foils*: scrutinise the blunt swords
Or with a little shuffling, you may choose
A sword unbated, and in a pass of practice   *unbated*: as distinct from a blunt foil
Requite him for your father.   *Requite*: revenge

LAERTES   I will do't,
And, for that purpose I'll anoint my sword.   140   *anoint*: smear
I bought an unction of a mountebank,₵
So mortal that but dip a knife in it,   *mortal*: deadly
Where it draws blood no cataplasm so rare,   *cataplasm*: poultice, compress
Collected from all simples that have virtue   *simples …*: medicinal herbs
Under the moon, can save the thing from death   145
That is but scratched withal: I'll touch my point   *point*: point of his sword
With this contagion, that, if I gall him slightly,   *gall*: graze
It may be death.

CLAUDIUS   Let's further think of this,
Weigh what convenience both of time and means   *Weigh*: consider carefully
May fit us to our shape. If this should fail,   150   *shape*: the role we're going to play
And that our drift look through our bad performance,   *that*: in case; *drift*: intention
'Twere better not assayed: therefore this project   *assayed*: attempted
Should have a back or second, that might hold**   *hold*: succeed
If this should blast in proof. Soft, let me see.††
We'll make a solemn wager on your cunnings –   155   *cunnings*: respective skills in fencing
I ha't!
When in your motion you are hot and dry,
As make your bouts more violent to that end,   *bouts*: attacks
And that he calls for drink, I'll have prepared him
A chalice for the nonce, whereon but sipping,   160   *nonce*: occasion
If he by chance escape your venomed stuck,   *venomed stuck*: thrust with poisoned sword
Our purpose may hold there. But stay, what noise?

Enter GERTRUDE

How, sweet queen!

---

* 121   *tongues … accidents*: people and events that
        deter us
† 122   *'should' is like a spendthrift sigh … hurts
        by easing*: to speak of 'should' is like a sigh
        that wastes life, damaging the person whilst
        easing the conscience. (Sighs were thought to
        draw life-blood from the heart.)
‡ 123   *quick o' th'ulcer*: the point of the diseased
        matter
§ 126   *To cut his throat i' the church*: contrast
        Hamlet's reluctance to kill Claudius while he
        was praying (Act 3 Scene 3, line 87)
₵ 141   *unction … mountebank*: ointment from a
        quack
** 153 *Should have a back or second*: should have an
        alternative plan
†† 154 *blast in proof*: if this should fail when put to
        the test, like a cannon that explodes when it
        is tested by being fired

GERTRUDE	One woe doth tread upon another's heel,	
	So fast they follow, your sister's drowned, Laertes.	165
LAERTES	Drowned! Oh where?	
GERTRUDE	There is a willow grows aslant a brook,	

GERTRUDE   There is a willow grows aslant a brook,
That shows his hoar leaves in the glassy stream.
Therewith fantastic garlands did she make
Of crow-flowers, nettles, daisies, and long purples, *   170
That liberal shepherds give a grosser name,
But our cold maids do dead men's fingers call them.
There, on the pendent boughs her cronet weeds
Clamb'ring to hang, an envious sliver broke,†
When down her weedy trophies and herself   175
Fell in the weeping brook. Her clothes spread wide,
And mermaid-like awhile they bore her up,
Which time she chanted snatches of old lauds
As one incapable of her own distress,
Or like a creature native and indued   180
Unto that element. But long it could not be†
Till that her garments, heavy with their drink,
Pulled the poor wretch from her melodious lay
To muddy death.

LAERTES   Alas, then, she is drown'd?
GERTRUDE   Drowned, drowned.   185
LAERTES   Too much of water hast thou, poor Ophelia,
And therefore I forbid my tears. But yet
It is our trick; nature her custom holds,
Let shame say what it will. When these are gone,
The woman will be out. Adieu, my lord,§   190
I have a speech of fire, that fain would blaze,
But that this folly douts it.

Exit

CLAUDIUS   Let's follow, Gertrude.
How much I had to do to calm his rage!
Now fear I this will give it start again.
Therefore let's follow.

Exeunt

---

willow: symbol of forsaken love

his hoar: its silver (underside colour of leaves)

cold maids: chaste, modest maids

cronet: shaped like a wreath or crown

lauds: hymns

incapable: unable to comprehend

our trick: the way of humankind, to shed tears

these: these tears

of fire: of manly anger

folly douts: crying extinguishes

follow: react in the same way

---

* 170   *Of crow-flowers ... long purples*: but-
        tercups ... purple orchises

† 173–4 *There, on the pendent boughs ...
        envious sliver broke*: by tradition,
        the willow is a tree representing lost
        love from which those who mourn
        make garlands that they then hang
        like monuments. To paraphrase
        Gertrude's lyrical unfolding of how
        Ophelia's dies, when climbing the
        drooping branches of the Willow
        tree in order to hang her wreath of
        weeds, the silver branch broke and
        Ophelia fell into the brook

‡ 180–1 *indued/ Unto that element*: endowed
        with the qualities that would make
        water her natural element

§ 190   *The woman will be out*: when these
        unmanly tears are shed, the female-
        like side of my nature will cease to
        appear

LAERTES & CLAUDIUS

The king has convinced Laertes that Hamlet was responsible for Polonius' death. He explains that he could not punish Hamlet properly for the crime because of his love for Gertrude and also because of the Danish people's affection for the prince.

A letter is brought to the king from Hamlet telling how the prince has returned to Denmark. Claudius quickly devises a plan to have Hamlet killed. He will arrange to have Hamlet and Laertes fight a fencing match in which Laertes' sword will be sharp instead of blunt. Laertes, hungry for revenge for his father's death, agrees to the plan and says that he will coat his sword with poison. The king also decides that he will have a cup of poisoned wine to hand that he will give to Hamlet during the fight.

Gertrude arrives with news that Ophelia has drowned.

A CLOSER LOOK

LINES 1–35: CLAUDIUS WINS OVER LAERTES

In Act 4 Scene 5 Claudius promised Laertes that he would explain the circumstances of his father's death, thereby proving his own innocence in the matter. This scene begins with Claudius having just given an account of Polonius' murder. The king has told Laertes how Hamlet killed Polonius. He says that Hamlet also attempted to kill him: 'Sith you have heard, and with a knowing ear,/ That he which hath your noble father slain/ Pursued my life'. (3–4) Claudius tells Laertes that he must now consider the king his friend: 'you must put me in your heart for friend'. (2)

Laertes believes what the king tells him, but he wonders why, if Hamlet is guilty of murder, he has not been appropriately punished (5–6)

Claudius gives him two reasons:

CLAUDIUS

MANIPULATIVE
In this scene we see just how effectively Claudius can manipulate others to suit his own interests. The king has carefully convinced Laertes that he was not responsible for Polonius' death. He has also clearly explained that Hamlet is guilty of the crime. He tells Laertes that they share a common enemy in Hamlet, and that they should therefore be friends.

When Claudius receives Hamlet's letter telling how the prince has returned to Denmark, the king needs to quickly think of a way to deal with the situation. Not wanting to bloody his hands with the deed, he sees how he can effectively use Laertes' grief and anger to get the job done. To ensure that Laertes will go through with his plan, he pushes him regarding his feelings for his father. He carefully stokes Laertes' need for revenge by suggesting that he might only be pretending to grieve Polonius' death. He is also careful to not get Laertes too worked up, knowing that things can easily go wrong if emotions are running too high. It is for this very reason that he is annoyed at the end of the scene. Having carefully brought Laertes to the right temperament to go through with his plan, he fears that news of Ophelia's death will cause him to be violently angry and act in a rash and reckless manner.

CALM AND COMPOSED
Once again, Claudius is faced with something of a crisis, and once again he responds in a calm and collected manner. When he receives the letter from Hamlet telling how the prince has returned to Denmark, Claudius is obviously shocked. However, he quickly thinks of a way of dealing with the situation. His plan to have Hamlet fence with Laertes, should it succeed, will not only result in Hamlet's death but will appear a tragic accident.

LOVE FOR GERTRUDE
When Laertes asks why Claudius has not taken action already against Hamlet, one of the reasons the king gives him is that the prince is so beloved of Gertrude that he would not harm him for her sake: 'She's so conjunctive to my life and soul,/ That, as the star moves but not in his sphere,/ I could not but by her'. (14–16) We must wonder, however, just how much the king actually loves his wife. So much of what Claudius does is out of self-interest that we have to question whether he simply wooed her as a means to gain the throne. He is confident that his new scheme will deceive even his queen: 'But even his mother shall uncharge the practice/ And call it accident'. (66–7)

HEARTLESS AND COLD
This scene also shows us Claudius' total insensitivity to other people's feelings. Laertes is devastated by the news of Ophelia's death and has to leave the chamber. The only thing that Claudius can think about is how his anger may upset their scheme to have Hamlet murdered: 'How much I had to do to calm his rage!/ Now fear I this will give it start again'. (193–4) He shows no empathy for Laertes' grief, and can think only of himself.

This repeats a trend begun at the start of the play. He could not understand Hamlet's reaction toward his mother's grief, nor later did he appear to show any sorrow over the death of Polonius. Claudius uses the emotions felt by those around him as a means by which to further his own ends.

LAERTES

VENGEFUL
Laertes is burning with desire to avenge his father's death and his sister's madness. Once he has satisfied himself as to Claudius' innocence in both affairs, he readily joins the king's scheme to have Hamlet murdered. He even says that he would be willing to cut the prince's throat in a church, such is his violent need for revenge. This is in stark contrast to Hamlet's hesitation when he found Claudius at prayer and declined to take advantage of a perfect opportunity to take his revenge. When the king describes his plan to have Laertes and Hamlet fight a fencing match, Laertes proposes to coat the tip of his sword with poison in order to ensure the prince's death.

A LOVING BROTHER
As well as having to cope with his father's death, Laertes now has to deal with the loss of his sister. In spite of his attempt to not cry ('I forbid my tears'), he cannot control his grief. However, though his grief is obviously genuine and heartfelt, we have to question the way that Laertes treated Ophelia when she was alive. Seeing her in a mad and troubled state upon his return to Elsinore, Laertes lamented her condition but did not actually do anything to comfort or help her. When his sister seemed most in need of loving support, Laertes chose to remain with the king, listening to him speak of Polonius' death and plotting Hamlet's murder. All the while Ophelia was wandering alone outside the castle.

- Gertrude loves Hamlet dearly and Claudius claims that he loves his wife so much that he will not harm his stepson for her sake: 'She's so conjunctive to my life and soul/ That, as the star moves not but in his sphere,/ I could not but by her'. (14–16)
- Hamlet is much loved by the Danish people. (18) A public trial would be very unpopular and possibly threaten Claudius' reign. The people would forgive Hamlet anything and a prosecution on Claudius' part would backfire badly. (21–4)

Laertes is outraged that his personal misfortunes should go unanswered. He has lost a father and has had a sister 'driven into desperate terms'. (25–6) Knowing that Hamlet is being sent to England seems scant justice for the crime committed. Laertes vows to avenge the deeds himself: 'But my revenge will come'. (29)

Claudius has not, of course, only sent Hamlet to England; he has also arranged for him to be killed when he arrives. However, the king has not told Laertes that this will happen. But still he does not wish Laertes to think that he has been casual and soft in his dealings with the whole affair: 'you must not think/ That we are made of stuff so flat and dull/ That we can let our beard be shook with danger/ And think it pastime'. (30–3) He tells Laertes that his revenge will come and that he will learn more about this shortly. (33–5)

LINES 36–57: CLAUDIUS LEARNS OF HAMLET'S RETURN

A messenger arrives with letters from Hamlet. He tells the king how sailors delivered them to the palace. The king is surprised at the news. He opens a letter and reads it to Laertes. The letter informs the king that the prince is back in Denmark without any of his belongings: 'I am set naked on your kingdom'. (43–4) Hamlet also writes that he will meet with the king tomorrow and explain his 'sudden and most strange return'. (46–7)

Claudius is puzzled by the letter, and wonders if Hamlet is deceiving him. (46–7) He seeks Laertes' opinion about the matter. (53) Laertes admits to being puzzled also, but is glad that Hamlet is returning. (54) He intends to confront the prince and kill him in revenge for Polonius' death and Ophelia's madness: 'It warms the very sickness in my heart/ that I shall live and tell him to his teeth, "Thus didest thou!"' (55–7)

LINES 57–162: CLAUDIUS CREATES A NEW PLAN TO KILL HAMLET

Claudius knows that he needs to take control of the situation. It is important that Hamlet be dealt with properly. The king does not need Laertes to pursue reckless vengeance and cause an even greater mess than already exists. He therefore asks Laertes if he will follow his command in dealing with Hamlet: 'Will you be ruled by me?' (59) Laertes says that he will.

The king quickly thinks of a way to have Hamlet killed that will appear like an accident. (64–8) He will lure Hamlet into a fencing match with Laertes. Fencing contests are fought with blunt swords so as to avoid injury to the participants, but Claudius plans to have Laertes fight with a sharpened rapier. He is confident that Hamlet will not notice that Laertes has chosen a deadly weapon, as he is 'most generous and free from all contriving'. (135) When the two join in combat, Laertes will kill Hamlet: 'in a pass of practise/ Requite him for your father'. (138–9)

The king is confident that Hamlet will agree to the fencing match because he knows how the prince envies Laertes' skills. Claudius tells how a great French horseman named Lamord recently praised Laertes' fencing skills, saying that he was more skilled than any fencer in France. (81–98) Hamlet heard report of Lamord's opinion and was filled with envy. The king says that the prince wished and begged that Laertes would return from France so that they might compete in a fencing match. (103–5)

Claudius wants to make sure that Laertes will go through with the plan to kill the prince. He asks Laertes if he really loved his father or if his grief is merely a show. (107–9) He says that he does not doubt that Laertes loved Polonius, only that time can have a softening effect on love: 'love is begun by time; And that I see, in passages of proof,/ Time qualifies the spark and fire of it'. (111–13) There is also within love a quality that brings about a lessening in its intensity; the emotion cannot remain at the same pitch forever: 'There lives within the flame of love/ A kind of wick or snuff that will abate it,/ And nothing is at a like goodness still'. (114–16) Therefore, the king tells Laertes, we should act when we must and when we say we will, as failure to do so will lead to endless delays and procrastination. (118–23)

Claudius asks Laertes what he is prepared to do to prove the reality of his grief. (124–6)

Laertes replies by saying that he is willing 'To cut his [Hamlet's] throat i'th'church'. (126)

The king then asks him to remain in his quarters until the time for action arrives. (129) When Hamlet returns to Elsinore, he will be told that Laertes is present and will have to listen to the king's courtiers praise the latter's fencing skills even more lavishly than Lamord did. (131–3) Hamlet will be so stirred by this that he will agree to the two of them having a fencing match.

Laertes agrees immediately to the plan: 'I will do't'. (139) He even has his own suggestion: he has bought a deadly ointment and will smear the tip of his sword with it in order to ensure Hamlet's death: 'I'll touch my point/ With this contagion, that, if I gall him slightly,/ It may be death'. (146–8)

Claudius likes this idea. But he wants to be absolutely sure that the plan to kill Hamlet succeeds. Should the plan fail, there could be terrible consequences. In order to ensure Hamlet will fight, the king will make a bet on the outcome of the fight. (155) And

just in case the poison-tipped sword does not kill the prince, Claudius decides that he will prepare a cup of poisoned wine. He believes that in the heat of combat, Hamlet will call for refreshments. When this happens, the king will hand the prince the poisoned cup. (158–61)

LINES 162–95: THE QUEEN ARRIVES WITH NEWS OF OPHELIA'S DEATH

The queen arrives with news that Ophelia has drowned. (164–5) Laertes is devastated: 'Drown'd! O, where?' (166) Gertrude recounts the circumstances of his sister's death.

Ophelia climbed out upon the branch of a willow tree overhanging a stream in order to hang a garland of flowers on the end of the branch. However, the branch broke and she fell into the water. She floated in the water for a while, singing and oblivious to the danger she was in. (178–9) After a while, however, the water dragged her down and she drowned: 'but long it could not be/ Till that her garments, heavy with their drink,/ Pulled the poor wretch from her melodious lay/ To muddy death'. (181–4)

Laertes attempts to hold back his tears, but he cannot. He has to leave the room, his grief preventing him from expressing his anger toward Hamlet: 'Adieu, my lord,/ I have a speech of fire, that fain would blaze,/ But that this folly douts it'. (190–2)

Claudius expresses no sympathy for Ophelia or Laertes. He can only think that Laertes' grief and rage may interfere with their new plan to have Hamlet murdered: 'How much I had to do to calm his rage!/ Now fear I this will give it start again'. (193–4)

SOME LINES TO LEARN

She's so conjunctive to my life and soul,
That, as the star moves not but in his sphere,
I could not by her
                                    Claudius (14–16)

I know love is begun by time,
And that I see, in passages of proof,
Time qualifies the spark and fire of it.
There lives within the very flame of love
A kind of wick or snuff that will abate it
                                    Claudius (111–15)

I forbid my tears. But yet
It is our trick; nature her custom holds,
Let shame say what it will. When these are gone,
The woman will be out.
                                    Laertes (187–90)

CHARACTER DEVELOPMENT

OPHELIA

AN INNOCENT VICTIM

Ophelia's death is the culmination of her tragic fate in the play. In the atmosphere of intrigue and deception that dominates Elsinore, she was the only figure who acted naturally and spoke what she felt. Unfortunately, nobody seemed to care enough about her. Hamlet, the man who swore he loved her, treated her extremely badly, seemingly using her to vent his anger and disgust at his own mother. He then murdered her father. Polonius was subsequently buried in a rushed manner, preventing Ophelia from being able to grieve in the proper manner. When he was alive, Polonius used her as a prop in his plan to prove to the king that Hamlet's madness stemmed from his love for Ophelia. Laertes was away in France and came back too late to save his sister from falling into madness. When eventually he returned from France, he did not spend any time with his sister, spending his time instead in plotting to overthrow the king, and then scheming with Claudius to kill Hamlet.

ACT 5 SCENE 1

A graveyard near the castle

Enter two CLOWNS (gravediggers)

CLOWN	Is she to be buried in Christian burial when she wilfully seeks her own salvation?*
OTHER	I tell thee she is: and therefore make her grave straight: the crowner hath sat on her, and finds it Christian burial.†
CLOWN	How can that be, unless she drowned herself in her own defence?
OTHER	Why, 'tis found so.
CLOWN	It must be se offendendo; it cannot be else. For here lies‡ the point: if I drown myself wittingly, it argues an act: and an act hath three branches – it is to act, to do, to perform. Argal, she drowned herself wittingly.
OTHER	Nay, but hear you goodman delver –
CLOWN	Give me leave. Here lies the water – good. Here stands the man – good. If the man go to this water and drown himself, it is will he, nill he, he goes – mark you that. But if the water come to him, and drown him, he drowns not himself. Argal, he that is not guilty of his own death shortens not his own life.
OTHER	But is this law?
CLOWN	Ay, marry, is't; crowner's quest law.
OTHER	Will you ha' the truth on't? If this had not been a gentle woman, she should have been buried out o' Christian burial.
CLOWN	Why, there thou say'st – and the more pity that great folk should have countenance in this world to drown or hang themselves more than their even-Christen. Come, my spade; there is no ancient gentleman but gardeners, ditchers, and grave-makers: they hold up Adam's profession.
OTHER	Was he a gentleman?
CLOWN	He was the first that ever bore arms.§
OTHER	Why, he had none.
CLOWN	What, art a heathen? How dost thou understand the scripture? The Scripture says Adam digged. Could he dig without arms? I'll put another question to thee. If thou answerest me not to the purpose, confess thyself –

wilfully seeks: committed suicide

straight: straightaway

5

own defence: plea relevant to homicide

wittingly: intentionally

10

Argal: ergo, therefore
delver: gravedigger
Give me leave: allow me continue

15 *will he, nill he*: willy-nilly

20 *crowner's quest*: coroner's inquest

there thou say'st: now that's the truth
25 *countenance*: approval, privilege
even-Christen: fellow Christians

hold up: continue

30

none: no coat of arms

art a heathen: are you a pagan

35 *confess thyself*: as fool

* 1–2   *Christian burial … her own salvation*: the suggestion in these lines is that Ophelia took her own life, that through her own will, rather than God's, she sought deliverance from her earthly life. Christian funeral services and burial in consecrated ground were denied to suicides, a practice that continued into the nineteenth century.

† 4   *the crowner hath sat on her*: the coroner conducted an inquest into the cause of her death

‡ 8   *'se offendendo'*: deliberate comic misapplication of *se defendendo*, meaning in self-defence

§ 30   *He was the first that ever bore arms*: Adam was the first man, therefore the first to have arms to labour the earth. The word 'arms' puns on weapons, and gentleman's heraldry being 'a coat of arms'

OTHER	Go to!
CLOWN	What is he that builds stronger than either the mason, the shipwright, or the carpenter?
OTHER	The gallows-maker, for that frame outlives a thousand tenants.
CLOWN	I like thy wit well, in good faith. The gallows does well, but how does it well? It does well to those that do ill. Now, thou dost ill to say the gallows is built stronger than the church; argal, the gallows may do well to thee. To't again, come.
OTHER	Who builds stronger than a mason, a shipwright, or a carpenter?
CLOWN	Ay, tell me that, and unyoke.
OTHER	Marry, now I can tell.
CLOWN	To't.
OTHER	Mass, I cannot tell.

Enter HAMLET and HORATIO, at a distance

CLOWN	Cudgel thy brains no more about it, for your dull ass will not mend his pace with beating and, when you are asked this question next, say a grave-maker. The houses that he makes last till doomsday. Go, get thee to Yaughan: fetch me a stoup of liquor.

Exit Second Clown

Song

> In youth, when I did love, did love,
>   Methought it was very sweet,
> To contract-o the time for-a my behove,
> Oh methought there-a was nothing-a meet.

HAMLET	Has this fellow no feeling of his business? A sings in grave-making.
HORATIO	Custom hath made it in him a property of easiness.
HAMLET	'Tis e'en so, the hand of little employment hath the daintier sense.
CLOWN	*Sings*

> But age with his stealing steps
>   Hath clawed me in his clutch,
> And hath shipped me intil the land,
>   As if I had never been such.

Throws up a skull

HAMLET	That skull had a tongue in it, and could sing once. How the knave jowls it to th'ground, as if 'twere Cain's jawbone, that did the first murder. This might be the pate of a politician which this ass now o'erreaches, one that would circumvent God, might it not?
HORATIO	It might my lord.
HAMLET	Or of a courtier, which could say 'Good morrow sweet, lord how dost thou, sweet lord?' This might be my lord Such-a-one, that praised my lord Such-a-one's horse, when a meant to beg it, might it not?
HORATIO	Ay, my lord.

Go to: Get on with it!

how does it well?: it has many tenants

To't: answer it

unyoke: have done with it

Mass: by the holy Mass

Cudgel: beat
mend his pace: get any faster

'Yaughan': unknown word
stoup: flagon

contract: shorten
meet: as good

Custom: habit

daintier sense: more delicate feeling

shipped ... intil: dispatched me to

jowls: throws
pate: head
ass: gravedigger; *o'er-reaches:* gets the better of

courtier: associated with false flattery

beg: borrow

40

45

50

55

60

65

70

75

80

* 73–4 *one that would circumvent God:* the politician is being referred to disparagingly as one who would run circles around God

HAMLET	Why, e'en so, and now my Lady Worm's; chopless, and knocked about the mazard with a sexton's spade. Here's fine revolution, and we had the trick to see't. Did these bones cost no more the breeding but to play at loggets with 'em? Mine ache to think on't.†	
		85

CLOWN	*Sings*
	A pickaxe, and a spade, a spade,
	  For and a shrowding sheet,
	Oh a pit of clay for to be made
	  For such a guest is meet.	

Throws up another skull		
HAMLET	There's another. Why may not that be the skull of a lawyer? Where be his quiddities now, his quillets, his‡ cases, his tenures, and his tricks? Why does he suffer this rude knave now to knock him about the sconce with a dirty shovel, and will not tell him of his action of battery? Hum! This fellow might be in's time a great buyer of land, with his statutes, his recognizances, his fines, his double vouchers, his recoveries. Is this the fine of his fines and the recovery of his recoveries, to have his fine pate full of fine dirt? Will his vouchers vouch him no more of his purchases, and double ones too, than the length and breadth of a pair of indentures? The very conveyances of§ his lands will hardly lie in this box, and must th'inheritor himself have no more, ha?	90
		95
		100
HORATIO	Not a jot more my lord.	
HAMLET	Is not parchment made of sheepskins?	105
HORATIO	Ay my lord, and of calves' skins too.	
HAMLET	They are sheep and calves which seek out assurance in that. I will speak to this fellow. Whose grave's this sirrah?	
CLOWN	Mine, sir.	
	Sings Oh a pit of clay for to be made For such a guest is meet.	110
HAMLET	I think it be thine indeed; for thou liest in't.	
CLOWN	You lie out on't, sir, and therefore 'tis not yours. For my part, I do not lie in't, and yet it is mine.	
HAMLET	Thou dost lie in't, to be in't and say 'tis thine. 'Tis for the dead, not for the quick, therefore thou liest.	115
CLOWN	'Tis a quick lie, sir, 'twill away again from me to you.	
HAMLET	What man dost thou dig it for?	
CLOWN	For no man, sir.	
HAMLET	What woman, then?	
CLOWN	For none neither.	120
HAMLET	Who is to be buried in't?	
CLOWN	One that was a woman, sir, but rest her soul she's dead.	
HAMLET	How absolute the knave is! We must speak by the card, or equivocation will undo us. By the Lord, Horatio, these three years I have taken a note of it: the age is grown so picked, that the toe of the peasant comes so near the heel of the courtier, he galls his kibe. How long hast thou been¶ a grave-maker?	125

chopless: without the lower jaw
mzard: upper part of skull
trick: knack
loggets: skittles

shrowding sheet: shroud

quiddities: legal subtleties
tenures: property holdings
sconce: head
action: legal action
in's: in his
statutes: legal documents
recognizances: particular type of statutes

box: coffin, grave

assurance: security
in that: in documents made of parchment

quick: living

absolute: strict, particular; *card*: accurately
equivocation: double-meaning

picked: over-refined, dainty, finicky
kibe: sore on the heel, chilblain

---

* 81   *now my Lady Worm's*: now the skull belongs to the worm
† 83–5   *Did these bones … loggats with 'em?*: is the raising of these bones not worth any more than that men should play throw-about games with them?
‡ 91   *quillets*: petty distinctions
§ 101   *indentures*: duplicate document, with indented edge; *conveyances*: documents showing ownership
¶ 128   *peasant comes so near the heel/ of the courtier, he galls his kibe*: the peasant's mannerisms are so close to that of the courtier's that he, metaphorically, hits off the courtier's diseased heel

141

CLOWN	Of all the days i'th'year, I came to't that day that our last king Hamlet o'ercame Fortinbras.	130
HAMLET	How long is that since?	
CLOWN	Cannot you tell that? Every fool can tell that. It was the very day that young Hamlet was born; he that is mad, and sent into England.	135
HAMLET	Ay, marry, why was he sent into England?	
CLOWN	Why, because he was mad. A shall recover his wits there, a or if do not, it's no great matter there.	
HAMLET	Why?	
CLOWN	'Twill not be seen in him there. There the men are as mad as he.	140
HAMLET	How came he mad?	
CLOWN	Very strangely they say.	
HAMLET	How, strangely?	
CLOWN	Faith, e'en with losing his wits.	145
HAMLET	Upon what ground?*	
CLOWN	Why, here in Denmark: I have been sexton here man and boy thirty years.	
HAMLET	How long will a man lie i'th'earth ere he rot?	
CLOWN	Faith, if a be not rotten before he die, as we have many pocky corses nowadays, that will scarce hold the laying in, a will last you some eight year, or nine year. A tanner will last you nine year.	150
HAMLET	Why he more than another?	
CLOWN	Why, sir, his hide is so tanned with his trade, that a will keep out water a great while, and your water is a sore decayer of your whoreson dead body. Here's a skull now: this skull hath lien you i'th'earth three and twenty years.	155
HAMLET	Whose was it?	
CLOWN	A whoreson mad fellow's it was. Whose do you think it was?	160
HAMLET	Nay I know not.	
CLOWN	A pestilence on him for a mad rogue, a' poured a flagon of Rhenish on my head once. This same skull sir, was Yorick's skull, the king's jester.	165
HAMLET	This?	
CLOWN	E'en that.	
HAMLET	Let me see. *Takes the skull* Alas, poor Yorick! I knew him Horatio, a fellow of infinite jest, of most excellent fancy, he hath borne me on his back a thousand times – and now how abhorred in my imagination it is! My gorge rises at it. Here hung those lips that I have kissed I know not how oft. Where be your gibes now? your gambols, your songs, your flashes of merriment, that were wont to set the table on a roar? Not one now, to mock your own grinning? Quite chop-fallen? Now get you to my lady's chamber, and tell her, let her paint an inch thick, to this favour she must come. Make her laugh at that. –† Prithee, Horatio, tell me one thing.	170 / 175
HORATIO	What's that, my lord?	180

last king Hamlet: Hamlet's father

pocky corses: corpses ravaged by syphilis
hold: last; *laying in*: in the ground
tanner: one who tans hides for a living

whoreson: expression of scornful familiarity

Rhenish: Rhine wine

gorge: gullet (stomach turns)

gibes: teasing jokes; *gambols*: frolics

chap-fallen: crestfallen (down in the mouth)

favour: appearance

* 146   *Upon what ground?*: from what cause? (The gravedigger chooses to interpret 'ground' literally in his reply.)

† 177–8   *let her paint an inch thick, to this favour she must come*: satirises women's attempt to look younger through the application of face make-up when she is destined also to become as this skull

HAMLET	Dost thou think Alexander looked o' this fashion i'th'earth?
HORATIO	E'en so.
HAMLET	And smelt so? Pah! *Puts down the skull*
HORATIO	E'en so, my lord.
HAMLET	To what base uses we may return, Horatio! Why may not 185
	imagination trace the noble dust of Alexander, till a find
	it stopping a bunghole?
HORATIO	'Twere to consider too curiously to consider so.
HAMLET	No faith, not a jot, but to follow him thither with modesty
	enough, and likelihood to lead it: as thus: Alexander died, 190
	Alexander was buried, Alexander returneth into dust; the
	dust is earth, of earth we make loam, and why of that
	loam whereto he was converted might they not stop a
	beer-barrel?

> Imperious Caesar, dead and turned to clay,   195
> Might stop a hole, to keep the wind away:
> Oh that that earth which kept the world in awe
> Should patch a wall to expel the winter's flaw!

	But soft, but soft! Aside – here comes the king.,
	The queen, the courtiers.

Enter CLAUDIUS, GERTRUDE, LAERTES, and a coffin, with PRIEST and LORDS attendant

> Who is this they follow?   200
> And with such maimèd rites? This doth betoken
> The corse they follow did with desperate hand
> Fordo it own life. 'Twas of some estate.
> Couch we awhile, and mark. *Retiring with HORATIO*

LAERTES	What ceremony else? 205
HAMLET	That is Laertes, a very noble youth. Mark.
LAERTES	What ceremony else?
PRIEST	Her obsequies have been as far enlarged
	As we have warranty. Her death was doubtful,
	And but that great command o'ersways the order, 210
	She should in ground unsanctified have lodged
	Till the last trumpet. For charitable prayers,*
	Shards, flints, and pebbles should be thrown on her;
	Yet here she is allowed her virgin crants,
	Her maiden strewments and the bringing home 215
	Of bell and burial.†
LAERTES	Must there no more be done?
PRIEST	No more be done:
	We should profane the service of the dead
	To sing a requiem and such rest to her
	As to peace-parted souls.
LAERTES	Lay her i' the earth: 220
	And from her fair and unpolluted flesh
	May violets spring. I tell thee, churlish priest,
	A ministering angel shall my sister be
	When thou liest howling.
HAMLET	What, the fair Ophelia!
GERTRUDE	Sweets to the sweet: farewell! *Scattering flowers* 225
	I hoped thou shouldst have been my Hamlet's wife.
	I thought thy bride-bed to have decked, sweet maid,
	And not have strewed thy grave.

Alexander: Alexander the Great

bunghole: hole in a beer barrel
too curiously: too ingeniously
follow him: to trace his steps to decay
modesty: reasonable speculation
lead: direct

Imperious: Imperial

that earth: Caesar's body

maimèd: incomplete, broken

Fordo: destroy; *estate:* rank
Couch: hide

What … else?: ref. to the incomplete rites

enlarged: extended
warranty: authority to command
o'ersways: overrides
unsanctified: unblessed
For: instead of
Shards: broken pieces of glass and pottery
crants: garlands
strewments: flowers strewn on the grave

profane: disrespect

churlish: boorish

howling: as a damned soul

decked: covered in flowers

---

* 212 *Till the last trumpet:* Till the last Day of Judgement, when the angels blow their trumpets from each corner of the earth

† 216 *bell and burial:* burial custom of ringing church bell

LAERTES   Oh treble woe
Fall ten times treble on that cursèd head,
Whose wicked deed thy most ingenious sense   230   *wicked deed*: the murder of Polonius
Deprived thee of. Hold off the earth awhile
Till I have caught her once more in mine arms.

Leaps into the grave

Now pile your dust upon the quick and dead   *the quick*: the living
Till of this flat a mountain you have made,
To o'ertop old Pelion or the skyish head   235   *Pelion*: mountain, mentioned in ancient myth
Of blue Olympus.   *Olympus*: lofty mountain, home of the gods

HAMLET   *Advancing*   What is he whose grief
Bears such an emphasis? whose phrase of sorrow   *an emphasis*: an excess
Conjures the wandering stars, and makes them stand   *Conjures*: places a spell on
Like wonder-wounded hearers? This is I,
Hamlet the Dane.

Laertes climbs out of the grave

LAERTES   The devil take thy soul!   240

Grappling with him

HAMLET   Thou pray'st not well.
I prithee take thy fingers from my throat,
For, though I am not splenitive and rash,*
Yet have I something in me dangerous
Which let thy wisdom fear. Hold off thy hand.   245   *wisdom*: good sense

CLAUDIUS   Pluck them asunder.

GERTRUDE   Hamlet, Hamlet!

ALL   Gentlemen!

HORATIO   Good my lord, be quiet.

The Attendants part them

HAMLET   Why, I will fight with him upon this theme
Until my eyelids will no longer wag.   *wag*: move, show signs of life

GERTRUDE   O my son, what theme?   250

HAMLET   I loved Ophelia; forty thousand brothers
Could not with all their quantity of love
Make up my sum. What wilt thou do for her?

CLAUDIUS   Oh he is mad Laertes.

GERTRUDE   For love of God forbear him.   255   *forbear*: leave, refrain from

HAMLET   'Swounds, show me what thou't do.
Woo't weep? woo't fight? woo't fast? woo't tear thyself?   *woo't*: would you
Woo't drink up eisel? eat a crocodile?   *eisel*: vinegar
I'll do't. Dost thou come here to whine,
To outface me with leaping in her grave?   260
Be buried quick with her, and so will I.   *quick*: alive
And, if thou prate of mountains, let them throw   *prate*: prattle, talk
Millions of acres on us, till our ground,
Singeing his pate against the burning zone,†
Make Ossa like a wart. Nay, and thou'lt mouth,   265   *Ossa*: another mountain in Greece
I'll rant as well as thou.

GERTRUDE   This is mere madness:
And thus awhile the fit will work on him;
Anon, as patient as the female dove   *dove*: associated with peace
When that her golden couplets are disclosed,‡   *disclosed*: hatched, brought to life
His silence will sit drooping.

---

*   243   *splenitive*: full of anger, associated
                 with the spleen
†   264   *the burning zone*: the celestial sphere,
                 associated with the element of fire
‡   269   *her golden couplets*: the dove lays two
                 eggs, and the newly hatched birds
                 have golden down

HAMLET   Hear you sir,   270
What is the reason that you use me thus?
I loved you ever – but it is no matter.
Let Hercules himself do what he may,
The cat will mew, and dog will have his day.*

Exit

CLAUDIUS   I pray thee good Horatio wait upon him.   275

Exit HORATIO

To LAERTES Strengthen your patience in our last night's speech;
We'll put the matter to the present push. –
Good Gertrude, set some watch over your son. –
This grave shall have a living monument.
An hour of quiet shortly shall we see;   280
Till then in patience our proceeding be.

Exeunt

use: behave towards

wait upon: follow

the present push: immediate action

a living: an enduring

* 273–4 *Let Hercules … dog will have his
      day*: no matter what courageous and
      noble action is performed, natural
      (animal) instinct will assert itself

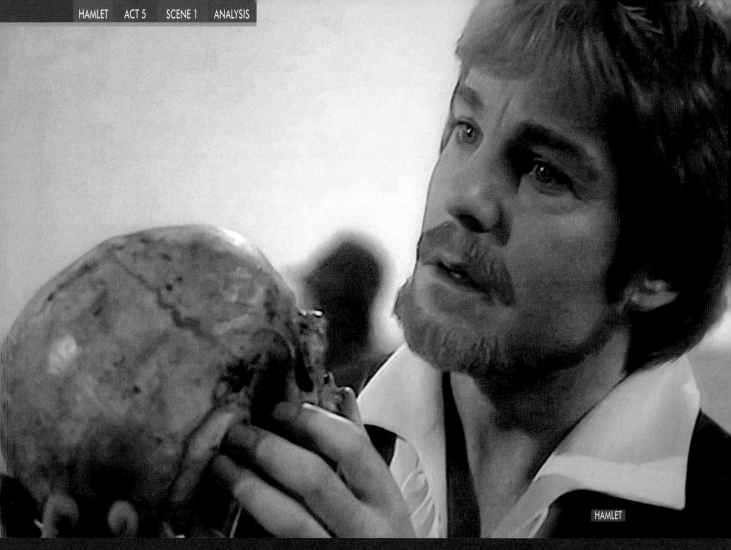

HAMLET

Two gravediggers banter while working. Hamlet and Horatio arrive. Hamlet mediates on death, decomposition and the transience of life, being particularly moved when he comes across the skull of Yorrick, a jester he knew in his youth. They watch Ophelia's funeral approach the graveyard. The priest refuses to give Ophelia full funeral rites because she may have committed suicide. Laertes poetically mourns his sister and even demands to be buried alive with her. Hamlet, seemingly offended by his eloquence, emerges from his hiding place and interrupts. He and Laertes fight.

A CLOSER LOOK

✍ LINES 1–69: THE GRAVEDIGGERS

Two gravediggers are working in a graveyard. The first asks if the person whose grave they're digging will be given a full Christian burial even though she took her own life: 'Is she to be buried in Christian burial when she wilfully seeks her own salvation?' (1–2) We can immediately guess that they are talking about Ophelia. The question is prompted by the fact that suicides were denied full Christian rites of burial.

The second gravedigger answers that she is indeed to receive the full rites because the coroner has judged she died a natural death. (3–4) After a clownish conversation about the legal issues surrounding suicide, the second gravedigger declares that Ophelia is only getting a Christian burial because she belonged to the upper class. (21–3) The first agrees and comments on the unfairness of this special treatment. (24–8)

As the gravediggers work, they engage in witty banter of a morbid nature. Hamlet and Horatio arrive unnoticed, and listen in on their conversation. The first gravedigger sends the second to fetch him a drink. (55–6) He then continues digging, singing a song about youthful love as he does so. (58–60)

✍ LINES 70–108: HAMLET'S MORBID REFLECTIONS

Hamlet seems offended that the gravedigger can sing

so cheerily while digging someone's grave: 'Has this fellow no feeling of his business? A sings in/ grave-making?' (61–2) Horatio comments that he has grown so accustomed to his job that he has lost all sensitivity to it. (63) The gravedigger continues singing, now about the process of aging and death, and throws a skull from the grave. (66–9)

Hamlet is struck by the transience of life: 'That skull had a tongue in it, and could sing once'. (70–6) The skull was once part of a living person but is now a gravedigger's plaything. It is treated with no more respect than if it had belonged to Cain, the first murderer. (71–2) We live, it seems, only to become bones that are kicked around a cemetery: 'Did these bones cost no more the breeding but to play at loggets with 'em?' (83–5)

Hamlet imagines that various skulls in the graveyard belonged to members of four fairly unpopular professions: a politician, a courtier, a lawyer and a property dealer. In life, these were important and influential figures. In death, however, these powerful gentlemen moulder and rot the same as everybody else. Hamlet takes delight in describing how these mighty figures have fallen:

- The powerful politician, who in life had the skill to outwit God himself, has his skull tossed around like a football by the gravedigger.
- The courtier who in life fawned on powerful lords and ladies is now a servant of 'Lady Worm'. (81)
- The lawyer's political skills cannot help skills cannot help him as his skull is kicked around by the gravedigger. (90–4)
- The property developer, who in life owned great tracts of land, ends up like the rest of us with only a plot of ground in a graveyard. (95–100)

There is an element of comic relief in these lines. Shakespeare's audience would have enjoyed seeing these unpopular professions and their devious practices being made fun of. They would also have taken satisfaction in being reminded that in the graveyard everyone, rich and poor alike, rots in the same way.

LINES 108–67: HAMLET BANTERS WITH THE GRAVEDIGGER

This element of comic relief continues when Hamlet decides to speak with the gravedigger. The humour here stems from the fact that the gravedigger answers Hamlet's questions in an extremely literal fashion. There is also an element of punning, with Hamlet

playing on the two meanings of the word lie – to tell an untruth and to lay down: 'Thou dost lie in't, to be in't and say 'tis thine. 'Tis for the dead, not for the quick, therefore thou liest'. (115–16)

Hamlet asks the man how long he has been a gravedigger. (128–9) He answers that he started on the day Hamlet's father defeated the elder Fortinbras in battle. (130–1) This was also the birthday of Denmark's beloved Prince Hamlet, a day all Danes remember: 'Cannot you tell that? Every fool can tell that. It was the very day that young Hamlet was born'. (133–4)

The gravedigger clearly doesn't realise who Hamlet is. The prince exploits this in order to find out what rumours have been circulating about him. (136) The gravedigger says that Hamlet has gone insane and has been set to England to recover. If he does not, it will not matter because everyone is mad in England. (137–41)

LINES 168–200: HAMLET REMEMBERS YORICK

The clown picks up a skull and says that it has lain in the earth for twenty-three years. (158) Hamlet asks whose skull it is. (160) The gravedigger answers that it belonged to Yorick, who used to be the court jester. (164-5) Hamlet is shocked by the identity of the skull, and asks to look at it more closely. (168)

When Hamlet was growing up, he had a close relationship with Yorick, who seems to have been like an uncle to him: 'Alas, poor Yorick! I knew him Horatio'. (168–9) He remembers Yorick's wit and imagination: 'a fellow of infinite jest, of most excellent fancy'. (169) The jester would playfully cart the young prince around the castle on his back: 'he hath borne me on his back a thousand times'. (170)

Hamlet is 'abhorred' or disgusted by the fact that he holds Yorick's skull in his hand and feels almost nauseous: 'My gorge rises at it'. (171) He is struck again buy the fleeting nature of life: 'Here hung those lips that I have kissed I know not how oft'. (172–3) He rhetorically asks the skull 'Where be your gibes now? your gambols, your songs'? (173–4)

Hamlet morbidly remarks how even the greatest of men die and turn to dust. Even Alexander the Great and Julius Caesar turned into dust and clay, which has all kinds of industrial uses. He is struck by the fact that the bodies of these great men might end up being turned into the stopper for a beer bottle or patching the wall of a house.

A NEGATIVE STATE OF MIND

This prince's morbid obsession with decomposition and decay finds its most potent expression in this scene. He asks the gravedigger how long it takes for a human body to rot once it has been buried: 'How long will a man lie ere 'i the earth ere he rot?' (149) He imagines the bodies of great men like Alexander the Great and Julius Caesar turning to dust and clay and eventually being put to practical uses. (190–6) He imagines how Alexander's remains might end up as the stopper of a beer barrel and how Caesar's might end up patching the wall of a house.

He seems fascinated by the skulls that are tossed around the graveyard as the gravediggers do their work, imagining the different people they belonged to. (70–103) He is both hor-rified and mesmerised by Yorick's skull; by that the fact that where the play. He seems both fascinated and horrified that the skulls being so unceremoniously tossed around the graveyard once belonged to living people: 'That skull had a tongue in it, and could sing once'. (71) He is similarly both repelled and mes-merised that Yorick, who was so full of joy and good humour, is now only a jawless skull: 'Where be your gibes now? your gambols, your songs?' (173–4)

It doesn't matter what skills or achievements we have in life, whether a politician, a lawyer or a great businessman. Each of us will die and rot in the ground. Even a great man like Alexander the Great ends up as only a stinking skull. In this scene, then, Hamlet is also struck by the notion of death as the 'great leveller', by the idea that death treats all of us, great and humble alike, in the very same way. One

Hamlet accuses Laertes of trying to somehow upstage or outdo him with his extravagant mourning: 'Dost thou come here to whine, To outface me with leaping in her grave?' (259–60) He says that he can lament and wail as well as Laertes can: 'I'll rant as well as thou'. (266) He even offers to be buried alive with him in Ophelia's grave: 'Be buried quick with her, and so will I'. (261)

Hamlet's behaviour here can only be described as self-absorbed, selfish and self-important. He disrupts the funeral in a manner that is extremely disrespectful to the dead Ophelia, to her brother, and to the other mourners. His only concern at this point is his bizarre belief that Laertes is trying to show him up with his ostentatious mourning. It seems that in Hamlet's mind, every-thing is about him. It has even been suggested that he gate-crashes the

It may seem sincere given how he baited and verbally tortured Ophelia earlier in the play. Yet we should also remember the love letters and love tokens he gave her in the past, before the action of the play began.

A RUTHLESS STEAK
The prince's ruthless streak, which we have seen throughout the paly, is also hinted at in this scene. He refers to this ruthless streak when he says 'Yet have I something in me dangerous/ Which let thy wisdom fear'. (244–5) He warns Laertes not to risk his life by fighting with him. His last lines are a warning to Laertes to leave him alone. Yet they can also be taken as a veiled threat to Claudius himself: 'Let Hercules himself do what he may,/ The cat will mew, and dog will have his day'. (273–4)

Hamlet's most powerful declaration comes when he reveals himself to the funeral, announcing himself by saying 'This is I,/ Hamlet the Dane'. (239–4) By calling himself 'the Dane', Hamlet suggests that he is the true king of Denmark. This is more or less a direct threat to Claudius: Hamlet suggests he is going to do away with the king and claim the throne that is rightfully his. Hamlet means business now that he is back in Denmark.

LINES 200–36: OPHELIA'S FUNERAL
At that moment, Ophelia's funeral cortege approaches. Hamlet notices that the funeral is proceeding with 'maimed' or incomplete rites. (201) He reasons, therefore, that the person being buried must have taken their own life, because the Church did not permit suicides to receive the full funeral ceremony. (201–3) Hamlet and Horatio conceal themselves to watch the funeral.

Laertes, Claudius and Gertrude are with the funeral party. Laertes repeatedly asks the priest if there will be proper rites for his sister. (205) The priest bluntly says that no further rites will be performed. He says that Ophelia's death was 'doubtful', a possible suicide. She should there-fore be buried without any rites at all, outside the holy ground of the churchyard: 'She should in ground unsanctified have lodged'. (211–12) However, because Claudius commanded it, she will receive some of the benefits of a normal funeral. (215–17)

Laertes curses the priest for his uncharitable attitude, saying that Ophelia will be a 'ministering angel' in Heaven while the priest lies 'howling' in hell. (223–4)

He also expresses his rage toward Hamlet, who he blames for driving his sister to madness and suicide: 'O, treble woe/ Fall ten times treble on that cursed head,/ Whose wicked deed thy most ingenious sense/ Deprived thee off'. (228–32)

Laertes tells the gravediggers to halt their work while he says a final farewell to Ophelia: 'Hold off the earth awhile/ Till I have caught her once more in mine arms'. (231–2) He then leaps into the grave. Seemingly crazed with sorrow, he demands to be buried alive with his sister. (233–4)

LINES 236–81: HAMLET AND LAERTES FIGHT
The watching Hamlet has figured out whose funeral it is (236) He now decides to reveal himself to the funeral party. He seems somehow offended by Laertes' poetic words of mourning and extrava-gant display of grief. He emerges from his hiding place, announcing himself in terms that suggest he is the true king of the realm: 'This is I,/ Hamlet the Dane'. (238–9)

Hamlet and Laertes begin to fight. Hamlet warns Laertes to leave him alone, saying that while he is not 'splenetic' or hot-headed he is still a danger-ous foe: 'Yet have I something in me dangerous/ Which let thy wisdom fear'. (244–5)

Claudius orders his attendants to separate the two men. (246) Hamlet declares that he's willing to fight with Laertes over who loved Ophelia most, saying that he himself loved Ophelia far

It is unclear where the fight takes place. In some productions, Hamlet, enraged by Laertes' extravagant display of grief, leaps into the grave after him and attacks him.

In other productions, Laertes emerges from the grave to attack Hamlet, enraged by the sight of the man who killed his father and who he blames for his sister's death.

more than anybody else: 'I loved Ophelia; forty thousand brothers/ Could not with all their quantity of love/ Make up my sum'. (251–3) He also suggests that he was willing to do far more for Ophelia than Laertes ever was. (256–8)

Hamlet rather arrogantly asks if Laertes was deliberately trying to upstage him with his passionate display of grief: 'Dost thou come here to whine,/ To outface me with leaping in her grave?' (259–60) He offers to be buried alive along with Laertes in Ophelia's grave. (261) He also expresses puzzlement as to why Laertes is angry with him: 'What is the reason that you use me thus?/ I loved you ever'. (271–2) Hamlet departs and Claudius instructs Horatio to follow him. (275)

Claudius tells Laertes they will act against Hamlet very soon: 'We'll put the matter to the present push'. (277) Hamlet, he promises Laertes, will soon be dead: 'This grave shall have a living monument'. (279) He advises Laertes to be patient a little while longer before the murderous plan they came up with in the previous scene is put into action. (280–1)

LAERTES

A BROTHER IN MOURNING

Laertes' love for his sister and his intense grief over her death are highly evident in this scene. He expresses his sorrow over her passing in poetic and moving terms. He repeatedly asks the priest to perform more funeral rites in order that her soul might have a better chance of reaching Heaven. He asks the gravediggers to halt their work so he can bid Ophelia a final farewell. Finally, he jumps into the grave and demands to be buried alive with her. (233–4)

Hamlet seems to accuse Laertes of merely playacting and exaggerating his grief. Yet we have no reason to doubt the sincerity of his emotions. There can also be no doubt that the priest's uncharitable response to his request for more prayers exacerbates his grief and anger.

VENGEFUL

Laertes' rage at Hamlet is still very intense. He curses the man he holds responsible for his sister's death: 'Oh treble woe/ Fall ten times treble on that cursèd head,/ Whose wicked deed thy most ingenious sense/ Deprived thee of' (228–31) His reaction to the sight of Hamlet is one of total hatred: 'The devil take thy soul!' (240) Laertes' almost uncontrollable anger at the prince makes it very easy for Claudius to manipulate him.

SOME LINES TO LEARN

Now get you to my lady's chamber, and tell her, let her paint an inch thick, to this favour she must come. Make her laugh at that
                                        Hamlet (176–8)

Imperious Caesar, dead and turned to clay,
Might stop a hole, to keep the wind away:
Oh that that earth which kept the world in awe
Should patch a wall to expel the winter's flaw!
                                        Hamlet (195–8)

or, though I am not splenitive and rash,
Yet have I something in me dangerous
Which let thy wisdom fear.
                                        Hamlet (243–5)

Let Hercules himself do what he may,
The cat will mew, and dog will have his day
                                        Hamlet (273–4)

CHARACTER DEVELOPMENT

GERTRUDE

SADNESS OVER OPHELIA'S DEATH
Gertrude seems genuinely saddened by the death of Ophelia, the woman she once hoped would become her daughter-in-law: 'I hoped thou shouldst have been my Hamlet's wife'. (226) She spreads flowers on the graveside and remarks sadly that she expected she would one day decorate Ophelia's marriage bed, not her grave. (227–8)

MATERNAL FEELING FOR HAMLET?
There is also a sense in which Gertrude appears protective of Hamlet in this scene. When the prince reveals himself, he suggests that he – not Claudius – is Denmark's true ruler, and makes barely veiled threats against the king. Gertrude declares that Hamlet is merely ranting: 'This is mere madness:/ And thus awhile the fit will work on him'. (266–7) Is she trying to protect her son by convincing Claudius he doesn't know what he's saying? Throughout the play, Gertrude has been intensely loyal to Claudius. Yet here, perhaps, we see her feelings toward her son come to the fore.

CLAUDIUS

MANIPULATIVE
In this scene Claudius comes across yet again as a master manipulator. When Hamlet declares to Laertes that he loved his sister, Claudius says the prince is only speaking out of madness: 'Oh he is mad, Laertes'. (254) He doesn't want Laertes' hatred of Hamlet to soften. After Hamlet departs, he quickly moves to calm Laertes: 'Strengthen your patience'. (276) He reassures Laertes that Hamlet will soon be dead. (279) He doesn't want Laertes to do anything rash and spoil the plot they hatched to kill the prince.

Hamlet has reappeared, referred to himself as the true ruler of Denmark, and made barely veiled threats against the king. This will no doubt have fuelled Claudius' desire to deal with his stepson once and for all.

HORATIO

HAMLET'S LOYAL FRIEND
Horatio continues to be Hamlet's loyal friend in this scene. He dutifully listens to and plays along with the prince's morbid musings on death and the transitory nature of human existence. Eventually, though, he fears that Hamlet is brooding excessively on these matters, and advises him to no avail to stop obsessing: "Twere to consider too curiously, to consider so'. (188)

Horatio attempts to restrain the prince in his confrontation with Laertes: 'Good my lord, be quiet'. (247) Even Claudius acknowledges that Horatio is the only person who Hamlet will listen to, and asks him to go and watch over the prince: 'I pray you, good Horatio, wait upon him'. (275)

Enter HAMLET and HORATIO

HAMLET	So much for this sir, now shall you see the other.[*]
	You do remember all the circumstance?
HORATIO	Remember it my lord!
HAMLET	Sir, in my heart there was a kind of fighting
	That would not let me sleep. Methought I lay
	Worse than the mutines in the bilboes. Rashly,^{††}
	And praised be rashness for it – let us know,
	Our indiscretion sometimes serves us well
	When our deep plots do pall, and that should learn us
	There's a divinity that shapes our ends,
	Rough-hew them how we will –
HORATIO	That is most certain.
HAMLET	Up from my cabin,
	My sea-gown scarfed about me, in the dark
	Groped I to find out them, had my desire,
	Fingered their packet, and in fine withdrew
	To mine own room again, making so bold,
	My fears forgetting manners, to unseal
	Their grand commission; where I found, Horatio –
	O royal knavery! – an exact command,
	Larded with many several sorts of reasons,
	Importing Denmark's health, and England's too,
	With, ho! such bugs and goblins in my life,[§]
	That, on the supervise, no leisure bated,
	No, not to stay the grinding of the axe,
	My head should be struck off.
HORATIO	Is't possible?
HAMLET	Here's the commission, read it at more leisure.
	But wilt thou hear me how I did proceed?
HORATIO	I beseech you.

fighting: agitation

5

Worse: more uncomfortably
let us know: consider
indiscretion: lack of good judgement
deep: deeply thought through; *pall:* falter
10 *shapes our ends:* determines our fate
Rough-hew: (like a piece of timber)

sea-gown: high-collared gown of coarse fabric
them: Rosencrantz and Guildenstern
15 *Fingered:* stole; *in fine:* finally

commission: (see Act 3 Scene 3, lines 3–7)

20 *Larded:* garnished, embellished
Importing: regarding

supervise: viewing; *no … bated:* without delay
stay: wait for

25

beseech: entreat

[*] 1   *this … other:* 'this' refers to Hamlet's letter to Horatio (Act 4 Scene 6, lines 11–26), the 'other' being a reference to the commission given to Rosencrantz and Guildenstern

† 6   *mutines in the bilboes:* mutineers in iron shackles

‡ 6   *Rashly:* Impulsively – the word is followed by a parenthetic reflection; the events that 'Rashly' introduces resume at line 12

§ 22   *With, ho! … my life:* 'ho!' is an expression of astonishment. The terms 'bugs' and 'goblins' ridicule, as far-fetched lies, the claims the letter makes about how dangerous Hamlet is if left alive.

HAMLET	Being thus benetted round with villanies, –
	Or I could make a prologue to my brains,*
	They had begun the play. I sat me down,
	Devised a new commission, wrote it fair.
	I once did hold it, as our statists do,
	A baseness to write fair and laboured much
	How to forget that learning; but, sir, now
	It did me yeoman's service. Wilt thou know
	Th'effect of what I wrote?
HORATIO	Ay, good my lord.
HAMLET	An earnest conjuration from the king,
	As England was his faithful tributary,
	As love between them like the palm might flourish,
	As peace should still her wheaten garland wear,†
	And stand a comma 'tween their amities,
	And many suchlike as-es of great charge,‡
	That on the view and knowing of these contents,
	Without debatement further, more, or less,
	He should those bearers put to sudden death,
	Not shriving time allowed.
HORATIO	How was this sealed?
HAMLET	Why, even in that was heaven ordinant.
	I had my father's signet in my purse,
	Which was the model of that Danish seal;
	Folded the writ up in the form of th'other,
	Subscribed it, gave't th'impression, placed it safely,§
	The changeling never known. Now, the next day
	Was our sea-fight, and what to this was sequent
	Thou know'st already.
HORATIO	So Guildenstern and Rosencrantz go to't.
HAMLET	Why man, they did make love to this employment;
	They are not near my conscience. Their defeat
	Does by their own insinuation grow.
	'Tis dangerous when the baser nature comes
	Between the pass and fell incensèd points
	Of mighty opposites.
HORATIO	Why, what a king is this!
HAMLET	Does it not, think thee, stand me now upon –◊
	He that hath killed my king, and whored my mother,
	Popped in between th'election and my hopes,
	Thrown out his angle for my proper life,
	And with such cozenage – is't not perfect conscience
	To quit him with this arm? And is't not to be damned
	To let this canker of our nature come
	In further evil?
HORATIO	It must be shortly known to him from England
	What is the issue of the business there.

30

benetted: trapped in a net

fair: as a clerk would write it
statists: statesmen, politicians

35

yeoman's service: servant that gives loyal service
effect: import

conjuration: appeal

40

amities: friendship

45
debatement further: further discussion
the bearers: Rosencrantz and Guildenstern
shriving time: time for confession of sins

ordinant: ordaining, directing

50
model: exact likeness

changeling: substitution (as a fairy-child)
sequent: to follow

55
to't: to their death
they did make love to: willingly embrace

insinuation: suggestion, interference

60

pass … points: thrust of sword-points
opposites: antagonists (Hamlet and Claudius)

whored: made a whore of
Popped in between: divided
65
angle: fish-hook
cozenage: deception

canker: contagious sore

70

issue: outcome

* 30   make a prologue: outline the action to be performed
† 41   wheaten garland: symbol of plenty and prosperity
‡ 43   as-es … charge: 'as' clauses of import – also a pun on the word 'asses'
§ 52   Subscribed: signed; impression: of the seal on wax
◊ 63   Does it not, think'st thee, stand me now upon: do you not think that it is now incumbent on me, that it is my duty

HAMLET	It will be short. The interim's mine,	
	And a man's life's no more than to say 'one.'*	
	But I am very sorry, good Horatio,	75
	That to Laertes I forgot myself,	*I forgot myself*: lost my self-control
	For by the image of my cause, I see	
	The portraiture of his. I'll court his favours.†	*favours*: friendship
	But sure the bravery of his grief did put me	
	Into a towering passion.	
HORATIO	Peace, who comes here?	80

Enter young OSRIC

OSRIC	Your lordship is right welcome back to Denmark.
HAMLET	I humbly thank you, sir. – Dost know this water-fly?
HORATIO	No, my good lord.
HAMLET	Thy state is the more gracious, for 'tis a vice to know him.

water-fly: small, meddling creature

	He hath much land, and fertile; let a beast be lord of	85
	beasts, and his crib shall stand at the king's mess. 'Tis a‡	
	chough, but as I say, spacious in the possession of dirt.	*chough*: crow; *of dirt*: of land, which is but dirt
OSRIC	Sweet lord, if your lordship were at leisure, I should	*Sweet lord*: courtly address
	impart a thing to you from his majesty.	
HAMLET	I will receive it sir with all diligence of spirit. Put your	90
	bonnet to his right use, 'tis for the head.	*bonnet*: hat (put it back on)
OSRIC	I thank your lordship, it is very hot.	
HAMLET	No believe me, 'tis very cold, the wind is northerly.	
OSRIC	It is indifferent cold my lord, indeed.	*indifferent*: fairly
HAMLET	But yet methinks it is very sultry and hot for my	95
	complexion.	*complexion*: bodily state
OSRIC	Exceedingly my lord, it is very sultry, as 'twere – I cannot	
	tell how. But, my lord, his majesty bade me signify to you	
	that he has laid a great wager on your head. Sir, this is the	*wager*: bet
	matter –	100
HAMLET	I beseech you, remember.	

Hamlet moves him to put on his hat

OSRIC	Nay good my lord, for mine ease in good faith. Sir, here is	
	newly come to court Laertes; believe me an absolute	
	gentleman, full of most excellent differences, of very soft	*differences*: distinctions; *soft*: refined
	society and great showing Indeed, to speak feelingly of	105
	him, he is the card or calendar of gentry, for you shall find	*card or calendar*: pattern
	in him the continent of what part a gentleman would see.	*continent*: physical container, embodiment

* 74   *And a man's life's no more than to say 'One.'*: A man's life lasts as long as the time it takes to count to one

† 77–8   *the image of my cause … portraiture of his*: my desire for revenge is reflected in Laertes

‡ 85–6   *let a beast be lord of beasts … the king's mess*: even though he is no better than the beasts he lords over, because of his large possessions he is received at the king's table

HAMLET	Sir, his definement suffers no perdition in you, though I know to divide him inventorially would dozy th'arithmetic of memory, and yet but yaw neither in respect of his quick sail. But in the verity of extolment, I take him to be a soul of great article, and his infusion of such dearth and rareness as, to make true diction of him, his semblable is his mirror, and who else would trace him, his umbrage, nothing more.	*yaw:* to move off course (sailing metaphor) *verity of extolment:* true appraisal *trace:* closely follow *umbrage:* shadow
OSRIC	Your lordship speaks most infallibly of him.	
HAMLET	The concernancy, sir? why do we wrap the gentleman in our more rawer breath?	*concernancy:* what is the point (concern) of this *rawer breath:* coarse language
OSRIC	Sir?	
HORATIO	Is't not possible to understand in another tongue? You will to't sir, really.	
HAMLET	What imports the nomination of this gentleman?	
OSRIC	Of Laertes?	
HORATIO	His purse is empty already; all's golden words are spent.	
HAMLET	Of him sir.	
OSRIC	I know you are not ignorant –	
HAMLET	I would you did sir, yet in faith if you did, it would not much approve me. Well, sir?	
OSRIC	You are not ignorant of what excellence Laertes is.	
HAMLET	I dare not confess that, lest I should compare with him in excellence, but to know a man well were to know himself.	
OSRIC	I mean sir for his weapon; but in the imputation laid on him by them, in his meed he's unfellowed.	*imputation:* estimation *meed:* merit, talent, service *unfellowed:* unmatched
HAMLET	What's his weapon?	
OSRIC	Rapier and dagger.	
HAMLET	That's two of his weapons, but well.	
OSRIC	The king sir hath wagered with him six Barbary horses, against the which he has impawned, as I take it, six French rapiers and poniards, with their assigns, as girdle, hangers, and so. Three of the carriages in faith are very dear to fancy, very responsive to the hilts, most delicate carriages, and of very liberal conceit.	*Barbary horses:* prized for their swiftness *impawned:* staked *poniards:* small daggers; *assigns:* fittings *carriages:* straps *responsive:* coordinated (in style) *liberal conceit:* elaborate design
HAMLET	What call you the carriages?	
HORATIO	I knew you must be edified by the margent ere you had done.	*margent:* explanatory gloss in the margin
OSRIC	The carriages sir are the hangers.	
HAMLET	The phrase would be more germane to the matter if we could carry cannon by our sides; I would it might be hangers till then. But on, six Barbary horses against six French swords, their assigns, and three liberal-conceited carriages – that's the French bet against the Danish. Why is this impawned, as you call it?	*germane:* useful, appropriate

110
115

120

125

130

135

140

145

150

* 108   *definement ... perdition:* description suffers no loss

† 109–10 *to divide him inventorially ... memory:* to list his attributes one by one would bewilder the memory's ability to add up (remember) the many parts

‡ 112   *article:* importance; *infusion:* mixture

§ 112–14 *infusion of such ... semblable is his mirror:* he is a mixture of such qualities that are generally lacking and rare that, to speak truly of him, his only likeness is his own image in a mirror

¶ 121   *Is't not possible to understand in another tongue ... really:* Horatio is growing impatient with the courtly flattery and grandiose language being used by Osric and mimicked by Hamlet, and with Osric's inability to understand Hamlet's meaning. He urges for a simpler language that would get to the point of the matter.

** 122   *What ... gentleman:* why do you mention his name

OSRIC	The king sir, hath laid sir, that in a dozen passes between yourself and him, he shall not exceed you three hits. He hath laid on twelve for nine. And it would come to immediate trial, if your lordship would vouchsafe the answer.* 155
HAMLET	How if I answer no?
OSRIC	I mean my lord, the opposition of your person in trial.
HAMLET	Sir, I will walk here in the hall. If it please his majesty, it is the breathing time of day with me. Let the foils be brought, the gentleman willing, and the king hold his 160 purpose, I will win for him and I can. If not, I will gain nothing but my shame and the odd hits.
OSRIC	Shall I redeliver you e'en so?
HAMLET	To this effect sir, after what flourish your nature will.
OSRIC	I commend my duty to your lordship. 165
HAMLET	Yours, yours.

Exit Osric

	He does well to commend it himself, there are no tongues else for's turn.
HORATIO	This lapwing runs away with the shell on his head.†
HAMLET	A did comply with his dug before he sucked it. Thus has‡ 170 he, and many more of the same bevy that I know the drossy age dotes on, only got the tune of the time and§ outward habit of encounter, a kind of yesty collection,¶ which carries them through and through the most fanned and winnowed opinions; and do but blow them to their 175 trial, the bubbles are out.**

Enter a LORD

LORD	My lord, his majesty commended him to you by young Osric, who brings back to him that you attend him in the hall. He sends to know if your pleasure hold to play with Laertes, or that you will take longer time. 180
HAMLET	I am constant to my purposes, they follow the king's pleasure. If his fitness speaks, mine is ready; now or whensoever, provided I be so able as now.
LORD	The king and queen, and all, are coming down.
HAMLET	In happy time. 185
LORD	The queen desires you to use some gentle entertainment to Laertes, before you fall to play.
HAMLET	She well instructs me.

Exit Lord

Glossary (right margin):

laid: wagered

him: Laertes

twelve for nine: the final score

trial: contest

breathing time: time for exercise
foils: weapons

redeliver: report what you've said

flourish: pretentious language

commend my duty: conventional phrase

for's turn: to serve his purpose

bevy: horde

winnowed: well-sifted, carefully considered

attend: await

play: fight with swords

if … ready: once the king is ready then so am I

gentle: friendly

---

*   155   *vouchsafe the answer:* accept the challenge (Hamlet deliberately misinterprets the phrase to mean simply 'give a reply')

†   169   *This lapwing runs away with the shell on his head:* presumably, it is only now, on his departure, that Osric puts his hat on his head. The image is of a young bird running off with a piece of its eggshell still stuck to his head

‡   170   *He did comply with his dug, before he sucked it:* he ingratiated himself with his nurse's breast before he sucked it – that is to say, he was a flattering courtier from the day he was born

§   172   *drossy age:* superficial times; *outward … encounter:* habitual formal meetings that are all show

¶   173   *yesty:* yeasty, swollen with ambition (fungus-like), frothy like foam on beer

**   176   *but blow them to their trial, the bubbles are out:* put them to the test, by so much as talking simply to them (blow them), and their high-blown language is shown to be empty of meaning, their 'bubbles' have burst

HORATIO	You will lose, my lord.	
HAMLET	I do not think so. Since he went into France, I have been	190
	in continual practice; I shall win at the odds. But thou	
	wouldst not think how ill all's here about my heart – but	
	it is no matter.	
HORATIO	Nay good my lord –	
HAMLET	It is but foolery, but it is such a kind of gaingiving as would	195
	perhaps trouble a woman.	
HORATIO	If your mind dislike anything, obey it. I will forestall their	
	repair hither, and say you are not fit.	
HAMLET	Not a whit, we defy augury. There is a special providence	
	in the fall of a sparrow. If it be now, 'tis not to come; if it	200
	be not to come, it will be now; if it be not now, yet it will	
	come – the readiness is all. Since no man of aught he	
	leaves knows, what is't to leave betimes? Let be.	

A table prepared, with flagons of wine on it. Trumpets, Drums and Officers with cushions.

Enter CLAUDIUS, GERTRUDE, LAERTES, and LORDS, with other Attendants with foils,

daggers and gauntlets

CLAUDIUS	Come Hamlet, come and take this hand from me.	

Hamlet takes Laertes by the hand

HAMLET	Give me your pardon sir, I've done you wrong;	205
	But pardon't as you are a gentleman.	
	This presence knows,	
	And you must needs have heard, how I am punished	
	With a sore distraction. What I have done,	
	That might your nature, honour and exception	210
	Roughly awake, I here proclaim was madness.*	
	Was't Hamlet wrong'd Laertes? Never Hamlet:	
	If Hamlet from himself be tane away,	
	And when he's not himself does wrong Laertes,	
	Then Hamlet does it not, Hamlet denies it.	215
	Who does it then? His madness. If't be so,	
	Hamlet is of the faction that is wronged;	
	His madness is poor Hamlet's enemy.	
	Sir, in this audience,	
	Let my disclaiming from a purposed evil	220
	Free me so far in your most generous thoughts,	
	That I have shot my arrow o'er the house	
	And hurt my brother.	
LAERTES	I am satisfied in nature,	
	Whose motive in this case should stir me most	
	To my revenge; but in my terms of honour	225
	I stand aloof, and will no reconcilement	
	Till by some elder masters of known honour	
	I have a voice and precedent of peace†	
	To keep my name ungored. But till that time,	
	I do receive your offered love like love,	230
	And will not wrong it.	
HAMLET	I embrace it freely,	
	And will this brother's wager frankly play.	
	Give us the foils, come on.	
LAERTES	Come, one for me.	

---

foolery: foolishness; *gaingiving*: misgiving

obey it: follow your instinct
repair: coming
augury: omens, forebodings
providence ... sparrow: see Matthew 10:28–31
it: death

betimes: beforetime, have an early death

presence: royal assembly

tane: taken, by madness

faction: party

purposed: deliberate, willed and intended

That I have: as if I had

nature: natural, personal feeling

honour: public pride

ungored: unwounded, unstained

frankly: with honesty

---

* 209–11 *What I have done ... Roughly awake*:
         What offence I may have caused
         your nature and honour

† 228   *voice and precedent*: till I have an
             authoritative opinion and example

HAMLET	I'll be your foil, Laertes. In mine ignorance
	Your skill shall like a star i'th'darkest night, 235
	Stick fiery off indeed.
LAERTES	You mock me, sir.
HAMLET	No, by this hand.
CLAUDIUS	Give them the foils, young Osric. Cousin Hamlet,
	You know the wager?
HAMLET	Very well, my lord
	Your grace hath laid the odds a'th'weaker side. 240
CLAUDIUS	I do not fear it, I have seen you both.
	But since he is bettered, we have therefore odds.
LAERTES	This is too heavy, let me see another.
HAMLET	This likes me well. These foils have all a length?
Prepare to play	
OSRIC	Ay, my good lord. 245
CLAUDIUS	Set me the stoups of wine upon that table.
	If Hamlet give the first or second hit,
	Or quit in answer of the third exchange,
	Let all the battlements their ordnance fire.*
	The king shall drink to Hamlet's better breath. 250
	And in the cup an union shall he throw
	Richer than that which four successive kings
	In Denmark's crown have worn. Give me the cups
	And let the kettle to the trumpet speak,
	The trumpet to the cannoneer without, 255
	The cannons to the heavens, the heaven to earth,
	'Now the king drinks to Hamlet!' Come, begin,
	And you the judges bear a wary eye.
HAMLET	Come on sir.
LAERTES	Come, my lord. 260
They play	
HAMLET	One.
LAERTES	No.
HAMLET	Judgement.
OSRIC	A hit, a very palpable hit.
LAERTES	Well, again. 265
CLAUDIUS	Stay, give me drink. Hamlet, this pearl is thine.†
	Here's to thy health.
Drum, trumpets sound, and shot goes off	
	Give him the cup.
HAMLET	I'll play this bout first, set it by awhile.
	Come.
They play	
	Another hit. What say you?
LAERTES	A touch, a touch, I do confess't. 270
CLAUDIUS	Our son shall win.
GERTRUDE	He's fat, and scant of breath.
	Here Hamlet, take my napkin, rub thy brows.
	The queen carouses to thy fortune, Hamlet.
HAMLET	Good madam.
CLAUDIUS	Gertrude, do not drink! 275
GERTRUDE	I will, my lord, I pray you pardon me.
Drinks	
CLAUDIUS	*Aside* It is the poisoned cup. It is too late.
HAMLET	I dare not drink yet madam, by and by.

foil: background to display a Jewel's brilliance

Stick fiery off: stand out majestically

bettered: more skilful

all a length: the same length

better breath: improvement
an union: pearl (as was the king's custom)

kettle: drum

wary: careful

fat: out of condition, sweaty

* 249   *Let all the battlements their ordnance fire*: let all our plans and means to kill Hamlet come into play – in other words, Claudius will then offer him the poisoned wine to drink

† 266   *this pearl is thine*: instead of a pearl, the king throws poison in the chalice, as Hamlet suggests later in this scene (line 313)

GERTRUDE	Come, let me wipe thy face.	
LAERTES	My lord, I'll hit him now.	
CLAUDIUS	I do not think't.	280
LAERTES	And yet it is almost against my conscience.	
HAMLET	Come, for the third, Laertes. You but dally.	
	I pray you pass with your best violence.	
	I am afeard you make a wanton of me.	
LAERTES	Say you so? Come on.	285

Play

OSRIC	Nothing neither way.	
LAERTES	Have at you now!	

Wounds Hamlet

In scuffling they change rapiers

CLAUDIUS	Part them. They are incensed.	
HAMLET	Nay, come again.	

Wounds Laertes

Gertrude falls

OSRIC	Look to the queen there, ho!	290
HORATIO	They bleed on both sides. How is it, my lord?	
OSRIC	How is't Laertes?	
LAERTES	Why, as a woodcock to mine own springe, Osric.	
	I am justly killed with mine own treachery.	
HAMLET	How does the queen?	
CLAUDIUS	She swounds to see them bleed.	295
GERTRUDE	No, no, the drink, the drink – O my dear Hamlet –	
	The drink, the drink – I am poisoned.	

Dies

HAMLET	Oh villainy! – Ho, let the door be locked!	
	Treachery! Seek it out!	
LAERTES	It is here, Hamlet. Hamlet, thou art slain,	300
	No medicine in the world can do thee good,	
	In thee there is not half an hour of life –	
	The treacherous instrument is in thy hand,	
	Unbated and envenomed. The foul practice	
	Hath turned itself on me; lo, here I lie,	305
	Never to rise again. Thy mother's poisoned –	
	I can no more – the king, the king's to blame.	
HAMLET	The point envenomed too! Then, venom, to thy work!	

Hurts the king

ALL	Treason, treason!	
CLAUDIUS	Oh yet defend me friends, I am but hurt.	310
HAMLET	Here, thou incestuous, murderous, damnèd Dane,	
	Drink off this potion. Is thy union here?	
	Follow my mother.	

King dies

LAERTES	He is justly served,	
	It is a poison tempered by himself.	315
	Exchange forgiveness with me, noble Hamlet.	
	Mine and my father's death come not upon thee,	
	Nor thine on me.	

Dies

pass: thrust

springe: woodcocks often ensnared themselves

swounds: swoons, faints

Unbated and envenom'd: see 4.7.136–47

union: pearl (poison)/ symbol of his marriage

tempered: concocted

285   *I am afeard you make a wanton of me*:
I think you're just toying with me as
if I were a child

HAMLET	Heaven make thee free of it! I follow thee.		free: absolved
	I am dead, Horatio. Wretched queen, adieu.	320	Wretched: pitiable
	You that look pale, and tremble at this chance,		You that look pale: (the attendants)
	That are but mutes or audience to this act,		but mutes: play no speaking part in these acts
	Had I but time, as this fell sergeant death		
	Is strict in his arrest, oh I could tell you –		
	But let it be. Horatio, I am dead,	325	
	Thou livest; report me and my cause aright		
	To the unsatisfied.*		
HORATIO	Never believe it:		
	I am more an antique Roman than a Dane.		
	Here's yet some liquor left.†		
HAMLET	As th'art a man,		
	Give me the cup. Let go, by heaven, I'll ha't.	330	
	O God, Horatio, what a wounded name,		wounded name: damaged reputation
	Things standing thus unknown, shall live behind me!		
	If thou didst ever hold me in thy heart,		
	Absent thee from felicity awhile,‡		
	And in this harsh world draw thy breath in pain	335	
	To tell my story.		

March afar off, and shot within

	What warlike noise is this?		
OSRIC	Young Fortinbras, with conquest come from Poland,		
	To the ambassadors of England gives		
	This warlike volley.		
HAMLET	Oh I die, Horatio;		
	The potent poison quite o'ercrows my spirit.	340	o'er-crows: triumphs over
	I cannot live to hear the news from England.		
	But I do prophesy th'election lights		th'election: for the new king of Denmark
	On Fortinbras; he has my dying voice.		
	So tell him, with th'occurrents more and less		occurrents …: occurrences, big and small
	Which have solicited – the rest is silence.	345	solicited: incited … (breaks off mid-sentence)

Dies

HORATIO	Now cracks a noble heart. Good night sweet prince,		sweet: conventional term of affection
	And flights of angels sing thee to thy rest. –		
	Why does the drum come hither?		

Enter FORTINBRAS and ENGLISH AMBASSADORS, with drum, colours and Attendants

FORTINBRAS	Where is this sight?		
HORATIO	What is it ye would see?		
	If aught of woe or wonder, cease your search.	350	wonder: strange sights
			cease your search: look no further
FORTINBRAS	This quarry cries on havoc. O proud death,§		toward: in preparation
	What feast is toward in thine eternal cell		thine … cell: death's grave; thou: (death)
	That thou so many princes at a shot		
	So bloodily hast struck?		

*   328   *unsatisfied*: those that do not know the whole story

†   329–30 *I am more an antique Roman … liquor left*: The ancient Romans believed that suicide was an honourable way to die when faced with an intolerable situation – Horatio is about to drink from the poisoned chalice himself

‡   335   *Absent thee from felicity awhile*: do not yet seek the happiness of death (as a release from life's miseries)

§   352   *This quarry cries on havoc*: this heap of dead bodies proclaims that general slaughter has taken place

AMBASSADOR   The sight is dismal,
And our affairs from England come too late.   355
The ears are senseless that should give us hearing,*
To tell him his commandment is fulfilled,
That Rosencrantz and Guildenstern are dead.
Where should we have our thanks?†
HORATIO   Not from his mouth,‡
Had it th'ability of life to thank you;   360
He never gave commandment for their death.
But since, so jump upon this bloody question,§
You from the Polack wars, and you from England,
Are here arrived, give order that these bodies
High on a stage be placèd to the view;   365
And let me speak to th'yet unknowing world
How these things came about. So shall you hear
Of carnal, bloody, and unnatural acts,ℂ
Of accidental judgements, casual slaughters,**
Of deaths put on by cunning and forced cause,   370
And in this upshot, purposes mistook
Fall'n on th'inventors' heads: all this can I††
Truly deliver.
FORTINBRAS   Let us haste to hear it,
And call the noblest to the audience.
For me, with sorrow I embrace my fortune.   375
I have some rights of memory in this kingdom,‡‡
Which now to claim my vantage doth invite me.
HORATIO   Of that I shall have also cause to speak,
And from his mouth whose voice will draw on more.§§
But let this same be presently performed,ℂℂ   380
Even while men's minds are wild, lest more mischance
On plots and errors happen.
FORTINBRAS   Let four captains
Bear Hamlet like a soldier to the stage,
For he was likely, had he been put on,
To have proved most royal; and for his passage,   385
The soldiers' music and the rite of war
Speak loudly for him.
Take up the bodies. Such a sight as this
Becomes the field, but here shows much amiss.
Go bid the soldiers shoot.   390

Exeunt marching, after the which a peal of ordnance are shot off

---

dismal: dreadful

jump upon: at the moment of

carnal: refers to incestuous marriage

put on: brought about; *forced:* contrived
in this upshot: as a final result

vantage: favourable opportunity

whose voice: whose authority

wild: passionately enraged

put on: put to the test
for his passage: to mark his passing away

Becomes the field: suits the battlefield

---

* 356   *The ears are senseless:* (i.e. deaf because dead) here belong to Claudius

† 358   *Where should we have our thanks?:* A polite way of asking, Who is now in command?

‡ 359   Horatio tells the English ambassador that it wasn't Claudius who ordered the deaths of Rosencrantz and Guildenstern. Claudius is dead, but if his dead mouth could speak, it would not thank the ambassador's English masters for killing them

§ 363   *question:* conflict

ℂ 369   *unnatural acts:* fratricide (the killing of one's brother)

** 370   *accidental judgements:* unpremeditated killings that manifest divine judgement; *casual:* due to chance

†† 373   *purposes mistook ... inventors' heads:* plots to kill others backfired and killed the schemers themselves

‡‡ 376   *rights ... memory:* unforgotten (long-standing) claims

§§ 379   *draw on:* persuade

ℂℂ 380 *same:* Horatio's promised explanation of events

HAMLET & LAERTES

Hamlet tells Horatio what happened aboard the ship that was bringing him to England. A courtier called Osric arrives and invites Hamlet to participate in a fencing match with Laertes. He declares that Claudius has bet Laertes that he will be unable to beat Hamlet by more than three points. Despite feelings of foreboding, Hamlet agrees to take part in the contest. Before the match starts, Hamlet apologises to Laertes for the fracas at the graveyard, and Laertes declares that he is at least satisfied 'in honour'.

Laertes chooses a poisoned blade with which he intends to kill the prince. Claudius also produces a chalice of poisoned wine which he plans to trick Hamlet into drinking. However, Gertrude accidentally drinks some of the wine. In a scuffle, both Hamlet and Laertes are stabbed by the poisoned foil. Gertrude dies. Before dying, Laertes confesses the plot he was involved in. Hamlet kills Claudius. Horatio tries to kill himself, but the dying Hamlet asks him to live on and preserve his memory. Fortinbras arrives and declares himself the new ruler of Denmark. He decrees that Hamlet's corpse be treated with full military honours.

A CLOSER LOOK

LINES 1–80: HAMLET'S ESCAPE

Hamlet and Horatio are talking in the palace. Hamlet tells Horatio what happened on the ship that was taking him to England:

- He was lying in his cabin unable to sleep due to a feeling of uneasiness: 'in my heart there was a kind of fighting'. (4)
- He went to Rosencrantz and Guildenstern's cabin and stole the letter they were taking from Claudius

to the king of England. (13–16) The letter instructed the English king to execute Hamlet: 'My head should be struck off'. (24)

- Hamlet replaced Claudius' letter with one he wrote himself. He managed to imitate Claudius' wordy writing style. (31–43) He had his father's seal with him, which he used to mark the envelope, giving it the appearance of coming from Claudius. (48–50)
- This new letter instructed the English king to execute its bearers immediately. (46–7) Therefore,

once Rosencrantz and Guildenstern present this new letter to the English king, they will be put to death.

- The following day the Danish ship was attacked by the pirates allowing Hamlet to return to Denmark. (53–5)

Horatio is shocked by Hamlet's ruthlessness in sending Rosencrantz and Guildenstern to their deaths: 'So Guildenstern and Rosencrantz go to't'. (56) Hamlet, however, feels no guilt over their deaths: 'They are not near my conscience'. (58) He says they got what they deserved for being lackeys of Claudius: 'Why man, they did make love to this employment'. (57)

Hamlet then asks Horatio if he is not now justified in killing the king. (67–8) He says that it would be immoral to let the this wicked man continue to rule Denmark: 'And is't not damned/ To let this canker of our nature come/ In further evil?' (68–70)

The prince expresses regret over his confrontation with Laertes in the graveyard: 'But I am very sorry, good Horatio,/ That to Laertes I forgot myself'. (75–6) He promises to make up with Laertes, and blames their spat at the graveyard on high emotion. (78–9) Hamlet realises that Laertes seeks the same thing he does: revenge for a father's death: 'For, by the image of my cause, I see/ The portraiture of his'. (77–8)

LINES 80–136: HAMLET TOYS WITH OSRIC
At that moment Osric arrives with a message from Claudius. Hamlet regards Osric with utter contempt, describing him as a 'water-fly' and a fawning lackey of the king's. (82, 84–8) He torments Osric, insisting he puts his hat back on before delivering his message, then changing his mind, then insisting once more. (90–101)

Osric launches into a wordy and long-winded description of Laertes: 'an absolute gentleman, full of most excellent/ differences, of very soft society and great showing'. (103–4) Hamlet seems to make fun of Osric's long-windedness by providing an even more elaborate description of Laertes' qualities. (108–15) He bamboozles the poor messenger, continually interrupting him with confusing statements.

LINES 137–89: THE WAGER
Osric at last gets to the point of his message. He states how fine a swordsman Laertes is and that Claudius has made a bet with him. The king has put up six prize horses; Laertes has put up six French rapiers

and daggers. (137–40) Claudius has wagered that in a twelve-round fencing match Laertes could not beat Hamlet by more than three hits. (152–3)

The king wants to know if Hamlet is willing to participate in this match immediately. (154–7) Hamlet answers that it is his time of day for exercise and he will be walking in the hall. (158–9) If it suits the king and Laertes, the duel can take place now and Hamlet will do his best to win for Claudius. (159–61)

Osric says he will take Hamlet's answer to the king, and exits. (163) Horatio condemns Osric as a lackey, and Hamlet adds that he is typical of the kind of grovelling flunky that worships power but have no real substance. (170–6)

A lord enters, declaring that the king and queen are on their way to witness the fencing match. (184) The lord adds that Gertrude wants Hamlet to make his peace with Laertes before the duelling begins: 'The queen desires you to use some gentle entertainment/ to Laertes, before you fall to play'. (186–7) Hamlet agrees: 'She well instructs me'. (188)

LINES 190–203: HAMLET'S SENSE OF FOREBODING
Horatio tells Hamlet that he cannot win the bet: 'You will lose, my lord'. (189) Hamlet disagrees, saying he's been practising his swordsmanship while Laertes was in France: 'I shall win at the odds'. (191) However, he hints that his mind is filled with foreboding and apprehension: 'But thou wouldst not think how ill all's hereabout my heart'. (192–3)

Horatio says he will have the duel cancelled if Hamlet does not want it to go ahead. (197–8) Hamlet refuses, however, and says he will ignore his foreboding: 'Not a whit, we defy augury'. (199) He dismisses his apprehension as 'womanly' and resolves to go ahead with the fencing match: 'It is but foolery; but it is such a kind of gaingiving as would perhaps trouble a woman'. (195–6)

He declares that death ('it') is inevitable and unavoidable. Hamlet says that since we own so little of the world, it doesn't matter if we die prematurely: 'Since no man of aught he leaves knows, what is't to leave betimes?' (202–3) All that matters is that we are ready at all times for death's possible arrival. (202)

LINES 204–40: HAMLET APOLOGISES TO LAERTES
The royal couple, Laertes, Osric and the court

attendants enter the hall. Claudius acts as a peacemaker and puts Laertes' hand into Hamlet's. (204) Hamlet apologises to Laertes for his behaviour in the graveyard, blaming his actions on madness. (205–11) Due to madness he was not himself when he behaved in such an offensive manner: 'If Hamlet from himself be tane [taken] away,/ And when he's not himself does wrong Laertes,/ Then Hamlet does it not, Hamlet denies it'. (213–15)

Laertes makes a stiff reply. He says that in personal terms he is satisfied: 'I am satisfied in nature'. (223) However, he still needs to satisfy his public pride: 'but in my terms of honour/ I stand aloof; and will no reconcilement'. (225–6) He is content though with the prince's apology: 'I do receive your offered love like love,/ And will not wrong it'. (230–1)

LINES 241–58: PREPARATIONS FOR THE FENCING MATCH

Hamlet asks for the foils. (232) He then appears to flatter Laertes' fencing skills with elaborate language: 'I'll be your foil, Laertes. In mine ignorance/ Your skill shall like a star i'th'darkest night,/ Strike fiery off indeed'. (234–6) Laertes thinks he is being sarcastic, but Hamlet denies it. (236–7)

Claudius instructs Osric to give them the foils or fencing swords. (238) Laertes refuses the first foil Osric offers him, and asks to see another, presumably so he can choose the one whose tip has been poisoned. (243)

Claudius asks that wine be set out on a table. (246) He says that if Hamlet scores a hit he will also drink a toast to the prince's health. He will place a priceless pearl ('an union') in the cup which will be Hamlet's to keep. (251–3) In reality, however, the pearl contains poison. Once Claudius has placed it in the cup, he will coax Hamlet to have a drink, thereby killing him.

LINES 259–74: THE FENCING MATCH BEGINS

Hamlet and Laertes start duelling. Hamlet claims a touch on Laertes. (261) Laertes denies it but Osric, who's acting as judge, confirms the hit. (262–3) The king drinks to Hamlet's health and the cannon is fired off. He orders Hamlet to be given the cup. (266) (Presumably Claudius has placed the poisoned pearl in the cup before handing it over.)

Hamlet declines the drink, however, and asks Laertes to continue with the match. (268) The match resumes and Hamlet claims another hit. This time Laertes concedes that he is struck. (269–70)

> **REMEMBER:** Gertrude doesn't know the wine she drinks is poisoned. She is completely unaware of the plan by Claudius and Laertes to murder the prince.

LINES 275–8: GERTRUDE UNKNOWINGLY DRINKS THE POISON

Gertrude says that Hamlet is sweaty and short of breath. (271) She offers him her napkin to wipe himself. (272) She toasts the good fortune he has so far enjoyed in the match, lifting the poisoned cup to her lips. Claudius calls on her to stop but she insists on drinking. (275–6) Claudius laments to himself that his wife is doomed: 'It is the poisoned cup. It is too late'. (277) The queen offers Hamlet the cup, but he again refuses to take a drink. (278)

LINES 279–94: HAMLET AND LAERTES ARE BOTH WOUNDED WITH THE POISONED FOIL

Laertes asks Claudius if he should now wound Hamlet with his poisoned foil. (279) Claudius agrees, but Laertes expresses doubts about what he is doing: 'And yet it is almost against my conscience'. (281) Hamlet asks Laertes to return to the match and not to mock him by delaying. (283–4)

They duel, and for a brief time neither can strike the other. Finally, Laertes manages to wound Hamlet with the poisoned foil. They scuffle and somehow the poisoned foil ends up in Hamlet's hand, who wounds Laertes with it. Claudius orders the two men to be separated, but Hamlet wants to fight on. (288–9)

LINES 295–300: GERTRUDE DIES

The poison Gertrude has drunk begins to take effect and she falls to the ground. Claudius tries to conceal his crime, pretending she has merely fainted at the sight of the fencers' wounds: 'She swounds to see them bleed'. (295) Gertrude, however, will not allow this deception. With her last breath she calls out to warn Hamlet that the drink is poisoned; 'No, no, the drink, the drink – O my dear Hamlet –/ The drink, the drink – I am poisoned'. (296–7)

LINES 300–14: HAMLET KILLS CLAUDIUS

Hamlet is shocked that his mother has been poisoned. He orders that the doors of the hall be locked until the guilty parties can be discovered. (298–9) Laertes confesses and declares that Claudius is behind the whole plot: 'the king, the king's to blame'. (307) He tells Hamlet the foil that wounded both of them was poisoned and that they have only a short time to live:

'The treacherous instrument is in thy hand,/ Unbated and envenomed'. (303–4)

Hamlet reacts quickly and decisively to this news. He stabs Claudius with the poisoned foil: 'The point envenomed too!' Then, venom, to thy work'. (307–8) He then forces the poisoned wine down the king's throat: 'Here, thou incestuous, murderous, damnèd Dane,/ Drink off this poison'. (311–12) At last, Hamlet has taken his revenge.

✍ LINES 315–18: LAERTES DIES

Laertes is quickly dying having been wounded by the poisoned foil. He declares that Claudius is a villain who has got what he deserved: 'He is justly served/ It is a poison tempered by himself'. (314–15) With his last breath, he asks to be reconciled with Hamlet. (316) He wants them to forgive the wrongs they have done each other: 'Mine and my father's death come not upon thee,/ Nor thine on me'. (317–18)

✍ LINES 319–45: HAMLET DIES

Hamlet forgives the dead Laertes: 'Heaven make thee free of it! I follow thee'. (319) He also bids farewell to his dead mother: 'Wretched queen, adieu.' (320) He asks Horatio to remember his story to the world: 'Horatio, I am dead/ Thou livest; report me and my cause aright/ To the unsatisfied'. (325–7)

Horatio intends to kill himself by drinking from the poisoned cup. (327–9) Hamlet, however, manages to wrestle the cup from his friend. (329–30) The prince does not want his reputation defamed after his death. (331–2) He asks Horatio to keep living for the sake of their friendship and to tell the world the truth about the dramatic events at Elsinore: ' If thou didst ever hold me in thy heart,/ Absent thee from felicity awhile,/ And in this harsh world draw thy breath in pain/ To tell my story'. (333–5)

A disturbance and some cannon-fire are heard, signalling the arrival of both Fortinbras' troops and the English ambassadors. (336–9) Hamlet makes a last request, declaring that Fortinbras is his choice to become new king of Denmark: 'But I do prophesy th'election lights/ On Fortinbras; he has my dying

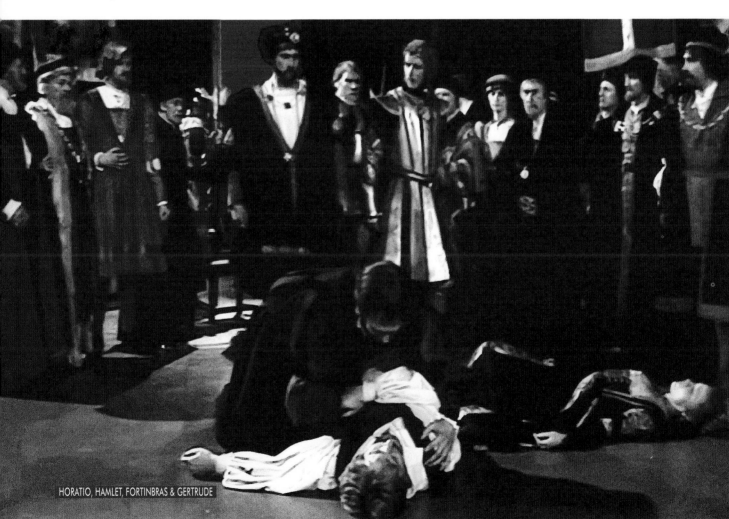

HORATIO, HAMLET, FORTINBRAS & GERTRUDE

voice'. (342–3) He asks Horatio to tell the Norwegian prince everything that has happened, but falters in mid-sentence, his last words being 'the rest is silence'. (345)

✒ LINES 346–90: FORTINBRAS AND THE ENGLISH AMBASSADORS ARRIVE

The doors open and Fortinbras and the English ambassadors enter. Fortinbras is shocked by the sight of the dead bodies, and wonders what has happened:

> O proud death,
> What feast is toward in thine eternal cell
> That thou so many princes at a shot
> So bloodily hast struck? (351–4)

The English ambassador declares that he has arrived too late to tell Claudius that his command has been carried out: 'Rosencrantz and Guildenstern are dead:/ Where should we have our thanks?' (354–8) Horatio reveals that it was not Claudius who ordered their deaths: 'He never gave commandment for their death'. (361)

Horatio requests of the new arrivals that the dead bodies be placed on a stage for all to view. (364–5) He then declares that he will fulfil Hamlet's request and tell the world the events that have led to such a bloodbath. He wants to tell his story immediately, but warns that his tale will be a bloody and chaotic one: 'So shall you hear/ Of carnal, bloody, and unnatural acts,/ Of accidental judgements, casual slaughters,/Of deaths put on by cunning and forced cause'. (367–70) Fortinbras is eager to hear Horatio's tale: 'Let us haste to hear it'. (373)

He says that he will take possession of Denmark with a heavy heart, but also informs those present that he has a long-standing claim to the throne. (375–7)

He orders that Hamlet's body should be carried to the stage with military honours. (382–7) He also orders the other bodies to be carried, saying the sight of so many bodies is more suited to a battlefield. (388–9) A funeral dirge is played as the bodies are carried out. A volley of cannon shot is fired.

A RUTHLESS STREAK

The prince's ruthless streak is once again evident in this scene. It comes across most forcibly when he describes sending Rosencrantz and Guildenstern to their deaths. This shows he has fulfilled the promise he made himself in Act 4 to become ruthless in his actions. Hamlet says he acted on instinct rather than reason: 'Our indiscretion sometimes serves us well,/ When our deep plots do pall'. (8–9) He sprung into action immediately, rather than 'unpacking his heart with words' as he has done throughout the play.

Yet we might ask, as Horatio seems to, if Hamlet's old school friends really deserved their fate. There is no reason to suspect that they knew they were bringing Hamlet to his death. The prince could instead have put an instruction in the letter condemning them to exile or imprisonment. Hamlet, however, shows no remorse. In his eyes, his two old friends had betrayed him by their unquestioning servitude to Claudius and so deserved to die: 'Why, man, they did make love to this employment;/ They are not near my conscience'. (57–8)

This new found ruthlessness is also evident when he suggests to Horatio that he intends to kill the king: 'is't not perfect conscience/ To quit him with this arm?' (67–8) He declares it would be wrong to let an evil man like Claudius continue to occupy the throne: 'and is't not to be damn'd/ To let this canker of our nature come/ In further evil?' (68–70)

It is arguable that Hamlet also shows this ruthless streak when

---

he kills Claudius toward the end of the scene, stabbing him with the poisoned blade and pouring poisoned wine down his throat. (311–12) At this stage, Hamlet himself is dying and most of the other main characters are dead. However, the prince does at last take his long-awaited revenge.

A NEGATIVE STATE OF MIND

Hamlet displays what can only be described as a sense of weary resignation in this scene. He seems untroubled that Claudius will soon learn the fate of his messengers and no doubt act against him, saying it doesn't really matter because life is so short anyway. (73–4) 'A man's life', he says, is 'no more than to say 'One'. (74)

This sense of resignation is also evident when Horatio offers to have the duel postponed. Hamlet will not even consider the suggestion. If he is to die now, then that is his destiny and there is no point in fighting it: 'If it be now, 'tis not to come; if it be not to come, it will be now; if it be not now, yet it will come – the readiness is all'. (200–2)

Hamlet also experiences a sense of dread and misgiving in this scene. Despite his confidence that he will defeat Laertes, he confesses to Horatio that he is filled with feelings of apprehension: 'But thou wouldst not think how ill all's here about my heart – but it is no matter'. (191–2) The prince dismisses these misgivings as 'foolery', but we can be sure they continue to haunt him. (195)

Hamlet's negative state of mind is offset by his apparent faith in divine purpose. He suggests that our lives are not our own to control but are shaped by a higher power: 'that should learn us/ There's a divinity that shapes our ends,/ Rough-hew them how we will'. (9–11) God's will,

he says, governs even the tiniest and most insignificant things that happen: 'there's a special providence/ in the fall of a sparrow'. (199–200) Heavenly influence, he says, even ensured he had his father's ring with him on the boat to England, allowing him to forge the letter from Claudius: 'even in that was heaven ordinant'. (48)

Throughout the play, Hamlet has expressed a deep weariness and disgust with life, regarding human existence has futile, meaningless and pointless. Now, however, he seems to have regained some of his faith in human existence, suggesting that each aspect of creation is guided by God and that all things serve a purpose decided by him.

SELF-IMPORTANCE

Hamlet's typically high opinion of himself is in evidence when he is challenged to the fencing match. He is confident of his ability to match Laertes, who is well known for his skill with the blade. Hamlet is convinced he will able to hold his own, saying he's been practising while Laertes was away in France. (190–1)

This sense of self-importance is also evident when Horatio attempts to kill himself by drinking from the poisoned cup. Hamlet prevents him from doing so, saying he cannot bear that he should be spoken ill of after his death: 'O God, Horatio, what a wounded name,/ Things standing thus unknown, shall live behind me!' (331–2)

He emotionally blackmails Horatio into fulfilling this wish, saying that if he is a true friend he will live on 'To tell my story'. (333–5) Hamlet, it seems, does not want Horatio to die so that he can tell his story and protect his posthumous reputation.

A CONCERN FOR HIS REPUTATION

As he lies dying, Hamlet expresses great concern that he should have a reputation after death. He exhorts Horatio to tell the world that he was justified in his actions: 'report me and my cause aright/ To the unsatisfied'. (326–7) He makes a similar request with his last breath, urging Horatio to tell Fortinbras the events that have taken place in Elsinore: 'So tell him, with th'occurents more and less/ Which have solicited'. (344–5)

Although it is a dying man's wish, we might perhaps find Hamlet's desperate desire to have himself completely exonerated of all guilt a little questionable, especially when we recall his murder of Polonius and baiting of Ophelia.

GERTRUDE

MATERNAL AFFECTION

Gertrude's deep maternal affection for Hamlet is evident throughout this scene. She urges him to make his peace with Laertes. During the fencing match she voices concern for his physical state: 'He's fat, and scant of breath'. (271) She offers him her napkin to wipe himself. She drinks a toasts to his good fortune, a toast that tragically leads to her own accidental death. With her final breath she warns her son that his life in his danger: 'O my dear Hamlet –/ The drink, the drink – I am poisoned'. (296–7) Her loyalty to her husband has been rewarded in a most terrible way. He has gone behind her back in an attempt to murder her son, accidentally killing her in the process.

CLAUDIUS

A SHREWD POLITICIAN

Claudius plans for Hamlet to die but doesn't want anyone at court to suspect him of involvement in the murder. He therefore plays the role of the forgiving stepfather, letting on that he has nothing against the prince. He backs Hamlet in the bet on the fencing match, declaring he will celebrate his nephew's scores by drinking wine and having cannon fired. He even offers Hamlet a priceless jewel as a reward for doing well. (Only, he knows, of course, that the jewel actually contains poison.)

His political acumen is also evident when he plays the role of peacemaker between Hamlet and Laertes: 'Come, Hamlet, come, and take this hand from me'. Doing so makes him appear as a king fully in control of his court.

In this scene Claudius goes ahead with his plan to offer Hamlet poisoned wine, a plan he came up with in Act 4 Scene 7. This is intended as a failsafe in case Laertes fails to kill Hamlet with the poisoned foil. We might, however, question the wisdom of this decision.

The poisoned wine introduces an element of chance and randomness to proceedings. Something can easily go wrong, as happens when Gertrude accidentally drinks from the poisoned chalice and ruins the entire scheme

MANIPULATIVE AND DECEPTIVE

This scene also shows Claudius at his most manipulative. The whole story of the bet between him and Laertes is perfectly contrived to prick Hamlet's pride and goad him into participating in the fencing match. We can imagine he instructed Osric to emphasise Laertes' qualities and skill as a swordsman, further pricking the prince's pride.

As we've noted, he pretends to be a loving and forgiving stepfather and plays the role of peacemaker between Hamlet and Laertes. Both deceptions, no doubt, are also intended to make sure the prince doesn't suspect the plot against him. His most despicable deception comes as Gertrude lies dying. He attempts to cover up what's happening, claiming she's only fainted at the sight of blood: 'She swounds [swoons] to see them bleed'. (295)

LAERTES

VENGEFUL

Throughout the previous scenes Laertes has come

As he lies dying he confesses about the plot he's been involved in. He tells Hamlet that Gertrude has indeed

HORATIO

HAMLET'S LOYAL FRIEND
As ever, Horatio continues to be Hamlet's loyal and protective friend.

+ He warns Hamlet that the king will soon discover what Hamlet has done to Rosencrantz and Guildenstern. (71-2)
+ He is wary of anyone approaching Hamlet. When Osric appears he is immediately watchful: 'Peace! Who comes here?' (80)
+ He plays along with Hamlet's baiting and mockery of Osric.
+ He is concerned that Hamlet will be defeated by Laertes in the duel: 'You will lose, my lord'. (189)
+ When Hamlet expresses his feelings of foreboding he offers to have the fencing match postponed.
+ Finally, when he sees that Hamlet has been wounded he rushes to his side: 'They bleed on both sides. How is it, my lord?' (291)

Horatio, it seems, cannot bear the prospect of life without Hamlet, and decides to join his friend in death: 'I am more an antique Roman than a Dane'. (328) He is talked out of it by Hamlet, who wants him to live on and tell his story. Horatio memorably expresses the sorrow he feels at his friend's passing: 'Now cracks a noble heart. Good night sweet prince,/ And flights of angels sing thee to thy rest', (346-7)

Horatio is determined to safeguard Hamlet's memory and give a truthful account of the bloody events at Elsinore: 'And let me speak to th'yet unknowing world/ How these things came about'. (366-7) He is confident he can carry out this final request of Hamlet's: 'all this can I/ Truly deliver'. (371-2) He believes that if he his rendition of Hamlet's saga will prevent further bloodshed. (378-82) Even though Hamlet is dead, Horatio will continue to serve him as a loyal friend.

FORTINBRAS

Fortinbras was described as a war-like young man in Act 1 Scene 1. His brief appearance here certainly confirms that impression. His troops needlessly fire on the English ambassadors who approach Elsinore at the same time he does. While he disapproves of dead bodies in a castle hall, he thinks they 'become' or suit a battlefield. (388-9) The greatest honour he think of giving Hamlet is a soldier's funeral: 'Bear Hamlet like a soldier to the stage'. (383) He will honour his fellow prince with 'soldier's music and the rite of war'. (386) This is someone who loves war and everything about it.

Throughout the play Fortinbras has come across as an aggressive and decisive person. In Act 1 we learned he rustled up his own army with which to invade Denmark. (He did this without even asking the permission of his uncle, the Norwegian king.) He then took an invasion force to Poland, risking thousands of lives over a meaningless piece of ground. Now he acts aggressively once more, asserting what he sees as his family's right to the Danish throne: 'I have some rights of memory in this kingdom'. (376) He takes charge of the situation, issuing instructions to the Danish courtiers. He claims that it is with sorrow he embrace kingship of Denmark. (375) However, we may question his sincerity here.

CONSIDER THIS

Fortinbras' appearance at the play's conclusion is something of a surprise. The last we saw of him was in Act 4 Scene 4 when he was crossing Denmark on his way to fight the Poles. We might ask ourselves exactly how he came to be at Elsinore.
Some readers feel that Fortinbras, having met with success in his Polish venture, is now invading Denmark. Yet why was this invasion never mentioned by any of the characters in the preceding scenes? And why did he find it seemingly so easy to penetrate the royal castle itself? (After all, in Act 1 we're told the Danish army is on high alert.) Is this a sudden, surprise attack?
It is also possible that Fortinbras, re-crossing Denmark on his way home to Norway, has simply come to visit the Danish court (he mentioned the possibility of such a visit in Act 4 Scene 4). Much to his surprise, he finds the Danish royal family dead and the throne his for the taking. We know he has troops with him because they fire on the English ambassadors. Yet it is not clear whether this is a full invasion force or merely a small group of men-at-arms.
Although Hamlet has nominated Fortinbras as king, we might ask ourselves if this is another instance of irony on Shakespeare's part. From what we have seen and know of Fortinbras, he appears as a ruthless character, determined to have his own way regardless of the cost in blood. Shakespeare may be telling us that Denmark's troubles will continue.

CHARACTERS & THEMES

CHARACTERS

HAMLET

HAMLET BEFORE HIS FATHER'S DEATH

We are occasionally given glimpses of what Hamlet was like prior to the events portrayed in the play. From those hints we can see that the prince was a noble and well-respected figure.

Hamlet is much loved by the Danish people. As Claudius puts it, 'He's loved of the distracted multitude'. (4.3.4) Ophelia suggests that everybody in Denmark looks up to him: 'The observed of all observers'. (3.1.156) He is considered the crowning glory of the Danish state: 'The expectancy and rose of the fair state'. (3.1.154)

We also get the sense that he was an active and good-humoured individual. (2.2.295) According to Ophelia, he was a gifted scholar, soldier and politician: 'The courtier's, soldier's, scholar's, eye, tongue, sword'. (3.1.153) However, the character that we meet at the start of the play has been affected deeply by his father's death and his mother's hasty remarriage. He has become listless, melancholic, self-obsessed and possibly even a little bitter.

ACT 1

LOYALTY TO HIS FATHER
In Act 1 Scene 2 we learn that Hamlet had extremely high regard for his father. He tells Horatio, 'I shall not look upon his like again'. (1.2.188) In his long soliloquy he describes him as 'So excellent a king', and praises the intense and tender love he showed his mother (1.2) As he puts it, he continues to see his father in his mind's eye. (1.2.185)

A NEGATIVE STATE OF MIND
It is obvious, then, that this great man's passing would have a negative impact on the prince's emotional state. However, Hamlet has also been deeply affected by his mother's hasty remarriage.

These events have cast Hamlet into a deep depression:

· He is harbouring thoughts of suicide and wishes that God hadn't decreed suicide a sin: 'that the Everlasting had not fixed/ His canon 'gainst self-slaughter'. (1.2.131–2)
· He would like to simply melt away and cease to exist. (129–30)
· Life seems grey, pointless and fruitless: 'How weary, stale, flat and unprofitable/ Seem to me all the uses of this world!' (133–4)
· The whole world now fills him with disgust. He describes it as an 'unweeded garden' full of 'things rank and gross in nature'. (135–6)

It is important to note that what Hamlet is experiencing is more than everyday depression or sorrow. This is a man gripped by a profound sense of futility and meaninglessness, someone for whom life no longer holds any value whatsoever.

We see this when Hamlet encounters the ghost on the battlements. He is unsure whether the ghost is a 'spirit' of health from Heaven or a 'goblin' damned from hell. (1.4.40) He disregards his friends' warnings, and follows the ghost's summons, heading off to speak with it in private. He also seems to place such little value on his own life that he doesn't care if the ghost leads him to his death: 'I do not set my life at a pin's fee'. (65)

ANGER & BITTERNESS
Yet Hamlet's depression is mixed with bitterness and anger caused by his mother's remarriage. The prince simply cannot believe that his mother has remarried less than two months after his father's death: 'That it should come to this!/ But two months dead – nay not so much, not two'. (1.2.137–8) Hamlet is even more appalled that she has married his uncle, a union he regards as incestuous. (152) To make matters even worse, Hamlet believes Claudius isn't half the man his father was: 'no more like my father/ Than I to Hercules'. (152–3)

The more he thinks about his mother's speedy remarriage, the angrier Hamlet becomes: 'Let me not think on't; frailty, thy name is woman'. (1.2.146) He condemns the 'wicked speed' with which she entered the 'incestuous sheets' of Claudius' bed. (156–7) This bitterness is evident in the smart remarks he makes while in the royal couple's presence. It is, perhaps, also evident when he publicly stresses that his grief over his father's loss is genuine: 'Seems madam? Nay it is, I know not seems'. (1.2.76) By doing so, he suggests that the royal couple are only pretending to grieve.

Claudius is eager to wrap-up the grieving period for Hamlet's father. He wants the court to move on and for things to get back to normal. He is eager to get on with his own kingship. Hamlet, however, refuses to go along with this. He continues to wear black and to mope mournfully around the court. We get a sense that this is a kind of silent protest against his mother's hasty remarriage and his father's replacement by this lesser man. It is not surprising, therefore, that Gertrude and Claudius urge him to stop mourning:

To give these mourning duties to your father;
But, you must know, your father lost a father,
That father lost, lost his, and the survivor bound
In filial obligation for some term
To do obsequious sorrow; but to persevere
In obstinate condolement is a course
Of impious stubbornness; 'tis unmanly grief (1.2.88–94)

HAMLET'S ENCOUNTER WITH THE GHOST

The ghost's story has a profound effect on Hamlet. It has given him a mission and a sense of purpose. He declares that from now on he will focus only on the ghost's demand for revenge and forget everything else: 'thy commandment all alone shall live/ Within the book and volume of my brain'. (1.5.102–3) Now he has been given a real reason to hate Claudius. The resentment he feels towards his uncle has found a concrete focus, for he has been told that Claudius is a 'villain, villain, smiling, damnèd villain'. (1.5.106)

However, he seems to feel daunted by the task that now faces him, and uncertain about how he will accomplish it: 'O cursed spite/ That ever I was born to set it right'. (2.1.186–7) The task he has been given is a brutal one – after all, it is not every day that your father's ghost appears and tells you to kill your uncle.

It is not surprising, then, that when Hamlet meets Horatio and Marcellus he is in a strange and agitated state of mind. He speaks in a giddy and confused fashion, with what Horatio describes as 'wild and whirling words'. (1.5.132) Hamlet is no doubt shaken and disturbed by the supernatural encounter he has just experienced. But he also seems exhilarated and excited by the meeting with the ghost, and the task it has given him.

ACT 2 :

HAMLET PRETENDS TO BE MAD

What happens next is surprising and confusing. A number of weeks have passed between the closing of Act 1 and the beginning of Act 2. We might expect Hamlet to have taken some form of action against Claudius as a step towards fulfilling the ghost's demand for vengeance. Instead, he has started behaving in an extremely peculiar manner. His behaviour could only be described as that of a madman.

According to Claudius, Hamlet has undergone a 'transformation'. Hamlet, he says, is behaving as though he has lost his reason. He behaves as if he has been removed 'from th'understanding of himself'. (2.2.9) Polonius refers to the 'lunacy' that has begun to characterise the prince's behaviour. (2.2.49)

Ophelia tells how Hamlet came to her in a dishevelled and agitated state. He was dirty and half undressed, and staring into space with a piteous look. She says that he looked like a creature released from hell to 'speak of horrors'. (2.1.80) She describes how he held her at arm's length, with one hand on his brow, staring at her face. He then walked out of the room, staring back at her over his shoulder.

Hamlet also behaves in a deranged fashion during his encounter with Polonius. He seems to think that Polonius is a 'fishmonger'. (2.2.171) He asks Polonius if he has a daughter even though he knows Ophelia well. (179) He says some strange things about maggots, dogs and women getting pregnant if they walk in the sun. He seems to suggest that he is older than Polonius when in fact he is much younger: 'For yourself, sir, shall grow old as I am – if, like a crab, you could go backward'. (2.2.199–201)

TO WHAT EXTENT IS HAMLET'S MADNESS AN ACT?

There can be little doubt that Hamlet's mad behaviour is largely an act. At the end of Act 1 he signalled to his friends that he may start acting in a crazy manner: 'I perchance hereafter shall think meet/ To put an antic disposition on'. (1.5.170–1) In Act 2 Scene 2 he tells Rosencrantz and Guildenstern that he is 'but mad north-north-west', suggesting that at most he is only the tiniest bit mad. (2.2.363)

Hamlet comes across as rational and perceptive in his conversation with Rosencrantz and Guildenstern. He engages in some laddish banter of a sexual nature when they arrive. He quickly realises that Rosencrantz and Guildenstern have been sent to spy on him by Claudius: 'You were sent for, and there is a kind of confession in your looks'. (2.2.275–6) He persuades them to admit this even though they deny it at first.

The prince also comes across as very sane in his dealings with the players, giving them a warm welcome to Elsinore and enthusiastically discussing his favourite speech. His soliloquy at the end of the act reveals the workings of a rational, logical mind. There can be no doubt, therefore, that Hamlet is sane, and that the peculiar behaviour he exhibits is an act.

WHY DOES HAMLET PRETEND TO BE MAD?
It is unclear why Hamlet decides to pretend to act like a madman. It is often suggested that it is the first stage of his plan to get revenge on Claudius. Yet the prince never actually reveals what he hopes to accomplish by putting on an 'antic disposition'. It is far from clear how behaving in this strange fashion brings revenge any closer.

It has been suggested that the act is a smokescreen so that Claudius will not suspect that Hamlet is out to get him. If he thinks Hamlet is a simple-minded lunatic, he won't be on his guard against him. However, there are two problems with this: firstly, Claudius has no reason at all to suspect that Hamlet knows about his crime; secondly, by behaving in this bizarre fashion, Hamlet only draws attention to himself, presumably making his mission only more difficult to accomplish.

Another reason given for Hamlet's mad behaviour is that it allows him to say anything he wants. As we have seen in Act 1, and will see in the next section, Hamlet is in an extremely negative state of mind. Pretending to be mad means that Hamlet can say horrible things to people and use madness as an excuse. This allows him to vent the anger and bitterness he feels about his mother's remarriage, his hatred of Claudius and the general feelings of despair and futility that have gripped him.

HAMLET'S NEGATIVE STATE OF MIND
SUICIDAL THOUGHTS
In Act 1 Hamlet expressed what can only be described as suicidal thoughts, wishing that his body would just dissolve and melt away. Similar sentiments are expressed here. When Polonius leaves him, he says that there is nothing he would part with more readily than his life: 'You cannot take from me anything that I will not more willingly part withal – except my life'. (2.2.216–18) It is also perhaps evident when he says that he might walk into his grave. (2.2.208)

HIS DISGUST AT THE WORLD
As in Act 1, Hamlet expresses his disgust at the world in which he is forced to live. He describes the world as a prison and Denmark as the worst of its 'many confines,/ wards and dungeons'. (2.2.245–6) The earth, he says, is nothing but a 'sterile promontory' and the air no more than 'a foul and pestilent congregation of vapours'. (2.2.302–6) Perhaps a similar disgust is evident when he describes to Polonius how the 'sun breed maggots in a dead dog'. (2.2.181)

THE FUTILITY OF LIFE
As in Act 1, Hamlet expresses how pointless life seems to him. Humanity is considered the 'paragon of animals', God-like, yet to him it is no more than the 'quintessence of dust'. (2.2.312) Given this sense of life's futility, it is hardly surprising that Hamlet has given up exercising and no longer takes any joy in the world around him: 'Man delights not me; no, nor woman neither'. (2.2.309–10) This sense of futility is perhaps also evident when he tells Polonius that the book he is reading contains 'Words, words, words'. (2.2.192)

PROCRASTINATION & SELF-ACCUSATION
Hamlet bitterly accuses himself of being a procrastinator, someone who thinks too much and over-analyses situations rather than taking direct action. He is disgusted by what he sees as this negative aspect of his personality, wondering why he must 'like a whore unpack my heart with words'. (582)

The prince is amazed that the player could move himself to tears while speaking about Hecuba, a fictional character: 'What's Hecuba to him, or he to Hecuba,/ that he should weep for her?' (554–5) Hamlet has a much greater 'motive and cue for passion' than the player, yet so far he has done nor said nothing against the murderer of his father. (561–4) He mentions all the reasons he has for taking action:

· He has been asked to avenge his 'dear father' on

whose 'property and most dear life / A damn'd defeat was made'. (565–6)

· He has been commanded to act by a presence from beyond the grave: 'Prompted to my revenge by heaven and hell'. (581)

· The man he's been asked to kill is nothing but a 'remorseless, treacherous, lecherous, kindless villain!' (577)

Despite all this, however, he has done nothing. His disgust at his own procrastination is evident in the stream of insults the prince throws at himself. He bitterly describes himself as a 'rogue', a 'peasant slave', an 'ass', a 'drab' and a 'scullion'. He condemns himself as weak-willed and unreliable, a 'dull and muddy-mettled rascal'. (562) He declares that he must be a coward for not having already killed the king:

But I am pigeon-livered and lack gall
To make oppression bitter, or ere this
I should have fatted all the region kites
With this slave's offal (573–6)

We get a sense here that Hamlet wishes he could be driven by raw emotion rather than having to think about and analyse every situation. Hamlet accuses himself of cowardice, of lacking the 'gall', the bitter, raw emotion to take revenge. (2.2.512)

WHY DOES HAMLET NOT TAKE MORE DIRECT ACTION AGAINST CLAUDIUS?

Critics generally believe that a number of weeks have passed between Act 1 and Act 2. There is reason to believe that for most of this time Hamlet has done nothing productive in terms of avenging his father. It seems that all he has done is begin to act in an insane fashion. There are a number of potential reasons for Hamlet's lack of action:

1. PERSONALITY REASONS

Hamlet accuses himself of being a procrastinator, someone who thinks too much and over-analyses situations rather than taking direct action. He is disgusted by what he sees as this negative aspect of his personality, wondering how he must 'like a whore unpack my heart with words' instead of just getting on with it and killing Claudius. (2.2.520) This is especially so because he is the son of a murdered man, 'Prompted to my revenge by heaven and hell'. (2.2.518–19)

The prince seems amazed that the player could move himself to tears while thinking about Hecuba, a fictional character. Hamlet has a much greater motive

and 'cue for passion' than the player, yet he has done nor said nothing against the murderer of his father so far. He curses his procrastination, saying 'O what a rogue and peasant slave am I!' (2.2.485)

2. PSYCHOLOGICAL REASONS

We should also remember that Hamlet is not in what we might call a normal or healthy state of mind. As we've seen, he is grappling with suicidal thoughts, he regards life as futile, and is full of contempt and disgust for the life around him. There is also the matter of his burning rage towards his mother and towards women in general. All in all, then, Hamlet is perhaps not in the best state of mind to take on a dangerous mission of vengeance.

3. MORAL REASONS

Hamlet is deeply worried that the ghost is not telling the truth and that Claudius may in fact be innocent of his father's murder. He worries that the spirit he has seen 'may be a devil' that's trying to damn his soul by tricking him into killing an innocent man. (2.2.533–9) He is, therefore, desperate to have proof of Claudius' guilt.

We should also bear in mind that Hamlet has been asked to perform a terrible deed – the murder of another person. To make matters worse, the man he is being asked to kill is not only the king – God's representative on earth – but also his uncle.

4. PRACTICAL REASONS

There are also practical reasons that make it difficult for Hamlet to carry out his revenge. Claudius is a formidable adversary – shrewd, cunning and devious. In Act 1 Scene 2 we get the impression that the king has the entire Danish court behind him.

Hamlet cannot be sure whom, if anyone, he can trust. Rosencrantz and Guildenstern, his old school friends, have been brought to spy on him. The woman he loved, Ophelia, will be used as bait in order to determine the cause of his madness: 'I'll loose my daughter to him'. (2.2.159) He cannot even trust his own mother. As we see in Act 3, he suspects that she may even have been involved in the plot to murder his father.

There is also the question of what would happen to Hamlet after he kills the king. He would have to be in a position to mount a coup and seize the position himself, otherwise he would surely be put to death for murdering Denmark's rightful monarch.

While it was easy for Hamlet to swear immediate

vengeance in Act 1 Scene 5, we should remember that this was on the battlements in the dead of night, just after his encounter with the ghost. The prince has found that it is not so easy to fulfil that promise in the cold light of day.

HAMLET'S LOVE OF THEATRE

The prince has a deep and passionate love of theatre. Rosencrantz is certain that the players' arrival will bring him joy, and remarks how much Hamlet enjoyed the 'tragedians of the city'. (2.2.292)

Hamlet immediately remarks how the players will be given great hospitality during their stay in Elsinore. He stresses this to Polonius, saying that the players must be 'well bestowed' during their stay. When the players arrive, he welcomes them warmly, calling them 'masters' and 'good friends'.

Hamlet displays an excellent knowledge of the theatrical world:

- He is curious about the new fashion for child performers that threatens to drive the established companies out of business.
- It is obvious that he is familiar with this particular troupe, and has seen them perform before.
- He immediately asks to hear a speech, and asks them to perform *The Murder of Gonzago* later at court.
- He asks about an obscure play, one that was almost never performed because it was considered too deep and complex for the general public.
- He seems to know entire speeches off by heart, and is clearly a good speaker of theatrical verse, earning Polonius' praise for his efforts.
- He is also capable of writing for the theatre, asking the first player if he can insert some dozen or sixteen lines into the performance of *The Murder of Gonzago*.

HAMLET'S PLAN TO DISCOVER IF THE GHOST IS LYING

The unexpected arrival of the players provides Hamlet with an opportunity to prove to himself that Claudius is guilty. He has heard that criminals sometimes act guiltily when they see a performance that mirrors their own crimes: 'I have heard/ That guilty creatures suiting at a play/ Have by the very cunning of the scene … proclaimed their malefaction'. (2.2.565–70) He has therefore asked the players to perform *The Murder of Gonzago*, a play whose plot closely resembles the murder of his father: 'I'll have these players/ Play something like the murder of my

father/ Before mine uncle'. (2.2.573–5) Presumably, the lines that Hamlet will add himself will make the similarity even more striking. By observing Claudius' reaction, Hamlet will be able to tell if the king is guilty of the murder or not: 'The play's the thing/ Wherein I'll catch the conscience of the king'. (2.2.582–3)

ACT 3

HAMLET PRETENDS TO BE MAD

Hamlet continues his act of being a madman. This is especially evident before the performance of *The Murder of Gonzago*. As the royal couple arrives to watch the show, Hamlet tells Horatio that it is time for him to 'be idle' once more, meaning that he must once again pretend to be insane.

- He responds to Claudius' greeting with what seems like gibberish. (3.2.92–3)
- He makes a similar response when Polonius tells him that he once played the part of Julius Caesar in a play: 'It was a brute part of him to kill so capital a calf there'. (3.2.102–3)
- He makes several comments about Ophelia's genitalia that are both highly socially inappropriate and weird and disjointed.
- He pretends to not know how long it has been since his father's death.

His rantings have a disconnected and disjointed quality, making them sound like the products of an irrational mind. He denies he ever gave Ophelia gifts, though he obviously did, and repeatedly switches from denying he ever loved her to telling her that he once did. (3.1.90–151)

Hamlet gives a similar performance when he meets Rosencrantz and Guildenstern after the players have performed. He speaks to them in a manner that is somehow wild and disconnected, telling them that his 'wit's diseased'. (3.2.300) Rosencrantz is baffled and frustrated by Hamlet's strange talk, and asks him to speak normally: 'put your discourse into some frame, and start not so wildly from my affair'. (198–9)

It is important to realise that Hamlet does not act like someone who has gone completely and utterly insane. As Claudius puts it, 'what he spake, though it lack'd form a little,/ Was not like madness'. (3.1.165–6) Though what he says is disjointed and peculiar, it makes a strange kind of sense. His crazy remarks are often sharp and punning observations of the world around him.

In Act 3 Scene 4 he reveals to Gertrude that he is only pretending to be mad: 'it is not madness/ That I have utter'd'. (3.4.142–3) However, he is desperate that Claudius not find this out, asking Gertrude not to tell the king that he is essentially 'not in madness/ But mad in craft'. (3.4.190–1)

We might ask ourselves again why Hamlet is so keen for Claudius to believe that he is insane. After all, as we noted in our discussion of Act 2, it is hard to know what Hamlet wishes to achieve from this pretence.

HAMLET'S NEGATIVE STATE OF MIND
In this Act Hamlet continues to think about suicide. He wonders whether it is better to be dead than alive: 'To be, or not to be: that is the question'. (3.1.56) He regards death as a restful sleep that soothes us after the toil and hardship of living. (60–5) He himself longs for the soothing sleep of death: ''tis a consummation/ Devoutly to be wish'd'. (63–4) He wonders why we endure the trials of living, why we 'bear the whips and scorns of time', when we could end it all with a dagger: 'When he himself might his quietus make/ With a bare bodkin'. (75–6)

According to Hamlet, all that stops us from committing suicide is fear of what awaits us in the next life. We do not know what awaits us in the 'undiscover'd country' of death. (3.1.79) There is always a possibility that the eternity of death will be filled with terrible dreams. Therefore, we prefer to stick with the devil we know, enduring the ills of this world rather than risking whatever awaits us in the next.

THE FUTILITY OF LIFE & DISGUST AT THE WORLD
In the 'To be, or not to be' speech Hamlet expounds upon the sense of futility and disgust he expressed in Acts 1 and 2. He depicts life as being full of trials and difficulties, wondering why any of us continue to bear the 'whips and scorns of time'. (3.1.70) A similar attitude seems evident when he tells Ophelia to become a nun and not bother having any children: 'Get thee to a nunnery: why wouldst thou be a breeder of sinners'. (3.1.121–2) It's as though Hamlet thinks there is no point bringing children into the world. He considers the world to be full of 'arrant knaves', none of whom are to be trusted. (3.1.128–9)

ANGER & BITTERNESS
In this act, as in Act 1, Hamlet expresses the intense bitterness and anger his mother's remarriage has caused him. From the very beginning of the play Hamlet has been filled with rage caused by his

mother's remarriage. Let's remind ourselves that the remarriage upset Hamlet for three different reasons: he felt that it came much too soon after his father's death, that Claudius isn't half the man his father was, and that the union is incestuous.

This is evident during the player's performance, when Hamlet pretends to think that his father has been dead only two hours. (3.2.121) He sarcastically remarks that we don't remember great men for very long after their deaths. (3.2.126) These statements are no doubt veiled criticisms of his mother for having married so quickly and seemingly forgetting about his father. He also bitterly remarks that his mother looks cheerful despite having recently been widowed. (3.2.120)

In Act 3 Scene 4 Hamlet expresses his anger towards his mother in no uncertain terms, essentially raging at her for its entire first half. In Act 3 Scene 2 he vowed to verbally torment his mother for what he perceives as her great sin. Now he does so, attempting to 'wring her heart' with his harsh words. (3.4.35) His aim is to 'set up a glass' or mirror in which Gertrude 'may see the inmost part' of herself. (3.4.18–19) He refuses to let her leave until his rage is vented: 'you shall not budge'. (3.4.16)

His volcanic anger is also evident when he describes his mother as having a 'wicked tongue' and especially when he cruelly wishes she was not his mother at all. (3.4.10, 14) He violently rants at Gertrude, saying how her actions have stolen the very soul from the institution of marriage, branded 'innocent love' like a prostitute, and have made even Heaven blush. (3.4.40–51)

He seems filled with incomprehension at his mother's actions, simply failing to understand how she could marry Claudius having previously been with a great man like his father. Repeatedly he asks her 'Have you eyes?' (65–7) Either her reason was paralysed when she made this choice or she must have been possessed by a devil. (71–5)

Hamlet also vents his anger at Claudius in this scene, referring to him as 'a murderer and a villain;/ A slave'. (96–7) He describes the king in no uncertain terms as a thief or 'cutpurse' who stole the 'rule and empire' from its rightful owner.

NEGATIVE ATTITUDE TOWARDS WOMEN & SEXUALITY
In Act 3 Scene 1 the prince's encounter with Ophelia reveals his negative view of women:

- He seems to suggest that beautiful women cannot be honest: 'Your honesty should admit no discourse to your beauty'. (3.1.107–8)
- He suggests that women are dangerous temptresses that make monsters out of men. (3.1.139–41)
- The prince suggests that women are false and deceitful, especially in their use of make-up: 'God has given you one face, and you make yourselves another'. (3.1.143–4)
- He suggests that women are shallow, lisping, silly creatures. (3.1.144–7)

Hamlet's negative view of women causes him to attack the institution of marriage: 'I say we will have no more marriages. Those that are married already – all but one – shall live'. (148–9) He urges Ophelia to become a nun rather than marry. (3.1.136–9) He curses any marriage she might have.

Throughout this act, Hamlet also reveals a strange attitude towards female sexuality. This is evident in the various vulgar sexual remarks he makes to Ophelia. We see this when he tells her to go to a nunnery, a 'nunnery' being not only a convent but also a slang term for brothel. We also see this tendency during the players' performance, when Hamlet makes several oblique but vulgar remarks to Ophelia:

- He makes a reference to oral sex ('country matters').
- He makes a reference to genitalia ('the puppets dallying').
- He also says that if Ophelia took the edge off his sexual desire it would cost her a 'groaning' in childbirth.

This disgust or discomfort with female sexuality is also evident in Act 3 Scene 4. He declares that it's impossible for an older woman like Gertrude to fall in love: 'You cannot call it love … at your age'. (3.4.68) He says that women of Gertrude's age feel little passion or sexual desire: 'The hey-day in the blood is tame, it's humble'. (3.4.69)

He presents Gertrude's sexual relations with Claudius as being sinful and corrupt, describing how the king caresses her with his 'damn'd fingers'. (3.4.188) He describes her marriage bed as a sewer of lust and corruption: 'but to live/ In the rank sweat of an enseamed bed,/ Stew'd in corruption, honeying and making love/ Over the nasty sty'. (3.4.91–4)

It is notable that while Hamlet regards his mother's sexual behavior as disgusting, sinful and corrupt, he cannot avoid dwelling on it and describing it in some detail. (3.4.184–9) The prince seems to have a disturbed and disturbing fascination with his mother's sexuality. He finds it simultaneously repulsive and fascinating.

A RUTHLESS STREAK

After the player's performance, Hamlet is certain that the ghost spoke the truth, and that Claudius is guilty of murder. At the end of Act 3 Scene 2 he speaks in a dark and violent manner, suggesting that he could 'drink hot blood'. (3.2.363) This is the first time in the play when Hamlet seems to be in the right frame of mind to avenge his father's death.

The prince has been asked to visit his mother. He worries that in his bloodthirsty state he will attack her, or that visiting her will diminish his bloodthirstiness. Hamlet speaks to himself at the end of the scene in an effort to restrain himself from causing his mother harm: 'Let me be cruel, not unnatural:/ I will speak daggers to her but use none'. (3.2.368–9)

Hamlet's decision not to murder Claudius while the king is at prayer reveals the ruthless side of his personality. His father was murdered in cold blood, without the opportunity to confess his sins, and he suffers torment in Purgatory as a result. If Hamlet murders Claudius while he's praying, the king's soul will be in a state of grace and go straight to Heaven. Hamlet feels it's wrong that Claudius should go straight to paradise while his own father languishes in Purgatory. He wants Claudius not only to die but also to suffer in the next life.

The death of Polonius provides further evidence of this ruthlessness. Hamlet assumes that Claudius is spying on him from behind the screen. (3.4.24) Yet he doesn't bother to lift the screen before driving his sword into it. If there's even a chance the hidden observer is Claudius, then that person is going to die. At this stage, the prince definitely means business.

Hamlet claims to regret killing Polonius: 'I do repent'. (3.4.174) His regret, however, seems a little insincere, especially given the way he taunts the corpse. He refers to Polonius as a 'fool' and a as a 'foolish prating knave'. (3.4.31, 216) He spends only a moment contemplating Polonius' demise before turning his attention back to his mother. We get the impression that Hamlet's only regret is that he killed the wrong man.

This steely side to his character is also evident when he says he plans to deal clinically with Rosencrantz and Guildenstern. He claims that their betrayal of him will 'marshal' or lead him to 'knavery' of his own. He seems to admit he will take a kind of pleasure in the prospect of dealing them back in kind: 'For 'tis the sport to have the engineer/ Hoist with his own petard'. (3.4.207–8) He ominously says that it will 'go hard' with his two old school friends. (3.4.208)

A SENSE OF SUPERIORITY

Hamlet's sense of superiority is evident throughout this Act. We see it in the way he speaks to the players in Act 3 Scene 2. Hamlet speaks to them like a true prince. There is an element of arrogance in the way he tells them exactly how he wants them to perform his piece. This is a man who knows what he wants, and is used to getting it. (3.2.1–39)

Throughout this Act Hamlet displays what many feel is an unpleasant sense of superiority. In Act 3 Scene 1 he stresses his own virtue to Ophelia. Similarily in Act 3 Scene 4 he credits himself as being more or less the only person in Elsinore to have any sense of what is right and wrong: 'Forgive me this my virtue;/ For in the fatness of these pursy times/ Virtue itself of vice must pardon beg'. (3.4.153–5)

This self-righteousness is most evident in Act 3 Scene 4 when he essentially preaches at his mother declaring that he will force her to confront her sins. (3.4.19–20) We also see it when he urges her to 'Confess yourself to heaven,/ Repent what's past; avoid what is to come'. (3.4.150–1) A similar preachiness is evident when he advises his mother that she can overcome her sinful lust by getting into the habit of not sleeping with Claudius: 'Refrain tonight,/ And that shall lend a kind of easiness/ To the next abstinence, the next more easy'. (3.4.166–8)

He rages against his mother, pointing out what he perceives as her faults. However, he offers her no chance to explain or justify herself. Instead he is a self-appointed judge and jury. Hamlet seems convinced that he and only he knows what is right and proper.

LOYALTY TO HIS FATHER

Act 3 Scene 4 stresses once again just how much Hamlet reveres and misses his father. His depiction of the dead king is unreserved in its admiration and respect: 'A combination and a form indeed,/ Where every god did seem to set his seal,/ To give the world assurance of a man'. (3.4.60–2) His love for his father is evident when he is almost moved to tears by the ghost's terrible state. (3.4.126–8)

A LOVE OF THEATRE

In Act 2 Scene 2 we witnessed Hamlet's great excitement upon hearing of the players coming to court. In Act 3 Scene 2 he reveals just how knowledgeable he is about theatrical performance, describing in great detail how he wishes the players to perform their lines. He is confident of his views and opinions and tells them exactly what he likes and dislikes in a performance. The prince is deeply passionate about theatre and loathes to see bad acting.

ACT 4

Act 4 swiftly follows on from Act 3. Hamlet has hidden the body of Polonius somewhere in the castle and Rosencrantz and Guildenstern have been sent by the king to find him.

Hamlet's intention – after the king's reaction to the performance of the play proved the ghost's words to be true – was to kill the king. He seemed to have been in the right frame of mind to go through with the deed. However, when he found Claudius seemingly at prayer, Hamlet hesitated and decided that the time was not right. He then paid a visit to his mother's room where, hearing a voice behind the arras, he stabbed Polonius to death.

By so doing he lost the initiative and perhaps the necessary blood-thirstiness to seek out the king and kill him. The king has also had time to re-group and he now has men looking for Hamlet. Claudius will not take any chances with the prince now that he has heard how Polonius was killed.

PRETENDING TO BE MAD

When we first meet Hamlet in Act 4 Scene 2 he seems to be in a highly excited and somewhat playful state of mind, not too dissimilar to how he was after he spoke to the ghost on the ramparts (Act 1 Scene 5). He speaks in a strange and sometimes cryptic manner to Rosencrantz and Guildenstern and runs away from them at the end of the scene as though they are playing some schoolyard game: 'Hide fox, and all after!' (4.2.28)

However, though his former schoolmates are bamboozled by what he says, the prince's words are at times sharp and pertinent. He tells Rosencrantz and Guildenstern that they are little more than the king's 'sponges'. Claudius will flatter and reward them while they are useful to him, but he will also quickly discard them when he has gotten what he needs.

In Scene 3 Hamlet continues to act in a mad fashion. His responses to Claudius' questions are strange. When asked where Polonius is, the prince replies 'At supper', by which he means that Polonius is being eaten by worms. He then speaks about worms and maggots and describes how 'a king may go a progress through the guts of a beggar'.

However, as we have just noted, though the prince may be acting somewhat madly, what he says is not mindless gibberish. His responses to the king are certainly bizarre, but they contain sharp and logical observations about death.

A SENSE OF SUPERIORITY

The prince's usual sense of superiority is on display throughout this Act. It is evident when he verbally toys with Rosencrantz and Guildenstern, asking them why he, 'the son of a king', should answer their questions. (4.2.13) It is also evident in Hamlet's encounter with the king in Act 3 Scene 3.

Although Hamlet is now at the mercy of the king, he does not appear greatly distressed. He greets Claudius' news that he is to be sent to England with a nonchalant 'Good'. His confident behavior before the king is perhaps designed to unsettled Claudius. Hamlet knows that he will not be harmed openly before the court, and that he can say more or less what he wants.

SELF-CRITICAL

By the time Hamlet is being led to the ship that will take him to England he seems to have once again lost the rage and violence that he felt after the play, and which enabled him to act in a bloody manner. His speech upon seeing Fortinbras leading an army to Poland is reminiscent of his soliloquy in Act 2 Scene 2 after witnessing the Player's emotional performance of lines from a play about Hecuba. Again Hamlet berates himself for his lack of action. He is appalled that he, having greater personal motivation than Fortinbras seems to have for attacking Poland, cannot kill Claudius. He vows once again to act in a determined and bloody manner: 'Oh from this time forth,/ My thoughts be bloody, or be nothing worth.' (65–6)

RUTHLESS & DECISIVE

The prince seems to act on this promise to be more ruthless as he sails to England. Horatio receives a startling letter from Hamlet describing how the princes' ship came under attack from a pirate vessel. Hamlet describes how he single-handedly fought his way aboard the pirates' ship and somehow managed to negotiate his return to Denmark.

ACT 5

A RUTHLESS STREAK

In Act 4 Scene 4 Hamlet swore he would become more ruthless and decisive. He demonstrated this when he boarded the pirate ship and made his way back to Denmark. We also see it in the ruthless way he dealt with Rosencrantz and Guildenstern. Hamlet says he acted on instinct rather than reason: 'Our indiscretion sometimes serves us well/ When our deep plots do pall'. (5.2.8–9) There, he sprang into action immediately, rather than 'unpacking his heart with words' as he has done throughout the play.

Hamlet declares that now he is back in Denmark he means business. He warns Laertes not to trifle with him: 'Yet have I something in me dangerous/ Which let thy wisdom fear'. (244–5) His last lines In Act 5 Scene 1 can be taken as a warning to Laertes and to Claudius: 'Let Hercules himself do what he may,/ The cat will mew, and dog will have his day'. (5.1.273–4)

The prince also threatens Claudius when he announces himself to the funeral by saying 'This is I,/ Hamlet the Dane'. (5.1.239–40) By calling himself 'the Dane' Hamlet suggests that he is the true king of Denmark. He seems to be suggesting that he is going to do away with Claudius and claim the throne that is rightfully his.

He tells Horatio that he intends to kill the king: 'is't not perfect conscience/ To quit him with this arm?' (5.2.67–8) He declares it would be wrong to let an evil man like Claudius continue to occupy the throne: 'and is't not to be damned/ To let this canker of our nature come/ In further evil?' (5.2.68–70)

PROCRASTINATION

Yet despite these strong words, once back in Denmark Hamlet does little or nothing to destroy Claudius. He takes no direct action against the king. Instead he spends his time pondering death in the graveyard, verbally toying with Osric, and even agrees to take part in the fencing match that is being staged for the king's amusement. It is difficult to reconcile the prince's behaviour with his words.

It is interesting to contrast Hamlet's behaviour in this regard with Laertes, something discussed in more detail in the section on revenge.

A NEGATIVE STATE OF MIND

In Act 5 Hamlet continues to be in an incredibly negative state of mind. His morbid obsession with decomposition and decay finds its most potent expression in the graveyard scene:

· He asks the gravedigger how long it takes for a human body to rot once it has been buried: 'How long will a man lie i'th'earth ere he rot?' (5.1.149)
· He imagines the bodies of great men like Alexander the Great and Julius Caesar turning to dust and clay and eventually being put to practical uses. (5.1.191–8)
· He seems fascinated by the skulls that are tossed around the graveyard as the gravediggers do their work, imagining the different people they belonged to. (5.1.70–91)
· He is both horrified and mesmerized by Yorick's skull, by that the fact that where the jester's lips once 'hung' where there is now only bare bone. (5.1.172)
· Hamlet is almost sickened by this stark sight, declaring his 'gorge rises at it'. (5.1.171–2) And yet he is too riveted to look away but continues addressing the skull of his childhood friend.

There is something unnerving about the almost professional interest Hamlet takes in the gravedigger's trade. He wants to know how long the gravedigger has been on the job, how long a body will take to rot, whose grave it is he's digging, and whom the skulls belonged to. Horatio warns him that he is brooding on the topic of death too much: 'Twere to consider too curiously, to consider so'. (5.1.188) Hamlet, however, will not be diverted from this morbid train of thought. This is truly a man obsessed with death and decay.

Throughout the play Hamlet has been haunted by the transience of life, by the awful but inescapable reality that after all too brief a time each of us must pass away.

In this final Act his brooding awareness of life's transience reaches a crescendo.

He seems both fascinated and horrified that the skulls being so unceremoniously tossed around the graveyard once belonged to living people: 'That skull had a tongue in it, and could sing once'. (5.1.70) He is both repelled and mesmerized that Yorick, who was so full of joy and good humour, is now only a jawless skull: 'Where be your gibes now? Your gambols? your songs?' (5.1.173–4)

It doesn't matter what skills or achievements we have in life, whether we be a politician, a lawyer or a great businessman. Each of us will die and rot in the ground. Even a great man like Alexander the Great ends up as only a stinking skull. In this scene, then, Hamlet is also struck by the notion of death as the 'great leveler', by the idea that death treats all of us, great and humble alike, in the very same way. One skull, after all, is indistinguishable from another.

This awareness of life's transience fills Hamlet with a sense of weary resignation. He seems untroubled that Claudius will soon learn of the fate of Rosencrantz and Guildenstern, and will no doubt act against him. He says it doesn't really matter because life is so short anyway. 'A man's life', he says, is 'no more than to say "one"'. (5.2.74) He feels that death is no great tragedy because we really own nothing in this life anyway.

A SENSE OF SUPERIORITY

Arguably Hamlet's least attractive quality is his self-importance and self-absorption.

We see this at its worst when emerges from his hiding place and interrupts Ophelia's funeral. Hamlet's behaviour here can only be described as self-absorbed, selfish and self-important. He disrupts the funeral in manner that is extremely disrespectful to the dead Ophelia, to her brother, and to the other mourners.

He seems to do this out of jealousy at Laertes' powerful words of mourning, rather than out of grief over Ophelia's death. The prince asks: 'What is he whose grief/ Bears such an emphasis?' (5.1.236–7) Throughout the play Hamlet has thought of himself as a master of language: a theatre lover, actor, writer and talker. He now seems to experience envy and resentment at the eloquence with which Laertes expresses his grief. In a sense he gatecrashes and ruins the funeral because he cannot bear to not be the centre of attention.

It seems that in Hamlet's mind everything is always about him. His self-absorption prevents him from seeing the effect his actions have on other people. He is more concerned that Laertes is somehow showing him up than he is with the emotional needs and dignity of the mourners. He becomes indignant over the fact that Laertes is angry with him. (5.1.271) The prince appears to forget that he has just ruined the funeral of Laertes' sister and has also murdered his father.

Hamlet at least has the good grace to later regret barging in on the funeral and insulting Laertes: 'I am very sorry, good Horatio,/ that to Laertes I forgot myself'. (5.2.75–6)

His apology to Laertes is long and eloquent. (5.2.205–22) Hamlet attributes his bad behaviour in the graveyard to a fit of madness. (5.2.213) Yet surely this is only an excuse. Throughout the play Hamlet has only been acting as if he were mad, and we have no reason to believe he was anything other than completely sane during the graveyard scene.

Hamlet's typically high opinion of himself is also in evidence when he challenged to the fencing match. He is confident of his ability to match Laertes, who is well known for his skill with the blade. Hamlet is convinced he will able to hold his own, saying he's been practicing while Laertes was away in France. (5.2.190–1)

A NEW FAITH IN DESTINY?

Throughout the play Hamlet has expressed a deep weariness and disgust with life. He has regarded the world as a foul place and human existence as futile, meaningless and pointless. In this final scene, however, his negative state of mind is offset by what seems to be a new faith in divine purpose. He suggests that our lives are not our own to control but are shaped by a higher power: 'that should teach us/ There's a divinity that shapes our ends,/ Rough-hew them how we will'. (5.2.10–11)

· God's will, he says, governs even the tiniest and most insignificant things that happen: 'There is a special providence/ in the fall of a sparrow'. (5.2.199–200)
· He feels that heavenly influence even ensured he had his father's ring with him on the boat to England, allowing him to forge the letter from Claudius: 'even in that was heaven ordinant'. (5.2.48)
· If he is to die today, then that is his destiny and there is no point in fighting it:. (5.2.200–3)

Hamlet, therefore, he seems to have regained at least some of his faith in human existence, suggesting that each aspect of creation is guided by God and that all things serve a purpose decided by him. He seems to have a newfound acceptance of death. Death, he says, will come to us at the time appointed by our each of our destinies. If it be now, ''tis not to come; if it/ be not to come, it will be now'; if it be not now, yet it will/ come'. (5.2.200–2) There is nothing we can do to affect or change this outcome. All we can do is

prepare ourselves to meet death when it does arrive: 'the readiness is all'. (5.2.202)

A CONCERN FOR HIS REPUTATION

Hamlet's concern for his posthumous reputation is evident when Horatio attempts to kill himself by drinking from the poisoned cup. Hamlet prevents him from doing so, saying he cannot bear that he should be spoken ill of after his death and that Horatio must live on to protect his good name: 'O God, Horatio, what a wounded name,/ Things standing thus unknown, shall live behind me!' (5.2.331–2)

As he lies dying, Hamlet expresses great concern that he should have a good reputation after his death. He exhorts Horatio to tell the world that he was justified in his actions: 'report me and my cause aright/ To the unsatisfied'. (5.2.326–7) He makes a similar request with his last breath, urging Horatio to tell Fortinbras of the events that have taken place in Elsinore: 'So tell him, with th'occurents, more and less/ Which have solicited'. (5.2.371–2)

HAMLET – THE FINAL JUDGEMENT

There can be little doubt that Hamlet is presented as a most impressive individual. Claudius refers several times to the great love that the Danish people have for the prince. In Act 4 Scene 3, for example, the king says that he cannot deal too harshly with Hamlet because 'He's loved of the distracted multitude'. (4.3.4) The admiration that the Danish populace have for Hamlet is also evident in Act 3 Scene 1 when Ophelia refers to the prince's noble mind and distinguished qualities, describing how he is the 'observed of all observers', the focus of the entire state. (3.1.154)

AN EXTRAORDINARY WAY WITH WORDS

Arguably the most notable of these qualities is the prince's extraordinary way with words. This is a man who expresses deep and complex feelings in memorably poetic lines. This love of language no doubt contributes to the Hamlet's love of theatre as described above in our section on Act 2.

The prince is an extraordinarily witty individual. He loves puns, wordplays and double-meanings. He also enjoys taking on other people in what can only be described as battles of wit. He does this several times with Polonius, as well as with Rosencrantz and Guildenstern. He also does it with the gravedigger in Act 5. In these encounters Hamlet enjoys playing with words and displaying his quick-wittedness, but he also seems to derive pleasure from bamboozling and confusing those with whom he speaks. This is especially evident in his encounter with Claudius in Act 4 Scene 3.

A SENSE OF SUPERIORITY

This leads us to one of Hamlet's less admirable traits, his extraordinary sense of superiority. To a large extent this sense of superiority is understandable; Hamlet is after all a prince, the second most important person in the realm. All his life he has been the centre of attention, deferred to by those around him. Yet for the modern reader Hamlet's elevated view of himself can be hard to swallow.

The prince's quick-wittedness and verbal jousting, for example, can be viewed as an attempt to prove his intellectual superiority to those around him. This is especially true in the case of Polonius whom Hamlet regards as a tedious old fool he can easily play with, manipulate and verbally outwit.

Even more grating is Hamlet's sense of moral superiority. He compares his own virtue with Ophelia's sinfulness in Act 3 Scene 1. He is particularly preachy and sanctimonious when he berates Gertrude in Act 3 Scene 4, accusing of sins that would make even the heavens blush. Once again he suggests that he is more good and virtuous than the other inhabitants at Elsinore.

One of the prince's least glorious moments comes in Act 5 Scene 1 when he assaults Laertes at Ophelia's funeral. This seems motivated by his over-riding sense of superiority. As noted above, Hamlet thinks of himself as a master of language and self-expression. He accuses of Laertes of somehow trying to show him up with his eloquent words of mourning. There is a sense here that Hamlet cannot bear that Laertes rather than he is the centre of attention. This is a moment of incredible insensitivity and self-absorption. The prince seems to care little for the feelings of those who have gathered to mourn for Ophelia.

A NEGATIVE STATE OF MIND

Hamlet is nothing if not a deep thinker. He broods obsessively on the topic of death. He is almost unhealthily fixated with the transience of life, on the inescapable reality that every living being must eventually die. The king and queen describe death as a natural part of life, something 'common' that we must accept, but to Hamlet the fact of death is a tragedy that he simply cannot come to terms with. To him the

human race is defined not by its qualities and achievements but by the fact that each of us must die and turn to dust: 'yet to me, what is this quintessence of dust?' (Act 2 Scene 2). Hamlet's obsession with death is also evident in his morbid fascination with rotting, decay and decomposition.

The prince's negative state of mind is also evident in the horror and disgust with which he views the world around him. He regards the world as a 'prison', 'an unweeded garden' and 'a sterile promontory'. He considers life to be pointless and futile: 'How weary, stale, flat and unprofitable,/ Seem to me all the uses of this world!' (1.2.133–4) Given this negative state of mind, it is hardly surprising that Hamlet expresses thoughts of suicide throughout the play. These thoughts are most eloquently expressed in the 'To be or not to be' soliloquy in Act 3 Scene 1.

ANGER & BITTERNESS AT CLAUDIUS & GERTRUDE

Hamlet's negative state of mind is linked to his mother's hasty remarriage. The rage and anger he feels towards Claudius is evident throughout the play. The prince despises this 'smiling, damned villain' who killed his father and stole the crown. Hamlet also feels great anger and bitterness towards his mother. He is hurt by both the speed of her remarriage and the fact that he regards it as incestuous. He also feels that his mother has married a far lesser man than his father. This bitterness is given full vent when the prince violently rants at his mother in Act 3 Scene 4.

LOYALTY TO HIS FATHER

Hamlet's negative of Gertrude and Claudius can be contrasted with the intense loyalty he feels towards his father. From the very beginning the prince stresses the high regard he has for Denmark's former king, saying 'I shall not look upon his like again'. (1.2.188) Hamlet also stresses the tenderness that the old king showed to Gertrude. His devotion to his father is most evident in Act 3 Scene 4 where he emphasises his father's almost God-like qualities: 'A combination and a form indeed,/ Where every god did seem to set his seal'. (3.4.60–1)

A NEGATIVE VIEW OF WOMEN & SEXUALITY

Gertrude's relationship with Claudius seems to have poisoned Hamlet's view of women and female sexuality. He has come regard women as weak-willed and easily tempted from the path of morality. He thinks of them as shallow, vain and false. They are temptresses who make monsters out of men.

Even more disturbing is the way Hamlet has come to regard normal sexual relations as foul and disgusting. He seems almost unhealthily fixated with his mother's sexual relationship with Claudius. He refers to her 'incestuous sheets' in Act 1 Scene 2 and later to 'the rank sweat of an enseamèd bed,/ Stewed in corruption'. (3.4.93–4) He says his mother is possessed by lust and calls on her to wean herself off sex with Claudius, the way an addict might give up a drug.

LOVE FOR OPHELIA

Hamlet's negative view of women causes him to berate and abuse Ophelia in Act 3 Scene 1. This no doubt contributes to her mental collapse later in the play. Yet the prince claims to truly and deeply love her: 'I loved Ophelia; forty thousand brothers/ Could not with all their quantity of love/ Make up my sum'. (5.1.251–3) We also know that Hamlet courted Ophelia before the action of the play, and gave her gifts and love tokens.

It is difficult, however, to square Hamlet's words of love with his actual behaviour. If he loves her so much, why does he abuse her so cruelly, especially when there seems to be nothing to be gained from this harsh treatment? It should also be noted that the prince's interruption of her funeral is prompted more by Laertes' eloquence than love for the poor dead girl. Furthermore, once the funeral is over, Hamlet never mentions Ophelia again, turning his attention back towards Claudius.

A PROCRASTINATOR?

Hamlet is often described as a procrastinator. In Act 2 the prince berates himself for unpacking his heart with words instead of taking action against Claudius. Yet, as we noted above there are reasons that partly explain or justify his lack of action. However, it is more difficult to justify his lack of action in Act 5. When Laertes returns to Denmark looking for revenge, he gathers a band of men and storms the castle. But when Hamlet returns to Denmark looking for revenge, he writes to the king, hangs around the graveyard, and agrees to participate in a fencing match.

However, the prince is also capable of being man of swift and decisive action. We see this when he changes the letters on board the ship taking him to England, and when he boards the pirate vessel. He also acts decisively in killing Claudius at the end of the play. However, we could argue that this is too little too late. Hamlet is also capable of acting too rashly, with arguably too little procrastination. We see this in Act 3 Scene 4 when he stabs the person hiding behind the arras without bothering to check who it is.

It should also not be forgotten that the prince has a pronounced ruthless streak. This is especially evident when he delays killing Claudius in order to send him to hell instead of Heaven and also when he sends Rosencrantz and Guildenstern to their deaths in England. Hamlet is then both an indecisive procrastinator and a ruthless man of action. One could almost chart his mindset on a long rolling graph, varying between moments of decisiveness and periods of unfocused procrastination.

ACTING MAD

Hamlet's procrastination is often considered alongside his decision to act mad. As noted above, faking madness seems a waste of time in practical terms, gaining him little or no strategic advantage in his quest for revenge. His decision to put on an 'antic disposition' is therefore a great mystery, especially as the prince doesn't specify the motivations that lie behind this choice. What is certain however is that acting mad allows Hamlet to speak his mind. By playing the role of a lunatic he can ignore social conventions and say or do what he wants.

CONCLUSION

Hamlet, then, is nothing if not a man of contradictions. He is both indecisive and rash, hesitant and ruthless, a highly rational individual and someone who does things that makes no sense. The prince is capable of the most poetic musings but also violent and ugly words of abuse. He is someone who thinks deeply about the great issues of existence but who can also be terribly self-absorbed and childishly self-interested. It is no exaggeration to say he is one of the most paradoxical and complex characters in all of English literature.

CLAUDIUS

We might say that Claudius is the villain in *Hamlet*. But the king is not a straightforwardly evil character. For one thing, we can't be absolutely sure that the king is guilty of the crime that Ghost accuses him of until the beginning of the third Act. For much of the play, therefore, we are unsure of his character. Secondly, when we do know with certainty that Claudius is a murderer and a liar we are given an insight into the king's conscience. Claudius may be an evil man, but at least he seems to suffer for the sins he has committed.

When we meet Claudius at the start of the play, we have no knowledge of his crimes, and he seems an able politician and a loving husband. Although Hamlet has an obvious dislike of his new stepfather, it is the prince who seems churlish in his behaviour at the start of the play. However, as the play progresses our suspicions grow. And once we know with certainty that Claudius murdered his brother to gain the throne we see just how false and ruthless a man he is.

Claudius is desperate to hold on to power and to ensure that his terrible crime remains a secret. He cares little for others and acts purely out of self-interest, manipulating those around him to serve his own ends. And yet at times it is difficult to not admire the skill with which he handles the problems that come his way.

SKILLED POLITICIAN

Claudius ultimately has to deal with a number of difficult issues in the play:

· Firstly, he has inherited an unsettled state with some bitter and vengeful neighbours. Norway in particular is smarting from having had to forfeit land to old Hamlet after he defeated the Norwegian king in battle.
· Secondly, Claudius is following on from a much loved and well-respected king. At the start of the play Horatio describes old Hamlet as 'a goodly king'. (1.2.186) Claudius must therefore battle with the Danish people to gain their loyalty and respect.
· The third battle that the king must fight is a battle of wits with his stepson. This battle is essentially linked with the king's need to earn the respect of the Danish people because Hamlet is a much-loved public figure. Before he can make any strong decisions regarding the prince, Claudius must consider how the Danish people will react.

In dealing with these issues the king demonstrates many essential political skills.

1. DIPLOMACY
Claudius is a very different kind of king to the 'warlike' old Hamlet. (1.1.47) We are told in Act 1 Scene 1 how the old king 'smote the sledded Polacks on the ice' (1.1.63) and fought the king of Norway to the death over some issue of pride: 'by Fortinbras of Norway,/ Thereto pricked on by a most emulate pride,/ Dared to the combat'. (1.1.82–4)

When faced with a threat from the young Prince Fortinbras, Claudius decides to try diplomacy before physical force. It is possible that by sending diplomats to Norway he wants to negate the threat of Fortinbras without a fight. Or perhaps he is doing it to buy time in order to continue the arms build-up described in the first scene before confronting his enemy. Whatever his reason, the approach is a success and a potentially messy and bloody situation is resolved without a single life being lost.

2. THE ABILITY TO LISTEN TO OTHERS & TAKE ADVICE
Claudius has a number of trusted councillors, of which Polonius is one. Throughout the play the king consults with these men, and seems to value their opinion. Polonius is especially important to Claudius when he is seeking to understand Hamlet's peculiar behaviour. He listens carefully to Polonius' claim that Hamlet is mad because of his love for Ophelia. The king also agrees to Polonius' plan to observe an encounter between Hamlet and Ophelia.

Polonius' death presents the king with a particularly tricky political situation. Claudius knows how rumours and stories will quickly spread throughout Denmark and that his leadership will be called into question. It is vital that the king control the message and protect his reputation. He therefore decides to summon the royal couple's wisest friends for an emergency conference on how to 'spin' or explain to the world at large the recent dramatic events at Elsinore. (4.1.38–40)

3. REMAINS CALM & LEVEL-HEADED
Though things start to get very complicated for Claudius as the play progresses, he never loses his cool. When faced with a pending attack from Norway at the start of the play, the king does not rush troops

into battle. He bides his time and successfully sends diplomats to resolve the situation with the Norwegian king.

It could be argued that Claudius' response to *The Murder of Gonzago*, the play that Hamlet has performed to prove the king's guilt, is calm and level-headed. He makes no comment about the performance, simply calling for light and leaving the room. His actions might tell Hamlet all he needs to know, but to the rest of the audience he rouses no suspicions. That a king should take offence at a play depicting the murder of a king would not have been considered unusual.

The best example of Claudius' ability to remain calm in the face of crisis is when Laertes storms the castle, thirsting for revenge for the death of his father. Claudius does not take fright even though his life is at risk. He carefully calms Laertes down and looks to explain that he was not responsible for Polonius' death.

4. MASTER OF 'SPIN'

Claudius is a very modern politician in the sense that he places great bearing on how his actions are perceived by the general public. This probably stems from the fact that he is replacing a strong and much-loved king, as well as from the controversy surrounding his 'incestuous' marriage. It seems that from the outset of his reign he is fighting a constant battle to keep the public on his side.

Things seem to be going pretty smoothly for Claudius at the start of the play. He addresses the court with a speech designed to put rest to the past and the discomfort surrounding the hasty marriage. Claudius diverts attention away from himself by focusing on the Norwegian threat. When his decision to try for a diplomatic resolution proves successful, the king seems to be on the path to silencing whatever critics he might have.

However, the fact that Hamlet is uncooperative and acting strangely causes the king problems. The prince is very popular with the Danish people and so Claudius must be very careful how he deals with him. When Hamlet kills Polonius and poses a clear threat to Claudius, the king must make it seem that his decision to send the prince away is warrented and reasonable. He declares that Hamlet now poses a threat to everyone: 'His liberty is full of threats to us all,/ To you yourself, to us, to everyone'. (4.1.14–15)

The king also anticipates how he might be partially blamed for Polonius' death. He will be asked why the prince was permitted to freely roam the palace when he knew that Hamlet was of unsound mind. Claudius will explain this by saying that he loved his stepson too much to confine him: 'but so much was our love,/ We would not understand what was most fit'. (4.1.19–20) Hamlet's exile must look like a carefully weighed political decision that serves the good of the state: 'This sudden sending him away must seem/ Deliberate pause'. (8–9)

5. ACTS DECISIVELY

Claudius must be admired for his ability to listen to the advice of others. However, the king never prevaricates. When a decision needs to be made he acts. A good example of this is just after the king has spied on Hamlet's encounter with Ophelia. Although he does not know what exactly lies behind the prince's strange behaviour, Claudius sees enought to make him uncomfortable. By deciding immediately to have Hamlet sent to England, the king displays his ability to act in a timely manner.

FALSE & MANIPULATIVE

Yet for all the political skill he demonstrates throughout the play, Claudius is ultimately a despicable character. Once we become aware of the fact that he murdered his brother to gain the throne we realise just how insincere and manipulative a person the king actually is. Claudius' words at the beginning of the play, addressed to the assembled court, about 'our dear brother's death' and how 'we with wisest sorrow think on him' are suddenly seen for what they are, false and spoken just for show. (1.2.1–6)

The king tells Hamlet that it is the most natural thing to lose a father when there was nothing natural about old Hamlet's death. Claudius also claims to love Hamlet when really the prince is nothing but a thorn in his side: 'with no less nobility of love/ Than that which dearest father bears his son/ Do I impart toward you'. (1.2.110–12) Of course Hamlet knows very well that Claudius is false and insincere: 'That one may smile, and smile, and be a villain'. (1.5.108)

In Act 2 Scene 2 Claudius reveals a manipulative streak that becomes more pronounced as the play continues. He effectively forces Rosencrantz and Guildenstern to spy on their old friend. They are promised a reward for their assistance, but of course they have no real choice but to obey what Rosencrantz describes as the 'sovereign power' and 'dread pleasures' of the king. (2.2.27–8)

However, it is only when he has to deal with Laertes that we really see how manipulative the king can be. He tells him that he is 'most sensible in grief' for Polonius' death when in fact he expressed no sadness upon hearing the news. (4.5.150) The king then plays on Laertes' genuine grief for his father in order to have him kill Hamlet: 'Laertes, was your father dear to you?/ Or are you like the painting of a sorrow,/ A face without a heart?' (4.7.107–9) Claudius skillfully manipulates this hot-headed young man in order to have him eliminate the greatest threat to his kingship.

SELFISH & COLD

Claudius only really seems to care about himself. His behaviour is dictated by his desperate need to conceal his crime and to hold on to power. When he hears that Polonius has been killed he expresses no sadness, just shock that he could so easily have been killed had he been the one hiding in Gertrude's bedroom: 'It had been so with us had we been there'. (4.1.13) Similarly, when he witnesses Ophelia's tragic descent into madness he can only think of his own troubles: 'O Gertrude, Gertrude,/ When sorrows come, they come not single spies'. (4.5.76–7) When he hears about Ophelia's death, the king can only express annoyance that the news will upset his careful manipulation of her brother: 'How much I had to do to calm his rage!/ Now fear I this will give it start again'. (4.7.193–4)

RELATIONSHIP WITH GERTRUDE

The one person that Claudius might genuinely care for is Gertrude. However, we are not given enough of an insight into their relationship for us to be able to say with certainty what the king feels for his wife.

The only time in the play that Claudius speaks of his love for Gertrude is in Act 4 Scene 7 when he is desperately trying to convince Laertes of his innocence in the matter of Polonius' death. He tells Laertes that he could not deal too harshly with Hamlet because he did not wish to upset Gertrude:

She's so conjunctive to my life and soul,
That, as the star moves not but in his sphere,
I could not but by her (4.7.14–16)

However, it is difficult at this point of the play to trust anything that the king is saying, considering how he is looking to manipulate Laertes.

Perhaps Claudius is too selfish to really love anyone but himself. At the end of the play he does little to

prevent the queen drinking the poison. To stop her raising the cup to her lips he would have to admit that it is poisoned, and that would destroy him. His fear that the truth might be known is stronger than any love he may feel for her.

A GUILTY CONSCIENCE

The king, however, is not a completely inhuman character. At moments throughout the play we are made aware that he is suffering a guilty conscience because of his crime. When Polonius speaks about how pious actions can be used to conceal the darkest sins, the king's conscience is troubled. In an aside he speaks of the 'heavy burden' of his crime:

O, 'tis too true:
How smart a lash that speech doth give my conscience!
The harlot's cheek, beautied with plastering art,
Is not more ugly to the thing that helps it
Than is my deed to my most painted word:
O heavy burden! (3.1.49–54)

When the king's conscience is again pricked by the performance of the play at court, he attempts to pray for forgiveness. Alone in his room he speaks about how great a crime he has committed: 'Oh my offence is rank, it smells to heaven'. (3.3.36) He knows that his soul is tainted with this terrible sin and this causes him to suffer greatly:

Oh wretched state! Oh bosom black as death!
Oh limèd soul that struggling to be free,
Art more engaged! (3.3.67–9)

He desperately wishes to pray and be forgiven and cleansed of his sin, but he senses that his crime is too great and that his soul is possibly beyond redemption: 'Is there not rain enough in the sweet heavens/ To wash it white as snow?' (3.3.45–6)

In the end he knows that he cannot be forgiven because he is unwilling to give up everything he gained when he murdered his brother. How, he asks, 'can one be pardoned' for their sins and still 'retain the offence'?

but oh, what form of prayer
Can serve my turn? 'Forgive me my foul murder'?
That cannot be, since I am still possess'd
Of those effects for which I did the murder,
My crown, mine own ambition, and my queen.
May one be pardoned and retain the offence? (3.3.51–6)

CLAUDIUS & HAMLET

Hamlet despises and loathes Claudius. From the very beginning of the play he has nothing good to say about the king. Claudius is 'no more like my father [old Hamlet]/ Than I [Hamlet] am to Hercules'. (1.2.152–3) The prince finds the king's love of drink and feasting deplorable, thinking such behavior detrimental to the Danish reputation abroad. (1.4.17–21) When Hamlet is told by the ghost that Claudius is a murderer he has a solid reason to hate the king, and his suspicion that Claudius is a false and despicable person is confirmed: 'O villain, villain, smiling, damnèd villain'. (1.5.106)

Claudius in turn claims to love Hamlet and says that he thinks of him as a son. In Act 1 Scene 2 he states that Hamlet is next in succession for the throne:

You are the most immediate to our throne,
And with no less nobility of love
Than that which dearest father bears his son,
Do I impart towards you (1.2.109–12)

However, as we mentioned above the king's sentiments never seem genuine, even at this early stage of the play. From the moment Claudius becomes king, Hamlet is a problem that he has to deal with.

But Claudius has to treat Hamlet with the greatest of care. There are three reasons for this:

· He is the prince, the next in line for the throne, and a very public figure.
· He is much loved by the Danish people.
· He is Gertrude's beloved son.

It is important to note, however, that for much of the play Claudius does not suspect that Hamlet knows he killed the old king. There is no possible reason why the prince should know of his crime – Claudius could hardly suspect that his brother's ghost has come from the grave to speak to Hamlet. Therefore, the prince is not initially a serious threat in the king's eyes. But as the play progresses, Claudius' discomfort grows and Hamlet becomes more and more of a concern.

We can chart the way the prince's behaviour increasingly troubles Claudius, and the action that the king takes to deal with it:

1. HAMLET IN MOURNING
At the start of the play Claudius is not overly-concerned about Hamlet. The fact that the prince is still dressing in black and mourning the death of his father does provide an awkward reminder of the past. Hamlet is also a member of the royal family with a claim to the throne, and he is very popular with the Danish people. It is important that Claudius does not make an enemy of him, and that he keeps him under careful watch. The king responds to this potential threat by ingratiating himself with the prince, declaring Hamlet to be his heir and saying he loves him like his own son. It is also quite possible that he asks Hamlet to remain in Denmark so he can keep him under close observation.

2. HAMLET STARTS TO BEHAVE MADLY
When Hamlet starts to behave madly, the king takes a closer interest in his behaviour. It is troubling for Claudius to have the prince acting in a strange and irrational manner. The king wants everything to settle at court, and for normal life to resume as quickly as possible. Hamlet remains the one element that he cannot fathom or address with diplomacy and political skill. The cause of Hamlet's bizarre behaviour must be discovered and eliminated for the Claudius' peace of mind.

In order to get to the bottom of the prince's peculiar behaviour, Claudius summons Rosencrantz and Guildenstern – Hamlet's old friends from his school days – to Elsinore. Claudius feels Hamlet will open up to these old companions. Their mission is to talk with the prince and learn the reason for his apparent madness: 'you may glean,/ Whether aught to us unknown afflicts him'. (2.2.16–17) He also goes along with Polonius' suggestion that they spy on Hamlet in order to learn if his mad behaviour has been caused by love for Ophelia. (12.2.168)

3. HAMLET SPEAKS ANGRILY WITH OPHELIA
After observing Hamlet's encounter with Ophelia, the king is quite troubled. Despite the fact that Polonius is still convinced that Hamlet's madness is a result of his love for Ophelia, the Claudius remains unsure: 'There's something in his soul,/ O'er which his melancholy sits on brood'. (164–5) However, he still has no reason to think that Hamlet knows anything about how he murdered the old king.

Although he does not know what else might be behind the prince's strange behaviour, Claudius has seen enough, and is no longer comfortable having Hamlet at court. By deciding immediately to have Hamlet sent to England, the king looks to act in a timely and decisive manner.

4. HAMLET PUTS ON THE PLAY & KILLS POLONIUS

The performance of the play reveals to Claudius that the prince knows he murdered old Hamlet. When he hears that Hamlet has killed Polonius in Gertrude's room alarm bells ring. Had he been in the bedroom instead of his councillor Claudius would now likely be dead.

Hamlet now poses a real and immediate threat to the king. He could ruin him by exposing his terrible secret. He also now seems capable of taking bloody revenge for the death of his father. Claudius describes the prince as 'the hectic in my blood' and knows that he cannot relax until Hamlet is dead: 'Till I know 'tis done,/ Howe'er my haps, my joys were ne'er begun'. (4.3.63–4)

In spite of the pressure he must be feeling, Claudius retains his composure and acts in a decisive manner. He has already stated that Hamlet will be sent to England. (3.1.169) He now decides to make this happen as quickly as possible. However, at this stage Claudius is no longer content to have Hamlet simply sent far away from Elsinore; he now wants prince to be killed. He therefore sends a letter with Rosencrantz and Guildenstern instructing the king of England to execute Hamlet upon his arrival.

5. HAMLET ESCAPES FROM THE SHIP & RETURNS TO DENMARK

When Claudius tackles Laertes and masterfully brings him on side, he seems to be in a position of considerable control. He almost relaxes enough to boast to Laertes about how he has arranged to have Hamlet killed in England. When Hamlet's letter arrives, however, informing the king that the prince is back in Denmark, Claudius is shocked. For once in the play the king seems flabbergasted and at a loss about what to do. His initial plan to have Hamlet killed in England was perfect because he could not be blamed for the prince's death. Now that Hamlet has returned the king must once again work out how to deal with this most complicated of issues.

Claudius' plan to have Hamlet fence with Laertes is quite clever. Once again he thinks of a way to have the prince killed by someone else, so keeping his hands clean. However, Claudius' shock at discovering that his first plan failed means that he wants to be absolutely certain that his next scheme will work. Not only will Laertes' sword be sharp but it will be coated in poison. And not only will the sword be poisoned but the king will have a cup of poisoned wine at hand to give to the prince during the fight. It can be argued that this over-determination of the plan borne out of desperation to deal with a too-long concern ultimately leads to the death of the queen and of the king himself.

CONCLUSION

Claudius is a despicable person and deserves little or none of our sympathy. He murdered his own brother and stole the crown. He cares little for others and never expresses any genuine feelings for the sufferings of those around him. When Polonius is killed the king displays no grief for his trusted advisor, and the news of Ophelia's death only causes him to lament the fact that he will again have to soothe Laertes' rage so that he will go through with their plan to kill the prince.

Throughout the play Claudius is living a lie, and everything he does is ultimately geared toward a desperate effort to hide that lie from those around him. This is a very difficult thing to do, and we are given insights into Claudius' troubled mind on several occasions throughout the play. But the king has chosen his fate and he is not willing to sacrifice all he has gained from his crimes in order to save his soul. As he attempts to pray, he acknowledges that forgiveness cannot come to those who continue to profit from their sins. He lives his lie to the very end, and cannot even bring himself to tell the queen that the cup of wine she is about to drink is poisoned. Such an act might have saved her life, but such is his fear of exposure that he decides to remain silent. The king's fear of the truth is stronger than his love for the queen, and this is a damning fact. In the end, however, Claudius' battle to preserve the lie by which he lives is defeated by the prince's fight to expose the truth.

POLONIUS

LONG-WINDED

Polonius comes across as someone who loves the sound of his own voice. We first see this in Act 1 Scene 3 with the long-winded advice he gives to Laertes. To be fair much of this advice is reasonable. Polonius, however, expresses it in an unnecessarily wordy and convoluted fashion. We should also remember that this not Laertes' first time away from home. This scene is often acted with a bored and exasperated Laertes listening to his father's long-winded words of wisdom for the umpteenth time.

Polonius is similarly verbose in the instructions he gives to Reynaldo in Act 2 Scene 1. We also see this tendency when he tells the royal couple about his theory that love for Ophelia has the caused Hamlet's apparent madness, in what can only be described as an irritatingly long-winded manner. He does this in a particularly elaborate and over-the-top fashion. An irritated Gertrude tells him to get to the point: 'More matter, with less art'. (2.2.97) Polonius, however, is just as long-winded when he goes on tell them about how he told Ophelia to ignore the prince's advances. (2.2.135–55)

CONVINCED OF HIS OWN WISDOM

Throughout the play Polonius comes across as someone convinced of his own wisdom. He explicitly states this in when he tells Claudius he's never been proved wrong in anything before. (2.2.154–6) He is convinced of his wisdom as a political councillor, declaring that his brain 'hunts' the 'trail of policy' in a way that is 'sure'. (2.2.46–7) Throughout the play Polonius is convinced that he and only he knows best. This faith in his own wisdom is one of his most prominent characteristics:

- We see it in the extremely lengthy advice he gives Laertes before the latter leaves for college in France. (1.3.55–81)
- We see it when Ophelia tells him Hamlet has been pursuing her. He immediately assumes that Hamlet's intentions must be dishonourable: 'Do not believe his vows'. (1.3.127) Polonius, of course, feels no need to explore the situation further before jumping to this conclusion.
- He straightaway urges Ophelia to ignore the prince and rebuff his advances. (1.3.132–5) He simply dismisses Ophelia's suggestion that Hamlet's affections toward her might be genuine: 'Affection! Puh! you

speak like a green girl'. (1.3.101)
- We see it when he tells Reynaldo how best to go about spying on Laertes. (2.1.38–68)
- We see it when he tells Ophelia how she should behave during her meeting the prince: 'Ophelia, walk you here … Read on this book' (3.1.43–4)
- We also see it when he tells Gertrude what she should say when the prince comes to meet her in her chamber. (3.4.1–5)

Polonius' unwarranted faith in his own brilliance is also evident when Ophelia tells him about Hamlet's strange behaviour. He immediately assumes that love for his daughter has caused the prince's apparent madness: 'This is the very ecstasy of love'. (2.1.102) He is certain that his theory about the prince's madness is correct, telling the king that if he's wrong he's only fit to work as a farmer. (2.2.168) He is convinced he will be able to 'board' Hamlet, to get inside the prince's head and confirm his theory about the prince's state of mind: 'I'll board him presently'. (2.2.171)

His conversations with the prince further convince him that he's right in thinking Hamlet's been driven mad by love for Ophelia. He interprets several of Hamlet's cryptic and crazy-sounding remarks as references to his daughter: 'How say you by that?/ Still harping on my daughter'. (2.2.188–9) These conversations convince him that Hamlet is 'far gone, far gone' with love for Ophelia. (2.2.190) He clings to this theory even after he has watched Hamlet berate and insult his daughter. (3.1.176–8)

Polonius also fancies himself as something of an expert on theatre and poetry. He tells Hamlet that he has dabbled in drama in the past and was 'accounted a good actor'. (3.2.92) He is free with his criticisms of the dramatic speech performed in Act 2 Scene 2. He praises Hamlet's recitation and the playwright's choice of the word 'mobled'. (2.2.447–8, 485) However, he criticises the speech for being too long, much to Hamlet's annoyance. (2.2.479–81) In similar fashion he criticises certain poetic phrases in Hamlet's love letters to Ophelia: 'That's an ill phrase, a vile phrase'. (2.2.113)

A FLATTERER

Polonius also displays an unpleasant tendency to fawn on those in power. We see this when he gives Claudius the credit for coming up with the idea of spying on a meeting between Hamlet and Gertrude: 'And, as you said, and wisely was it said'. (3.3.30) It was in fact Polonius himself who suggested doing this back in Act 3 Scene 1. This tendency is arguably also evident when he praises Hamlet's verse-reciting skills in Act 2 Scene 2.

We also see this tendency toward flattery in Act 3 Scene 2. Hamlet says that a cloud floating in the sky looks like a camel. Then he changes his mind and says it looks like a weasel. Finally he says it looks like a whale. Each time Polonius agrees with him. (3.2.352–56) Polonius, it seems, will agree with anything as along as it is uttered by the royal and powerful Prince Hamlet. (Some readers, however, feel that Polonius is merely humouring Hamlet in this scene, acting out of his belief that the prince has lost his reason).

LONGS TO BE AT THE CENTRE OF COURT'S AFFAIRS

Polonius' self-importance makes him long to be at the centre of the court's affairs. We see this in Act 2 Scene 1 when he thinks he has discovered the cause of Hamlet's apparent madness, and rushes to share this 'knowledge' with the king and queen. He prolongs this moment of importance, telling them he has found the 'cause of Hamlet's lunacy' but then not sharing his theory till after the ambassadors have departed: 'My news shall be the fruit to that great feast'. (2.2.52) Throughout the play he meddles in the affairs of the royal family, coming up with various schemes to get to the bottom of Hamlet's madness.

Polonius declares that his family is far too humble to provide a wife for Prince Hamlet. (2.2.142–3) Yet does he secretly hopes that a marriage between Hamlet and Ophelia will after all take place, thereby greatly increasing his own status? Perhaps this hope is at the back of his mind when he rushes to the king to share his belief that Hamlet's madness is caused by love for Ophelia. It may also be in his thoughts when he subtly suggests to the royal couple that Ophelia is now of marriageable age. (2.2.108)

Polonius seems to love being the one to bring the royal family news, to tell them something they don't already know. We see this when he excitedly brings Hamlet news of the players' arrival to Elsinore. (2.2.374) This tendency may also be evident when he tells Claudius and Gertrude about Hamlet's enthusiasm for the players and adds that the prince wishes for the royal couple to attend the performance. (3.1.21–3)

AN UNCARING FATHER

Polonius displays a distinct lack of care for Ophelia throughout the play. In Act 2 Scene 1 Ophelia comes to him in a extremely distressed state, upset by Hamlet's bizarre behaviour toward her: 'I have been so affrighted!' (2.1.79) Polonius, however, spends little or no time comforting his daughter. Instead he rushes to tell the king his belief that Hamlet's apparent madness is caused by love for Ophelia. He seems more focused on meddling in royal affairs than on the concerns of his own daughter.

In Act 3 he uses Ophelia in order demonstrate this theory. He treats her like bait in his scheming, declaring that he will 'loose' her to Hamlet as if she was some kind of animal. (2.2.163) He uses Ophelia like a prop in his plan, telling her where to walk and what to do: 'Ophelia, walk you here... Read on this book'. (3.1.43–4)

Polonius also treats Ophelia very badly after her traumatic encounter with the prince. He has heard Hamlet say terrible things to her that have made her visibly distraught. Yet Polonius offers her no emotional support. Caught up in his schemes and in his conversation with the king he barely acknowledges his heart-broken daughter: 'How now, Ophelia!/ You need not tell us what Lord Hamlet said;/ We heard it all'. (3.1.178–80) She has served her purpose in his plan and her grief seems of little consequence to him.

A SCHEMER

Polonius has an inbuilt tendency toward plotting and scheming:

· We first see this in Act 2 Scene 1 when he sends Reynaldo to spy on his son while he's away studying in France.
· He comes up with a plan to observe Hamlet while the prince encounters Ophelia and thereby prove his theory of Hamlet's 'madness'. (2.2.164–6)
· He ushers Claudius and Gertrude away so he can speak to Hamlet alone and learn more about the prince's state of mind: 'both, away/ I'll board him presently'. (2.2.170–1)

Polonius, then, is something of a meddler who can't resist involving himself in other people's business; especially the affairs of the royal family. His meddling has grave consequences for him, leading to him getting stabbed by Hamlet as he lurks behind the cover in the queen's bedroom. (3.4.24–5) Getting himself killed in this somewhat ridiculous fashion has indirect but extremely negative consequences for his son and daughter. It is difficult not to agree with Hamlet that he is a 'wretched, rash, intruding fool'. (3.4.33)

OPHELIA

AN OBEDIENT DAUGHTER

Ophelia, perhaps more than anything else, is an obedient young girl. In Act 1 Laertes warns her not to take Hamlet's affections seriously: 'Hold it a fashion, and a toy in blood'. (1.3.6) Hamlet, he adds, is not free to choose his own bride but must marry for reasons of state. (1.3.19–20) Ophelia listens without interruption and promises to heed his words: 'I shall th' effect of this good lesson keep'. (1.1.45) She promises that his warning will be kept in her memory: ''Tis in my memory lock'd,/ And you yourself shall keep the key of it'. (1.3.85–6)

She also displays obedience toward her father. Polonius asks her what has been going on between her and Hamlet and she immediately answers, telling him how the prince has made her 'many tenders/ of his affection'. (1.3.99–100) Polonius is convinced that Hamlet's intentions toward his daughter are dishonorable and urges her to stay away from him. (1.3.108–10) Ophelia immediately agrees to follow his instructions: 'I shall obey my lord'. (1.3.136) We later learn that she does indeed obey her father's command to the letter. (2.1.108–10)

Her obedience is also evident when she goes straight to her father with news of Hamlet's extremely strange behaviour toward her. (2.1.75) We also see it in Act 3 Scene 1 where she obediently participates in Polonius' scheming. She does what he tells her to do, walking where she'll meet Hamlet 'as t'were by accident' and carrying herself as her father suggests. (3.1.30)

INNOCENT & TRUSTING

Ophelia, then, is an innocent and trusting young woman, one who trust's her father and brother's guidance and advice. She follows her Polonius' instructions in all matters, never questioning or disagreeing with his judgment.

Ophelia also comes across as someone who is inexperienced when it comes to love and matters of the heart. She is uncertain what to make of Hamlet's advances: 'I do not know my lord what I should think'. (1.3.104) Some productions further emphasize her innocence by suggesting she doesn't understand the prince's vulgar sexual remarks in Act 3 Scene 2.

Ophelia's trusting personality inclines her to take his professions of love at face value. (3.1.116) Her innocent and trusting nature comes most poignantly across in her bewilderment and distress after Hamlet's savage attack on her in Act 3 Scene 1. Ophelia's innocent trust in those around her will prove sadly misplaced before the end of the play. For their plotting and lack of regard for her will lead to her destruction.

LOVE FOR HAMLET

There can be little doubt that Ophelia has genuine love and affection toward the prince:

- She seems disappointed that Laertes believes his interest in her to be only a passing fancy: 'No more but so?' (1.3.10)
- At the beginning of the play she sincerely believes in the honourable nature of Hamlet's romantic approaches toward her: 'he hath importuned me with love/ In honourable fashion'. (1.3.110–11)
- She shares Gertrude's hope that she and Hamlet might get together, thereby healing the prince's apparent madness: 'Madam, I wish it may'. (3.1.42)
- Her affection is evident when she laments the prince's apparent madness: 'Oh what a noble mind is here o'erthrown!' (3.1.144)
- We also see it when she calls on heaven to restore Hamlet's sanity: 'Oh help him you sweet heavens!' (3.1.134)

Ophelia's feelings toward Hamlet are perhaps most eloquently expressed in Act 3 Scene 1. She describes his striking physical attractiveness, referring to him as the 'glass of fashion and the mould of form'. (1.3.153) She also stresses his unmatched abilities as a courtier, soldier and scholar. (3.1.151) Her love for him is obvious when she calls him 'that unmatched form and feature of blown youth'. (3.3.159)

HAMLET'S ABUSE OF OPHELIA

It is Ophelia's misfortune that she is victimised and tormented by the man she loves. We first see this in Act 2 Scene 1 where she describes how Hamlet came to her chamber in a dishevelled and half-dressed state. (2.1.78–80) The prince, she says, had a demented look on his face: 'As if he had been loosèd out of hell/ To speak of horrors'. (2.1.83–4)

Hamlet behaves in an absolutely bizarre way toward her: he holds her by the wrist, stares into her face without speaking for a long time, sighs pitifully and walks out of the room while looking back over his shoulder. (2.1.87–100) The prince did all this without speaking a single word. Ophelia is naturally upset and horrified by this bizarre behaviour: 'I have been so affrighted'. (2.1.75)

Hamlet treats Ophelia even more terribly in Act 3 Scene 1:

· When she attempts to return the love tokens he gave her he denies he ever gave her anything. (3.1.96)
· He torments her by saying he loved her then taking it back: 'I did love you once … You should not have believed me … I loved you not'. (3.1.115–19)
· He tells her that if she is beautiful she cannot be honest. (3.1.107–8)
· He repeatedly tells her should become a nun, saying that if she marries she will give birth to sinners: 'Get thee to a nunnery – why wouldst thou be a breeder of sinners?' (3.1.121–2)
· He launches into a violent misogynistic rant in which he criticises various aspects of female behaviour, attacking the institution of marriage and declaring that women make 'monsters' out of men. (3.1.139)

Ophelia is stunned by this abusive attack on her, and by the prince's agitated and demented-sounding rant. She is distraught to see how Hamlet has seemingly changed from the much-admired and talented prince she loved into a deranged and bitter madman: 'Oh woe is me/ T'have seen what I have seen'. (3.1.160–61)

Hamlet also speaks to Ophelia in a very unpleasant manner during the performance of the play, making a number of vulgar sexual remarks to her. (3.2.106–8) Ophelia repeatedly and innocently asks about the meaning of the only to be answered by angry comments on the untrustworthiness of women. (3.2.139, 230) Perhaps his crudest and most aggressive comment comes when he hints that to take the edge off his desire he'd have to leave her 'groaning' in pregnancy and childbirth. (3.2.232) We can only imagine how hurtful these vulgar and misogynistic comments must be to Ophelia, the woman that he once swore to love.

DESCENT INTO MADNESS

When we next encounter Ophelia she is in a terrible and pitiful state. A gentleman describes how she has gone over the edge into what can only be described as madness, saying how she 'beats her heart' and speaks things 'that carry but half sense'. (4.5.5–7)

There are several reasons for Ophelia's descent into madness:

· Hamlet, as we noted above, has turned on her, denying he ever loved her and abusing her terribly.

· Her father completely failed to comfort and support her following her traumatic confrontation with the prince. Polonius barely spares his distraught daughter a thought, so caught up is he in scheming with the king. (3.1)
· Her father has been murdered. To make matters worse he has been killed by the man she loved.
· Her father has been buried secretly and quickly, without proper mourning and ceremony. (4.5.82–3)
· She seems to have been even more alone since her father's death. Her brother Laertes is away in France and even Gertrude has been refusing to see her.

Given all this it is hardly surprising that Ophelia has gone over the edge. She wanders about singing songs and speaking what can only be described as nonsense: 'They say the owl was a baker's daughter'. (4.5.42) Several of her crazy-sounding comments seem to relate to her father's death: 'White his shroud as the mountain snow … To think they would lay him I' th' cold ground'. (4.5.36–70)

Perhaps she is most pitiful of all when she hands out flowers and herbs to the various members of the court, once again occasionally bursting into song as she does so. (4.5.174–5) Laertes is understandably horrified at his sister's condition: 'O rose of May,/ Dear maid, kind sister, sweet Ophelia'. (4.5.157–8) He can hardly believe what she has become: 'Do you see this, O God?' (4.5.196)

AN INNOCENT VICTIM

Ophelia's death can only be described as tragic. Gertrude recounts how she came to a willow tree growing by a brook and climbed it in order to hang garlands of flowers on its branches. (4.7.167–74) However, a branch broke and she fell into the water. She floated there for a while, singing snatches of song, seemingly oblivious to the danger she was in. (4.7.176–9) After a while, however, the water dragged her down and she drowned: 'her garments, heavy with their drink,/ Pull'd the poor wretch from her melodious lay/ To muddy death'. (4.7.182–4)

Some readers feel that Ophelia effectively committed suicide, lying peacefully in the water till it finally sucked her under and she drowned. (This is suggested by the priest in Act 5 Scene 1). Others feel that in her death was accidental, that in her demented state she simply didn't know what was happening to her.

What is clear is that Ophelia is very much an innocent victim of the intrigue and scheming going on around her. Hamlet, while pretending to be mad, abuses her terribly. He also kills her father in the mistaken belief it's Claudius who is hiding in his mother's bedroom. Polonius uses her as bait in his scheme to discover the cause of the prince's madness, 'loosing' her to Hamlet as if she was an animal. As we noted above Polonius is too caught up in his scheming to care for her. Laertes, too, is guilty of this. In Act 4 Scene 5 he is caught up in his conversation with the king and lets his demented Ophelia wander off on her own.

Each of these factors contributes to the shattering of Ophelia's mental well-being and to her eventual death. She is caught in the crossfire of the other characters' scheming, ensnared in events she does not fully understand and over which she has no control. Her death is all the sadder because she is the only character who does nothing really wrong throughout the play. It seems that someone with Ophelia's innocent and trusting nature cannot survive in the treacherous and dangerous world of Elsinore.

GERTRUDE

A LOYAL WIFE

Throughout the early stages of play Gertrude exhibits great loyalty toward her new husband. In Act 1 Scene 2 she echoes Claudius' request that Hamlet cease mourning his father: 'Good Hamlet, cast thy nighted colour off,/ And let thine eye look like a friend on Denmark'. (1.2.68–9)

Gertrude and Claudius, no doubt, find Hamlet's public and ostentatious mourning something of an embarrassment. It draws attention to the fact that their marriage was unorthodox, and it is an unwelcome reminder of the old regime just as Claudius is trying to establish a new reign in Denmark.

They both stress to the prince that death is a common thing, and that mourning excessively is inappropriate: 'Thou know'st 'tis common; all that lives must die/ Passing through nature to eternity'. (1.2.71–2)

In Acts 2 and 3 she supports Claudius' schemes to discover the cause of Hamlet's apparent madness:

- In Act 2 Scene 2 she and Claudius welcome Rosencrantz and Guildenstern to Elsinore. They have been summoned to discover the cause of Hamlet's 'lunacy'. (2.2.15–19)

- Gertrude promises them they will be rewarded, essentially for spying on her son: 'Your visitation shall receive such thanks/ As fit's a king's remembrance'. (2.2.25–6)
- She seems fully supportive of Polonius and Claudius' plan to spy on a meeting between Hamlet and Ophelia, obediently leaving the great hall so it can be put into effect: 'I shall obey you'. (3.1.37)
- It seems that Gertrude is aware from an early of Claudius' plan to send Hamlet to England. Yet she doesn't share this information with her son until he asks her about it when he storms into her room. (3.4.203)

MATERNAL FEELING

While Gertrude is deeply loyal to Claudius, she also displays maternal affection toward her son. She is anxious that Hamlet remain with her at court rather than returning to his studies at Wittenberg. (1.2.118–19) She seems genuinely moved by Hamlet's apparent madness, referring to him as a 'poor wretch'. (2.2.169) She hopes the 'wildness' that has gripped his mind is caused by love for Ophelia, and that getting together with her will heal him of his lunacy: 'I hope your virtues/ Will bring him to his wonted way again'. (3.1.40–1) Her affection for her son is arguably also present when she asks him to sit beside her at the performance of the play. (3.2.99)

Her maternal feelings are also evident in Act 3 Scene 4. During the ghost's visit she fears for his sanity, desperately urging him to calm himself: 'O gentle son,/ Upon the heat and flame of thy distemper/ Sprinkle cool patience'. (3.4.122–3)

A CONFLICT OF LOYALTIES

Act 3 Scene 4 produces a conflict between Gertrude's loyalty toward her husband and affection for her son. Hamlet bursts into her room and accuses Claudius of being a murderer who stole the crown. (3.4.96–101) Gertrude responds to this outburst simply by saying 'No more!' (101)

She never asks Hamlet to elaborate on the accusation. She expresses no astonishment or horror at the charges Hamlet has leveled. She doesn't even defend her husband against them. She certainly doesn't leave her husband. Nor, as far as we can tell, does she question him about this matter.

It is possible that Gertrude regards Hamlet's accusations as ridiculous but fails to defend her husband in Act 3 Scene 4 because she is in an extremely stressful situation. After all, her son is raging at her and has just murdered her counselor before her very eyes. It is possible that Gertrude offer no denial simply to avoid aggravating the prince further.

Yet it is also possible that on some level Gertrude suspects Claudius was involved in her previous husband's death. Unwilling to fully confront this possibility she begs Hamlet to speak 'no more' about it.

GERTRUDE'S GUILT

Hamlet is convinced that his mother's remarriage is extremely sinful. As he first outlines in Act 1 Scene 3 he has three problems with the union:

· It was too hasty, coming much too soon after his father's death.
· Claudius isn't half the man his father was.
· The marriage is incestuous because Gertrude married her brother-in-law.

In Act 3 Scene 4 Hamlet makes these points to his mother in no uncertain terms, describing how she lies each night in the 'rank sweat of an enseamèd bed,/ Stew'd in corruption. (3.4.91–2) He accuses her of having committed a sin so terrible it makes even the heavens blush. (3.4.48)

Initially Gertrude claims to have no idea what the prince is talking about: 'What have I done, that thou darest wag thy tongue/ In noise so rude against me?' (3.4.39–40) Yet Gertrude clearly feels guilty about marrying Claudius. Three times in quick succession she pleads with Hamlet to 'speak no more' declaring that his criticisms of her marriage cut her 'like daggers'. (3.4.88, 94, 103)

She has already referred to her remarriage as 'o'erhasty'. (2.2.57) Now she admits the deep guilt it has caused her, saying her very soul is marked by 'black and grainèd spots' that cannot be washed away. (3.4.90) It is seems that deep down she shares Hamlet's view of the union as being incestuous and inappropriate.

Does her guilt make her listen silently when Hamlet tells her to avoid Claudius' bed? Does she contemplate taking Hamlet's advice and refraining from sex with her husband? It is also possible, however, that she remains silent in order to avoid aggravating the prince. Hamlet, after all, has violently raged at her, has murdered Polonius before her very eyes, and has been talking to himself with a crazed expression on his face.

DOES GERTRUDE BELIEVE HAMLET WHEN HE SAYS HE'S SANE?

In Act 3 Scene 4 Hamlet admits to his mother that he's only 'mad in craft', that his lunatic behaviour has all been an act. Gertrude appears to believe him, promising not to share this information with Claudius. Yet does she really think her son is sane? After all, throughout this scene Hamlet behaves in a fairly crazed fashion:

· He kills Polonius in cold blood.
· He violently rages at her and calls her a terrible sinner. (3.4.40–51)
· He accuses her husband of murdering his father. (3.4.96–101)
· He claims to be speaking to the ghost of his father when all she can see is empty air. (3.4.132)
· He has, she says, a deranged look in his eye. (3.4.118)

It is possible that Gertrude genuinely believes Hamlet when he says he's sane. However, it's also possible she thinks he really has lost his reason. She may pretend to believe his admission of sanity in order to avoid aggravating him further. After all, the prince is in such a state of rage and high emotion that she fears for her very life. (3.4.21–2)

WHO IS GERTRUDE LOYAL TO IN ACT 4 SCENE 1?

Throughout Acts 3 and 4 Claudius has been desperate to determine the cause of Hamlet's apparent madness. Finally Hamlet tells her that he is only pretending to be mad. (4.3.188–9) As we've seen she promises not to betray Hamlet by sharing this information with the king:

Be thou assured, if words be made of breath,
And breath of life, I have no life to breathe
What thou hast said to me (3.4.198–9)

In Act 4 Scene 1 she seems to keep this promise, telling Claudius that Hamlet is mad: 'Mad as the sea and wind, when both contend/ Which is the mightier'. (4.1.7–8)

Yet who is Gertrude actually loyal to here? It all comes down to whether she believed Hamlet's declaration of sanity in the previous scene. If she thinks Hamlet is actually mad she's being loyal to her husband, telling him the truth as she sees it. If she believes Hamlet is sane she's being loyal to her son, protecting his secret from the king.

THE FINAL SCENES: GERTRUDE'S CONFLICTED LOYALTIES CONTINUE

In the play's final scenes Gertrude continues to be torn between her husband and her son.

In Act 4 Scene 5 she seems to be experiencing intense feelings of guilt. She seems worried that she will blurt something out, revealing her guilt to those around her: 'So full of artless jealousy is guilt,/ It spills itself in fearing to be spilt'. (4.5.19–20) This guilt is no doubt caused by her feeling that her marriage is inappropriate. It may also stem from her suspicion that Claudius was involved in her previous husband's murder.

Yet Gertrude's guilt doesn't change her behaviour. She may feel that her marriage is incestuous, but she doesn't leave her husband or stop sleeping with him. She may suspect on some level that Claudius murdered her husband, but she remains loyal to him.

This loyalty is evident in Act 4 Scene 5 when she hears of the uprising lead by Laertes. Her immediate and instinctive reaction is one of allegiance to her husband and contempt for the Danish people who are rebelling against him: 'O, this is counter, you false Danish dogs!' (4.5.110) She attempts to physically defend Claudius from Laertes, and declares her husband is innocent of any part in Polonius' death: 'But not by him'. (4.5.128)

We get the impression that Gertrude supported Claudius' decision to bury Polonius quickly and without fuss. (4.5.82–3) She attends Ophelia's funeral at the king's side, and sits with him throughout the fencing match between Hamlet and Laertes.

Yet she also displays deep maternal feeling toward Hamlet in these final scenes. Hamlet reappears with a bang at Ophelia's funeral, assaulting Laertes and referring to himself as 'the Dane', the rightful king of Denmark. (5.1.240) This move is sure to antagonise Claudius. Gertrude attempts to protect her son, saying that he is only speaking out of a fit of madness: 'This is mere madness:/ And thus awhile the fit will work on him'. (5.1.266–7)

This maternal feeling is also evident in Act 5 Scene 2. She sends a messenger urging Hamlet to make his peace with Laertes. (5.2.186–7) She expresses concern over his fitness: 'He's fat, and scant of breath'. (5.2.271) She offers him her napkin to wipe away his sweat (5.2.272). Fatally, she drinks to his skill: 'The queen carouses to thy fortune, Hamlet'. (5.2.273) She falls to the ground and realises she's been poisoned.

Only when dying does Gertrude resolve the conflict that has divided her loyalties throughout the play. Only with her last breath does she choose her son's side against that of her husband. Claudius pretends she has collapsed due to shock at the sight of blood. She does not play along with his deception, however, and warns Hamlet about her husband's treachery: 'No, no, the drink, the drink, – O my dear Hamlet,/ The drink, the drink! I am poison'd'. (5.2.296–7)

CONCLUSION

Gertrude is sometimes thought of as a cold and unfeeling character. This insensitivity is perhaps evident at the beginning of the play when she urges Hamlet to cease mourning his father. We also see it when, wrapped up in her own affairs, she refuses to see Ophelia. (4.5.1)

Yet Gertrude is not totally unfeeling. She seems genuinely upset by Ophelia's death. (4.7.169–80) She speaks movingly at Ophelia's funeral, saying how she wished the poor girl would eventually have married her son: 'I thought thy bride-bed to have decked, sweet maid,/ And not have strewed thy grave'. (5.1.227–8) We can also have little doubt that she genuinely loves her son.

Her greatest failing is that she remains loyal to Claudius when she knows on some level that the marriage is wrong or inappropriate and may even slightly believe Hamlet's accusation that he killed her previous husband. This loyalty is rewarded in a most terrible way. Claudius goes behind her back in an attempt to murder her son, accidentally killing her in the process.

Yet it is difficult not to feel some sympathy for Gertrude. She spends the play torn between her husband and her son, troubled by feelings of intense guilt, before dying in what can only be described as a tragic and a pointless accident. We can only agree with Hamlet that she was unfortunate, miserable and wretched: 'Wretched queen, adieu!' (5.2.320)

LAERTES

A LOVING BROTHER

Laertes is Ophelia's brother and he seems to love her dearly. When he must leave to go to France in Act 2 he asks her to write him often and advises her to be wary of Hamlet's affections as they might not be sincere. He is also careful to advise her that, as Prince of Denmark, Hamlet may have to marry a foreign princess for political reasons.

When Laertes returns from France it is because he has heard of his father's death. He spends time in Denmark gathering men and information and plotting to kill the king before he arrives at Elsinore. He seems to be completely unaware of his sister's descent into madness until he sees her at the palace.

Seeing Ophelia acting in a deranged manner devastates Laertes: 'O heat, dry up my brains, tears seven times salt/ Burn out the sense and virtue of mine eye'. (4.5.154–5) He vows to avenge her madness: 'By heaven, thy madness shall be paid with weight,/ Till our scale turn the beam'. (156–7)

However, despite the obvious sincerity of his emotions, we might be critical of Laertes' response to his sister's troubled condition. When Ophelia clearly needs loving support and careful attention, Laertes chooses to stay with the king discussing revenge. It is while he is with the king that Ophelia falls into the stream and is drowned.

VENGEFUL & VIOLENTLY PASSIONATE

Laertes re-appearance in the play in Act 4 is very dramatic. Enraged at hearing of his father's death and inexplicably quick and undignified burial, he secretly returns from his studies in France to Denmark. Rumours are rife in Denmark that the king had something to do with Polonius' death and so Laertes quickly gathers together an army of men willing to revolt against Claudius. In Act 4 Scene 4 he manages to storm the castle and gain entry to the king and queen. Only Claudius' composure and carefully measured words prevent his own death.

It is remarkable how violently passionate Laertes is. Whereas Hamlet has to make an effort to feel such intense anger (and even then it seems a short-lived emotion), Laertes seems capable at a moment's notice of taking bloody revenge. When he sees his sister in her terrible state of madness his response is one of

shock followed swiftly by a pledge to avenge her condition: 'By heaven, thy madness shall be paid with weight'. (4.5.156) As we mentioned above, a more considerate and beneficial response might have been to spend time with Ophelia – vengeance, after all, will do nothing to ease her troubles. Even as he stands over her grave, Laertes is still swearing vengeance:

Oh treble woe
Fall ten times treble on that cursed head
Whose wicked deed thy most ingenious sense
Deprived thee of! (5.1.228–31)

Laertes' violently passionate nature is also indicated by the fact that he claims he would be willing to murder Hamlet in a church ('To cut his throat i'th'church'. (4.7.126) This is in stark contrast to Hamlet's hesitation when he found Claudius at prayer, the moment he decided not to act when he had a perfect opportunity to take his revenge.

Perhaps, however, Laertes is not given an opportunity in the play to reveal his better qualities. Circumstances have been hard, and to lose a father and a sister in such a short space of time is an extremely difficult thing to deal with. Hamlet speaks well of Laertes in the final scene of the play, sympathising with his loss:

I am very sorry, good Horatio,
That to Laertes I forgot myself,
For by the image of my cause, I see
The portraiture of his (5.2.75–8)

The prince also tells Osric that he takes Laertes 'to be a soul of great article'. (5.2.112) Indeed Laertes' better temperament is shown when he accepts Hamlet's apology for his behaviour at Ophelia's grave. (5.2.229–31) Just before he fatally wounds the prince, Laertes speaks of his discomfort at what he is about to do: 'And yet it is almost against my conscience'. (5.2.281) And when it is too late, he sees the king's treachery and realises that he has been used by Claudius in a foul scheme to have the prince killed. As he lies dying he asks Hamlet to 'exchange forgiveness' with him.

ROSENCRANTZ & GUILDENSTERN

OLD SCHOOL FRIENDS

Rosencrantz and Guildenstern are two of Hamlet's old school friends, summoned to Elsinore by the king and queen and asked to find out what is troubling the prince. In effect they have been ordered to spy on their friend, a difficult and uncomfortable task. Their discomfort is evident when they first meet Hamlet and he asks them why they have come to Elsinore. They are initially reluctant to admit that they are there under orders from the king, but Hamlet is well aware of the truth, and they quickly confirm his suspicions. (2.2.288)

Rosencrantz and Guildenstern's task is further complicated by the fact that they are dealing with a deeply troubled and vengeful prince. Had it simply been a matter of Hamlet being a little depressed, his friends' arrival might have done the trick and restored him to good spirits. As it is however, these two young men are out of their depth and don't know what they are dealing with. Hamlet is angry that people he once counted as friends are now acting on behalf of the man he despises most, Claudius. His frustration with Rosencrantz and Guildenstern is evident a number of times throughout the play and he confuses and baffles them with his verbal skills. In Act 3 Scene 2 he angrily asks if they think that he is to be played with like a musical instrument, made to make whatever sounds they please. (3.2.340–8)

In the end Rosencrantz and Guildenstern are more loyal to the king than to the prince. This is perhaps understandable. For one thing the king is a very powerful man and must be obeyed. Secondly, Hamlet seems to be mad and is not open to normal conversation. To his friends, therefore, he must seem someone who needs to be watched and controlled and they probably think the king is right to have them spy on the prince. However, they fail to heed Hamlet's warning about the king and their position as spies. (4.2.10–20) On the voyage to England the prince outwits them one final time and sends them to their deaths.

FORTINBRAS

A SECOND PRINCE

There is history between Fortinbras' family and Hamlet's family. About thirty years ago Hamlet's father killed Fortinbras' father in single combat. (1.1.84–6) As a result certain lands passed from Fortinbras' family to Hamlet's family. (1.1.86–89) There is also a sense that Fortinbras' family have a claim to the throne of Denmark itself. We see this when Hamlet nominates Fortinbras as his successor. (5.2.343) It is also evident when Fortinbras declares he has a right to the Danish kingdom. (5.2.377)

There are several important similarities between Hamlet and Fortinbras. Both are princes. Both live in kingdoms ruled by their uncles. Both are out to avenge their father's deaths.

In many respects Fortinbras is Hamlet's 'mirror image': the same but opposite. A more detailed discussion of the contrasts between them can be in found in the section on revenge.

DECISIVE & AGGRESSIVE

Throughout the play Fortinbras comes across as an aggressive and decisive person. Fortinbras' decisiveness is pronounced. Fortinbras assembles a rag-tag army with which to invade Denmark and avenge his father's death. (1.1.95–104) He acts alone, without the support or knowledge of the Norwegian king. (2.2.62–67) When he is prevented from invading Denmark he takes an invasion force to Poland instead. (2.2.74–75)

In the final scene he acts decisively and aggressively once more, being quick to assert his family's right to the Danish throne: 'I have some rights of memory in this kingdom'. (5.2.377) He is quick to take advantage of the fact that the Danish royal family are all dead, leaving the throne his for the taking. He asserts himself immediately, issuing instructions to the Danish courtiers. He claims that it is with sorrow he embraces kingship of Denmark. (5.2.375) However, we may question his sincerity here.

A WARLIKE PRINCE

Fortinbras is described as a warlike young man in Act 1 Scene 1: 'of unimproved mettle hot and full'. (1.1.96) This is evident in the way he plans to regain the lands lost by his father in that long-ago duel: 'But to recover of us, by strong hand/ And terms compulsatory, those foresaid lands/ So by his father lost'. (1.1.102–4) His warlike nature is also evident in his invasion of Poland. Fortinbras has no qualms about marching his army off to Poland to fight for a meaningless piece of ground: 'a little patch of ground/ That hath in it no profit'. (4.4.18–19) Hamlet is horrified that thousands of men will die for a 'fantasy and a trick of fame'. (4.4.61) It seems that for Fortinbras, however, fame on the battleground is of paramount importance.

THEMES

THE MEANING OF LIFE

SIN & THE AFTERLIFE

The world of Hamlet is one where people are haunted by a concern with the afterlife. For the medieval Danes portrayed in the play, life after death is a very real thing. After all, this is a play where the ghost of a dead person appears in the very first scene. Particularly pronounced is their awareness of hell and purgatory; their fear that dying in a state of sin will send their souls to unspeakable torments in the afterlife. This awareness of sin and the afterlife occurs again and again throughout the play:

· The ghost of Hamlet's father describes how he died in a state of sin: 'No reckoning made, but sent to my account/ With all my imperfections on my head'. (1.5.78–9) He therefore suffers unbearable and unmentionable tortures in purgatory. (1.5.11–22)
· The ghost makes the point that Gertrude, too, will have to answer for her wrong-doings in the next life. (1.5.89–91)
· Hamlet laments that his father died 'full of bread', without the chance to fast or do penance, and therefore entered the next life in a sinful state. (3.3.80–4)
· Hamlet worries that the ghost is in reality the devil trying to trick him into murdering an innocent man, thereby damning his soul to hell for eternity: 'The spirit I have seen/ May be the devil ... [that] abuses me to damn me'. (2.2.576–81)

Hamlet declares that only a fear of suffering in the next life prevents us ending the torments of this one. We postpone the tempting 'sleep of death' because we fear the terrible dreams it may contain. (3.1.66) According to the prince only the 'dread of something after death' stops us taking our own lives. (3.1.78)

· Claudius is deeply aware of the sins he committed in killing his brother and stealing the throne: 'Oh my offence is rank it smells to heaven'. (3.3.36) He worries that he will suffer in the afterlife for these offences. (3.3.60–4)
· Laertes, too, is conscious of the possibility of damnation. But he is so enraged by his father's death

that he is will risk this fate in order to avenge the crime: 'Conscience and grace to the profoundest pit!/ I dare damnation'. (4.5.132–3)
· The priest suggests that because Ophelia is a (possible) suicide she died in a state of terrible sin and cannot enter Heaven. (5.1.208–12)
· Laertes answers that the priest himself will lie 'howling' in hell because of this un-Chrsitian attitude. (5.1.224)

This awareness of the afterlife is most brutally expressed in Act 3 Scene 3 when Hamlet delays killing Claudius. Claudius is praying and defenceless, providing Hamlet with the perfect opportunity to avenge his father's death: 'Now might I do it pat ... And so am I revenged'. (3.3.73–5) Yet Hamlet worries that because Claudius is praying he has purged his soul of sin: the king is in 'the purging of his soul ... fit and seasoned for his passage'. (3.3.85–6) Killing him, therefore would send his soul directly to Heaven. (3.3.76–8)

Hamlet decides it is no revenge to send Claudius directly to Heaven while his own father suffers in the fires of Purgatory. (3.3.84–7) He decides to kill Claudius when the he has committed a sinful act, such as drinking, swearing or making love to Gertrude: 'Or in th'incestuous pleasure of his bed;/ At gaming, swearing, or about some act/ That has no relish of salvation in't'. (3.3.90–2) That way Claudius will die in a state of sin and burn in Hell forever: 'that his soul may be as damned and black/ As hell, whereto it goes'. (3.3.94–5)

This awareness of sin and the afterlife also makes the deaths of Rosencrantz and Guildenstern particularly brutal. Hamlet specifically arranges for them to be killed without the opportunity to confess their sins: 'Not shriving time allowed'. (5.2.47) Does the prince deliberately intend for his old friends to suffer torment in the next life? If so, he exacts a terrible revenge for their betrayal.

DOES GOD GOVERN ALL THINGS?

The world of the play, then, is a religoius one. It is populated by people of faith, who have no doubt that God and the afterlife exiists. There are also several instances in the play where characters express the belief that God governs all things. Hamlet, in particular, expresses the view that God determines or shapes the course of our lives: 'There's a divinity that shapes our ends'. (5.2.10)

· God's will, he says, governs even the tiniest thing that happens, such as a sparrow falling in a forest: 'there's a special providence in the fall of a sparrow'. (5.2.199–200)
· Hamlet believes that even the seemingly accidental death of Polonius was willed by Heaven: 'heaven hath pleased it so'. (3.4.174)
· Hamlet believes it was God's will that he escape being executed in England. God, he says, even ensured he had his father's ring with him with which to brand the replacement letter: 'even in that was heaven ordinant'. (5.2.48)
· In Act 1 Scene 4 Horatio expresses a similar belief that God governs human affairs. When Marcellus declares that 'something is rotten in the state of Denmark', Horatio responds by saying that God will intervene to solve the troubled country's problems: 'Heaven will direct it'. (1.4.91)

Hamlet seems filled with a sense of destiny, that he is God's chosen instrument to right the wrongs that have been committed in Denmark: 'The time is out of joint: O cursèd spite/ That ever I was born to put it right'. (1.5.189–90) He feels he has been 'chosen' by God to avenge his father's death: 'Prompted to my revenge by heaven'. (2.2.562) He makes this point to Gertrude, declaring that he has been chosen by Heaven to be its 'scourge and minister'. (3.4.176)

On one hand Hamlet and Horatio believe that God governs all things. On the other hand we are presented with a series of gruesome and chaotic events, a string of random, bloody and largely pointless deaths:

· Polonius' death, for instance, is essentially an accident. He is killed in what can only be described as a case of mistaken identity while hiding behind a curtain.
· Gertrude's death is similarly accidental. She dies from drinking poisoned wine that was never meant for her.
· Ophelia's death is also something of an accident. It is possible that she accidentally drowns herself

while in a deranged state. However, even if she takes her own life there is still something grimly accidental about her death. She is 'collateral damage', the unintended victim of circumstances beyond her control.
· Laertes, too, dies an accidental death: the swords get mixed up during his scuffle with Hamlet, and he is accidentally stabbed by the poisoned one. (In this instance we can comfort ourselves that Laertes himself was out to kill the prince.)
· Fortinbras' army, meanwhile, is marched off to Poland to fight for 'a little patch of ground/ That hath in it no profit'. (4.4.18–19) As Hamlet puts it, thousands of men will die for a 'fantasy and a trick of fame', to own a piece of land too small to hold the corpses of those killed in the fight over it: 'not tomb enough and continent/ To hide the slain'. (4.4.64–5)
· Rosencrantz and Guildenstern, too, are victims of a struggle they only dimly comprehend, seeming to know nothing about Claudius' plan to have Hamlet put to death when the ship reaches England, or that Hamlet has switched the letter, ensuring they themselves will be executed.

We can only agree with Horatio that the play consists of 'carnal, bloody, and unnatural acts,/ Of accidental judgements, casual slaughters'. (5.2.368–9) What God could govern a world this chaotic, cruel and bloody? The play leaves us with the impression that if any God does govern the world he must be either distant and uncaring or downright cruel.

THE TRANSIENCE OF LIFE

One of the most pronounced aspects of the play is the prince's obsession with the transience of life. Throughout the play Hamlet struggles to come to grips with the notion that every living human being must die and eventually turn to dust. For Hamlet mankind is a 'quintessence of dust': the most significant thing about the human race is not our faculties, abilities and achievements but the fact that we are doomed to die and decompose. (2.2.303) A similar view is expressed in Act 4 Scene 3 when he bitterly declares that we spend our lives fattening ourselves for maggots.

The prince's most profound meditation on the briefness of human existence occurs in the graveyard scene. He is mesmerised by the skulls so casually tossed around by the gravediggers: 'That skull had a tongue in it, and could sing once'. (5.1.70) The skull was once part of a living person, but is now a gravedigger's plaything. It is treated with no more respect than if it had belonged to Cain, the first murderer. (5.1.76–7) We live, it seems, only to become bones that are kicked around a cemetery: 'Did these/ bones cost no more the breeding, but to play at loggats/ with 'em?' (5.1.83–5) The notion of life's transience is eerily reinforced by the fact that the gravedigger started work on the very day that Hamlet was born. (5.1.134)

Hamlet is also exercised by the fact that even the greatest of men die and turn to dust. Even Alexander the Great ended up, like the rest of us, as a stinking skull. (5.1.181–3) Both Alexander and Julius Caesar turned into dust and clay, which has all kinds of industrial uses. He is struck by the fact that the bodies of these great men might end being turned into the stopper for a beer bottle or patching the wall of a house. (5.1.193–6) Similarly, he imagines the body of a king being eaten by worms and eventually passing through the digestive system of a beggar. (4.3.28–9)

Particularly moving is Hamlet's encounter with Yorick's skull. The prince is deeply saddened that his childhood companion's humour and energy have dis-appeared in death:

'Where be your gibes now? your/ gambols, your songs? your flashes of merriment'? (5.1.173–4) He is both horrified and mesmerised by Yorick's skull, by that the fact that where the jester's lips once 'hung' there is now only bare bone. (5.1.172) Hamlet, then, can't seem to take his mind off the brevity of human life: 'a man's life's no more than to say "one"'. (5.2.74)

THE NATURE OF MAN
A central idea in the play is that human beings are made in God's image and possess faculties and abilities that make us god-like. This is eloquently expressed by Hamlet in a passage worth quoting in full:

What a piece of work is a man! how noble in reason, how infinite in/ faculties, in form and moving how express and admirable,/ in action how like an angel, in apprehension how like a/ god! The beauty of the world, the paragon of animals (2.2.298–302)

The prince also raises the idea of man's godlike nature when he describes his father in dead in terms of the gods of ancient Greece. He declares that old Hamlet had 'A combination and a form indeed,/ Where every god did seem to set his seal'. (3.4.60–1)

The play suggests that it is our faculty of reason and apprehension that makes us noble and god-like. We

were endowed with this great power, and must use it to rule our lives rather than let it lie idle:

Sure, he that made us with such large discourse, Looking before and after, gave us not That capability and god-like reason To fust in us unused (4.4.36–9)

Our reason is all that separates us from the animals. Claudius expresses this view when confronted with Ophelia's madness: 'poor Ophelia/ Divided from herself and her fair judgement,/ Without the which we are pictures, or mere beasts. (4.5.83–5) Ophelia expresses similar sentiments about the primacy of reason when she thinks Hamlet has gone insane: 'Now see that noble and most sovereign reason,/ Like sweet bells jangled, out of time and harsh'. (3.1.157–8)

Failure to use our reason reduces us to the level of beasts. Hamlet makes the point when he says we should not focus on bodily pleasures at the expense of our minds: 'What is a man/ If his chief good and market of his time/ Be but to sleep and feed? A beast, no more'. (4.4.33–5)

This is one of the main reasons the prince is so disgusted at Gertrude's hasty remarriage. When lamenting the short gap between his father's death and her marriage to Claudius he complains that 'a beast, that wants discourse of reason,/ Would have mourn'd longer'. (1.2.150–1) Hamlet feels that Gertrude's marriage to Claudius was motivated completely by physical passion rather than by reason. Her reason, he suggests, must have been 'aplopexed' or paralysed when she chose to marry Claudius. (3.4.73)

Hamlet is torn between his view of human beings as god-like, and his keen awareness of the transience of life. It could be argued Hamlet is torn between two very different views of humanity. One the one hand human beings, as long as we use our faculty of reason, are almost god-like. Yet on the other hand human beings are a 'quintessence of dust': our faculties, abilities and achievements are negated by the fact that we are doomed to die and decompose.

THE FUTILITY OF LIFE
The prince is gripped by a sense of futility throughout the play. He memorably expresses how pointless life seems to him in Act 1 Scene 2: 'How weary, stale, flat and unprofitable,/ Seem to me all the uses of this world!' (1.2.133–4) There are several reasons for this sense of futility and pointlessness:

- For Hamlet, life's very transience makes it futile. We exist for only the briefest moment before ending up as food for worms and as skulls in a graveyard. What are we but the 'quintessence of dust'?
- As the prince puts it so memorably, we exist in a world characterised by suffering and evil: 'the whips and scorns of time/ The oppressor's wrong'. (3.1.70–1)
- Hamlet has come to regard the world around him as miserable and disgusting, calling it an 'unweeded garden' (1.2.135), as a dungeon (2.2.246), and as a 'sterile promontory' surrounded by a 'foul and pestilent congregation of vapours'. (2.2.294–8) The prince can't even take joy in the other human beings that inhabit this foul place. (2.2.303–4)
- There can be little doubt that Hamlet's sense of life's futility also stems from the depression that grips him in the wake of his father's death and his mother's hasty remarriage. As he puts it to Rosencrantz and Guildenstern: 'I have of late … lost all my mirth'. (2.2.291–2)

A MEANINGLESS WORLD?

In once sense *Hamlet* takes place in world carefully managed by God. The presence of the ghost seems to prove that God exists and judges each of us after our death. Yet as we noted above, the world of the play is also chaotic, random and brutal. It is a place where terrible things happen for no good reason. It is one of the play's great paradoxes that it presents us with a world that on one hand is watched over by God but that on the other is filled with pointless and meaningless death.

DEATH

SUICIDE

Throughout the early part of the play Hamlet frequently expresses suicidal thoughts. The prince is in an extremely negative state of mind. To him life seems pointless and meaningless: 'How weary, stale, flat and unprofitable/ Seem to me all the uses of this world!' (1.2.133–4) He regards the world around him with disgust, thinking of it as an 'unweeded garden', a 'sterile promontory' and a 'foul and pestilent congregation of vapours'. (1.2.135, 2.2.246, 2.2.294–8)

It is perhaps not surprising, therefore, that Hamlet expresses what can only be described a suicidal thoughts. He says he longs for death, wishing that his body would simply melt away: 'O that this too solid flesh would melt,/ Thaw and resolve itself into a dew'. (1.2.129–30)

- He tells Horatio he places little value on his own life: 'I do not set my life in a pin's fee'. (1.4.65)
- When Polonius says he's leaving, Hamlet responds bitterly, declaring there is nothing he would part with more willingly 'except my life, except my life, except/ my life'. (2.2.217–18)
- The prince's suicidal tendencies also seem to be expressed when he tells Polonius he might walk into his grave. (2.2.208)

THE LOGIC OF SUICIDE

In the famous 'To be or not to be' soliloquy, Hamlet teases out the logic of suicide. Life he says his full of suffering: 'The heart-ache and the thousand natural shocks/ That flesh is heir to'. (3.1.62–3) We are forced to endure the 'whips and scorns of time,/ The oppressor's wrong' as well as many more evils and difficulties. (3.1.70–4) It would be logical for us, therefore, to take our own lives and end this miserable existence. We could find 'quietus' or peace simply by stabbing ourselves with a dagger (a 'bare bodkin') (3.1.76)

According to Hamlet all that prevents us committing suicide is fear of the unknown. The afterlife is an 'undiscovered country' about which we know nothing. This undiscovered country may contain even greater horrors than those we endure in this life. We only go on living, therefore, due to 'the dread of something after death'. (3.1.78) We would rather suffer the familiar pains of this world than face something even worse in the afterlife. (3.1.81–2)

THREE SUICIDE ATTEMPTS?

There are arguably three characters in the play who attempt to commit suicide. The first is Laertes. Distraught with grief at his sister's death he begs to buried alive with her in her grave. (5.1.233) The second comes when Horatio attempts to drink the poisoned wine, unable to face life without his beloved Hamlet. (5.2.328–9) It is difficult to know how seriously to take these events. They are often acted as showy and attention-seeking displays of grief rather than genuine suicide attempts. (This is particularly true of Laertes' display in the graveyard.)

The third suicide attempt is arguably that of Ophelia who simply floats along the river until the weight of her sopping garments drags her under and she drowns. (4.7.182–4) Did the distraught Ophelia want to die? (This seems to be the opinion of the priest in Act 5 Scene 1.) Or was she simply too deranged to realise the danger she was in? If Ophelia intended to commit suicide her death represents a supreme irony. After all Hamlet's talk and contemplation of suicide it is actually poor innocent Ophelia who goes through with this terrible and tragic act.

SUICIDE AS SIN

In the world of the play, suicide is regarded as a very great sin. This is evident in from the beginning when Hamlet refers to the fact that God has declared taking one's own life a great wrong: 'Or that the Everlasting had not fixed/ His canon 'gainst self-slaughter'. (1.2.131–2) A similar point is made by the priest in Act 5 Scene 1. Because Ophelia is a possible suicide he refuses to give her the full funeral rites. To do so, he says, would be disrespectful to those in the graveyard who died at peace with God. (5.1.217–20) If it wasn't for Claudius' influence she would have been buried outside the graveyard with no funeral rites at all: 'She should in ground unsanctified have lodged/ Till the last trumpet'. (5.1.211–12) The priest seems to be suggesting that if Ophelia committed suicide she will never enter Heaven.

DECOMPOSITION

The idea of death also enters the play through Hamlet's fascination with decomposition. Again and again the prince expresses what can only be described as a fascination with what happens to our bodies when we die, with the processes of rotting and decay that turn us into dust.

For Hamlet mankind is a 'quintessence of dust': the most significant thing about the human race is not our faculties, abilities and achievements but the fact that we are doomed to die and decompose. (2.2.303) This view is also evident when he declares that Polonius' corpse is 'kin' with dust.

Hamlet has a morbid fascination with the processes of bodily decay. We first see this when he speaks about maggots breeding in a dead dog. (2.2.183–4) It is also expressed when Hamlet bitterly declares that we spend our lives fattening ourselves for maggots. (4.3.21–2) It comes across again when he describes Polonius' corpse as being 'at supper … Not where he eats but where he is eaten'. (4.3.17–19)

This obsession with decay finds its most potent expression in the graveyard scene when he asks the gravedigger how long it takes for a human body to rot once it has been buried. (5.1.149) The prince is fascinated by the skulls that are tossed around the graveyard as the gravediggers do their work, imagin-

ing the different people they belonged to. (5.1.70_103) He is both horrified and mesmerised by Yorick's skull, by that the fact that where the jester's lips once 'hung' there is now only bare bone. (5.1.172) Hamlet is disgusted by this stark sight, declaring his 'gorge rises at it'. (5.1.171–2) Yet he is too riveted to look away, and continues addressing the skull of his childhood friend.

'DEATH THE LEVELLER'

Related to the theme of decomposition is that of death the leveller. Death does not discriminate between the humble and the powerful. Rich and poor alike must die, be laid in the ground and rot away.

Hamlet gleefully makes this point to Claudius in Act 4 Scene 3 when he points out that both kings and beggars end up being eaten by maggots: 'Your fat king and your lean beggar/ is but variable service, two dishes, but to one table: that's the end'. (4.3.22–3)

Hamlet seems fascinated by the various undignified things that might happen to the bodies of great men after they're dead. He imagines part of a dead king's body passing through the digestive system of a beggar. The beggar eats a fish which has eaten a worm which in turn has eaten the body of a king: 'A man may fish with the worm that hath eat of a king,/ and eat of the fish that hath fed of that worm'. (4.3.25–6)

Similarly, Hamlet imagines the dead body of Alexander the great ending up as the stopper for a beer barrel: 'Why may not/ imagination trace the noble dust of Alexander, till a find/ it stopping a bunghole?' (5.1.185–7) He imagines how Alexander's body returned to dust and earth from which loam stopper might have been manufactured. (5.1.193–4) In a similar vein he imagines Julius Caesar's remains ending up as a patch of clay keeping the draught out of a house. (5.1.191–8)

Hamlet imagines that various skulls in the graveyard belonged to members of four fairly unpopular professions: a politician, a courtier, a lawyer and a property dealer. In life these were important and influential figures. In death, however, these powerful gentlemen moulder and rot the same as everybody else. Hamlet takes delight in describing how these mighty figures have fallen:

- The powerful politician, who in life had the skill to outwit God himself, has his skull tossed around like a football by the gravedigger. (5.1.72–4)

· The courtier who in life fawned on powerful Lords and Ladies is now a servant of 'Lady Worm'. (5.1.76–81)
· The lawyer's legal skills cannot help him as his skull is kicked around by the gravedigger. (5.1.90–94)
· The property developer, who in life owned great tracts of land, ends up like the rest of us with only a plot of ground in a graveyard. (5.1.95–103)

There is an element of comic relief in these lines. Shakespeare's audience would have enjoyed seeing these unpopular professions and their devious practices being made fun of. They would also have taken satisfaction in being reminded that in the graveyard everyone, rich and poor alike, rots in the same way.

BEREAVEMENT & MOURNING

At the beginning of the play Hamlet mourns his father in the conventional fashion. He wears dark clothes ('suits of solemn black') and wanders about the palace crying and sighing with a dejected look upon his face. (1.2.77–82) Hamlet, however, is adamant that his behaviour is not merely show, but reflect the genuine and terrible sorrow he feels at the passing of his father: 'I have that within which passes show/ These but the trappings and the suits of woe'. (1.2.85–6)

We can have little doubt that Hamlet's grief is genuine for he held his father in the highest esteem, regarding him as 'so excellent a king' and declaring that he 'shall not look upon his like again'. (1.2.139, 188) This esteem is especially evident in Act 3 Scene 4, where Hamlet praises his father at some length, describing him as a blessed and almost god-like figure: 'A combination and a form indeed/ Where every God did seem to set his seal/ To give the world assurance of a man'. (3.4.60–2)

Ophelia also suffers the loss of a father. This bereavement sends her into the spiral of lunacy we see in Act 4 Scene 5, where she wanders around singing nonsense and talking what is essentially gibberish. As Claudius puts it she is 'divided from herself and her fair judgement'. (4.5.84) There can be little doubt that her father's death contributes greatly to this mental collapse: we are told that in her madness Ophelia 'speaks much of her father'. (4.5.4)

Horatio is bereaved at the play's conclusion when Hamlet, his companion and best friend, is poisoned before his very eyes. Horatio is so overcome with grief at this loss that he attempts to poison himself and join Hamlet in death. (5.2.328–9) Hamlet, it seems, has to wrench the cup of poisoned wine away from him. (5.2.330) Horatio's expresses his grief simply and movingly: 'Now cracks a noble heart. Good night sweet prince,/ And flights of angels sing thee to thy rest'. (5.2.346–7)

Laertes suffers a double bereavement, losing his father and his sister in quick succession. He is clearly effected by his the news that his father has apparently passed away. He returns from France, storms into Elsinore at the head of an armed gang and demands to know exactly what happened. (4.5.130) When he learns that Hamlet was responsible for his father's death he reacts with great anger. He will prove the depth of his feelings for his father by killing the prince. He viciously declares that he is willing to 'cut his throat i'th'church'. (4.7.126) (We should remember, however, that Laertes' emotions are being skilfully manipulated by Claudius in this scene.)

His response to Ophelia's death is much more tender. He seems stunned by the news that she has drowned herself. He pleads with the priest to give her full funeral rites even though she is possibly a suicide. (5.1.207, 217) He movingly declares that she will be an angel in Heaven and that violets will spring from the earth she lies in. (5.1.222–3) Finally he leaps into the grave and demands to be buried alive with her. (5.1.233) Some productions of the play suggest that Laertes is somewhat exaggerating his grief here, as if he's looking for attention. Others, however, suggest that he is genuinely overcome with emotion.

IMPROPER MOURNING

Hamlet accuses his mother of not properly mourning his father. He feels that she ceased morning and remarried far too early: 'a beast that wants discourse of reason/ Would have mourned longer'. (1.2.150–1) Hamlet bitterly says that she remarried before the shoes in which she followed the coffin were 'old', and that the food purchased for the funeral was used at her wedding feast. (1.2.147, 180–1) Hamlet also seems to suggest that his mother's grief at his father's passing wasn't entirely genuine. Her tears, he says, were 'unrighteous'. (1.2.154) Hamlet bitterly claims that his own grief is deep and real: 'I know not seems'. (1.2.76) By doing so he suggests that Gertrude's grief is only put on.

Both Claudius and Gertrude suggest that Hamlet himself is mourning improperly. Hamlet, they argue, is mourning his father too intensely and for too long. They urge him to accept his father's death as a natural part of life and move on. As Gertrude puts it: 'Thou knows't 'tis common; all that lives must die,/ Passing through nature to eternity'. (1.2.72–3) Claudius, meanwhile, tells Hamlet that 'your father lost a father,/ That father lost, lost his'. (1.2.89–90) Too much mourning, they suggest, is not unhealthy and unmanly but also sinful and disrespectful. (We should remember that Claudius has his own selfish reasons for wanting Hamlet to cheer up.)

RESPECT FOR & REMEMBRANCE OF THE DEAD

The notion of respecting the dead is one that comes up several times throughout the play. It leads to a clash between Laertes and the priest in Act 5 Scene 1. Laertes wants to afford his sister the respect of full funeral rites. (5.1.205–224) The priest, however, maintains that doing so would actually disrespect the other dead people lying in the graveyard. (5.1.218–20) He declares that as an apparent suicide Ophelia is lucky to receive any rites at all or to even be buried on holy ground. (5.1.211)

There are several other places where this notion of respect for the dead arises throughout the play:

- Rosencrantz and Guildenstern are ordered to recover Polonius' body so it can be brought to the chapel for proper treatment. (4.2.7–8)
- Claudius regrets holding Polonius' funeral in quickly and secretly (in 'hugger mugger'), rather than with pomp with circumstance. (4.5.82–3) (Claudius regrets this, however, at least partly because it makes him look bad and caused rumours to the spread among the Danish people rather than out of genuine love for Polonius).
- Laertes is enraged that his father wasn't buried with the ceremony appropriate to his station in life. (4.5.208–12)
- Hamlet seems offended by the fact that the gravedigger sings merrily while he works, presumably finding this behaviour disrespectful to the dead. (5.1.61–2)
- Fortinbras is keen to treat Hamlet's body with the military honours worthy of a great prince: 'Let four captains/ Bear Hamlet like a soldier to the stage'. (5.2.382–3)

It could be argued that there are several instances where the prince himself shows disrespect toward the dead. He chides Polonius' corpse, calling him a 'wretched, rash, intruding fool' and describing his corpse as a tub of 'guts' he'll have to lug around the place. (3.4.213) In Act 5 Scene 1 Hamlet essentially gatecrashes Ophelia's funeral and assaults her brother, in some productions even jumping into the grave to attack him.

As the poison takes effect, Hamlet entrusts Horatio with the task of telling the world his story: 'And in this harsh world draw thy breath in pain/ To tell my story'. (5.2.335–6) His dying wish is an extremely common one: that he be remembered after his death. In this regard his last request echoes the ghost's haunting and pitiful cry of 'Remember me'.

A MEANINGFUL DEATH?

There are many deaths in Hamlet, but very few people achieve anything by dying. In this sense they die for nothing and their deaths serve no greater purpose. Many characters die in pointless accidents:

- Polonius' death, for instance, is essentially an accident. He is killed in what can only be described as a case of mistaken identity while hiding behind a curtain.
- Gertrude's death is similarly accidental. She dies from drinking poisoned wine that was never meant for her.
- Ophelia's death is also something of an accident. It is possible that she accidentally drowns herself while in a deranged state. However, even if she takes her own life there is still something grimly accidental about her death. She is 'collateral damage', the unintended victim of circumstances beyond her control.
- Laertes, too, dies an accidental death: the swords get mixed up during his scuffle with Hamlet and he is accidentally stabbed by the poisoned one. (In this instance we can comfort ourselves that Laertes himself was out to kill the prince.)

Fortinbras' army, meanwhile, is marched of to Poland to fight for 'a little patch of ground/ That hath in it no profit'. (4.4.18–19) As Hamlet puts it, thousands of men will die for a 'fantasy and a trick of fame', to own a piece of land too small to hold the corpses of those killed in the fight over it: 'not tomb enough and continent/ To hide the slain'. (4.4.64–5) In other words Fortinbras' men die for nothing.

Rosencrantz and Guildenstern, like Ophelia are victims of a struggle they only dimly comprehend. They seem to know nothing about Claudius' plan to have Hamlet put to death when the ship reaches England. They are also blissfully unaware that

Hamlet has replaced the letter they carry with one of his own composition, meaning that when they present it to the English king, they are to be instantly put to death. (5.2.38–47)

There is also a sense of futility surrounding their deaths. Hamlet had no need to have his old school friends put to death, and it is not clear what purpose their deaths serve. Hamlet could just as easily have replaced Claudius' letter with something less blood-thirsty. Hamlet, however, has no scruples over his actions. Rosencrantz and Guildenstern betrayed him by siding with Claudius against him in Acts 3 and 4, and therefore they deserve to die.

The world of the play, then, is not one where people die glorious deaths in service of some higher purpose. Instead it is one where people face death suddenly, brutally and pointlessly. Small wonder, therefore, that Hamlet declares 'the readiness is all'. (5.2.202) We must be ready for death at any time for 'if it be now, 'tis not to come, if it be not to come, it will be now'. (5.2.200–1)

LOVE & LUST

TRUE LOVE

We might guess that prior to his father's death and his mother's hasty re-marriage to his uncle, Hamlet believed in true love. He was then courting Ophelia, writing her love letters that contained romantic verse and suggesting to her that she could doubt everything in the world except his love. His parents' marriage testified to the strength of love and the sanctity of the union of husband and wife.

Hamlet's father seems to have loved Gertrude deeply and considered marriage sacred. The Ghost tells the prince that his love 'was of that dignity/ That it went hand-in-hand even with the vow/ I made to her in marriage.' (1.5.48–50) Hamlet says that his father was 'so loving to my mother/ That he might not beteem the winds of heaven/ Visit her face too roughly'. (1.2.140–2) No doubt Hamlet has idealised notions of what his parents' relationship was like, but it does seem that old Hamlet was a loving husband and father.

TAINTED LOVE

The Ghost utters the following lines to Hamlet:

So lust, though to a radiant angel linked,
Will sate itself in a celestial bed
And prey on garbage (1.5.55–7)

Seeing his mother move swiftly from one husband to another destroys Hamlet's ability to believe in either the sanctity of marriage or the innocence and purity of love. He tells his mother that her marriage to Claudius 'makes marriage vows/ As false as dicers' oaths'. (3.4.44–5) Their relationship angers and repulses him. He is horrified that his mother could move with 'most wicked speed, to post/ With such dexterity to incestuous sheets'. (1.2.156–7) The Ghost reinforces the prince's feelings of disgust at the relationship, begging him to 'Let not the royal bed of Denmark be/ A couch for luxury and damnèd incest'. (1.5.82–3)

To Hamlet, the relationship between Claudius and Gertrude is something dirty and sinful. It makes a mockery of and taints the 'innocent love' once seemingly held by his father for his mother: 'takes off the rose/ From the fair forehead of an innocent love,/ And sets a blister there'. (3.4.42–4) Hamlet does not consider Claudius and his mother to be in love but in lust. In fact, he considers his mother to be incapable of falling in love again at her advanced age: 'You cannot call it love, for at your age/ The heyday in the blood is tame'. (3.4.68–9)

As the play progresses, Hamlet becomes more enraged with his mother for what she has done, and thoughts of her being with Claudius swell and fester in his mind. We get a sense of just how fixated and disgusted Hamlet has become with his mother's relationship when he speaks to her in Act 3 Scene 4. He imagines his mother to have been living 'In the rank sweat of an enseamèd bed,/ Stewed in corruption, honeying and making love/ Over the nasty sty'. (3.4.92–4) Hamlet seems to imagine that the relationship is purely sexual and that his mother is driven by a desperate sexual appetite. When he confronts her in her bedroom he looks to wean her off her addiction to Claudius, begging her to 'Refrain tonight,/ And that shall lend a kind of easiness/ To the next abstinence'. (3.4.166–8)

MEN & WOMEN AS SEDUCERS

According to the Ghost it is Claudius who is essentially responsible for the sinful relationship. He characterises the king as 'that incestuous, that adulterate beast' and tells Hamlet that Claudius 'won to his shameful lust/ The will of my most seeming virtuous queen. (1.5.45–6) Of course in this account the queen does not come off as completely pure and innocent – she is the 'seeming virtuous queen' – but it is Claudius who is seen as the corrupting force. His 'shameful lust' overpowers the will of the queen.

This notion of men being seducers driven by lust and untrustworthy in their sentiments fits in with Polonius' account of the prince's involvement with his daughter. He tells Ophelia not to trust Hamlet's pledges of love because they are false, and only used as a means to satisfy his lust:

Do not believe his vows, for they are brokers,
Not of that dye which their investments show,
But mere implorators of unholy suits,
Breathing like sanctified and pious bonds
The better to beguile (1.3.127–31)

But the prince has the very opposite notion. To him women are the false sex. He sees them as temptresses, luring men to their ruin. He tells Ophelia that 'wise men know/ well enough what monsters you make of them'. (3.1.138–9) According to Hamlet women wear make-up and act in a wanton manner to seduce men: 'God hath given you one face, and you make yourselves another. You/ jig, you amble, and you lisp'. (3.1.143–4) Woman's love is 'brief' and the hearts of women fickle. Yet this is probably not how the prince always viewed women and love.

HAMLET & OPHELIA

According to Laertes and Polonius, Hamlet's love for Ophelia is fleeting, a youthful romance that will not stand the test of time. Laertes describes it as a 'violet in the youth of primy nature,/ Forward, not permanent, sweet not lasting'. (1.3.7–8) Although Ophelia is convinced that Hamlet's affections are genuine, her father remains sceptical. When his daughter tells him that Hamlet has acted in an honourable fashion and 'hath given countenance to his speech … / With almost all the holy vows of heaven'. (1.3.113–14) Polonius is dismissive:

Ay, springes to catch woodcocks. I do know
When the blood burns, how prodigal the soul
Lends the tongue vows. These blazes, daughter,
Giving more light than heat, extinct in both
You must not take for fire (1.3.115–20)

And yet when he hears of how the prince appeared before his daughter in a dishevelled and disturbed state Polonius has to acknowledge that Hamlet's feelings might be a little more intense than he initially imagined. He tells Ophelia that the prince's desperate love for her is causing him to act in a crazy manner:

This is the very ecstasy of love,
Whose violent property fordoes itself
And leads the will to desperate undertakings (2.1.102–4)

We don't get to see how Hamlet behaved towards Ophelia before his father died and his mother remarried. However, we do get a sense of what the relationship was like. It seems that Hamlet did genuinely love Ophelia, and perhaps throughout the play continues to love her. The letter that Polonius reads to the king and queen from Hamlet to Ophelia seems genuine in its sentiment:

O dear Ophelia, I am ill at these numbers, I have not art
to reckon my groans, but that I love thee best,
    O most best, believe it. (2.2.119–21)

And even as she approaches him in Act 3 Scene 1 the prince seems to feel genuine affection for Ophelia, saying 'Soft you now!/ The fair Ophelia. – Nymph, in thy orisons. (3.1.88–9) However, only moments later he is berating and insulting her in the most horrible manner, saying that he loved her and that he never loved her. (3.1.115, 118–19)

How do we explain how Hamlet goes from writing romantic letters in which he proclaims his love to resting his head on Ophelia's lap in public and telling her that 'It would cost you a groaning to take off my edge'? (3.2.232) How can he tell the woman he purports to love 'best' to take herself off to a nunnery, when the very term 'nunnery' was commonly used to refer to a brothel? How can he suggest that Ophelia, the most innocent and virtuous character in the play, would become a 'breeder/ of sinners'? (3.1.121–2) And how can the prince say all these things to Ophelia and then claim upon her death to have loved her more than 'forty thousand brothers'? (5.1.251)

It would seem that Hamlet did indeed love Ophelia, and that he does love her throughout the play, but his relationship with her gets all messed up with the feelings of rage, betrayal and disgust he feels towards his mother. Ophelia becomes the whipping post for his anger and he uses her to give vent to the complex and horrible emotions built up inside him. The prince is so shaken and disturbed by his mother's actions that his view of women gets clouded, corrupted and damaged. When Hamlet finally gets to confront his mother and to let all his rage and disgust at her spill out, we might wonder: Does this in any way lead to a softening of his harsh opinions about women in general? Certainly the prince seems a calmer and less hostile character after this moment in the play. Unfortunately, however, he never gets to see Ophelia alive again. Had she lived, would the prince have come to treat her any better?

POLITICS

THE INTERNATIONAL SCENE

Although much of the play focuses on the affairs of Elsinore there is an important international political dimension to *Hamlet*. At the start of the play we quickly become aware of Denmark's insecurity. There is talk of a pending attack from Norway and preparations are being made for war. There is a history of conflict between Norway and Denmark. Old King Hamlet was challenged to fight the old king of Norway, old Fortinbras, in single combat. King Hamlet won this fight, killing the Norwegian king and Norway had to subsequently forfeit large amounts of its land to Denmark.

The son of the dead Norwegian king, young Fortinbras, is a hot-blooded young man, thirsty for revenge. Horatio tells us that this young prince has gathered together an army and intends to recover the land that his father lost:

> *young Fortinbras,*
> *Of unimprovèd mettle hot and full,*
> *Hath in the skirts of Norway here and there*
> *Sharked up a list of landless resolutes* (1.1.95–8)

It is for this very reason that Denmark is preparing itself for war at the start of the play. Claudius tells the court that Young Fortinbras thinks Denmark is weak and vulnerable following old Hamlet's death: 'thinking by our late dear brother's death/ Our state to be disjoint and out of frame'. (1.2.19–20)

Denmark also has a history of conflict with Poland and England. We hear early in the play how old King Hamlet fought and defeated 'the sledded Polacks on the ice'. (1.1.63) It seems that Denmark has also recently defeated the English in battle. When Claudius sends Hamlet to England he is confident that the English will obey his command to have the prince executed because they still fear Denmark: 'Since yet thy cicatrice looks raw and red/ After the Danish sword, and thy free awe/ Pays homage to us'. (4.3.56–8)

Norway too has issues with Poland, and in the middle of the play young Fortinbras marches an army through Denmark to reach and fight Poland. This puts Denmark at the centre of warring nations, and it means that the country is nervous and fearful of a foreign invasion. Indeed the play ends with young Fortinbras returning from his battle with Poland. Whether he actually had intended to conquer Denmark on his return to Norway we cannot be sure, but he finds the country in disarray and easily assumes command.

THE ROLE OF THE KING

When we read *Hamlet* we get a sense of just how powerful a person the king is. Rosencrantz and Guildenstern obey the king's wish that they spy on Hamlet, because they know that the royal couple have it in their power to force them to do so. Rosencrantz tells the king and queen that 'Both your majesties/ Might, by the sovereign power you have of us/ Put your dread pleasures more into command/ Than to entreaty'. (2.2.26–9)

However, not only is the king head of the state and so capable of punishing those who do not obey his commands, he is also considered divine. The king in Shakespeare time was thought to be linked with God. Polonius reminds us and Claudius of this fact when he tells the king, 'Assure you, my good liege,/ I hold my duty, as I hold my soul,/ Both to my God and to my gracious king'. (2.2.43–5) Claudius also speaks of the divinity of kings when Laertes storms the castle in Act 4 Scene 5. He tells Gertrude that he does not fear Laertes because his divine status as king will ensure his protection:

> *… do not fear our person:*
> *There's such divinity doth hedge a king,*
> *That treason can but peep to what it would,*
> *Acts little of his will* (4.5.123–6)

Claudius' words are supremely ironic considering how he did exactly what he says here cannot be done when he killed old Hamlet.

Laertes gives us a sense of how important the king is to society when he describes the pressure that Hamlet is under as future head of state. He tells Ophelia that the prince cannot act anyway he wishes:

> *… for on his choice depends*
> *The sanity and health of the whole state;*
> *And therefore must his choice be circumscribed*
> *Unto the voice and yielding of that body*
> *Whereof he is the head.* (1.3.20–4)

DENMARK SUFFERS BECAUSE OF CLAUDIUS' CORRUPTION

The king is, therefore, not only someone who legislates and enforces the law, he is said to be responsible for the very well-being of the country. When the king is corrupt the whole country suffers.

Denmark certainly seems to be suffering since Claudius came to power. Young Fortinbras considers it 'to be disjoint and out of frame' and senses an opportunity to conquer Denmark. (1.2.20–1) Claudius has an uneasy relationship with the public and seems to fear an uprising. Indeed his fears are realised when Laertes storms the castle in Act 4 and threatens the life of the king.

The citizens of Denmark sense that since the death of old Hamlet, there is something fundamentally wrong. Marcellus tells Horatio that 'Something is rotten in the state of Denmark'. (1.4.90) He does not know that the new king is a murderer and an adulterer, and therefore responsible for the country's unsettled state. The Ghost, however, knows exactly why the country is suffering, telling Hamlet that 'the whole ear of Denmark/ Is by a forgèd process of my death/ Rankly abused'. (1.5.36–8) Only the death of Claudius, it seems, can restore balance to the country.

DYNASTIC POLITICS

Hamlet's birth puts him in line for the throne. As Laertes tells Ophelia:

His greatness weigh'd, his will is not his own,
For he himself is subject to his birth.
He may not, as unvalued persons do,
Carve for himself (1.3.17–20)

It is possible that Hamlet might have had a legitimate claim to the throne when his father died. Claudius seems eager to pacify the prince when he tells him that he is next in line: 'You are the most immediate to our throne'. (1.2.109)

Both Denmark and Norway are ruled by kings. And when the king dies he is succeeded by a blood relative. Political power in these countries is, therefore, dynastic, in other words kept within the family. Individual families can continue to rule for generations, assuming there is an able male relative available to take over when the king dies. In the case of both Denmark and Norway the brother of the recently deceased king has come to power. Young Fortinbras and Hamlet are therefore in similar positions, awaiting the death of their uncles before they can become king.

SPYING & SURVEILLANCE

Claudius' regime is marked by the need to observe and control. This is probably not surprising considering that the king has a terrible secret to conceal. Claudius is bound to be paranoid, and he knows better than anyone how the king's life can be threatened by even those closest to him.

For this reason alone, he needs to keep a close eye on his stepson Hamlet, the prince who probably had a legitimate claim to the throne when his father died. It is also the case that Denmark is a troubled country, 'disjoint and out of frame' (1.2.20), fearful of foreign invasion and containing the possibility of an internal uprising.

The king's chief advisor Polonius certainly favours spying, and considers close surveillance necessary in order to maintain control. He tells Reynaldo that in order to get to the truth it is necessary to be devious:

And thus do we of wisdom and of reach,
With windlasses and with assays of bias,
By indirections find directions out (2.1.64–6)

Certainly the king seems to be in agreement. Claudius is happy to go along with Polonius' plan to hide and overhear Hamlet's encounter with Ophelia. He considers himself and Polonius 'Lawful espials', who by 'seeing unseen' learn what they can of the prince from behind the arras.

Having heard Hamlet speak with Ophelia the king is still uncertain as to the reason for his stepson's strange behaviour. Polonius is quick to suggest further surveillance, proposing to hide himself in the queen's bedroom after the play is performed at court. The queen will request that Hamlet visit her in her room and Polonius will hear all that is said: 'I'll be placed, so please you, in the ear/ Of all their conference'. (3.1.184–5)

However, Polonius is not only willing to use surveillance for political purposes, he also feels a need to have his own son spied on. Laertes is away at university in France and his father seems to have no qualms about sending Reynaldo to spy on him. Polonius gives his servant clear and detailed instructions as to how he should go about gathering the necessary information regarding Laertes' behaviour and conduct.

The king takes a leaf out of Polonius' book when he calls on Rosencrantz and Guildenstern, two old school friends of Hamlet, to come and spend time at Elsinore. He wants the two young men to engage Hamlet in conversation and to gather by 'drift of circumstance' what information they can about the prince's state of mind. However, Hamlet knows all too well why his friends have suddenly appeared in the palace and he chastises them for doing the king's dirty work and presuming to think that they could make him reveal his inner thoughts: 'Why look you now how unworthy a thing you make of me./ You would play upon me, you would seem to know my/ stops, you would pluck out the heart of my mystery'. (3.2.340–2)

The prince himself, however, is not averse to using unusual methods to gather information. He carefully plans the play that will be performed at court in order to prick the conscience of the king. Hamlet positions Horatio so that he might observe Claudius' face at the critical moment. The plan proves a success and Hamlet gets the proof he desperately needed that the ghost's words were true.

APPEARANCE & REALITY

Throughout the play we are made aware of the huge gap between the appearance of things and the truth of the underlying reality. The first instance of this comes in Act 1 Scene 2. Claudius has made a speech paying due tribute to his predecessor, emphasising the collective grief at his passing ('it us befitted/ To bear our hearts in grief'. (1.2.2–3)) The royal couple then attempt to talk Hamlet out of his grief.

Hamlet is disgusted by their efforts ('I know not seems' (1.2.76)) and makes a sharp speech on the superficial nature of public mourning that Gertrude and Claudius have presumably been adopting: wearing black, sighing, tears, and a gloomy appearance. Hamlet claims to be different. His grief is real:

For they are actions that a man might play;
But I have that within which passeth show –
These but the trappings and suits of woe. (1.2.84–6)

Hamlet thinks that he is above such empty conventionality. He will say what he thinks, regardless of the consequences.

In a similar vein, he believes that his mother's swift remarriage proves that her grief for his father was only a pretence: 'Ere yet the salt of most unrighteous tears/ Had left the flushing of her gallèd eyes,/ She married'. (1.2.154–6) The shock of recent unexpected events in the prince's life has made him cynical and wary of appearances.

HONESTY AS A VICE

That appearances are everything and honesty is a liability is most vividly expressed in Polonius' farewell speech to Laertes. The entire thrust of his advice is that wisdom lies in withholding one's true feelings and thoughts: 'Give thy thoughts no tongue'. (1.3.59) One should listen and take the measure of others so as to have control over them without revealing one's own position: 'Give every man thy ear, but few thy voice;/ Take each man's censure, but reserve thy judgement'. (1.3.68–9)

Polonius' distrust of other men is further expressed in the same scene when he mocks Ophelia for her belief in the sincerity of Hamlet's romantic declarations: 'I'll teach you. Think yourself a baby/ That you have tane these tenders for true pay'. (1.3.105–6) Polonius' instincts automatically tend toward distrust and suspicion.

A FALSE KING

The most obvious instance of the hypocrisy of appearance covering reality is, of course, Claudius' kingship. He has gained the throne through murder, yet plays at being a brother in mourning. He acts like a concerned stepfather to Hamlet, yet in reality is suspicious of him. He is contemptuous of the Danish people, while pretending he has their best interests at heart.

The Ghost's revelations to Hamlet completely confirm the prince's suspicion of the glittering façade of Claudius' court:

O villain, villain, smiling, damnèd villain!
My tables – meet it is I set down,
That one may smile, and smile, and be a villain;
At least I'm sure it may be so in Denmark (1.5.106–9)

Hamlet now knows that Claudius is a false king. He will no longer act as one of his subjects. Hamlet's contempt for Claudius' kingship is suggested by his remark when the players arrive at court. The prince will not acknowledge his uncle's reign, but he will pay tribute to the theatrical king: 'He that plays the king shall be welcome; his majesty/ shall have tribute of me'. (2.2.312–13)

Claudius himself is aware of the corrupt reality that lies beneath the pomp of his reign. Before he and Polonius spy on Hamlet, his minister remarks on how the appearance of righteousness can cover up evil: 'with devotion's visage/ And pious action we do sugar o'er/ The devil himself'. (3.1.47–9) Polonius' words cut the king to the quick:

How smart a lash that speech doth give my conscience!
The harlot's cheek, beautied with plastering art,
Is not more ugly to the thing that helps it
Than is my deed to my most painted word (3.1.50–3)

Claudius is only too aware of his kingship resting on lies, manipulation, and assuming the correct appearance.

ACTING AS REALITY

The questionable nature of the reality of life at Elsinore is emphasised by the strong symbolic role played by acting and actors in the play. It is difficult to see how Hamlet's decision to feign madness is supposed to aid him in his quest for vengeance, but it is easy to see how it allows him to speak his mind with impunity. One of the ways of thinking about what it means to be mad is to consider it as a departure from social norms and conventionality. By acting the lunatic, Hamlet absolves himself from the burden of playing the part of the dutiful prince at court. His decision to act insane is a means by which he can attack the false appearance of Claudius' court and hint at the underlying reality.

In a more direct fashion, the prince uses actors to help him in his mission against Claudius. His decision to stage a play in order to snare Claudius involves him using pretence to reveal reality: 'The play's the thing/ Wherein I'll catch the conscience of the king'. (2.2.582–3) Hamlet believes the king will betray himself at the play, because 'the purpose of playing, whose end both at the first and/ now, was and is, to hold, as 'twere, the mirror up to nature'. (3.2.19–20) Professional actors can represent reality on stage, whereas on the 'stage' of court life people 'act' in order to hide the reality of their true feelings and motives.

WOMEN AS DECEIVERS

The bitterness Hamlet feels over his mother's marriage to Claudius generates in his mind a very strong suspicion of women generally. He comes to believe that they are arch-deceivers, skilled in the art of lying and manipulation. As mentioned previously, the prince suspects his mother's grief over his father

was false, and throughout the play he attacks women's social behaviour as being deceitful and dishonest.

This is most sharply expressed in his attack on Ophelia in Act 3 Scene 1. The prince claims that beauty corrupts women's honesty:

the power of beauty will sooner transform honesty/
from what it is to a bawd, than the force of/ honesty
can translate beauty into his likeness (3.1.111–13)

In Hamlet's eyes, all women are identified with Gertrude. They are universally guilty of lying and deception. He condemns their use of make-up ('God hath/ given you one face, and you make yourselves another' (3.1.142–3)) and their general comportment:

You/ jig, you amble, and you lisp, you nickname
God's creatures,/ and make your wantonness your
ignorance (3.1.143–5)

Hamlet's paranoia about women is given further expression when he confronts Gertrude in her bedchamber. He damns her union with Claudius as being the ultimate in deceit. He describes it as:

… an act
That blurs the grace and blush of modesty,
Calls virtue hypocrite, takes off the rose
From the fair forehead of an innocent love
And sets a blister there (3.4.40–4)

When he urges her to change her ways, he tells her to try and appear virtuous, even if it is not genuine: 'Assume a virtue, if you have it not'. (3.4.161)

Even in Act 5, when Hamlet appears to have a new-found acceptance of reality, he cannot resist making one last jibe at what he perceives as women's falsity. While examining Yorick's skull he comments bitterly on how he wishes women would appreciate the reality of death: 'Now get you to/ my lady's chamber, and tell her, let her paint an inch thick,/ to this favour she must come; make her laugh at that'. (5.2.176–8)

REVENGE
....
VENGEANCE AS A MORAL DUTY

The world of the play is one where people are expected to avenge the wrongs done to members their family. Vengeance is depicted as a moral duty. We see this when the Ghost tells Hamlet that if he ever loved him he will 'revenge his foul and most unnatural murder'. (1.5.25) The ghost is pleased when Hamlet declares himself willing to perform this duty: 'I find thee apt'. (1.5.31)

In Act 4 Scene 7 Claudius echoes the Ghost's sentiments, telling Laertes that if he really loved his father he must show this in his deeds by avenging his death. Claudius asks: 'what would you undertake/ To show yourself in deed your father's son/ More than in words?' (4.7.124–6) The king, then, manipulates Laertes by playing on the notion of revenge as a moral duty.

The Ghost expects Hamlet to do his duty like any good son and go about the business of avenging his death. Only a son who lacked all human emotion, all 'nature', would fail to heed such a summons. (1.5.81) Failing to avenge his father's death will show Hamlet to be a 'dull', lazy and careless son. (1.5.32) This expectation is evident when the ghost reappears in Act 3 Scene 4 to 'chide' Hamlet for being slow in carrying out his duty.

The notion of revenge as moral duty also features during Fortinbras' brief appearance in Act 4 Scene 4. Fortinbras sends a captain to meet with Claudius to request passage across Denmark, but says he is willing to meet the king himself if need be: 'If that his majesty would aught with us,/ We shall express our duty in his eye'. (4.4.5–6) In one sense Fortinbras is simply saying that if necessary he will pay his respects ('express his duty') to Claudius. Yet there is also a sense in which these lines are a threat to Claudius. For Fortinbras is surely referring here to his 'duty' of revenge, to the vengeance he is morally bound to exact on Hamlet's family for the defeat his father suffered thirty years before.

It could be argued that Fortinbras also expresses the idea that revenge is a right and a duty at the play's conclusion: 'I have some rights of memory in this kingdom'. (5.2.376) These 'rights' no doubt relate to the lands his father lost and that he is bound by the moral code of vengeance to regain.

AN EYE FOR AN EYE

There is a sense in the play that the revenge taken must match the original crime. This is particularly evident when Hamlet delays killing Claudius in order to send him to Heaven rather than hell. Claudius is praying and defenceless, providing Hamlet with the perfect opportunity to avenge his father's death: 'Now

might I do it pat … And so am I revenged'. (3.3.73–5) Yet Hamlet worries that because Claudius is praying he has purged his soul of sin: the king is in 'the purging of his soul … fit and seasoned for his passage'. (3.3.85–6) Killing him, therefore, would send his soul directly to Heaven. (3.3.76–8)

Hamlet decides it is no revenge to send Claudius directly to Heaven while his own father suffers in the fires of Purgatory:

A villain kills my father, and for that,
I, his sole son, do this same villain send
To heaven.
Why, this is hire and salary, not revenge (3.3.76–9)

He decides it is better to kill Claudius when the king is committing a sinful act, such as drinking, swearing or making love to Gertrude: 'Or in th'incestuous pleasure of his bed;/ At gaming, swearing, or about some act/ That has no relish of salvation in't'. (3.3.90–2) That way Claudius will die in a state of sin and burn in Hell forever: 'that his soul may be as damned and black/ As hell whereto it goes'. (3.3.94–5)

THE CONTRAST BETWEEN HAMLET & LAERTES

Hamlet recognizes that Laertes has a similar motivation to himself. Both wish to avenge their father's deaths: 'by the image of my cause I see the portraiture of his'. (5.2.77–8) Yet the two are very much opposites. Laertes is hot headed and passionate while Hamlet is something of a procrastinator who tends to think too much and over-analyse situations rather than taking direct action. The prince acknowledges this failing at the conclusion of Act 2, bitterly wondering why he must 'like a whore unpack my heart with words'. (2.2.563)

In Act 1 Scene 5, Hamlet demands to know the identity of his father's killer so that he can immediately take revenge: 'Haste me to know't, that I … May sweep to my revenge'. (1.5.29–31) He declares that from now on his mission is all that matters. The task of killing Claudius will be all that occupies his mind: 'And thy commandment all alone shall live/ Within the book and volume of my brain'. (1.5.102–3)

However, Hamlet does not follow through on this promise. Weeks, possibly even months, pass between Acts 1 and 2, but the prince has done nothing concrete to being his revenge any closer. Even when he returns to Denmark in Act 5, Hamlet continues to procrastinate, sending a letter to the king, hanging around the graveyard and agreeing to participate in a fencing match.

The contrast with Laertes could not be starker. Upon hearing of his father's death, Laertes returns immediately to Denmark, rounds a band of supporters and storms the royal palace. (4.5.99–108) When he learns that Hamlet killed his father he immediately takes action, hatching a plan with Claudius to kill the prince that is very quickly put into effect. (4.1.145–7)

Hamlet delays partially because he has no concrete evidence against Claudius and worries that the king might in fact be innocent. Laertes seems to have no such concern with evidence. He automatically assumes that Claudius was involved in his father's death and will not let his allegiance to the king stop him taking revenge: 'I'll not be juggled with./ To hell allegiance, vows, to the blackest devil!' (4.5.130–1) He also seems to require little evidence to convince him that Hamlet was in fact the killer.

Hamlet worries that in his quest for vengeance he will accidentally damn himself to hell by killing an innocent man. He worries that the Ghost may be the devil in disguise, attempting to damn his soul by tricking him into murdering a blameless individual. (2.2.576–81) Laertes has no such scruples. He declares that he is more than willing to risk damnation if it means avenging his father's death. (4.5.133) He cares nothing for this world or for what awaits him in the afterlife: 'both the worlds I give to negligence,/ Let come what comes'. (4.7.134–5)

Laertes is even willing to commit the terrible sin of killing his father's murderer on the sanctified ground of the church. (4.7.126)

It should be noted that there are also practical reasons that prevent Hamlet taking revenge, especially in the early part of the play. We get the impression however that not even these practical issues would have delayed Laertes.

THE CONTRAST BETWEEN HAMLET & FORTINBRAS

Like Hamlet and Laertes, Fortinbras is also out to avenge the death of his father. Hamlet's father killed Fortinbras' father in single combat about thirty years before play begins. (1.1.84–6) As a result certain lands passed from Fortinbras' family to Hamlet's family. (1.1.88–92) Young Fortinbras is now determined to restore his father's honour by regaining the lands

lost in that long-ago duel: 'But to recover of us, by strong hand/ And terms compulsatory, those foresaid lands/ So by his father lost'. (1.1.102–4)

The contrast between Hamlet's constant delaying and Fortinbras' decisiveness is pronounced. Fortinbras assembles a rag-tag army with which to invade Denmark and avenge his father's death. (1.1.95–102) He acts alone, without the support or knowledge of the Norwegian king. (2.2.65–70) The King of Norway orders him to call off his invasion plans and attack Poland instead. Yet as we noted above, Act 4 Scene 4 suggests there can be little doubt that revenge on Hamlet's family remains Fortinbras' primary goal.

This is borne out when Fortinbras turns up in the play's final scene. Having met with success in Poland he heads straight to Elsinore, no doubt determined to take his revenge. (5.2.364) His warlike intentions are signalled when he fires on the English ambassadors. (5.2.338–9) When he sees the Danish royal family lying dead he immediately stakes his claim to Denmark's throne. (5.2.376)

The contrast between Fortinbras and Hamlet is particularly pronounced in Act 4 Scene 4.

Fortinbras has no qualms about marching his army off to Poland to fight for 'a little patch of ground/ That hath in it no profit'. (4.4.18–19) Hamlet is horrified that thousands of men will die for a 'fantasy and a trick of fame', to own a piece of land too small to hold the corpses of those killed in the fight over it: 'not tomb enough and continent/ To hide the slain'. (4.4.64–5)

In this respect Hamlet's sensibility is strangely modern:

· He requires proof of guilt before taking revenge.
· He abhors the pointless deaths caused in war.
· His thoughtful nature causes him to contemplate the consequences of his actions. (In some respects he is too sensitive and thoughtful to make an effective avenger.)

In contrast Fortinbras and Laertes are much more like mediaeval war chieftains. They are aggressive, impulsive and quick to act. They waste little time in worrying about or pondering the consequences of their actions. Laertes requires no proof of guilt before acting, and Fortinbras cares seems to care little for the lives of his soldiers. Honour is everything to them. (We might remember, however, that Hamlet isn't a complete procrastinator. He also has a decisive and a ruthless streak.)

THE TERRIBLE CONSEQUENCES OF REVENGE

Hamlet features three sons whose fathers have been killed: Fortinbras, Hamlet and Laertes. The play shows how each of them seeks to avenge their father's death. It could be said that all three sons succeed in their goal of vengeance. However they achieve this in ways they could never have expected and at a terrible cost.

Hamlet does indeed kill Claudius. However along the way he has more or less accidentally murdered the innocent Polonius. This, in turn leads, to Ophelia's madness and eventual death by suicide or misadventure. He has also sent Rosencrantz and Guildenstern, his two old school friends, to their doom. Laertes does indeed kill Hamlet. However, in the process he also accidentally kills himself. Fortinbras, too, tastes vengeance, gaining not only the lands lost by his father but the entire Danish kingdom. It is surely ironic and unexpected that revenge – and the throne – is more or less handed to him without a fight.

The play's message seems to be that revenge is not a straightforward business. Its consequences are often far-reaching, messy, unexpected and generally disastrous for all concerned.

REVENGE & RELIGION

All the characters in the play are deeply Christian and as such should be opposed to revenge, to murdering someone who murdered a member of your family. In some respects, then, the play features a clash between two outlooks: a Christian one that regards revenge as sinful and an earlier pagan one where revenge was a moral duty of the highest importance.

Yet Hamlet seems to regard his revenge as a holy duty, a quest he has been ordered to fulfill by Heaven itself: 'Prompted to my revenge by heaven'. (2.2.562) He makes this point to Gertrude, declaring that he has been chosen by Heaven to be its 'scourge and minister'. (3.4.176) Claudius makes a similar point when he declares we should be allowed take revenge even if our victim seeks refuge in the scared ground of a church. (4.7.127) Revenge, he seems to suggest, is a holy duty and nothing should be allowed stand in its way: 'Revenge should have no bounds'. (4.7.128)

PASSION & REASON
THE PRINCE'S CONFLICT BETWEEN PASSION & REASON

From the beginning of the play the prince finds himself filled with powerful emotions. He cannot reason away or ignore the negative emotions that fill him, and he finds the attempts by Claudius and Gertrude to do so monstrous and repellent. Yet he finds it difficult to act spontaneously on the emotions he experiences. His only recourse, therefore, is to verbalise his feelings, an aspect of his personality he finds loathsome. He is disgusted that he can only 'like a whore unpack my heart with words'.

Hamlet is tormented by the fact that the Player can summon up such false emotion that he moves himself to tears, where he himself has genuine emotion but cannot act upon it: 'What would he do,/ Had he the motive and the cue for passion/ That I have?' (2.2.537–8)

There is a sense in which the prince's reason often prevents him from acting directly. He analyses everything too closely to be capable of unmeditated action. He initially swears that he will act on the Ghost's command without hesitation. However, his reason will not allow him to do so. His mind becomes filled with questions and concerns, including the suspicion that the devil might be trying to trick him. (2.2.577–8) He seeks proof to satisfy his intellect while his emotions continue to bubble dangerously.

This clash between the conflicting demands of reason and passion captured perfectly in the 'To be or not to be' speech:

Thus conscience does make cowards of us all;
And thus the native hue of resolution
Is sicklied o'er with the pale cast of thought,
And enterprises of great pitch and moment
With this regard their currents turn awry
And lose the name of action (3.1.83–8)

Hamlet seeks the impossible: a perfect marriage between passion and reason that will result in a genuinely emotional but well-controlled manner of action. He expresses something of this ideal in Act 2 Scene 2: 'how noble in reason … in action how like an angel'. He makes this desire even clearer in his advice to the players:

for in the very torrent, tempest, and, as/ I may say,
the whirlwind of your passion, you must acquire/ and
beget a temperance that may give it smoothness (3.2.5–7)

Perhaps the reason the prince loves actors so much is that they can manage this balancing act successfully but he cannot. It is also the chief reason he admires Horatio and would like to emulate him. The prince's friend is a man 'That is not passion's slave'. (3.2.65) This also explains his misguided admiration for Fortinbras. He views his Norwegian counterpart as an example to model himself on, but he does not fully grasp the ruthless and brutal nature of the man he nominates as Danish king.

Only when he sends Rosencrantz and Guildenstern to their deaths does Hamlet succeed in acting on instinct without being tormented by doubt. He acknowledges his relief at being able to do so: 'Our indiscretion sometimes serves us well,/ When our deep plots do pall'. (5.2.8–9)

It is arguable that he also acts with an appropriate mix of reason and instinct when he escapes Claudius' clutches by boarding the pirate ship.

FADING PASSIONS

Given Hamlet's admiration for actors it is a little ironic that the most profound insight into the nature of passion comes in the speech made by the Player King. The Player Queen has emotionally promised that she will never remarry, but her husband knows that time changes everything:

What to ourselves in passion we propose,
The passion ending, doth the purpose lose,
The violence of either grief or joy
Their own enactures with themselves destroy (3.2.180–2)

Passion lasts only briefly, and what we swear in the heat of the moment may never be enacted. Hamlet receives a similar message when his father reappears to him: 'Do not forget. This visitation/ Is but to whet thy almost blunted purpose'. (3.4.109–10)

THE DANGER OF PASSION

Although Hamlet seems to laud passion, and wishes that he were a more direct individual, the abandonment of thought can have fatal and unforeseen consequences. Hamlet murders Polonius in a fit of rashness when his passions are high. This has disastrous consequences: the prince himself is more or less taken into custody and sent to England; Laertes is drawn into Claudius' plotting; and Ophelia is eventually driven insane.

However, it is Laertes who best exemplifies the risks of excess emotion. Polonius' son at no point stops to consider his actions. As soon he receives news of his father's death he rushes back to Denmark and is prepared to kill Claudius on the spot. This volatility makes Laertes easy prey for the king's calculated wiles. Claudius manipulates him by questioning his sincerity with a speech very like the Player's:

But that I know love is begun by time;
And that I see, in passages of proof,
Time qualifies the spark and fire of it.
There lives within the very flame of love
A kind of wick or snuff that will abate it (4.7.111–15)

Laertes responds immediately to the bait and swears revenge on Hamlet. If the latter is arguably guilty of too much reason, the former errs in the opposite direction. As a result of his explosive nature, Laertes becomes caught up in a scheme that leads to his own death.

Ironically, it is the outsider Fortinbras who seems to marry reason and passion perfectly. He is undoubtedly passionate in his quest for revenge: 'of unimproved mettle hot and full'. Yet he controls himself well enough to devise a plan of action to move against Denmark and eventually gains the Danish throne in the play's final scene. (It is unclear whether Fortinbras is in the processing of invading Denmark at this stage, or whether he has simply been lucky enough to visit Elsinore and find the throne of Denmark suddenly vacant.)

LANGUAGE & IMAGERY

SICKNESS & DISEASE

Hamlet abounds in images of sickness and decay. This reflects the corruption of the Danish state and the condition of its inhabitants' souls:

· At the very beginning Francisco reflects the general uneasiness that prevails when he says 'I am sick at heart'. (1.1.9) His comrade Marcellus echoes this sentiment when he says 'Something is rotten in the state of Denmark'. (1.4.90)

· The prince examines his own soul and finds that his natural impulses are 'sicklied o'er with the pale cast of thought'. (3.1.85) Later he tells Guildenstern that 'my wit's diseased'. (3.2.300)

· His mortal enemy Claudius also expresses similar sentiments about his inner state. When expressing his inner torment, he says 'my offence is rank, it smells to heaven'. (3.3.36) Hamlet later describes his stepfather as the 'bloat king' to Gertrude. (3.4.183)

· Claudius tells Laertes that he does not know if his love for the queen is 'My virtue or my plague'. (4.7.13)

· Shortly afterward, Laertes tells the king that the prospect of killing Hamlet 'warms the very sickness of my heart'. (4.7.55)

· When Hamlet attacks his mother over her marriage to Claudius, he speaks of how her shallow guilt will only 'skin and film the ulcerous place,/ While rank corruption, mining all within,/ Infects unseen'. (3.4.148–150)

· Claudius compares Hamlet's dangerous presence to a disease: 'Diseases desperate grown/ By desperate appliance are relieved,/ Or not at all'. (4.3.9–11) He compares the prince to a fever: 'like the hectic in my blood he rages'. (4.3.62)

The duplicity that prevails in Elsinore has corrupted the hearts of its inhabitants and has led to a general atmosphere of illness and disease.

WEEDS & PESTILENCE

Parallel to the prevalence of images of sickness and decay is the large number of references to a decayed and ugly state of nature.

· After listening to Claudius address the royal court, Hamlet expresses his disgust and disillusionment by describing the world as 'an unweeded garden/ That grows to seed, things rank and gross in nature/ Possess it merely'. (1.2.135–7)

· When he later confronts Gertrude and urges her to change her ways, he repeats the image: 'do not spread the compost on the weeds,/ To make them ranker'. (3.4.152–3)

· When advising Ophelia to stay away from Hamlet, Laertes employs negative images of nature. He tells his sister how 'The canker galls the infants of the spring,/ Too oft before their buttons be disclosed'. (1.3.39–40) He also describes how easily the innocence of youth can be corrupted: 'in the morn and liquid dew of youth/ Contagious blastments are most imminent'. (1.3.41–2)

· When the ghost appears to Hamlet, he warns him how inappropriate it would be for Hamlet to delay in taking revenge: 'And duller shouldst thou be than the fat weed/ That roots itself in ease on Lethe wharf,/ Wouldst thou not stir in this'. (1.5.32–4)

· He tells his son not to harm Gertrude, as her guilty feelings will torment her enough: 'Leave her to heaven/ And to those thorns that in her bosom lodge/ To prick and sting her'. (1.5.86–8)

For Hamlet life and death become inextricably linked in a grotesque way. Life breeds in even the most disgusting of places: 'For if the sun breed maggots in a dead dog, being a good/ kissing carrion'. (2.2.183–4) The prince later describes the earth as a 'sterile promontory'. (2.2.294) the sky is no more 'than a foul and pestilent congregation of vapours'. (2.2.298)

Hamlet returns to the image of maggots when he is brought as a captive before Claudius. He emphasises how, in spite of appearances, the king is just as mortal and prone to physical decay as anyone else: 'Your worm is your only/ emperor for diet: we fat all creatures else to fat us, and we fat/ ourselves for maggots'. (4.3.20–3)

LUST & DEGRADATION

The decay and corruption of morality in Denmark is also highlighted by the frequent uses of images of lust and base sexual appetite. Polonius believes that Hamlet's declarations of love for Ophelia are only a disguise for his real, baser intentions. They are 'mere implorators of unholy suits,/ Breathing like sanctified and pious bonds,/ The better to beguile'. (1.3.129–31) Ironically (especially in editions of *Hamlet* which read the word 'bonds' in the last quotation as 'bawds') Hamlet employs similar language in his tirade to Ophelia: 'for the power of beauty will sooner transform/ honesty from what it is to a bawd than the force of/ honesty can translate beauty into his likeness'. (3.1.111–113)

The ghost expresses sentiments of the same kind when describing lust's indiscriminating tendencies: 'So lust, though to a radiant angel linked,/ Will sate itself in a celestial bed,/ And prey on garbage'. (1.5.55–7) Hamlet compares Fate to an inconstant loose woman: 'In the secret parts of fortune? Oh most true; she is a/ strumpet'. (2.2.235–6) The prince uses images of bestiality of describe Gertrude's lust for Claudius: 'Nay, but to live/ In the rank sweat of an enseamèd bed,/ Stewed in corruption, honeying and making love/ Over the nasty sty'. (3.4.91–3)

When Hamlet berates himself for his tendency to speak instead of act, he compares himself to a prostitute: 'This is most brave,/ That I …//Must, like a whore unpack my heart with words,/ And fall a-cursing, like a very drab'. (2.2.560–64) Claudius also uses the image of prostitution to describe his sin: 'The harlot's cheek, beautified with plastering art,/ Is not more ugly to the thing that helps it/ Than is my deed to my most painted word'. (3.1.51–3) The prince also makes an allusion to the distorting power of women's make-up in the graveyard scene: 'Now get you to/ my lady's chamber, and tell her, let her paint an inch thick,/ to this favour she must come. Make her laugh at that'. (5.1.176–9)

IMAGERY OF DEATH

As might be expected in a play so concerned with mortality and decay, images of death are plentiful. Dust is a common image in this regard, used to emphasise the final fate of man and the vanity of his ambitions. Gertrude tells Hamlet not to 'for ever with thy vailed lids/ Seek for thy noble father in the dust'. (1.2.70–1) The prince speaks of man as being nothing but 'a quintessence of dust'. (3.2.303)

In the graveyard scene in Act 5 Hamlet refers to the 'noble dust of Alexander' and describes how 'Alexander died,/ Alexander was buried, Alexander returneth into dust; the dust/ is earth'. (5.1.190–2) When Laertes demands to be buried alive with Ophelia he shouts 'Now pile your dust upon the quick and dead'. (5.1.233)

Death is more directly personified by Hamlet in the 'To be or not to be' speech. He describes it as an eternal sleep and as being 'The undiscover'd country from whose bourn/ No traveller returns'. (3.1.79–80) As he lays dying Hamlet imagines himself as being apprehended by 'this fell sergeant, death,/ [who] Is strict in his arrest' (5.2.323–4) When viewing the scene of slaughter in the Danish court shortly afterwards

Fortinbras describes death as being 'proud'. The shadow of death is everywhere in the play.

POISON

Another recurring motif in the play is the frequent use of poison. Poison is the embodiment of deceit and treachery, and also reflects the tendency of corruption to work its way slowly through an individual. The most powerful image of poison comes when Hamlet's father is recounts his death. He describes how Claudius

In the porches of my ears did pour
The leperous distilment, whose effect
Holds such an enmity with blood of man
That swift as quicksilver it courses through
The natural gates and alleys of the body (1.5.63–7)

This scene is recreated by the players in the dumbshow they perform before their play, and Hamlet tells Claudius that they 'poison in jest'. (3.2.218) The words of the poisoner are designed to torment Claudius with his guilt: 'Thoughts black, hands apt, drugs fit, and time agreeing,/ Confederate season, else no creature seeing'. (3.2.237–8) Hamlet adds to it: 'A poisons him i'th'garden for's estate … You/ shall see anon how the murderer gets the love of/ Gonzago's wife'. (3.2.243–6) Claudius himself uses an image of poison to describe Ophelia's insanity: 'Oh this is the poison of deep grief'. (4.5.74)

Poison caused the death of Hamlet's father, and it is appropriate that it should feature heavily at the play's finale. Claudius employs envenomed rapiers as his weapon of choice to kill Hamlet, and he has a poisoned drink on standby as a fallback. Hamlet and Laertes die as a result of being cut by the poisoned rapiers, and Gertrude drinks from the cup and dies, so Claudius ironically ends up having poisoned both husband and wife. And, of course, Hamlet finally kills the king with his own poison too. Events come full circle.

CLOTHING, CONCEALMENT & DISGUISE

In keeping with the theme of appearance and reality that runs through the play there is also a large use of images of clothing, make-up and disguise used in *Hamlet*. The prince spends quite a lot of his time seeing through these camouflages. His first lengthy speech is a condemnation of 'the trappings and the suits of woe' (1.2.86) that he feels Claudius and Gertrude are using as a front to disguise their lack of grief over his father's death. Hamlet later describes how a major flaw in our characters is a part of 'nature's livery'. (1.4.32)

The hypocrite and deceiver Polonius knows the value of proper clothing and appearance. He advises Laertes not to dress too flashily, as people will get the wrong impression: 'Costly thy habit as thy purse can buy,/ But not express'd in fancy; rich, not gaudy;/ For the apparel oft proclaims the man'. (1.3.70–2) He condemns Hamlet's romantic declarations as being a romantic cover for his lustful desires: 'they are brokers,/ Not of that dye which their investments show'. (1.3.127–8)

The prince uses insanity as a social disguise and he wears a dishevelled appearance to convey his madness when he appears in Ophelia's chamber: 'with his doublet all unbraced;/ No hat upon his head, his stockings fouled,/ Ungartered, and down-gyvèd to his ankle'. (2.1.78–80) Claudius remarks on how 'nor th'exterior nor the inward man/ Resembles that it was'. (2.2.6–7)

Hamlet tells Rosencrantz and Guildenstern that they are not good enough at feigning the right appearance when they try to probe him: 'there is a kind of confession in your looks which/ your modesties have not craft enough to colour'. (2.2.276–7) He later shakes their hands, although he knows they are spies, because 'the appurtenance of welcome is fashion and/ ceremony'. (2.2.356–7)

He later thinks that Claudius' external reaction will tell him if the king is guilty of murder: 'I'll observe his looks'. (2.2.574) This connects well with Polonius' observations on how 'with devotion's visage/ And pious action we do sugar o'er/ the devil himself' (3.1.47–9), which in turn leads to Claudius' guilty comparison of his sin with 'the harlot's cheek, beautied with plastering art'. (3.1.51) Hamlet picks up the theme of women's use of deception shortly after: 'I have heard of your paintings too, well enough; God hath/ given you one face, and you make yourselves another'. (3.1.142–3)

Although Hamlet has no difficulty in using professional actors as a means to help him uncover Claudius' guilt, he despises acting in real life. When he tries to reform his mother's duplicity by encouraging her to get into the habit of goodness the prince uses another clothing metaphor. He speaks of how Custom 'is angel yet in this,/ That to the use of actions fair and good/ he likewise gives a frock or livery/ That aptly is put on'. (3.4.163–6)

Hamlet's determination to act honestly and authentically is well reflected in the note he sends to Claudius telling him he is returning to Denmark: 'You shall know I am set naked on/ your kingdom'. (4.7.43–4) His announcement when he dramatically appears at Ophelia's funeral also shows his determination to be honest. It is simple and straightforward: 'This is I, Hamlet the Dane'. (5.2.239–40) The prince will no longer tolerate deception and deceit.

IRONY

DRAMATIC IRONY

Dramatic irony occurs when the reader or the audience knows more about what's going on than the character who is speaking. The character's words, therefore, have a different meaning for us than they do for the character himself. There are several examples of this device in *Hamlet*.

When Hamlet is recalling his father to memory in front of Horatio, Marcellus and Barnardo, he says 'I shall not look upon his like again'. (1.2.188) Little does the prince know that he will be looking upon his father again very soon, and that his life will be turned upside down as a result.

After Ophelia has encountered the 'mad' Hamlet in Act 3 she laments 'that noble and most sovereign reason,/ Like sweet bells jangled, out of time and harsh'. (3.1.157–8) Not only does she not know that the prince is only feigning madness, but she cannot know that she will genuinely lose her sanity as a result of the man she loves murdering her father.

When Hamlet asks Gertrude what she thinks of the Player Queen's protestations of loyalty to her husband, she answers 'The lady doth protest too much'. (3.2.215) Her words are ironic in the sense that her son's rage against her comes from his belief that she did not 'protest' at all against the advances of her dead husband's brother. Shortly afterwards, Hamlet has the chance to murder Claudius, but declines because he believes the latter is praying and therefore in a state of grace. Little does the prince know that Claudius is not actually praying. He is attempting to do so, but cannot because of his guilt. Hamlet has therefore passed up a golden opportunity to take his revenge: 'My words fly up, my thoughts remain below:/ Words without thoughts never to heaven go'. (3.3.97–8)

VERBAL IRONY

Verbal irony occurs when a character's words have a double meaning. The prince has a particular attachment to this kind of wordplay. His first words in the play are an instance of verbal irony. In reply to Claudius calling him his nephew and his son, he remarks in an aside that he is 'A little more than kin, and less than kind'. (1.2.65) Hamlet is referring to fact that he is related to Claudius by being both his nephew (which is generally regarded as a closer relation than cousin) and now his stepson. He is also referring to the double meaning of 'kind' in that he is feeling anything but favourably disposed toward the new king.

Hamlet's first open words to Claudius are a denial that he is in deep mourning: 'I am too much i'the sun'. (1.2.67) Hamlet is punning on the fact that he is both in the sunshine of Claudius' favour, and that he is unhappy because he is too close to the king in being his new son.

Shortly afterwards when Gertrude is attempting to assuage her son's mourning she refers to death as 'common'. Hamlet replies 'Ay, madam, it is common'. (1.2.74) Hamlet is punning on the many meanings of 'common'. Death is common in being universal, but Gertrude's supposed grief for her husband is common in the sense of being cheap and commonplace. He may also be referring to the 'common' or vulgar nature of her speedy remarriage.

The 'mad' Hamlet tells Polonius that he should guard Ophelia carefully: 'Let her not walk i'th'sun. Conception is a blessing, but/ not as your daughter may conceive'. (2.2.186–7) Hamlet is making a double pun here. He uses 'sun' in the sense that Ophelia should avoid him as being the son of the king. There is also a multiple pun on 'conception', meaning the forming of ideas, impregnation, and the 'breeding' of maggots by the sun following death.

In Act 4 Scene 4, Fortinbras instructs his captain to tell Claudius that he is prepared to meet him: 'We shall express our duty in his eye'. (4.4.6) He means 'duty' in the sense of paying his respects as a guest in Danish territory, but also 'duty' in the sense of carrying out his duty of avenging his father by seizing the throne of Denmark.

The gravedigger is also an exponent of verbal irony. He specialises in the very literal use of the meanings of words. When Hamlet asks him what man the grave he is digging is meant for he replies 'For no man, sir'. When the prince then asks 'What woman, then?' he gives a similar negative answer. Finally he answers the question: 'One that was a woman, sir, but rest her soul she's dead'. (5.1.123) The ensuing verbal battle of wits between Hamlet and the gravedigger is based on this kind of literal interpretation of words.

SITUATIONAL IRONY

Situational irony occurs when a situation talked about by a character comes to pass in an unexpected way:

- In the Player King's speech the rampaging Pyrrhus is described as being 'horridly tricked/ With blood of fathers, mothers, daughters, sons'. (2.2.438–9) Little does the admiring Hamlet realise that the trail to his own botched revenge will lead to the blood of Polonius, Gertrude, Ophelia, Laertes and himself being shed.
- When Polonius tells Hamlet that he played the part of Julius Caesar and was killed by Brutus, the prince jokes that 'It was a brute part of him to kill so capital a calf there'. (3.2.96) Hamlet does not know that shortly afterwards he will end up killing Polonius in his mother's bedchamber.
- When Hamlet decides to forgo the opportunity to kill Claudius at prayer, he decides that he will wait until he is 'at gaming, swearing, or about some act/ That has no relish of salvation in't'. (3.3.91–2) The prince will indeed kill Claudius at an occasion of 'gaming', the duel that will also lead to his own death.
- When Rosencrantz is flattering Claudius by describing how the king's downfall brings with it many insignificant others, he says 'when it falls,/ Each small annexment, petty consequence,/ Attends the boisterous ruin'. (3.3.21–2) Little does Rosencrantz realise that he and Guildenstern will be two of the 'small annexments' whose deaths will occur in the process of Claudius' fall.
- In some versions of Hamlet, Claudius dies after Hamlet forces the poisoned drink down his throat. Hence irony in Claudius' declaration, just before the duel between Hamlet and Laertes, that 'The king shall drink to Hamlet's better breath'. (5.2.250) The king does not realise that his promise will be fulfilled in an unexpected way.

TRAGEDY

WHAT IS TRAGEDY?

Tragedy is typically defined as a drama or literary work in which the main character is brought to ruin or suffers extreme sorrow, especially as a consequence of a tragic flaw, moral weakness, or inability to cope with unfavourable circumstances. Tragic drama often shows us that we are terribly limited beings, powerless to control and determine our own fate. A hidden or malevolent God, blind fate, or the brute fury of our animal instincts waits for us in ambush, bringing about our downfall and destroying our hopes and dreams.

A tragedy often contains the following elements:

- It tells of a person who is highly renowned and prosperous, who falls as a result of some error or frailty, because of external or internal forces, or both.
- The tragic hero's powerful wish to achieve some goal inevitably encounters limits, usually those of human frailty, the gods, or nature.
- The tragic hero should have a flaw and/or make some mistake.
- The hero need not die at the end, but he must undergo a change in fortune.
- In addition, the tragic hero may achieve some revelation or recognition about human fate, destiny, and the will of the gods.

WHY IS HAMLET A TRAGEDY?

Hamlet is a tragedy because it conforms to the above criteria.

- It tells the story of a much-admired prince, who, as a result of his own weaknesses and because of the intervention of chance, falls from grace
- Hamlet's powerful wish to avenge his father is achieved, but in the process many others also die as an indirect result of the prince's torturous path to his goal.
- Hamlet's procrastination is commonly perceived to be his 'tragic flaw', that element of his character that brings about his ruin. As we have seen, however, it would be too simple to describe Hamlet as a straightforward procrastinator.
- The ghost of his father is the 'external force' who plays a significant role in Hamlet's downfall. The ghost's exhortation to avenge his death sends Hamlet on the chaotic path that will lead to his own death and the fall of the Danish royal family.
- Hamlet's experiences as an avenger, together with the meaningless deaths he sees all around him, lead him to state of mind where he comes to believe in a divine providence that controls events and which is beyond our understanding.

A little more than kin, and less than kind

Hamlet 2.1.65

This goodly frame, the earth, seems to me a sterile promontory

Hamlet 2.2.293

O that this too too solid flesh would melt,
Thaw and resolve itself into a dew,
Or that the Everlasting had not fixed
His canon 'gainst self-slaughter!

Hamlet 1.2.129–32

What a piece of work is a man! how noble in reason, how infinite in faculties, in form and moving how express and admirable, in action how like an angel, in apprehension how like a god! The beauty of the world, the paragon of animals – and yet to me, what is this quintessence of dust?

Hamlet 2.2.298–303

How weary, stale, flat and unprofitable,
Seem to me all the uses of this world!
Fie on't, ah fie, 'tis an unweeded garden
That grows to seed, things rank and gross in nature
Possess it merely

Hamlet 1.2.134–9

O what a rogue and peasant slave am I!

Hamlet 2.2.527

Neither a borrower nor a lender be,
For loan oft loses both itself and friend,
And borrowing dulls the edge of husbandry
This above all, to thine own self be true

Polonius 1.3.75–8

I'll have grounds
More relative than this. The play's the thing
Wherein I'll catch the conscience of the king

Hamlet 2.2.581–3

Haste me to know't, that I, with wings as swift
As meditation or the thoughts of love
May sweep to my revenge

Hamlet 1.5.29–31

How smart a lash that speech doth give my conscience!
The harlot's cheek, beautied with plastering art,
Is not more ugly to the thing that helps it
Than is my deed to my most painted word:
O heavy burden!

Claudius 3.1.50–4

O villain, villain, smiling, damnèd villain!

Hamlet 1.5.106

To be, or not to be, that is the question –
Whether 'tis nobler in the mind to suffer
The slings and arrows of outrageous fortune,
Or to take arms against a sea of troubles,
And by opposing end them.

Hamlet 3.1.56–60

There are more things in heaven and earth, Horatio,
Than are dreamt of in your philosophy

Hamlet 1.5.166–7

To die, to sleep –
To sleep: perchance to dream. Ay, there's the rub;
For in that sleep of death what dreams may come
When we have shuffled off this mortal coil,
Must give us pause

Hamlet 3.1.64–8

Get thee to a nunnery – why wouldst thou be a
breeder of sinners?

Hamlet 3.1.121–2

Such an act
That blurs the grace and blush of modesty,
Calls virtue hypocrite, takes off the rose
From the fair forehead of an innocent love
And sets a blister there, makes marriage vows
As false as dicers' oaths

Hamlet 3.4.40–5

God hath given you one face, and you make yourselves another. You jig, you amble, and you lisp, you
nickname God's creatures, and make your wantonness your ignorance

Hamlet 3.1.142–5

Nay, but to live
In the rank sweat of an enseamèd bed,
Stewed in corruption, honeying and making love
Over the nasty sty

Hamlet 3.4.91–4

Oh what a noble mind is here o'erthrown!
The courtier's, soldier's, scholar's, eye, tongue, sword,
Th'expectancy and rose of the fair state,
The glass of fashion and the mould of form,
Th'observed of all observers

Ophelia 3.1.150–4

A man may fish with the worm that hath eat of a
king, and eat of the fish that hath fed of that worm

Hamlet 4.3.25–6

---

the purpose of playing, whose end both at the first
and now, was and is, to hold, as 'twere, the mirror
up to nature; to show virtue her own feature, scorn
her own image, and the very age and body of the
time his form and pressure

Hamlet 3.2.19–22

Oh from this time forth,
My thoughts be bloody or be nothing worth

Hamlet 4.4.65–6

Give me that man
That is not passion's slave, and I will wear him
In my heart's core, ay in my heart of heart,
As I do thee

Hamlet 3.2.64–7

I loved Ophelia; forty thousand brothers
Could not with all their quantity of love
Make up my sum

Hamlet 5.1.251–3

You would play upon me, you would seem to know
my stops, you would pluck out the heart of my
mystery

Hamlet 3.2.341–2

But I do prophesy th'election lights
On Fortinbras; he has my dying voice.
So tell him, with th'occurrents more and less
Which have solicited – the rest is silence

Hamlet 5.2.342–5

Oh my offence is rank, it smells to heaven;
It hath the primal eldest curse upon't,
A brother's murder

Claudius 3.3.36–8